CW01024174

# THE LANDSCAPE IMAGINATION

# THE LANDSCAPE IMAGINATION

Collected Essays of James Corner 1990 – 2010

**James Corner and Alison Bick Hirsch, editors**

---

PRINCETON ARCHITECTURAL PRESS

NEW YORK

FIG. 1 — *Intaglio Marking*, Photograph by Alex S. MacLean, Blythe, California, 1996

# Preface

———

James Corner

Landscape architecture has enjoyed enormous growth and visibility over the past fifty years or so, and especially over the past ten to fifteen years. Think of the new parks, waterfronts, squares, public places, gardens, and revitalized urban spaces around the world. Yet, whereas the profession has clearly made significant advancements in recent years, intellectual and critical work remains sadly lacking, impeding the cultural enrichment of the broader field. It was precisely this lack that prompted my early writing in the late 1980s. Intellectual work seemed effervescent at that time in so many allied fields—ecology, land art, cultural geography, urbanism, architecture, and philosophy, for example; and yet landscape architecture was stalled, caught between strictly vocational, formulaic design practice, on the one hand, and a dichotomous split between the environmentalists and the artists on the other. My own efforts to try and overcome this inertia began with extensive reading and research, with writing then facilitating the actual thinking. Writing was, and still is for me, a powerful tool for recording, generating, and evolving ideas, as well as communicating those ideas to others.

The essays collected in this book are a series of speculations and arguments aimed toward advancing design, creativity, and cultural ideas in landscape architecture. They are the provisional conjectures of a landscape architect who is primarily interested in designing and making actual projects, but who is, at the same time, searching for a deeper raison d'etre and broader cultural relevance for that work. What, why, and how become fundamental and recurrent questions in this search.

In rereading these essays together after such a long time, there is one apparent theme that unites them all: the landscape imagination. The essays expose and expand the imagination that undergirds all landscape. After all, there is nothing natural about landscape: even though landscape invokes nature and engages natural processes over time, it is first a cultural construct, a product of the imagination. Landscapes are initially imagined and represented in images and words, modeled in miniature in gardens, and ultimately encoded in the planning, design, and construction of the larger built environment. The fact that designed and constructed landscapes inevitably signify the natural world—and ultimately succumb to naturalization over time—is the primary source of the delight and pleasure they provide and the source of what makes the medium so difficult.

The delight of landscape is obvious—its sensory richness, its ambulatory experience, its temporality, and its capacity to imbue a specific place with irreproducible charm and quality. Landscape's delights can be found in its many representations (paintings, books, maps, poems, films) as well as through the direct physical experience of the environment and exposure to nature. Gardens, public parks, urban piazzas, and promenades are all examples of designed places that have provided immeasurable joy and pleasure for millions of people throughout time. Like music, landscapes are forged by the imagination, while also themselves provoking and stimulating the imagination to see and figure new things. In this regard, consider the inspirational agency of landscape on painting, poetry, and folklore, or even the multitude of populist interpretations, projections, and effects spawned through the experience of New York's High Line and Central Park, not to mention the gardens at Versailles, Stowe, or Stourhead. These settings frame and dramatize life, while inspiring new forms of reception and making.

On the other hand, the challenge of the landscape medium is not easily recognized, hidden by the fact that it so beautifully masks and veils its own artifice. Landscape appears natural, as if it has always been that way. The genius of the painter's imagination in bodying a new and powerful impression of an otherwise overlooked environment is often masked by the palette; the poet's capacity to enable new forms of appreciation and insight can seem just descriptive; and the landscape architect's creativity in physically transforming and reshaping inert land into a more edifying and wholesome "place" is all too often hidden by the medium itself. And even if not so hidden at first, the naturalizing effects of time—both natural processes and cultural habit—inevitably reduce landscape to a passive and recessive background.

Now, just to be clear, the masking effects of the medium over genius and labor are not necessarily a problem to be overcome. I am not arguing for artifice or credit to be shouted out and visibly assigned to the inventor, author, or designer. After all, the incorporation and assimilation of landscapes is not all bad; the backdrop that landscape provides can be enormously enriching and valuable in terms of psychological well-being and feeling grounded in a particular place. Excessively foregrounded landscapes will often seem dissonant with the nature of the medium itself, appearing mannered and estranged. In this regard, I have always been taken by Walter Benjamin's characterization that architecture is an art form received by a collective in a "state of distraction." We do not pay attention to landscapes in the same way we do a painting or a sculpture. Landscape is background, but a setting that can nevertheless powerfully foreground and enrich the actual experience of being in a place.

So the frustration with landscape is not with appearance per se, or even with naturalization, but more with the fact that it is so easy to simply and habitually reproduce the *imagery* of landscape, as the image is what is most easily understood and consumed. This in turn makes it very difficult to innovate and chart new possibilities for the medium. Because landscape is already so preconditioned as being "of nature," and because its imagery is so deeply ingrained in a particular culture's sense of place, it is extremely challenging to imagine or project it differently. Landscape retards its own advancement.

The essays in this collection address both the delights and the challenges of working with the landscape medium. Key to this is the centrality of the imagination in both understanding and projecting new forms of landscape, as well as the tools and techniques available for such a task. Landscape remains a profoundly imaginative project, requiring both a creative "reading" and "writing" of sites. Along these lines, three trajectories can be charted through the development of the early essays to the more recent ones.

Most obvious might be the shift from a representational interest (how landscapes mean and signify) to more instrumental practices (what landscapes do and how they perform). *Taking Measures Across the American Landscape* (1996) best represents the essence of this shift by dissecting the form and appearance of the American landscape as a wholly pragmatic, instrumental creation, but an instrumentality that at the same time harbors poetic and significant content. The shift toward instrumentality and pragmatism does not preclude any concern for meaning and representation, but instead suggests that meaning will best derive from use and work as opposed to some kind of passive, distanced reading—the inhabited *landschaft* as distinct from the more objectified and painterly *landskip*. From a design perspective, this means paying more attention to the productive and performative aspects of design, to the consequences and effects of what a design might do, and to what its agency might be in and on the world. At the same time, while earlier essays seem to be overly critical of the scenic landscape (landskip), more recent work attempts to reconcile the scenic with the performative, favoring a theatrical, stage-set approach toward the design of settings for action. Indeed, it may well be the interplay between how a setting looks and is figured in relation to the action it supports that creates the most engaging and meaningful landscape architecture.

Related to this is a second thread in the evolution of these essays; a shift from speaking about landscapes generally to landscape architecture specifically. Here one might cite a movement from theory to practice, but it is more precise to recognize that both the writings and the designed works are in themselves projects, and they therefore share the same impulse: to project new possibilities for the field. For me, writing is part of the practice of landscape architecture, much like drawing or building. The shift from general landscape to landscape architecture is a more nuanced shift than just theory to practice, and speaks more to a focus upon what John Dixon Hunt has called a "third nature." That is, in general terms, if "first nature" refers to wilderness landscapes, and "second nature" to agricultural and cultural landscapes, then Hunt's "third nature" refers more specifically to those highly designed landscapes that concentrate ideas, experiences, and prompt insight and reflection on both the surrounding second and first natures. Landscape architecture of course inhabits this full spectrum, mediating most closely the second nature of the working landscape (program, performance, activity, productivity, and construction) with the third nature of the garden (reflection, insight, experience, and delight). It is this intersection that characterizes landscape architecture at its best, and it is here that most of these essays find their fullest force.

The third thread found in the collection is the increased focus upon urbanism. It is not easy or obvious to conjoin landscape with urbanism, for many of the same reasons outlined above. As media and milieu, they seem different and distinct. The first image for most people in any formulation of "landscape urbanism" is the role of greenery and green open spaces in the city. Think of the importance and the effect of Central Park on Manhattan, or the rich network of parks and public places that enrich cities like Paris, London, or Barcelona. And yet, the formulation of landscape urbanism is intended to suggest much more than this; it is intended to provoke a radically new understanding of the city as a kind of ecological metabolism that functions much like a "landscape"—it might not *look* like a landscape, but as a primarily horizontal foundation, the geometries and entities that shape the city *function* much like a landscape, channeling flows and energy, connecting and dispersing, and expanding and contracting with varying degrees of fixity and open-endedness over time. Ecology and landscape here are no longer confined to greenery and natural systems, but now include infrastructure, engineering, real estate, constructed systems, and cultural places. Landscape urbanism suggests a much more comprehensive, inclusive, and synthetic version of the city than previous architectural or urban planning models. Landscape techniques, such as analysis and information management (through mapping, organizing, and layering, for example), planning (through spatial and programmatic organization, geometrization, and systematization, for instance), staging (through phasing, cultivating, choreography, and so forth), and place-making (through scenography, dramatization, styling, and design) all prove fundamental in any attempt to reformulate the city.

These might be lofty claims and ambitions, and there are many challenges to their further development and advancement. But if the landscape of the eighteenth and nineteenth century was primarily bucolic and antidotal to the city, and that of the twentieth century was in some ways much more embedded, perhaps the contribution of landscape for the twenty-first century is that of providing a more primary foundation for the city—the very bedrock, matrix, and framework upon which a city can thrive, sustainably with nature and equitably with diverse cultures and programs.

These themes, then, are what I have been trying to articulate through the intertwined modes of writing and designing over the past twenty years or so. I believe that there is a certain resonance between the general content and aim of these essays with issues still confronting the field of landscape architecture today. By bringing these essays together in one volume, it is my hope that the thoughtful reader will find correlations that continue to inform, enrich, and broaden the landscape imagination—conjoining thinking with making in an effort to further advance the landscape project.

FIG. 1 — View across the lake toward the city's horizon, by James Corner, Toolonlahti Park, Helsinki, 1997

# Introduction

## THE LANDSCAPE IMAGINATION IN THEORY, METHOD, AND ACTION

——

Alison Bick Hirsch

For more than two decades, James Corner has profoundly impacted the field of landscape architecture—as both an intellectual discipline and a physical practice. Through early writings and, more recently, through built work (executed with his team at James Corner Field Operations), he has provoked and pushed the field to question its position, values, and scope. Bringing his most significant essays together in this consolidated volume not only gathers them out of their dispersed obscurity, but is intended as a stimulus for renewed interest and scholarly investment in the foundations of the discipline. This anthology exhibits the power of writing as a form of inquiry that enriches and informs our understanding of landscape, an elusive and complex medium that is dynamic and ever changing. As such, Corner's work has helped to propel the field of landscape architecture toward new horizons, opening the medium of landscape to a broader spectrum of interpretation and possibility.

While the essays collected herein have been carefully selected and curated into four thematic parts, they are comprehensively linked by Corner's search for the ideas that form the basis for understanding landscape and that provide the intellectual framework for landscape architecture, as well as for the creative methods of actively testing these ideas in action. The essays span Corner's evolution from academic to practitioner, revealing a shift in style and content, yet his investigation into methods and modes of imaginative inquiry remains primary throughout. As a productive prompt, this compilation intends to inspire continued investigation into the theories and methods of landscape architecture and to insist that the imagination remain our essential catalyst for moving forward.

Though Corner might be best known for his manifestos of Landscape Urbanism, these texts are only a fraction of what he has uncovered and expressed in writing. As a professor at the University of Pennsylvania, he began writing with the aim of bringing landscape architecture out of its then relatively marginalized intellectual and professional position. As a body of work, the essays frame the field's powerful potential to shape cultural values and practices of human settlement, lead efforts in sustainable urban and regional development, and unleash new sources and methods of creative inquiry.

Corner was both a devoted student of and critical reactionary to renowned landscape architect Ian McHarg at the University of Pennsylvania. He studied at Penn under McHarg between 1984 and 1986, and began teaching there in 1988. He chaired and led the department of landscape architecture from 2000 through 2012, during which time his professional design practice grew, acquiring significant public projects, such as Fresh Kills Park and the High Line in New York. While McHarg's book, *Design with Nature* (1969), and his thirty-year tenure at Penn brought landscape architecture into broader visibility as a productive practice essential to "solving" environmental "problems," his deterministic approach to ecological and land-use planning fueled Corner's rebellious insistence on the role of *imagination* in landscape architecture. Importantly, however, Corner has continuously sought a balance between poetic imagination and McHarg's sense of instrumentality and purpose. Corner might say that his work is in many ways a continuation or broadening of McHarg's fundamental concerns, even though McHarg himself might take issue with some of Corner's less scientific, or measurable, interpretations and conjectures. Essays in this collection should be read with this tension in mind.

In the following pages, I will introduce the essays as they have been organized in this volume, situating Corner's scholarship, distilling common and emergent themes, and drawing cursory links between his writings and practice. Finally, I will offer brief remarks on where I believe the gaps in his synthetic thinking remain and suggest some projections for the field as it moves forward.

In terms of methodology, the editorial intentions were not to ensure current-day applicability, but to consolidate the dispersed essays into a body of work that contributes to disciplinary footing. Therefore, arguments and ideas have not been changed, only unnecessary verbiage and digressions eliminated.

To Corner, writing (like design) is an exploratory process through which he has sought to gain a better grip on the elusive medium of landscape and the vocabulary and working methods of landscape architecture. The essays have been grouped into four themes that are central to his thinking and to the field as it continues to shape itself. Those themes—which typically correspond to the chronology of Corner's development—are (Part 1) theory and criticism, (Part 2) representation and working methods, (Part 3) strategic approaches to the contemporary metropolis, and (Part 4) innovation and experimentation in practice. The essays in each section consistently negotiate between poetic imagination in landscape architecture as a cultural practice and ecological performance in landscape architecture as an instrumental medium. Claiming the dialectical middle ground, Corner framed the field as a mediator, a bridge and ultimately a "synthetic and strategic art form."[1]

### On Part One: *Theory*

The field today is not plagued by the same deadening division between "ecology" and "art" that first prompted Corner to begin writing in the late 1980s. Rather, landscape architecture's growing complexity and scope has stimulated an exciting proliferation of new directions in design research. Yet Part One—on theory and design as a critical practice—is a reminder of the productivity of revisiting the theoretical foundation that grounds the field and prompts us to engage in a conversation about where we were, where we are, and where we might be headed. Landscape—as representation, as material, as process, as cultural register—eludes generalized definition, considered essential to theory. Yet rather than abandon it entirely, the complexity of the medium provides the impetus necessary for dynamic and engaged conversation that draws inspiration from debates at the end of the last millennium.

Still spinning from the political and economic transformations set in motion in the early 1970s, the 1980s and 1990s became a period of searching for alternatives. The failed inheritance of postwar modernization inspired a ubiquitous quest for new modes of cultural production. By 1990, when Corner started writing, architecture as an intellectual discipline had been overtaken by theory—adopted and adapted from philosophers such as Jacques Derrida and Gilles Deleuze, whose work was packaged into "fast" and "portable" form.[2] Because Corner recognized the vacuum of critical debate within his own field, he looked sideways to allied disciplines for creative dialogue. Despite the popular trends in architecture, Corner did not rely on the same sources but did find inspiration from the renewed critical discourse.[3]

It is fitting then to begin this book of essays with Corner's response to the questions posed at the 1990 Council of Educators in Landscape Architecture (CELA) conference: "What is critical inquiry? What does it mean in the context of landscape architecture? What is its role in landscape architectural education and practice?" These questions contextualize Corner's early career when he and the other respondents recognized a clear lack of "theoretical infrastructure" or framework to situate ideas and "make criticism feasible and meaningful."[4] Corner's response also provides an introductory glimpse into some consistent themes that appear in all his writings, most primarily his insistence that criticism—particularly in the form of critical practices of design (*poiesis*)—should be simultaneously emancipatory and conservative (i.e. *situated*), acting as a reconciliatory medium between "prophecy" and "memory." Corner acknowledges the nihilism inherent to modern culture and looks to landscape as the literal and figurative (or physical and ideational) *ground* for dialogic relations between the achievements of technology and the conditions of human existence and inherited culture.

Responding to the cultural estrangement caused by the denial of history and overreliance on science, Corner asks in 1990, "How can we make the ordinariness of everyday situations into something imaginative or fresh, pertinent to our time but not estranged from tradition?" He explores this question in "Critical Thinking" through architectural critic Kenneth Frampton's idea of "Critical Regionalism," as a possible response to philosopher Paul Ricoeur's oft-cited dilemma: "How to become modern and return to sources."[5] While Corner does not adopt the term "critical regionalism" in his subsequent essays—perhaps because it had been widely adopted by design schools and had devolved into the formulaic—he similarly considers how landscape might mediate or reconcile this timeless paradox.[6]

Frampton's assertions in "Towards a Critical Regionalism: Six Points for an Architecture of Resistance" (1983) appeal to Corner because he believes in the importance of criticism which does not come from without, but *within*, through "circumstantial action—the building of critical landscapes."[7] It is here in his essay on "Critical Thinking" that Corner introduces the projective practice of "plotting," a critical drawing process, or the re-presentation of a given condition that, through interpretive and imaginative action, discloses "previously unforeseen relationships" that provoke newly inscribed "patterns for inhabitation in the landscape." As a generative form of representation, these early remarks on plotting in the context of critical thinking provide a well-rounded base to understand Corner's most fundamental motivations.

### Crisis and Recovery

In *Architecture and the Crisis of Modern Science* (1983), the title and ideas of which build on philosopher Edmund Husserl's *The Crisis of European Sciences and Transcendental Phenomenology* (1970), architectural historian Alberto Péréz-Gomez declares:

> When a physician talks about *crisis* in the condition of a patient, he is describing a moment when it is unclear whether the patient will survive or succumb. In a true sense this is now the condition of Western culture. In the last century

and a half, man has done his utmost to define the human condition and ironically has lost the capacity to come to terms with it; he is unable to reconcile the
eternal and immutable dimension of ideas with the finite and mutable dimension of everyday life. Moreover, contemporary man, while recognizing this
dilemma, seems incapable of deriving from this tension the ultimate meaning of
his existence.[8]

Building on these ideas, in "Sounding the Depths—Origins, Theory, and
Representation" (1990), Corner likewise argues, "The contemporary crisis of meaning is due in large part to the epistemological break with tradition
during the eighteenth century, and [he then concludes] that modern technological thinking works merely to perpetuate an excessively 'hard' world in which
culture simply cannot figure or recollect itself."[9] To Péréz-Gomez and subsequently Corner, the theories of Jean-Nicolas-Louis Durand signify the culmi-
nation of the crisis of meaning. Durand's books—including *Recueil et parallèle
des édifices de tout genre, anciens et moderns* (1800), the frontispiece of which
Corner features in this essay, and *Précis des leçons d'architecture données à
l'École royale polytechnique* (1805)—present architectural *types* neutralized of
idiosyncrasy and circumstance, as ideals that "reduced nature to a mathematical
manifold," in Husserl's words (and quoted by Corner).[10]

This dissociation from and reduction of the natural world also stimulated Corner's predecessor, Ian McHarg. Though Corner's concern with
*meaning* was partly a reaction to the rationality of McHarg's analytic method,
Corner couples the ecological crisis with the crisis of meaning, explaining, "if
humans were truly in accord with the world, with nature, and did not look at
things as mere phenomena to be measured and manipulated, then the current
ecological and existential crises, focusing on an aggressive technology and supported by an excessively rational thinking, would not arise."[11] Corner calls on
the landscape architect—working with the processes of nature as his/her primary cultural medium—to reconcile this conflict. He thus declares, "As the
great mediator between nature and culture, landscape architecture has a profound role to play in the reconstitution of meaning and value in our relations
with the Earth."[12]

Corner was not alone grappling with the question of meaning in landscape
architecture at this time. Two years prior, Laurie Olin wrote "Form, Meaning,
and Expression in Landscape Architecture" for *Landscape Journal*.[13] Reading
Corner's "Sounding the Depths" and "Three Tyrannies" essays alongside Olin's
text reveals the designers' generational differences, yet their primary motivation
is similar. Evoking Frampton/Ricoeur's paradox, Olin states: "The only thing

that we can ever know for certain about the world is that which exists now or has existed in the past. To make something new we must start with what is or has been and change it in some way to make it fresh…How to make old things new, how to see something common and banal in a new and fresh way is the central problem." Similar to Corner's rejection of the "avant-garde" as a "tyranny" of contemporary theory in "Three Tyrannies," Olin likewise rejects artists who simply "set out to be revolutionary," stating "many of the best works of the moment are inquiries into the validity of past expressions and their extension into the present." I mention these similarities to illustrate that Corner was not working in a disciplinary vacuum but was part of a small group of practitioners and scholars who were similarly engaged in theoretical inquiry.[14]

In fact, Corner's early writings built on a foundation of criticism directed at McHargian thought by individuals such as Anne Whiston Spirn, the chair of the Landscape Architecture Department at Penn following McHarg (1986–1994). Spirn's publications, particularly *The Granite Garden* (1984), challenge McHarg's declaratory dismissal of the inherited city and assert the necessity of enriched conversation about practices of human dwelling rather than devolve into simplistic binaries (i.e., art v. science, city v. landscape, etc.) that contributed to the field's stagnation.[15] Similarly, many of Corner's concerns about landscape architecture's stunted development were the focus of writings by Elizabeth Meyer, then professor at Harvard. Meyer, the initial respondent to the 1990 CELA inquiries about "critical thinking" in landscape architecture, likewise acknowledges a crisis in the field and poses theory and its critical application through landscape architectural practice as a "bridging, mediating, and reconciling" agent working *in between* the binaries that triggered this crisis.[16] While she traces the detrimental impact of this dichotomous thinking to the devolution of the Picturesque in the nineteenth century, tracing a thread through the history of the discipline that diverged somewhat from Corner's investigation of the "epistemological break with tradition during the eighteenth century," their shared hopes for and methods of recovery—situating landscape architecture as a productive and dialectical middle ground—suggest a reciprocal influence.

In "Three Tyrannies of Contemporary Theory" (1991), Corner builds on "Sounding the Depths" to argue that the inadequacies of theoretical practice in landscape architecture grew out of techno-scientific methods developed during the Enlightenment. Adopting hermeneutics as an "alternative" and "reconciliatory" approach, he proposes a renewed practice of theory that is simultaneously reflective and projective, acting as both "prompt and stabilizer." Philosopher Martin Heidegger's adaptation of hermeneutics, steering it away from the codification of interpretive principles, was later examined by philosopher

Hans-Georg Gadamer, who serves as Corner's primary reference. Gadamer's hermeneutics sought to uncover the nature of human understanding, which is continually shaped by our historically determined situatedness (i.e., tradition). While Gadamer was criticized by philosopher Jürgen Habermas for being conservative—with his focus on tradition supposedly undermining possibilities for transformation—Gadamer recognized that our situated horizon constantly changes, thus our understanding of the world likewise is always evolving. Such a dynamic means of interpreting the world seems particularly suitable for those who work with landscape, which is constantly undergoing transformation—through natural process and human endeavor. Corner thus sets hermeneutics in favorable contrast to the "three tyrannies of contemporary theory"—positivism, paradigms, and the avant-garde. While he consistently reassures his reader that he does not suggest we revert to nostalgic reclamations of the (obsolete) past, Corner's insistence on rootedness in tradition (in Gadamer's sense of the term, as the background that instigates all inquiry), on physical manifestations of time, and on situated criticism is embodied in the alternative of hermeneutics. A hermeneutical practice—whether performed through critical acts of drawing, writing, or constructing landscape—interprets, thus re-presents, the world in a new way.[17] Rather than the avant-garde insistence on constant rupture and denial of tradition, Corner sets to frame landscape architecture as a practice that uses the grounding conditions of the past as a "repository of meaning" that may be mined to prompt new possibilities that transcend the given present for the construction of new horizons.

"Recovering Landscape as a Critical Cultural Practice" (originally the introduction to *Recovering Landscape: Essays in Contemporary Landscape Architecture*, 1999) provokes us to harness such transcendental potential of the medium. In it, Corner introduces the idea of the *agency* of landscape. Rather than a regressive instrument of nostalgia or an ameliorative service, Corner resituates landscape architecture as an "innovative cultural agent." He consequently describes the book's intentions—"There is little mention of what landscape is or what it means; the focus is on what landscape *does*, as in its efficacy and scope of influence." Therefore, while landscape architect Richard Weller notes in 2001 the "inherent conservatism" of the term "recovering landscape," here recovery is not just about unearthing site memory, but also about reclaiming landscape as a means to actively and critically challenge "cultural habit and convention." Recognizing the devolved understanding and shaping of landscape—as a "scenic object, a subjugated resource, or a scientistic ecosystem"—Corner attempts to *re*claim and *re*situate its position and purpose in society. His "preferred prefix" *re-*, (v. *de-*) noted by Weller, appropriately implies to do something again, yet anew; to Corner, landscape is something that is consistently made and remade—it is in the perpetual process of transformation.[18]

In "Recovering Landscape," Corner also identifies areas of urgency for landscape architectural leadership, framing landscape first as a means through which to critically resist the homogenizing forces of globalization; second, as a means through which to engage in conversation about and react to environmental challenges such as waste treatment, diminished biodiversity, and resource depletion; and third, as a primary medium through which to evaluate and shape the process and outcome of massive deindustrialization in the West. In this view, landscape architecture is not simply a service profession that ameliorates the effects of modernization, but rather a cultural practice that actively shapes the world in an engaged dialogue with these dynamic forces of change.

Finally, "Recovering Landscape" provides the first thorough reference to practitioners Corner deemed successful at bridging the instrumental and expressive potentials of landscape (the essays of his colleagues included in the book greatly expands on these references). Recognizing the enormous impact of 1970s land art as a catalytic moment for landscape's recovery (the work of Robert Smithson in particular), Corner also cites the accomplishments of architects Rem Koolhaas/OMA and Bernard Tschumi, particularly for their success at challenging the conventions of what a *park* means and does through proposals for Parc de la Villette (Koolhaas and Tschumi's contribution to this competition are referenced frequently in Corner's writings). While he also mentions Adriaan Geuze and Peter Latz as landscape architects he admires, Corner's recognition of George Hargreaves followed an essay he wrote on the poetic agency of Hargreaves's practice.[19] More than simply "bridging the gap between artistic expression and ecological technique," as Corner describes Hargreaves in "Recovering Landscape," he notes in this earlier work: "For Hargreaves, the arrangement of water and other material elements across a landscape is not simply a utilitarian, restorative, and ameliorative, or scenographic practice, but a deeply material, symbolic, and ethical project, one that makes demands upon a society to critically reflect upon their relationship to the natural world."[20] This final statement underlies the primary motivation of Corner's recovery of landscape and practice of landscape architecture.

### On Part Two: *Representation and Creativity*

Part Two is the most fundamental and perpetuating focus of Corner's design investigations. It is an obvious extension of the ideas he began unpacking in "Sounding the Depths" and "Three Tyrannies," but here he more explicitly searches for "agents of creativity," which he discovers in various forms of eidetic imaging and ecology. [FIG. 1] If the essays in Part One present Corner's thoughts on the theory of landscape architecture, then Part Two is about uncovering the methods to test such ideas in action. Like the elusive challenges of theorizing landscape architecture, creative or working methods in the field have expanded rather than become more specific. It is for this reason that the practice of landscape architecture is so enriching; we arrive at new design possibilities through experimental processes and practices of visualization and construction. Though clearly today's "toolbox" swells with the growing potentials of computer technology, the essays in this section are less about the tools themselves but more comprehensively about representation as critical action—as ideational process and inquiry, rather than communication and delivery. Thus they remind us that while the field continues to invest its energy into the latest digital tools, it is how we deploy them that is most essential to the imaginative project.

Rather than focus exclusively on drawing and other intermediary acts of creative making, Corner is invested in the broader conflicts (and "crises") over representation, as once the art of *mimesis*—not mere imitation, but a "metaphor of the a priori order of the world."[21] Here, Corner builds on arguments of architectural theorist Dalibor Vesely, who identifies the seventeenth century as the "age of divided representation," when the ambiguities of traditional symbolic- and cosmologically-based representation were eclipsed and replaced by the precision of modern instrumental thinking. In fact, at this time, modern science is no longer seen as a *representation* of reality and truth but taken for "real nature" itself.[22] This divide—or *aporia*—provides the primary fuel for Corner's persistent investigation into the dialectical potentials of his medium—to negotiate and challenge the dualism that polarizes modern science and art.

In *Taking Measures Across the American Landscape* (1996), for instance, a collaborative project with aerial photographer Alex MacLean, Corner undertakes a critical reading of measurement in an effort to describe its potential as a reconciliatory agent between symbolic representation and modern technology. Citing the etymological roots of *geometry*—earth (*geo*) and measure (*metry*)—his argument is built on Husserlian concepts that trace the "crises" of modern existence to the end of classical geometry.[23] As he addresses in "Sounding the Depths," geometry, prior to the revolution in scientific thinking, had served as a mediator between the lived world and the cosmos. As a *representation* of the ideal world of divine order, it contained profound symbolic content that was purged when mathematics and geometry became an autonomous, self-referential construct—an instrument of modern technology. Examining its continued use as "earth measure," Corner investigates how geometry has shaped the American landscape in both emancipatory and exploitative ways.

In the photographs and collages in *Taking Measures'* culminating section, titled "Measures of Faith," Corner includes a quotation by Heidegger: "Measure-taking is no science. Measure-taking gauges the between which brings the two, heaven and earth, to one another. This measure-taking has its own metron, and thus its own metric."[24] The synthesizing power of the *metron*, as a unit of poetic measure, fuels Corner's insistence on the human imagination in shaping and structuring landscape.

By contrast, as vehicles of domination and control, modern measure can be situated within geographer John Barrell's "dark side of landscape," which Corner presents in "Recovering Landscape," additionally citing visual culture and literary scholar W. J. T. Mitchell and relations of power as they are translated in the structuring of land and economy. Corner also uses economic historian Witold Kula's book, *Measures and Men* (trans. 1986), as a foundational reference for *Taking Measures*. Kula's study considers the metrological history of land, grain, and bread in France under the ancien régime. The state-imposed transition to abstract measurement (from "traditional" to "modern measures") for taxation caused the inevitable disconnect between producer (generating goods for "abstract markets") and consumer—thus becoming an instrument of alienation.

Yet Corner likewise identifies the value of the universal standards of modern measure to "foster global cooperation and mutual understanding"— bringing humans closer to the earth and to one another through advancements in such areas as medicine and communication. While the Jeffersonian grid may be regarded as the distanced abstraction of Cartesian thinking imposed on the land—re-presented as an exploitable resource (commodity)—Corner considers its egalitarian intentions and uses it as an example of the liberating potentials of modern measure. Its neutral, nonhierarchical nature—while abstract and homogenous—provides a scaffold for endless appropriation and creative forms of dwelling—a democratic framework.

Therefore, while modern measure might be deployed as an agent of homogenization and alienation from the concrete circumstances of time and place, it may also ensure a common datum from which to relate to the world and one another. Thus is the "heart of the aporia of modern measure," according to Corner—its ambiguous value as a shared foundation and an instigatory scaffold for creative appropriation while at the same time an alienating agent of technocratic power and the homogenization of the world.[25] Yet rather than remain conflicted over this ambiguity, like urbanist Marshall Berman who celebrates the dynamic contradictions inherent to modernity, Corner is activated by these tensions and the possibilities for enhanced reciprocity between creativity and efficacy enabled by modern measure.[26] He concludes,

We do not wish to suggest a return to a pre-technological age or to promote romantic illusions of Arcadian life upon the land; instead we seek to restore to measure its full metaphoricity—its full capacity for representation— especially as this might forge new forms of interrelationship between people and land. Although we hope to disclose various imaginative extensions of measure and geometry, we do not deny the emancipating power of modern technology.[27]

The consistent logic of the U.S. Geological Survey (USGS) maps become a medium for exploring the liberating forces of modern measure—as an "objective field" that stimulates diverse forms of collagic intervention. Weller is accurate in his criticism of what is really the "irony and contradiction" of Corner's collages—the continued use of the aerial view—the synoptic and detached gaze at the height of which the actualities of everyday life (or *landschaft*) disappear.[28] Rather than experience the land as lived, worked, or inhabited (consider studies of the American landscape by cultural geographer J.B. Jackson for compelling comparison), Corner's collages remain distanced from the situated horizon he argues for in his earlier essays (with the exception, of the Hopi and Chacoan examples; see Figures 5 and 6, pp. 143 and 144).[29]

However, while Weller criticizes the collages as "gorgeous graphic designs" that merely indicate "what a hermeneutic site analysis might be," I believe they are more.[30] Corner uses the USGS maps of the land as the consistent measure on which to inflict various collagic techniques (splicing, overlay, extraction, etc.) and build in visual information latent with symbolic content in order to re-present the world to his readers in a way that might stimulate a new mode of seeing and thus shaping the land. The collages are the "plots," the strategic provocations, he presents in "Critical Thinking and Landscape Architecture" (1991). They present analytical information while also allowing for suggestive readings that stimulate the imagination.

About artist Emmet Gowin's *Geography Pages* (1974), reproduced in "Drawing and Making in the Landscape Medium" (1992), Corner states, "The experience of landscape space is never simply and only an aesthetic one, but is more deeply experienced as a lived-within topological field or as a highly situated network of relationships and associations that is perhaps best represented as a geographical map of collagic dimensions."[31] In this compilation of Corner's essays, the *Taking Measures* collages and all their "ironies" and "contradictions" serve as a transition into this important text, which he published five years earlier. While the essay is primarily about the secondary medium of drawing as essential to the practice of landscape architecture, Corner initially introduces landscape itself as "a way of seeing" (to use cultural geographer Denis Cosgrove's oft-cited phrase), or as a cultural construct or projection that reflects or represents humans' situation in Nature and a particular milieu.

### Drawing as vehicle of creativity and realization

"Drawing and Making" is one of Corner's most potent and clear essays and is still absolutely fundamental for landscape architectural education today. Published just after "Sounding the Depths" and "Three Tyrannies," Corner writes in his own voice, rather than through the frame of others, such as Gadamer or Vesely. He instead uses his earlier reliance on these figures as a foundation from which to build a powerful argument about *representation as critical creative practice*—an agenda that came to define the landscape architecture curriculum at Penn, most rigorously explored through the his own design studio teaching, and the work of his colleagues Anuradha Mathur and Dilip da Cunha.

Citing Robin Evans' "Translations from Drawing to Building" (1986), Corner recognizes the unique relationship a landscape architect has to his/her material of manipulation or object of thought (landscape)—through the intervening translatory medium of drawing. Translation, from the Latin *translatio*, to move or carry from one place to another, implies a displacement of effort, a lack of directness, but it is in this place *in between* that creativity—as *trans*figuration, *trans*formation, *trans*cendence—can occur. It is thus something to be exploited for its revelatory potential. An architect may expect a drawing to be translated with precise exactitude into built form, yet as Evans states, "we can never be quite certain, before the event, how things will travel and what will happen to them on the way."[32] While this may provoke anxiety for many in the architectural professions, it is a uniquely inherent aspect of our working process. As an "eidetic medium" that indicates a *process* rather than an object of composition and communication, drawing negotiates between a given reality and an idea and between an idea and its physical embodiment. Corner again recalls *poiesis*—suggesting that the actual *work* of making is the creative act, citing Heidegger who recognized "the hidden 'truth' of things…is something brought forth through human agency."[33] Again, Corner's stance is not the desire for novelty but to uncover what might remain hidden—it is thus a process of revelatory excavation—a "finding and founding," intended for "construal *and* construction."[34] In other words, it both follows (through interpretation of a given circumstance) and precedes the world it represents. While Evans states, "it is not so much produced by reflection on the reality outside the drawing, as productive of a reality that will end up outside the drawing," landscape architectural drawing is both a reflection and a productive prompt.[35]

## Mapping

The final statement in "Drawing and Making" — "the drawing is a plot, necessarily strategic, maplike, and acted out" — provides a preemptive transition into its sequel, "The Agency of Mapping" (1999). While maps (noun pl.) are long associated with technocratic instruments of imperialist authority and control, Corner attempts to recover the original "exploratory and entrepreneurial character" of *mapping* (verb) as a liberating and productive activity.

The process of mapping is, by necessity, both measured and abstract. A map is "analogous" in the sense that it is a measured projection of the ground, yet in order to remain useful and provide orientation, it re-presents (re-territorializes) the world — through omissions, symbols, annotations, and delineations. As a result of such deliberate decisions, a map is not an objective reproduction of reality but contains both symbolic and instrumental content that can provoke (through its "agency") changes in cultural practice and modes of understanding.

As a process of negotiation and translation, Corner's mapping provides an alternative to both technocratic conventions of twentieth-century "master-planning" and McHargian land-use planning and suitability analysis that preceded the development of Geographical Information Systems (GIS), for which maps serve as neutral "data." While McHarg's value overlays embody a *process* without preconceived outcome, the analytical mapping inventory is deployed to uncover (determine) an unwavering "truth" — a final map that reveals the proper land-use suitabilities.[36]

Corner cites Marxist geographers Edward Soja and particularly David Harvey (along with anthropologist Marc Augé and his concept of "non-space") to situate mapping as a reactionary alternative to the failures of twentieth-century urban planning. The spatiotemporal complexities and interrelated processes of urbanization visualized and understood through mapping (as a "utopia of process") replaces the static object-space reductionism of urban planning ("utopia of form").

While Corner presents mapping as a "strategic" medium and the militaristic language of "strategy" continues in his later essays on Landscape Urbanism (consider also the name of his firm, Field Operations), he culminates with a similar yet distinguishable term for his process of subverting traditional planning practice — "a *tactical* enterprise" (see cultural theorist Michel de Certeau on strategies and tactics) — that is "rhetorical and active" (as distinct from the passive neutrality of the map as a tool of objective analysis).[37] As an instrument of persuasion, analytical research through mapping is necessary but not the end goal. The "artistry lies in the use of the technique [of mapping], in the way in which things are framed and set up," to create "new realities out of existing constraints, quantities, facts, and conditions."[38] It is thus an active and creative process that can be used for highly productive (and convincing) ends.

In addition, Corner builds a vocabulary for mapping—drift, layering, gameboard, rhizome (the latter from Deleuze and Guattari's *A Thousand Plateaus*, 1980)—all of which are still deployed as creative methods of reterritorialization and activate different readings of place. As Weller notes, the essay reveals Corner's progressive attitude toward deconstructivism (from 1991) as no longer a perpetuation of the "irreconcilable contradiction of our times."[39] Rather, in "Agency of Mapping," he presents Peter Eisenman's scaling and layering as a productive working method that makes a "radically new fiction out of old facts," working with memory based in language and history driven through a study of site. Perhaps most compelling is Corner's presentation of gameboard methods since they have proliferated in planning circles as a means to activate public input and negotiate spatial conflicts; however, they have yet to succeed as transformative and generative tools (i.e., agents of creativity). This potential for creative inquiry thus deserves persistent attention.

### The metaphoric agency of ecology

The extensive section on "Representation and Creativity" ends with a different agent of creativity—ecology—which remains particularly manifest in Corner's later writings and professional design proposals, beginning with Fresh Kills landfill and Downsview Park. As a clear reaction to the privileging of "scientistic ecology" in the field, in the essay "Ecology and Landscape as Agents of Creativity" (1997), Corner mines the richness of the synthetic discipline for its metaphoric content. Rather than an instrument of technocratic thinking, Corner reminds us that ecology is yet another way of seeing and relating to Nature, a representational medium that views and projects the world as a dynamic network of interdependent forces. He challenges the objectifying logic of McHargian analysis, the exploitative perspective of resourcist ecological practice and the passivity and naivete of the restorative model. Ecology, instead, has the reconciliatory power to negotiate the representational divide or dualism between modern science and art—or the unproductive separation of the subjective sensibility of the artist and the objective rationality of the scientist—which emerged in the eighteenth century.

Recognizing the shift in the 1980s away from the "equilibrium paradigm" that represented ecological systems (of which humans were not considered a part) as closed and self-regulating—Corner embraces the indeterminacy of the renewed model. This model resituated humans' integral position in the complex and dynamic processes of the Natural world. These systems exhibit a wide range of adaptive responses to disturbance—all contingent on the specificity of history and context (versus the highly predictable and universal process of succession). The content, concepts, and vocabulary (indeterminacy, instability, chance, disturbance, adaptation, resilience) of this new understanding of earthly existence provides the foundation for Corner's subsequent design investigations explored in writing, drawing, and building. However, the existential search for fundamental sources of meaning Corner continues to express in this essay largely disappear after the turn of the millennium.

### On Part Three: *Landscape Urbanism*

Instead, from 2000 through 2004, Corner's writings take on a more rhetorical and pragmatic tone. This is partly attributable to his developing practice (for which "the art of rhetoric and persuasion is key") and confidence in his position in the field.[40] Rather than organizing Part Three chronologically, it begins with "Not Unlike Life Itself: Landscape Strategy Now" (2004), the most lucid of his essays that address design in the city of late capitalism and that encapsulate Corner's ideas about Landscape Urbanism. Ecology serves as the linchpin between the last essay of Part Two and this initial essay in Part Three. This juxtaposition should convey how the 1997 text provided a foundation for his developing ideas, yet also how Corner's appropriation of the principles of ecology evolve away from ecology as cultural metaphor and representational medium and toward ecology as an operational model. Strategy, resilience, adaptability, and "fitness" (a word often used by McHarg) are harnessed by Corner as a means to grapple with the inheritance passed on from predecessors whose urban schemes were destined for obsolescence and a vacuity of public life.

Corner's writings on Landscape Urbanism are significant to the genesis of the term and its key ideas, yet are distinct from persistent attempts at branding it into a new discipline that misrepresents the history of landscape architecture to justify its territorial claims. What is particularly unique about "Not Unlike Life Itself" in the context of Landscape Urbanism discourse is Corner's insistence on spatial form: "Design practices that are contextually responsive, temporal and open-ended, adaptive and flexible, and ecologically strategic do not imply that formal, material precision is irrelevant."[41] While he aligns himself with Harvey's criticism of exclusively spatial approaches to urban design intended to yield specific patterns of socialization, instead endorsing a strategic approach that prioritizes *processes* of urbanization, Corner insists that designing for "indeterminacy" and "flexibility" (the problematic language of Landscape Urbanism) does not imply formlessness. In 2001, Corner writes the short piece called "Landscraping," in which he uses the vagaries of language such as "setting up reserves of indeterminacy," yet it is most likely owing to his interactions with landscape architecture critic Anita Berrizbeitia at Penn that he is careful in subsequent writings to assert the significance of spatial structure. As early as 2001, in her essay about the Downsview Park competition, for which Field Operations was a finalist, Berrizbeitia states, "Instead of flexibility, thus we might now think, more precisely, in terms of scales of undecidability. By this I mean a landscape's capacity for precision of form notwithstanding flexibility of program — for the precisely open rather than the vaguely loose. Through this framework we are able to reject the notion that landscapes are either naturalistic and formless or object-like and form-full."[42] If Landscape Urbanism comprehensively adopted this insistence on formal precision, as Corner does, it could contribute more productively to informed discourse about the future of our cities.

Corner's facility with form and geometry was intrinsic to his education and his subsequent teaching. His combined studies in both landscape architecture and urban design provoked his interests during the 1980s in people, such as Richard Rogers, Edmund Bacon, Colin Rowe, Aldo Rossi, and others committed to an urban project. In fact, his 1986 Master's thesis at the University of Pennsylvania developed a radical new vision for the entire city of Philadelphia, which won an ASLA Award that year. [FIG. 2] Dramatic, even strident, geometries evoke the overlay and programming techniques of both collage and Suprematism in a plannerly (horizontal) format. With time, Corner's formal capacity and range have both softened and become much more nuanced and subtle (consider his High Line or Tongva Park, for example), but my point here is simply to reiterate that for Corner, Landscape Urbanism is as much a physical and formal affair as it is ideological.

His subsequent development of Landscape Urbanism is motivated by frustration at the continued marginalization of landscape as the city's antidote, respite or "salve," and at misguided ignorance of landscape architecture as integral to, effective of, and resultant from the processes of modernization and urbanization.[43] Regardless of Corner's evolved insistence on clarity of principles, Landscape Urbanism — with its often ambiguous definitions and hermetic jargon — has overshadowed the depth of landscape architecture (Landscape Urbanism is generally more about surface rather than depth). Clearly there is still great thirst for these ideas, however, which were largely birthed by Corner and his colleagues Mohsen Mostafavi and Charles Waldheim at Penn in the late 1980s and 1990s (building particularly on ideas launched by Rem Koolhaas).[44] City officials have developed a curiosity in this conflation of terms as well — particularly because of the success of the High Line (which is less an example of Landscape Urbanism than it is a refined example of landscape

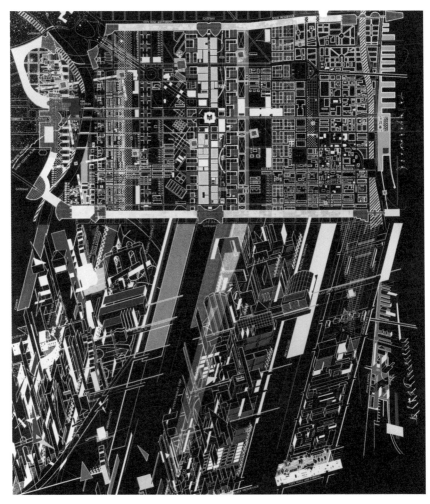

FIG. 2 — *City Vision for Philadelphia*, by James Corner, 1986

architecture) and the real estate and economic development it has stimulated and because it sounds like a marketable "green" model for growth. Yet I do not express skepticism about the current state of Landscape Urbanism in order to align myself with the most recent expression of "discontents," which contributes little depth to what could be an enriched conversation about the priorities of urban design.[45] Rather, I think it is worth revisiting some of its fundamental principles and clarifying some of its ambiguities so landscape architects, architects, and planners can have a more productive dialogue about how it may or may not have sustained relevance for the shaping of public life in the city today.

Some of the questions over the social responsibility (or lack thereof) of Landscape Urbanism are actually direct reactions to Corner's early statements. For instance, taking on the rhetoric of the Italian Futurists, in "Landscape Urbanism" (2003) Corner celebrates market-driven sprawl and other socially destructive forces of urbanization rather than those that are creative and productive. He declares, "The contemporary metropolis is out of control—and this is not a weakness but its strength," celebrating "postindustrial 'meta-urbanism,' replete with brutalist layers of concrete intersections flying over densely packed houses, distribution centers, and parking structures…"[46] Yet within the same text he aligns himself with Harvey's declaration that design and planning must focus on "the advancement of a more socially just, politically emancipating, and ecologically sane mix of spatiotemporal production processes," rather than acquiesce to the forces of "uncontrolled capital accumulation, backed by class privilege and gross inequalities of political-economic power."[47] The celebration of market-driven urbanism while later integrating Marxist geography focused on equity and justice has fueled some recent attacks against "the Landscape Urbanists."

By contrast, despite the passive ambiguity implied by its title, in "Terra Fluxus" (2006) Corner very concretely attempts to situate his ideas in the twentieth-century history of design approaches to the city, citing Jens Jensen, Le Corbusier, Frederick Law Olmsted, and urbanist Victor Gruen (to limited extent) as early precursors to the ideals of Landscape Urbanism (i.e., landscape provides the framework for development to ensue). It is in the same essay that his five "characteristics" of Landscape Urbanism from 2003 (horizontality, infrastructures, forms of process, techniques, and ecology) evolve into "four provisional themes": processes over time, the staging of surfaces, the operational or working method, and the imaginary. Corner's insistence on the *imagination* as integral to the Landscape Urbanism ethos is his most important and yet least recognized contribution. He contrasts the "imaginative project" of Landscape

Urbanism with the "oversimplification and reduction of the phenomenal richness of physical life" inflicted by the twentieth-century urban planner.[48] He continues, "A good designer must be able to weave the diagram and the strategy in relationship to the tactile and poetic."[49] Clearly, Corner had learned from previous failed attempts at this integral weaving (see, for instance, OMA and Bruce Mau's failed Downsview Park scheme, a direct translation from diagram to ground) and instead revisits some of the themes and thoughts of his writings from the early 1990s.

While many cite Fresh Kills Park as a realized example of Landscape Urbanism, Corner instead insists that it provided a metaphoric testing ground to work through some of the ideas fueling the discourse (similar to earlier experiments in the garden later applied to the city; see Baroque gardens and French urban planning in the eighteenth and nineteenth centuries, for example).[50] He does consider his work at the University of Puerto Rico (see "Botanical Urbanism" in Part Four) an early example of Landscape Urbanism because it integrates transit, development, ecological, and cultural agendas. Yet he has recently deployed the principles of Landscape Urbanism on a much larger scale in his scheme for Qianhai, a new dense urban district on the western edge of Shenzen in China's Pearl River Delta with an anticipated population of four million people. In his Afterword to this compilation, Weller examines this project, which may well serve as a model for planning cities undergoing rapid growth. In its maximization of limited open space for water cleansing and catchment combined with recreational amenity as the structuring element, it is landscape as infrastructure—beautiful in its legibility and anticipated performance. How it will withstand threats of cultural obsolescence, inevitably posed by the capitalist city (which China's cities have become), has yet to be determined.

### On Part Four: *Practice*

The final section in this book is not about commercial practice and describing recent commissions, but about creative or working methods that have been tested and deployed to generate built works and proposals for the contemporary city. As a finalist in the Downsview Park competition in 1999 (with architect Stan Allen), winner of the Fresh Kills Landfill park competition in 2001, and the selected designer for New York's High Line in 2004, Corner rapidly transitioned out of the confines of the academy and into practice in the largest and densest city in the United States. Navigating the complexities of public projects in New York and subsequently all over the world clearly impacts both the content of his essays and his writing style. His essays become more succinct and lack the suggestive ambiguities of his earlier texts, and thus do not necessitate the same analytical and contextual description I have undertaken in the introduction to Parts One through Three. Despite this palpable shift in his writing, however, uncovering methods of creative inquiry (now in practice) remains Corner's primary focus in part four. In addition, while essays from the years 2000 to 2004 were largely void of reference to cultural metaphor and meaning, writings like "Botanical Urbanism" and "Hunt's Haunts" reveal that instrumentality is never Corner's exclusive concern, but are subservient to a broader insistence on activating and provoking the imagination in the process of making and experiencing places.

Part Four begins most lucidly with a short piece from the 2010 *Harvard Design Magazine* issue devoted to landscape architecture and urban design practices. It provides significant insight into what occupies Corner's critical attention as a leading practitioner in the field. Though it exudes pragmatism, the essay challenges the field to continue searching for new modes of creative inquiry, specifically in areas of (1) "critical experimentation in action," rather than the hermeticism of academic inquiry, (2) public engagement "that supports imagination and innovation," and (3) the necessities for productive collaboration. The latter two are most revealing of a matured landscape architect who juggles large-scale public projects in some of the most socially progressive cities in the country (including New York, Seattle, and Santa Monica). It is in such contexts that Corner has been provoked to develop new creative methods and techniques.

For instance "Botanical Urbanism" is an essay rich in description of working method. It provides a clear example of client engagement that Corner adapts for broader constituent involvement in many of his subsequent professional projects. The presentation of "three purposefully provocative scenarios" to the university president and his board, each of which contained a range of characteristics that were equivalently desirable, elicited dynamic discussion. Through these initial provocations and the subsequent dialog they prompted, Field Operations was able to get a sense of primary values and priorities and generate a "hybrid graft" that synthesized the three concepts into one. Without bringing initial provocative ideas to the table to ensure productive and engaged discourse, the public process has the tendency to denigrate into checklists of stakeholder expectations and the design becomes more about subservient appeasement than developing stimulating and imaginative places. One might hope that in moving forward Corner frames these uncovered potentials in community engagement and collaboration as new "agents of creativity."

Part of both public and client involvement is the art of persuasion as a working method. Persuasion does not imply manipulation, but rather creatively crafting an argument, most productively achieved through visual material. In this

FIG. 3 — The High Line, Photograph by Iwan Baan, 2011

way, ideas can be *seen* and made to inspire, rather than simply heard in abstract. While "plotting" and unearthing design ideas through critical practices of eidetic imaging are not part of Field Operations' everyday working process, persuasive imaging and argumentation has ensured continued success. These images are used as instruments for challenging others (often nonprofessionals) to think critically about the expectations they have of their environment and their values about their city. That said, because of the pervasiveness of computer generated photo-realistic renderings today, many such imaging tools have diminished capacity for provocation. Corner should remain self-evaluative in this case, if he is to sustain a fresh and compelling form of critical action in practice.

The essays culminate in a previously unpublished tribute to the immensely prolific and influential landscape historian, John Dixon Hunt, whose career Corner celebrates through the lens of the High Line. While this anomalous text may seem out of character with the rest, it reveals a kind of full circle in Corner's writings about landscape and its construction. It is also a long-awaited recognition of the impact Hunt inevitably had on Corner during their nearly two decades of working closely in the Department of Landscape Architecture at Penn. With the attention generated around the High Line, which has stimulated billions of dollars of luxury development in what was a more slowly transitioning area, it is difficult to appreciate the less flashy subtleties of design that make this place such a successful backdrop for socialization and performance of public life. [FIG. 3] In "Hunt's Haunts," Corner refers to the High Line as a *garden*, which it undoubtedly is, yet with this word as associated with Hunt (see Hunt's essay "What on earth is a garden?" for instance) comes implications of metaphoric content and symbolic meaning.[51]

Seen through this lens, the High Line challenges us to understand our relationship to the Natural world. It is both inspired by the persistence of natural process—voluntary seeding and succession—and the surreal artificiality of vegetal lushness elevated off the ground on industrial artifact. It becomes Corner's hermeneutical middle ground, a tangible reconciliation of the aporia that "haunts" Corner—between the achievements of technology and science and the phenomenology of dwelling. Corner asks in "Sounding the Depths," "how can we make the ordinariness of everyday situations into something imaginative or fresh, pertinent to our time but not estranged from tradition?" The High Line is one response.

### Looking forward

In sum, this compilation of Corner's essays should serve as a provocation for continued inquiry into the theories and methods of landscape architecture. Since landscape is an elusive and ever-changing medium, the field is now challenged by sparse and dispersed discourse that could benefit from periodically revisiting its foundations and the methods and modes of inquiry that fundamentally enrich it.

On a few occasions, Corner has adopted anthropologist Clifford Geertz's notion of "thick description" (see "Recovering Landscape" and a recent lecture he delivered called "The Thick and the Thin of It").[52] Yet what Corner's writings seem to leave for future scholarship is how such ethnographic investigation into sociocultural dynamics of a particular place might also serve as an "agent of creativity." While the relationship between "eidetic operations" and the productivity of the term *landschaft* remains ambiguous in his 1999 essay "Eidetic Operations and New Landscapes," perhaps one resolution is how the cultural processes and spatial practices that shape an "occupied milieu" might be more fully construed as an imaginative stimulus for design generation. Looking forward, we await the next volume of Corner's written project—his reflections on and projections for practice. With this, let us hope it stimulates renewed conversation on publicness, on maximizing cultural assets and rituals, and on the importance of urban places that are meaningful for the diversity of people that use them.

The essays that follow here are full of compelling ideas that continue to resonate and shape how landscape architecture is theorized and practiced. The most fundamental of these ideas is Corner's insistence on the *imagination* as essential to the making of landscapes *and* the insistence on making landscapes that provoke and challenge the imaginations of those who inhabit and experience them.

NOTES

**1** James Corner, "Recovering Landscape as a Critical Cultural Practice," in *Recovering Landscape: Essays in Contemporary Landscape Architecture*, ed. James Corner (New York: Princeton Architectural Press, 1999), 2.

**2** See Michael Speaks, who declared American "theory was fast philosophy" arriving to architecture late (according to Mark Wigley), in "Theory was interesting…but now we have work," *arq* 6/3 (2002), 210.

**3** Corner's theoretical stance was shaped by the lineage (in reverse) of Alberto Péréz-Gomez and David Leatherbarrow, their teacher Dalibor Vesley (the latter two of whom teach at the University of Pennsylvania), Vesely's teacher Hans-Georg Gadamer (see *Truth and Method*, 1960), who was profoundly affected by Heidegger and the hermeneutical tradition (see *Being and Time*, 1927).

**4** Margaret McAvin's introduction to the multiple responses printed in "Landscape Architecture and Critical Inquiry," *Landscape Journal* 10/2 (Fall 1991), 156.

**5** See Kenneth Frampton, "Towards a Critical Regionalism: Six Points for an Architecture of Resistance," in *The Anti-Aesthetic*, ed. Hal Foster (Seattle: Bay Press, 1983).

**6** This possibility was noted by Richard Weller in response to an earlier draft of this introduction.

**7** This quotation is from Corner's "Postscript" in "Critical Thinking and Landscape Architecture," which was eliminated for this book. See *Landscape Journal* 10/2 (Fall 1991), 162.

**8** Alberto Péréz-Gomez, *Architecture and the Crisis of Modern Science* (Cambridge, MA: MIT Press, 1983), 4.

**9** Corner, in "Three Tyrannies" explains, "By crisis, of course, one refers to the moment when one is not sure whether a problem may be solved or not, *a time of both anxiety and hope*" (italics added). See *Landscape Journal* 10/2 (Fall 1991), 131, n. 2.

**10** Edmund Husserl, *The Crisis of European Sciences and Transcendental Phenomenology*, trans. D. Carr (Evanston, IL: Northwestern University Press, 1970) 21–60. Quoted in Corner, "Discourse on Theory I," *Landscape Journal* 9/2 (Fall 1990), 65.

**11** Corner, "Discourse on Theory I," 77.

**12** Ibid.

**13** See Laurie Olin, "Form, Meaning and Expression in Landscape Architecture" in *Landscape Journal* 7/2 (1988): 149–68.

**14** See also Catherine Howett's 1987 essay on meaning in landscape architecture, titled "Systems, Signs, Sensibilities: Sources for a New Landscape Aesthetic" (*Landscape Journal* 6/1), in which she identifies the impact of semiotics and phenomenology on landscape architectural practice. While her intentions were to articulate "a new aesthetic canon" for landscape architecture, Corner's essays of the early 1990s express more ambitious concerns about the practice and process of theory.

**15** In addition to Spirn, the peer-reviewer also noted the work of Michael Hough as a pioneer of ecological strategies for urbanism in the 1980s.

**16** See Elizabeth Meyer, "Situating Modern Landscape Architecture: Theory as a Bridging, Mediating, and Reconciling Practice," in *Design and Values*, ed. Elissa Rosenberg (*CELA Proceedings*, 1992), 167–75; "Landscape Architecture as Modern Other and Postmodern Ground" in *The Culture of Landscape Architecture*, ed. Harriet Edquist (Melbourne: Edge, 1994), 13–34; "The Expanded Field of Landscape Architecture," in *Ecological Design and Planning*, eds. George Thompson and Frederick Steiner (New York: Wiley and Sons, 1997), 45–79. The combined writings of

Meyer and Corner from the 1990s provide a fundamental footing for landscape architecture, even as it is practiced today.

17    While landscape critic Simon Swaffield makes a distinction between an interpretive and critical approach to theory, Corner's hermeneutical approach is both. See Swaffield, "Theory and Critique in Landscape Architecture: Making Connections," *Journal of Landscape Architecture* (Spring 2006): 22–29.

18    See Richard Weller, "Between hermeneutics and datascapes: a critical appreciation of emergent landscape design theory and praxis through the writings of James Corner, 1990–2000," *Landscape Review* 7/1 (2001), 9.

19    James Corner, "Aqueous Agents: the (re)-presentation of water in the landscape architecture of Hargreaves Associates," *Process Architecture* 108 (1996), 34–42.

20    Corner, "Aqueous Agents," ("Coda").

21    Péréz-Gomez, *Architecture and the Crisis*, 138. See also Paul Ricoeur, *The Rule of Metaphor* ("Study 1: Between poetics and metaphor: Aristotle"), trans. Robert Czerny (Toronto: University of Toronto, 1977).

22    See especially Dalibor Vesely, *Architecture in the Age of Divided Representation* (Cambridge, MA: MIT Press, 2004), 24–36.

23    See Husserl, *The Crisis of European Sciences* and "The Origin of Geometry" (1936), printed in *The Crisis*…as an Appendix.

24    Quoted in Corner and MacLean, *Taking Measures Across the American Landscape* (New Haven, CT: Yale University Press, 1996), 149.

25    Corner, *Taking Measures*, 36.

26    See Marshall Berman, *All that is Solid Melts into Air: The Experience of Modernity* (New York: Simon and Schuster, 1982).

27    Corner, *Taking Measures*, xix.

28    Weller, "Between hermeneutics and datascapes," 17–18.

29    See, for instance, J. B. Jackson, "The Accessible Landscape," *Whole Earth Review* 58 [March 8, 1988], 4–9 in which he states, "I was an early advocate of studying landscapes from the air…But…I recently drove from New Mexico to Illinois and Iowa in my pickup truck. It was a long trip with many monotonous hours, but I do not regret it. It broke the spell cast by the air-view of the grid system and reminded me that there is still much to be learned at ground level. What goes on *within* those beautifully abstract rectangles is also worth observing."

30    Weller, "Between hermeneutics and datascapes," 18.

31    Corner, "Representation and Landscape," *Word and Image* 8/3 (1992), 248.

32    Robin Evans, "Translations from Drawing to Building," *AA Files* 12 (1986), 3–18.

33    Corner, "Representation and Landscape," 244–45.

34    As Corner expresses later in "The Agency of Mapping" in *Mappings*, ed. Denis Cosgrove (London: Reaktion Books, 1999), 213; Corner, "Representation and Landscape," 265.

35    Evans, "Translations," 7.

36    See Ian McHarg, *Design with Nature* (New York: Natural History Press, 1969) and "Ecological Determinism," in *The Future Environments of North America*, ed. John P. Milton (New York: Natural History Press, 1966), 526–38.

37    See Michel de Certeau's distinction between "strategies" (as top-down) and "tactics" (as subversive; bottom-up) in *The Practice of Everyday Life*, trans. Steven Rendell (Berkeley: University of California Press, 1984), xviii–xix.

38    Corner, "The Agency of Mapping," 251.

39    Corner, "Discourse on Theory II," 124.

40    Corner, "Landscape Urbanism," in *Landscape Urbanism: A Manual for the Machinic Landscape* eds. Mohsen Mostafavi and Ciro Najle (London: Architectural Association, 2003), 61–62.

41    Corner, "Not Unlike Life Itself," *Harvard Design Magazine* 21 (Fall 2004/Winter 2005), 34.

42    Anita Berrizbeitia, "Scales of Undecidability," in *CASE: Downsview Park Toronto*, ed. Julia Czerniak (New York: Prestel, 2001), 124. Corner states with seasoned confidence, "If…staged groundwork is too constrained or too complicated or too mannered, it will eventually calcify under the weight of its own construction; if it is too loose or too open or too weak, it will eventually lose any form of legibility and order. The trick is to design a large park framework that is sufficiently robust to lend structure and identity while also having sufficient pliancy and 'give' to adapt to changing demands and ecologies over time." See "Introduction," in *Large Parks* ed. Julia Czerniak (New York: Princeton Architectural Press, 2007), 13.

43    Corner, "Terra Fluxus," in *The Landscape Urbanism Reader*, ed. Charles Waldheim (New York: Princeton Architectural Press, 2006), 24. He most certainly found solace in Robert Smithson's reading of the work of Frederick Law Olmsted as a dialectical practice, which achieved great feats of artificiality only possible by instruments of modernity [See Smithson, "Frederick Law Olmsted and the Dialectical Landscape," *Artforum* 11 (1973)]. While Corner repeatedly looked to Koolhaas and Tschumi's proposals for Parc de la Villette as examples of innovative landscape architecture, it is worth noting that both architects were ignorant of the history of landscape design essential to staking such claims. For a pointed criticism of Tschumi's proposal, the components of which have precedent in this history, see Elizabeth Meyer's "The Public Park as Avant-Garde (Landscape) Architecture: A Comparative Interpretation of Two Parisian Parks, Parc de la Villette (1983–1990) and Parc des Buttes-Chaumont (1864–1867)," *Landscape Journal* 10/1 (Spring 1991), 16–26.

44    For a well-researched description of the evolution of Landscape Urbanism beginning at Penn in the late 1980s, and Corner's contributions to the discourse, see Jeannette Sordi, *Landscape Ecological Urbanism*, PhD Dissertation (University of Genoa, 2013).

45    Andres Duany and Emily Talen, eds, *Landscape Urbanism and its Discontents* (Gabriola Island, BC: New Society Publishers, 2013).

46    Corner, "Landscape Urbanism," 58.

47    Harvey quoted in Corner, "Landscape Urbanism," 61.

48    Corner, "Terra Fluxus," 32.

49    Ibid., 32–33.

50    Field Operations' original intentions for Fresh Kills Lifescape was to "weave" the divisions of symbolic representation and modern science through three shaping processes: cultural practices of strip-cropping (the land-as-lived), the integration of cultural memory (earthworks of WTC debris), and seeding of native plantings to create biodiverse habitats over time.

51    "What on Earth is a Garden?" and see also "The Idea of a Garden and the Three Natures," from John Dixon Hunt, *Greater Perfections: The Practice of Garden Theory* (Philadelphia: University of Pennsylvania Press, 2000).

52    See, in particular, C. Geertz, "Thick Description: Toward an Interpretive Theory of Culture" in *The Interpretation of Cultures* (New York: Basic Books, 1973). See Corner, "Recovering Landscape," 24, n. 5 and his lecture, "The Thick and the Thin of It" presented at *Thinking the Contemporary Landscape* conference in Hanover, Germany, organized by ETH Zurich with the Volkswagen Foundation, June 22, 2013.

Part One

———

# THEORY

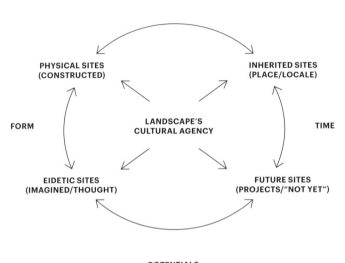

GIVENS

PHYSICAL SITES
(CONSTRUCTED)

INHERITED SITES
(PLACE/LOCALE)

FORM

LANDSCAPE'S
CULTURAL AGENCY

TIME

EIDETIC SITES
(IMAGINED/THOUGHT)

FUTURE SITES
(PROJECTS/"NOT YET")

POTENTIALS

FIG. 1 — Landscape's cultural agency diagram, by James Corner, 1996

# CRITICAL THINKING
# AND LANDSCAPE ARCHITECTURE

What is critical thinking? What is the point of it? We may find it easier to understand the validity of such discourse in literature, art history, or politics but what is its relevance to landscape architecture? One could quite convincingly argue that to talk of theory and criticism seems secondary and academic compared to the magnitude and severity of today's global problems. In such a light, perhaps, art itself may be seen as an eccentric practice, of little consequence in a world bestruck by more down-to-earth problems. To argue otherwise is often thought of as naive, and yet perhaps it is more naive to ignore the possibility that the two topics—theory and practice, art and life—might somehow be more significantly related, and fundamental to the landscape imagination.

Technocratic thinking has predominated Western culture for more than two centuries. The emphasis on objective and pragmatic reasoning has promoted a view of life that is more about the efficiency of means and ends, methods and techniques, than questions of existence and being. Critical thinking offers a more balanced perspective, focused as much on the "why" as the "what" and the "how." At its best, critical thinking strives to unite art with life, and as far as this pertains to the design and habitation of lived environments, critical thinking is of utmost significance to landscape architecture and placemaking.

Before I proceed with this argument, it might be useful to look back to the social institutions of late-seventeenth-century Europe—to the origins of modern criticism, according to literary theorist and critic Terry Eagleton in *The Function of Criticism* (1984). Eagleton explains how modern criticism was born of a struggle against the absolutist and the authoritarian state by a liberal and educated

*Originally published in:* Landscape Journal *10/2 (Fall 1991): 115–33. © 1991 Regents of the University of Wisconsin. Reproduced with permission.*

bourgeoisie seeking increased individual freedom and choice. Politicians, lawyers, theologians, physicians, actors, poets, artists, and so on would meet in the coffeehouses and clubs to exchange conversation, opinions, and ideas.

Richard Steele's *Tatler* and Joseph Addison's *Spectator* were periodicals central to the burgeoning public sphere of the early-eighteenth century and were indeed animated by notions of moral correction and satiric ridicule of the aristocracy. The *Tatler* and *Spectator* were catalysts for a new social grouping—"a reformative apparatus."[1] The *Spectator* also became Addison's platform for articulating much of the ideology behind the English landscape garden—its freedom from unnecessary constraints and its availability to a larger social group.

It is important to note four fundamental tenets of this early form of critical thinking. First, from its outset, modern criticism, or "the free, equal interchange of reasonable discourse," extended across all domains of social life and worked within a large public sphere.[2] It was not hermetic, nor was it solitary, but was rather a significant social and political force, operating from within and employing conventional languages.

Second, the eighteenth-century critical thinker was a generalist, a *bricoleur*, or dilettante—an amateur who rambled across many diverse social and intellectual territories. Multiple ideas and fields of discourse were drawn together into insightful observations and arguments by the roving critic. Addison, for example, was both informer and popularizer, interpreter and mediator. Critical judgment was therefore the fruit not of elitist dissociation, but of an energetic collusion with everyday life.[3]

Third, the rules and constitution of critical discourse were founded on a conversational and circumstantial sense, rather than on doctrines of absolute authority and certainty. The assumptions that underlaid ideas were reflected upon through dialogue and contemplation, in critical response to specific circumstances and particular situations.

Fourth, this early form of critical thinking was both emancipatory and conservative. On the one hand criticism sought radical rupture—a break from authoritarian politics—and on the other hand it sought to consolidate a new position through the codification and regulation of practice.[4] In this way, critical thinking acted as both prompt and stabilizer.

It is perhaps ironic that today critical thinking in landscape architecture is itself looked upon with skepticism and distrust by many. People are generally wary of it because it appears to lack any substantive social function, unlike the eighteenth-century equivalent. Unfortunately it is probably true to say that much of contemporary theory and criticism in the architectural arts is simply either the crutch for an ailing practice striving to keep up appearances through an illusory discourse of legitimation, or used primarily by an elite and hermetic group in academic circles, thus failing to gain traction in the broader field.

Unlike primary criticism—where the masters are the performers, the explicators who understand through doing and making—the discourse of secondary criticism is abstract and external.[5] If primary criticism has more to do with cultural politics as formed through the practice of one's own discipline, then secondary criticism is autonomous, focused on itself in a self-validating, self-generating manner. If primary criticism is grounded in authentic experience, in a human and ecological sense of creative activity, then secondary criticism belongs to the grammatical-logical discourse of mental concepts and structures detached from material practice.

So much of today's critical thinking is sadly less about the creative processes of making and action than it is about theories of theories. Today we find books about books about books, theories of texts of critiques of landscapes, four or more removes from real life. This parasitic form of secondary criticism is the trap and seduction of academic institutions, as well as of our critical journals and professional glossy magazines. Theory and criticism is in danger of becoming its own market, both producing and consuming its own images and discourse (prevalent in architecture today, for example). A disengaged and externalized rhetoric all too easily replaces the primary concern for the production of authentic and meaningful landscape architectural experience as embodied in built form. Paradoxically, the secondary criticism that seeks to disclose and examine the origins of the primary inevitably surrounds and suffocates the creative original through its own autonomous and self-referential mass.

But what, then, might be the key criteria for a primary and essential form of critical thinking, especially one pertinent to landscape architecture? What are the criteria by which critical thinking in landscape architecture may be deemed valid and significant?

Certain clues pointing toward an answer may be found in the characteristics of the discursive criticism of the eighteenth century, as well as in education scholar Stephen Brookfield's book, *Developing Critical Thinkers* (1987). Brookfield and Eagleton both explain how critical thinking begins with skepticism, particularly with regard to authority, rules, and conventions that have long gone unquestioned.[6] Although such skepticism may often be subversive, it is neither cynical nor destructive, but rather emerges from a discontentment or a lack of fulfillment.

Critical thinking also involves reflection, a considered and thoughtful analysis of the issues and values involved. This is followed by speculative contemplation, a formulation of alternatives and possibilities—necessarily fluid and unconstrained. Finally, critical thinking culminates in action: decisions are made, and work is done. The critical position is first established and then strategically acted out. Subsequently, the critical work itself becomes subject to future explication and critique.

The work of critical thinkers affecting landscape architecture, such as Addison, Richard Payne Knight, Uvedale Price, Lewis Mumford, Frederick Law Olmsted, and Robert Smithson, has shown us the rewards of a critical practice—a tradition that is continued today in the work of many leading practitioners. Indeed a critical stance is fundamental for any sort of clarity, legibility, and meaning in design. Critical practice is fundamental to any form of significant landscape architecture.

In my own work and studio teaching, I have often drawn from the practice of "plotting." This is a curious idea because of its fourfold meaning and suggestiveness. First, plotting refers to the marking and building of a piece of ground—a plot of land. Second, it refers to the graphic representation of that landscape, as in a plotted map or plan. Third, it refers to the construing of a narrative or time series, as in an unfolding or sequential plot. And fourth, it suggests the strategic, and perhaps subversive, act of devising and hatching a plot. Plotting therefore refers to the critical invention and inscription of new patterns for inhabitation in the landscape. We map and "lay out" our agendas and strategies, connecting and revealing previously unforeseen relationships. To plot is to critically cultivate our relationship to landscape.

Plotting is thus criticism participated within and through the work of landscape design in a specific place and time. It asks that one rethink, re-present, or replot those ideas that lie latent in landscape. Such restructuring is the function *par excellence* and justification of critical thinking in landscape architectural design. This is radically different from the grammatical-logical discourse of secondary criticism and academic chatter. Instead, critical making implies that the focus of valuation and interpretation lies in the work itself. "Work" is highlighted here to mean both the temporal process of puzzling and making—informed by the tactile perception of site and place with a critical, imaginative response—as well as the final product or built form.

In this light, Kenneth Frampton's coining of the term "critical regionalism" offers a useful approach toward balancing local phenomena with global technique and critical insight. In "Towards a Critical Regionalism" (1983), Frampton articulates an argument for a practice that resists the homogeneity promoted by monolithic processes of modernization—the ubiquitous landscape—and, at the same time, resists the sentimental urge to return to a preindustrial or vernacular regionalism.[7] Here, critical thinking in design mediates and bridges between the local and the global, between past inheritance and future potential, and between recovery and invention.

Thus, the most effective form of critical thinking in landscape architecture occurs through working in landscape architecture. Similarly, the best readings of landscape architecture are the specific works themselves, the reception of which is only enhanced and enriched through subsequent representations (painting, photographs, texts, etc.). Plotting is therefore an active critical process, enacted and embodied in built form and subsequently enriched through representation and discourse. It is a mode of work. The critical thinker is simultaneously critic, strategist, communicator, and maker.

The landscape imagination is a primary form of critical action in society, embodying creative reflection on the inheritance, context, and potential of designed landscapes. Works in the landscape are situated in space, time, and tradition, and inevitably become the site of future reflection, exposition, and projection. As such, there can be no significant landscape architecture without robust living and ongoing critical thought.

NOTES

1   See Terry Eagleton, *The Function of Criticism* (London: Verso Editions, 1984).
2   Ibid., 9.
3   Ibid., 23.
4   Ibid.
5   See George Steiner, *Real Presences* (Chicago: University of Chicago Press, 1990).
6   Stephen Brookfield, *Developing Critical Thinkers* (San Francisco: Jossey-Bass, 1987).
7   Kenneth Frampton, "Towards a Critical Regionalism," in Hal Foster, ed, *The Anti-Aesthetic* (Port Townsend, WA: Bay Press, 1983).

FIG. 1 — The Greek *Theatron* shares an etymological root with *theos,* or *theoria*. It was conceived as the stage upon which divine events were enacted and made manifest. Epidauros, Greece

Photograph courtesy of Douglas Stebila (www.douglas.stebila.ca)

# SOUNDING THE DEPTHS—

## ORIGINS, THEORY, AND REPRESENTATION

Specialists without spirit, sensualists without heart. This nullity imagines
that it has attained a level of civilization never before achieved.
—Max Weber, *The Protestant Ethic and the Spirit of Capitalism* (1905)

The modern concern for symbols implies a new contact with the sacred,
a movement beyond the forgetfulness of Being manifested today
in the arbitrary manipulation of empty signs and formalized languages.
—Paul Ricoeur, *The Conflict of Interpretations* (1969, translated 1974)

There has been a recent plea by practitioners and academics alike for the creation of a vibrant, all-encompassing body of landscape architectural theory. It is interesting and timely to ask why. What is theory, or what might it be, and why should we need it? What do we expect from theory?

Perhaps, concerned about the relative youth of the profession (certainly not the art itself) or the sparse distribution of work in space and time, we look for theory to provide a foundation, a shared basis and purpose for the practice and performance of the discipline. In this way, theory might be expected to provide a responsible structure, with attendant principles and axioms from which prescriptions for action may be drawn.

Alternatively, perhaps we look to theory not so much for stability and coherence, as for rupture and newness. Theory might act as a sort of disruptive catalyst, an inventive prompt, fostering new thought and inquiry within the discipline.

*Originally published in:* Landscape Journal 9/2 (Fall 1990): 60–78. © 1990 Regents of the University of Wisconsin. Reproduced with permission.

Theory may therefore be sought after, on the one hand, to stabilize and provide a set of codified principles of production or, on the other, to resist the status quo, maintaining heterogeneity and prompting change. In the former case, theory is a stabilizer, while in the latter, it is an innovative mechanism. This is neither a dichotomy nor a paradox, but remains a poorly understood relation. It may be discovered that theory in landscape architecture is in fact a much more elusive and enigmatic phenomenon than would first appear.[1]

There are those who would argue with conviction that there is no need or time for theory today. Others might remind us that landscape architecture is primarily a craft profession, an artisanal practice requiring multiple skills and talents. Such people may tell us of the lifetime commitment necessary to learn and master myriad technical skills, in which case theory would just get in the way. This may be true. In much of contemporary discourse, there is considerable divergent rhetoric having very little to do with a profession that is primarily a material endeavor, striving toward a greater artfulness and grace in its attendant skills.

However, there is a distinction between craft and motivation, between the skill of making and the purpose that motivates the skill. Craft may often win professional design competitions. It can be repeated and, to a degree, taught. Its skills can be deployed without any reference to feelings, history, or ideas. Motivation, however, necessitates the definition of a particular stance toward life—some idea of a culture's relationship toward the world and existential problems. It employs the feeling found in cultural memory and personal experience to generate meaning, wonder, and expression. Motivation engenders a heightened sense of purpose. At its greatest, it is an epiphany, a revelation, a new way of seeing the world. Motivation establishes a vital alertness, a sensitive curiosity, and an insatiable sense of marvel. A built landscape may well survive blemishes of craft, but will rarely survive a creative stillbirth.

This relation between craft and motivation, the how and the why, is the forgotten role of theory. Originally, art and architecture were understood as a unity between *techne* and *poiesis*.[2] Here, techne was the dimension of revelatory knowledge about the world, and poiesis was the dimension of creative, symbolic representation. Techne made no distinction between the theoretical and the practical. Making was understood as the embodiment of knowledge and ideas; we could say that craft was motivated. This unity fell apart in the seventeenth and eighteenth centuries. Techne became a separate body of instrumental or productive knowledge, and poiesis became an autonomous creation of subjective and aesthetic reality. This separation coincided with the origin of modern science (technology) and modern aesthetics (art).

It also involved an irretrievable alteration of the role of theory in architectural production.

In this essay, I hope to trace the nature of this shift and explain the various transformations in the use of theory. I argue that the contemporary crisis of meaning is due in large part to the epistemological break with tradition during the eighteenth century, and conclude that modern technological thinking works merely to perpetuate an excessively "hard" world in which culture and the landscape imagination remain difficult to reconcile.

### Theoria and Cosmology

The concept of *mathesis* emerged around the seventh century BC in preclassical Greece. It was an early form of mathematics that employed a numerical symbol system representative of the *lebenswelt* — an old German word that means the world-as-lived, the pre-reflective sphere of lived and subjective relations.[3] This implies that we come to know the world as we live in it, through our senses and instincts. It acknowledges human perception as the primary form of knowing, involving direct engagement and participation with the world. The symbols used in mathesis were never seen to be separate from the material and finite world given to perception. Instead, they were considered to be invariable entities that enabled the communication and transmission of knowledge. To engage these ideas was to tamper with the world itself, a very powerful form of magic.

Mathesis was the first step toward *theoria.* Theoria provided the first coherent conceptual system through which the lifeworld could be comprehended at a higher level. It enabled humans to disengage themselves from the ordinariness of the immediate world and enter into an independent universe of discourse.

Later, in the development of Greek philosophy, theoria was extended to astronomical and religious thinking, enabling a reconciliation between events in the immediate world and the divine order of the cosmos. From the term theoria came theology (the science of being), theophany (literally god appearance), and theater. The *theatron* was a stage upon which the deities would appear; the cosmos was made manifest and a spectacle enacted, in which the audience would transcend the banalities of everyday life. [FIG. 1] The *theoriai* were ancient Greek envoys who would visit distant theaters and festivals to observe and understand the "measured movements" of the "visible Gods." Through worldly observation, they looked forward to a kind of revelatory seeing that would momentarily clarify their being in the cosmos. The practice and explication of theoria was therefore limited to particular groups of theoreticians. Architects and gardeners, for example, were merely those who possessed technical skill, not theoretical knowledge. The ancient rites of site selection and orientation were governed by a special group of theoreticians within the priesthood.[4]

Another sense of the term theoria refers to the continual anticipation of something unexpected, something previously unforeseen, and something that would change one's life thereafter, like a revelation or vision. Architectural theorist David Leatherbarrow has written: "The experiences of longing, sighting something divine or true, and the onset of a new time or kind of life, are the necessary parts of ancient theoretical experience."[5] The classical understanding of theory, therefore, was a means by which a culture comprehended the lebenswelt; the way in which they could escape everyday life and marvel in wonder at the cosmos; and the way in which they awaited revelatory understanding to enact change of some sort in their lives.

In antiquity, and later in classical philosophy, artifacts and gardens were understood as figurative representations of the theoretical world. Greek theoria permitted the beginnings of an architectural theory, a *logos* of architecture. Architects became aware of their ability to transform the physical world, understood as a privileged form of metaphysics. The sacred world could be engaged and embodied. The Aristotelian notion of poiesis was the creative act by which raw matter, *hyle*, was given shape. It was figured according to an idea, *eidos*, to appear as a meaning-laden icon.[6] Early artifacts, especially temples, and gardens were thus visible embodiments of invisible ideas—they were idealizations understood under a variety of terms such as symbol, *typos*, emblem, and *figura*. In the Aristotelian world there was no separation between theory and practice; theory elucidated and justified practice, while practice retained its primordial meaning as poiesis. [**FIG. 2**]

It is important to recall that the origins of what we now call landscape architecture were buried deep within this symbolic ontology of myth and religion and that, as a profoundly traditional activity, its primary ideological role was as a representational art. Architecture critic Alan Colquhoun has described the aim of all such art as being the creation of "figurative and hierarchically organized form, to establish a sense of cultural centering and give the impression that the problems of modern life can be resolved at a transcendental level."[7] In this case, the essential idea in traditional representation lies latent in the verb "to edify," meaning to build to instruct or improve spiritually. For example, the enchanted gardens of Eden or Hesperides were mythically embodied places of both bodily and spiritual restoration, providing culture with some of the most consoling and enduring myths. As a different kind of example, one might consider the archaic acts of earth marking at Avebury, Stonehenge, and Carnac as being theoretically motivated constructs, sophisticated embodiments of ritual and astronomy.

FIG. 2 — An image of the world depicting the Aristotelian cosmos, holistic and complete,
by Cesare di Lorenzo Cesariano, from his edition of Vitruvius's *Ten Books on Architecture*, 1521

Courtesy Anne and Jerome Fisher Fine Arts Library, University of Pennsylvania

In ancient Mesopotamian culture, earth, air, fire, water, celestial movements, and seasonal patterns all possessed a profoundly sacred significance. The totality of earth and sky, gods and humans, was only assured through direct discourse with the deities. This was given through an orderly reenactment of celestial and terrestrial cycles, hierarchically embodied from house to temple. The Ziggurat temple was always built on the highest hill, vertically central and focal to the city and was symbolic of the hill itself. It was both celestial because it touched the heavens, each tier colored after one of the planets, and terrestrial because it mediated the underground tomb of God. Centrality and Symmetry were understood as symbolic gestures that represented the unity of the cosmos.[8]

The same depth of symbolic content, though of a completely different sort, can be seen in the Persian paradise gardens and later in the enclosed Moorish gardens of Granada: the Alhambra and the Generalife. Here, the sensual qualities of sight, sound, taste, and touch were controlled in such a way to give bodily pleasure and poetic delight, but they were still primarily understood as a representational iconography of a greater Islamic cosmos, idealized and embodied. The rich sensuality of these beautiful gardens was understood to be Allah himself—celestial paradise on earth.[9]

Later, inspired by the paradise gardens, the delicate sensuality of the European medieval gardens evolved, enclosed safely away from the wilds of untamed nature. While such gardens were a source of sensual comfort and delight, they also contained religious symbols and figuration. In Dante's *Divine Comedy,* the garden as *microtheos* was where God resided, and was therefore a much more divine and gentle place than the menacing world outside.

In all of these works, art was a *mimesis* of the primary reality given to perception—the primary reality being all that is tangible and mutable in the world. However, this mimesis was never just a mere reproduction, but rather a figurative representation of an eternal *idea,* something theoretical. Art provided the mediation between the human and the divine through a symbolic transfiguration of the real—plants, weather, seasons, and other physical elements. According to art historian Rudolf Wittkower, beauty was seen in things that were beheld theoretically and was inseparable from mathematics, music, and laws of nature.[10] For example, the symbols by which early medieval painters depicted nature bore little relation to actual appearance. [FIG. 3] Rather, many of these paintings and gardens conveyed symbols of divine perfection—idealized nature, eternal and sacred—as distinct from everyday life.

Many of the built landscapes before the Enlightenment were conceived and understood as figurative embodiments of divine order. They were manifestations of theoretical knowledge. Gardens during this time provided a kind of

. Cucurbite .

Cucurbite. oplo. fri a bū. ci f. Siceno recies unices. uuusinctun unciginr. sium Jo cunirum. cre lubricanr. Jemio norunin. ci mun i finapi. Quo gnif / mazimini medicai a frin. ouenuir colicr inunnbs estate omibe regioibes pripue inuioiusbi.

FIG. 3 — The picture is an iconography of symbols depicting God's generosity toward fruit and bloom. Manuscript illustration from *Tacuinum Sanitatis*

Courtesy Austrian National Library, Vienna

cosmic "quarry," gravid with histories and myth. Theoria remained very much a unifying concept of cosmic order. As a representational art, such gardens provided symbolic settings that situated a culture in relation to its history and the cosmos.

The cultural sharing of theoretical knowledge through idealized mimesis and iconographic content continued through the late Renaissance and Baroque eras. For example, the iconography of many villas, such as the Villa Lante or the Villa Aldobrandini, was rich with classical figures, symbolic fountains, and hidden grottos expressing aspects of classical mythology.[11] Here, form, geometry, and pattern possessed a profound symbolic content, embodying, communicating, and mapping ideas.

### The Scientific Revolution

The traditional symbolic system of theory and representation was radically altered during the late-seventeenth and early-eighteenth centuries, largely because of the revolution in scientific thinking. Previously, the medieval and Renaissance cosmologies asserted that number and geometry were a universal science, the link between the human and the divine. Even as late as 1619, mathematician and astronomer Johannes Kepler, in his *Harmonices Mundi*, wrote:

> The Christians know that the mathematical principles according to which the corporeal world was to be created are coeternal with God, that God is the soul and mind in the most supernally true sense of the word.[12] [FIG. 4]

And elsewhere:

> God, from the very beginning, and purposefully, has selected the curved and the straight for stamping the world with the divinity of the creator.[13]

During the early-seventeenth century, Galileo first brought this relation into question as he began to suggest that not only ideal but also empirical reality was mathematical in nature. Galileo opened the way for objectivism by making mathematic nature an "in-itself," a pure construct. Mathematics detached from the lived world was to become the object. The increased use of mathematics as an instrument for objective reasoning eventually superseded its use as an idealized representation. This transition occurred during the seventeenth and eighteenth centuries, during a period that Dalibor Vesely has called a time of "divided representation."[14] That is, there was a period when mathematics was still part of traditional cosmology, endowed with divine properties, while at the same time emerging as the basis for a new kind of representation: the instrumentality of modern science.

This time of transition was sustained during the eighteenth century in large part because of the myth of divine nature, grounded in Newtonian natural philosophy. Although Isaac Newton's empirical work was agreed upon and accepted during this time and would later evolve as the basis of nineteenth-century positivism, there remained a potent Neoplatonic cosmology in which geometry and mathematics still held transcendental value for many people. Newton and others still believed that God had composed the great masses in the universe and had set them into motion. The creation of matter from pure space was a notion that appeared in Plato's *Timaeus* (circa 360 BC).

The final transformation occurred around 1800, when geometry, mathematics, and other symbol systems became purely formal disciplines, shedding any last vestiges of metaphysical content.[15] The advocates of modern instrumentality assumed that mathematical precision and empirical clarity were radically superior to the ambiguous indeterminacy of symbolic, cosmological representation. It is at this point where the phenomenologist Edmund Husserl positioned

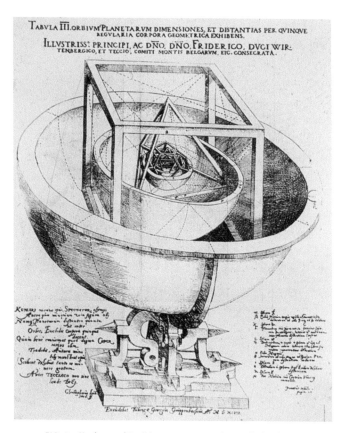

FIG. 4 — Kepler used Euclidean geometry and numerical orders to theoretically chart the divine, harmonic movements of the universe. Engraving by Johannes Kepler, from *Mysterium Cosmographicum*, 1596

the "crisis" of modern science and theory. He argued that the displacement of knowledge from the world as lived, or as sensibly perceived, created a distance between human life and nature. The freeing of science from its basis in the lebenswelt and its founding subjective nature was undoubtedly a necessary condition for all of its conquests, but Husserl argued that this freeing also carried the threat of an alienation, an objectivist occultation that makes the world increasingly abstract and inaccessible. For Husserl, the autonomous instrumentality of modern science "reduced nature to a mathematical manifold."[16]

Alongside this transformation occurred a similar shift in religious order. The religious metaphors began to lose their compelling force in the face of new, fresh ones. There followed a diminishment in the church's influence over human imagination, and religion lost much of its secular and moral power for several centuries after this. Therefore, the break with tradition during the seventeenth and eighteenth centuries was not solely due to advances in reason and science, but also to the deterioration of religious unity and sacred values.

A significant outcome of these changes was the splintering of the previous traditional cosmology, once holistic and complete, into separate categories. During the eighteenth and nineteenth centuries, art, science, language, religion, and myth were each differentiated and packaged neatly into contained bodies of knowledge. Jürgen Habermas has written that:

> The project of modernity, formulated in the eighteenth century by the philosophers of the Enlightenment, consisted in their efforts to develop objective science, universal morality and law, and autonomous art according to their inner logic. At the same time, the project intended to release the cognitive potentials of each of these domains from their esoteric forms. The Enlightenment philosophers wanted to utilize this accumulation of specialized culture for the enrichment of everyday life—that is to say, for the rational organization of everyday life.[17]

These separate spheres of knowledge were to move increasingly apart as each divergent specialization became more autonomous and self-referential, isolated in great institutions away from public life. Philosopher Michel Foucault has related this phenomenon to that of a panopticon—knowledge became trapped in a spherical prison wall. On the one hand, it could be surveyed and closely studied, while on the other hand, it could not escape. Estranged from the larger world of shared discourse, the possibility of creative exchange was severed, constituting a radical discontinuity with history and shared knowledge.[18]

Throughout the eighteenth and nineteenth centuries, institutions and academies were formed for specialists to engage in the project of reason. For example, the French Royal Academy of Sciences was founded in 1666. This academy, together with the Royal Society of London, regarded itself as contributing to Francis Bacon's "utopia."[19] Looking toward an enlightened world, the academies embraced the ideals of a positivistic science, building their theories and practice around reason and certainty. Less and less could the arts be based on mimesis, since the material world was reduced to a cortege of facts, drained or neutralized of any divine content.

During this time, schools of architecture and the associated arts were also changing. In 1671, the Royal Academy of Architecture was founded in Paris. The traditional apprenticeship provided by the Masonic guilds was superseded by an unprecedented emphasis on rational theory. The École Polytechnique was formed in Paris during the late years of the eighteenth century. It was a

FIG. 5 — Frontispiece from J. N. L. Durand's *Recueil et Parallèle des Édifices de Tout Genre, Anciens et Modernes*, 1801

Courtesy Adam Fetterolf Collection, Anne and Jerome Fisher Fine Arts Library, University of Pennsylvania

progressive institution, which taught, for the first time, architecture as a science, emphasizing logic and rational method. Principles of Euclidean geometry, algebraic analysis, order, and style were classified into various typologies and systems, which were then put forth as universal methods of technique and design.

The professor of architectural theory in the school was Jean-Nicolas-Louis Durand, who in 1801 published the *Recueil et Parallèle des Edifices de Tout Genre, Anciens et Modernes*. [FIG. 5] This work is used by Alberto Péréz-Gomez to exemplify, in architecture, the complete deterioration of theoria into a self-referential instrument used solely for the control of *praxis.*[20] That is, Durand successfully laid the foundation for an architectural order that was based neither in tradition nor in life experience, but referred instead to an architectural autonomy. Durand stressed the irrelevance of transcendental justification in architecture, rejecting outright the powers of intuition and metaphor. For Durand, architecture needed only to validate itself as something useful and rational in a material world governed by pragmatic values.

From Durand and the École Polytechnique emerged an architectural theory grounded in pure methodology and technique. Theory was reduced to a set

**FIG. 6** — Design for an English garden based on the new geometry, by Batty Langley in *New Principles of Gardening*, 1727

Courtesy Anne and Jerome Fisher Fine Arts Library, University of Pennsylvania

of technical operations, promoting an architectural discipline suspicious of intuition and sensible perception. Vesely states that architecture became "an instrumental discipline, with a formal purpose but with no explicit meaning, making it an instrument of pure *ars inveniendi.*"[21]

Another example of the reduction of theory to rules and method is designer Batty Langley's *Practical Geometry as Applied to Building, Surveying, Gardening and Mensuration,* published in 1726, and *New Principles of Gardening,* published in 1727. These works provided all the necessary principles and theorems of Euclidean geometry as a basis for all the building crafts. Langley applied it methodically and practically to the description of lines and layout in gardening, drawing plans for labyrinths, groves, cities, and estates, and even "wildernesses." [FIG. 6] For Langley, geometry was a scientific tool, "the basis of any layout," and he seemed unable to comprehend the symbolic implications of a geometry that imposed its form on nature in the stylistic manner of Baroque gardens.

Durand, Langley, and others, following on from Descartes, increasingly discredited the humanities by showing them to be matters of subjective caprice and ambiguity.[22] Artifacts made as a result of the application of mathematical laws of physical science and reasoned logic were considered to be of a higher value than those made as a result of mimesis and intuition. Beauty and aesthetic delight, once integral with mathematics, music, and knowledge, now became separated. Ambiguous and subjective, art presented modern people of reason with something untidy and illogical.

In 1750, Alexander Baumgarten published *Aesthetica.* This was the first reasoned discourse on the philosophy and theory of art, especially regarding beauty and taste. Baumgarten asserted that precise and distinct cognition achieves its clarity by abstracting from the confusions of the concrete, that is, by focusing in and discarding the irrelevant. But he also went on to discuss another mode of cognition, that of subjective sensibility. This, said Baumgarten, was not necessarily clear and distinct, but possessed a richness that did not sacrifice the sensual complexity of the concrete.

For Baumgarten, scientific thinking caused an inevitable devaluation of the sensual. He therefore favored subjective sensibility as a superior mode of looking at the world. He argued that art, which reveals the richness of the world, was a necessary complement to the sciences, which reveal the underlying structure of the world. The mid-eighteenth century therefore oscillated between these two poles of aesthetic and scientific thought. Although Baumgarten conceived their original relationship to be complementary, they were later to move farther apart with increasing antagonism.

Part of the reason for this was the evolution of "taste." Taste, as formulated by Baumgarten, was that by which an educated person intuitively deems something to be true, without any need, or ability, to explain why. Taste was to aesthetics what reason was to science. The people who possessed such innate good taste were free to discover their own sensibilities toward the world. However, this presented a problem for those concerned about people who lack taste: How could a standard be made by which to guide and control taste? In an attempt to provide some tangible criteria for beauty, the Earl of Shaftesbury wrote extensively about the importance of rules and examples.

Thereafter developed the notion of "good taste," with the academies becoming the educational arbiters. They provided their scholars with principles and standards that would assure good and reasoned taste. Ironically, the freedom granted the artist by Baumgarten's original conception of subjective taste now deteriorated into a kind of standard, governed by the elite members of an academic club.[23]

The point here is to show that the traditional symbolic system of representation, of which theoria was an integral part, was replaced not only by the autonomy of instrumental representation grounded in scientism, but also by an aesthetic representation grounded in the fallacies of taste.

Contemporary with this evolution emerged the practice of historicism. This is too complex a topic to cover here, but it should be noted that the Enlightenment philosophers, in their quest for reason, also sought an objective account of history and tradition.[24] A result of this practice was the treatment of history as a rational evolution of periods, factual occurrences, and formal styles. As with the sensual world, the realm of history was largely reduced and objectified. Landscape and architectural traditions were compounded into an ensemble of forms and types, all classified and measured. This project contributed to the eighteenth-century degeneration of the cultural foundation of meaning previously attached to architectural orders and forms. It was with this mind-set that the European Grand Tour not only provided an aesthetic acquisition of Classical taste, but also presented historical styles and forms as emblematic icons of the ideals of previous "higher" cultures.

This skeletal account of the development of Enlightenment aesthetics and historicism serves to set the ground for the way theory was to evolve during the past two centuries. When one traces the development of landscape architectural work since the late-seventeenth century, the aestheticization of landscape, the increased borrowing of emblematic forms from history, and the altered nature of theory and practice become clear.

### The Aestheticization of Landscape

Versailles may be used as an example to represent the beginning of secularization during the seventeenth century and the increased influence of Cartesian reasoning. [FIG. 7] No longer clustered around churches, the plan of Versailles centers around the king's palace. The centrality of the palace is reinforced by the park, attended by infinite vistas and limitless domain. Everything receives its place in relation to the royal point of view. This is truly secular in that only the point of view of the ruler is admitted—a kind of "divine kingship." Although it is idealized, it is no longer a mediation between humans and God. Philosophy scholar Karsten Harries has written:

> An art such as that presented at Versailles is born out of an awareness of man's metaphysical loneliness. Man's search for a measure finds an answer, if only an aesthetic answer.…The work of art provides man with an illusion of completeness; but now the price to be paid for this illusion is man's autonomy. Man himself becomes part of such a work.[25]

However, the geometry at Versailles still held symbolic power for the people at that time. Although this was not directly related to God, it was clearly a symbolic operation that evoked ideal truth and excellence. Baroque perspectivism was not in any way equivalent to that of the nineteenth century. One cannot compare the vistas at Versailles to Haussmann's boulevards. As Pérez-Gomez writes:

> In seventeenth-century Versailles, color, smell, light, water games, fireworks, and indeed the full richness of mythology played a major role. The meaning of the place as the seat of government and the dwelling of the Sun King derived from a synthesis of the power of geometry and its potential to enhance sensuality.[26]

It is not insignificant that, in 1657, designer Andre Mollet published *Le Jardin de Plaisirs,* the first work to stress aspects of bodily and aesthetic pleasure as exemplified through the formal geometries of French formalism. In his book, Mollet offered some practical advice, but most of the text is spent in an Aristotelian discourse. Praxis for Mollet was inextricably linked to the conception of an animistic cosmos. The gardener's life was supposed to be a part of the rhythms of cosmic time. Similarly, designer J. Boyceau's *Traité du Jardinage* (1638) postulated that the gardener should have some practical knowledge, but that ultimately the traditional poesis of gardening, connecting humans to the

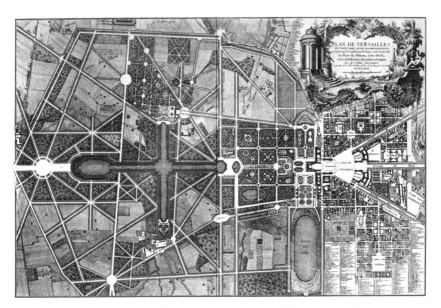

FIG. 7 — Plan of Versailles, from a plan made by the Abbé Delagrive, 1746

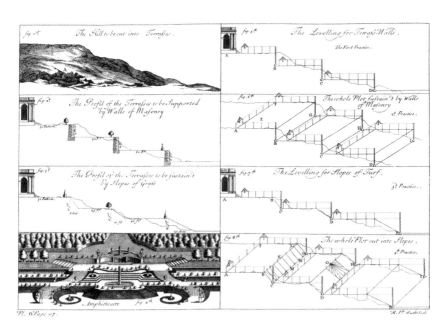

FIG. 8 — Techniques of leveling and terrace construction, from John James's English adaptation of Dezallier d'Argenville's *La Théorie et la Pratique du Jardinage* (1709), 1712

FIG. 9 — Gothic Temple with Palladian Bridge in foreground at Stowe House,
Photograph by Roger Bennion, Buckinghamshire, England, 2012

Courtesy Roger Bennion (http://www.flickr.com/photos/53783410@N03/)

earth, was the primary objective. The object of gardening was never simply the production of crops or the domination of nature.

In 1709, landscape gardener Dezallier d'Argenville published *La Théorie et la Pratique du Jardinage,* codifying the art form into rules and axioms. A much adapted translation to English, by John James, appeared in 1712. This work stood in contrast to that of Mollet and Boyceau. There was no metaphysical dimension in d'Argenville's work, merely practical guidelines, rules, and methods applied to site construction, plant propagation, and planting techniques. The geometry of the Baroque garden was now identified with the practical geometry of the surveyor. This work, as with Durand's, constituted the emergence of a new concept of "theory": theory as *ars fabricandi,* mere method and technique. [FIG. 8]

Increased travel across Europe and into the Americas and China later provided the impetus for a reaction against the rigid geometries of the French garden. As early as 1685, author Sir William Temple had written about the "natural" and irregular gardens of China, noting extensively the pleasurable "aesthetic" experiences of grottos and wild places. Later, architect William Chambers wrote a dissertation on Oriental gardening, citing formal principles of variety and contrast.[27] In England, between 1700 and 1720, there was a shift from the French and Dutch models to a landscape of irregularity, contrast, variety, and distant views. Poet Alexander Pope, with Addison, Langley, and designer Stephen Switzer, articulated the principles of this new model in writings considered as theory, articulating the necessary technical know-how for a particular aesthetic to be achieved.[28]

The customary European Grand Tour and the landscape paintings of Claude Lorrain and Nicolas Poussin ignited an interest in the classical literary genre and the Arcadian-agricultural landscapes of Italy. Moreover, it inspired the eclectic borrowing of both foreign and historical styles. A landscape informed by a pictorial and literary genre, and strewn with figural fragments of history, was further permeated by a fourth influence, theater and stage design.[29]

Stowe may be used as an excellent example of this new movement. These early gardens were a kind of bricolage of figural fragments, literary allegories, and theatrical scenography. [FIG. 9] Here, from Enlightenment aesthetics emerged the manipulation of the landscape for sensory and imaginary stimulation, while from the Enlightenment project of origins and history emerged the eclectic distribution of ruins and figural fragments—emblems of historical time arranged along allegorical narratives.

During the late-eighteenth century, the nature of theory was largely centered on the debate about landscape aesthetics and taste. Sir Uvedale Price published *An Essay on the Picturesque, as compared with the Sublime and the Beautiful* in 1874. Artist William Gilpin also published *Three Essays on Picturesque Beauty* in the same year. Richard Payne Knight was a rhetorical member of the group, taking an adversarial stance toward Gilpin and Price. Herein ensued a war of aesthetic taste; the "roughness of the Picturesque" being preferred over the "smoothness of the Beautiful"—the latter castigated for its lack of natural drama and elemental melancholy. [FIG. 10] Price labeled landscape architect Capability Brown "the genius of the bare and bald." He wrote: "The worst is that Brown fixes and stamps such a character of monotony on all that he does."[30] In Price's writing, there emerged a striking and radical importance attached to purely visual criteria. With Gilpin, too, there was a visual aesthetic that he clearly favored, a quality that was singular in his understanding of landscape.

Citing paintings by Salvator Rosa and John Constable, the protagonists of the Picturesque debate developed a new formal syntax emphasizing things such as "foregrounds and sidescreens," "roughness and variety," "contrast and chiaroscuro," and "gradation and effect." The landscape was to be contrived as a picture. Even though William Kent had worked in a pictorial manner seventy-five years earlier, there was so much more to Kent's landscape, each scene possessing some literary or allegorical content. With the rusticated Picturesque, however, the landscape was pure image, reduced to a singular pictorial representation.[31] The result was an aestheticized landscape, where form and picture became the primary content or meaning.

The Picturesque "formula"—or perhaps we might call it, in a now much depreciated sense of the word, "theory"—caught the imagination of designer Humphry Repton, who synthesized it in 1794, when he wrote *Sketches and Hints on Landscape Gardening*, and later in 1805, *Observations on the Theory and Practice of Landscape Gardening.* Repton, whose work certainly played a preliminary role in the beginning of an aestheticized nineteenth-century eclecticism, wrote:

> I do not profess to follow either Le Nôtre or Brown, but selecting beauties from the style of each, to adopt so much of the grandeur of the former as may accord with a palace, and so much of the grace of the latter as may call forth the charms of natural landscape. Each has its proper situation; and good taste will make fashion subservient to common sense.[32]

Here, Repton suggests that any number of aesthetic approaches and codified styles may be mixed and matched, once again all in the name of "good taste."

FIG. 10 — The garden undressed (top) and the garden dressed (bottom), or the picturesque and the beautiful, from Richard Payne-Knight, in *The Landscape*, 1794

However, if we remove the superficial and stylistic from Repton's treatise, we can see that he is intimating at an understanding of landscape as something somehow possessed with primordial content and meaning. He writes:

> I confess that the great object of my ambition is not merely to produce a book of pictures, but to furnish some hints for establishing the fact that true taste in landscape gardening, as well as in the other polite arts, is not an accidental effect, operating on the outward senses, but an appeal to the understanding, which is to compare, to separate, and to combine the various sources of pleasure derived from external objects and to trace them to some preexisting causes in the human mind.[33]

Repton seemed to be aware that art still primarily belonged to human ideas and the creative mind. His writing and theory inspired his friend, botanist J. C. Loudon to compile, edit, and disseminate the work after his death. In 1843, architect Joseph Paxton, a colleague of Loudon, designed Birkenhead Park, which ultimately caught the imagination of Olmsted and horticulturist Albert Downing. In 1841, Downing published *A Treatise on the Theory and Practice of Landscape Gardening*.

From Durand to Repton, d'Argenville to Downing, theory was clearly something different from that of the pre-Enlightenment period. Slowly, over the course of a century, theory's very form and purpose were altered. Theory had degenerated into a kind of technical knowledge, a methodology with attendant standards and principles. It became a practical "language," something that enabled production and repetition. Yet before 1800, art was primarily understood to be an embodiment of ideas and knowledge, imaginatively expressive of a culture and more analogous to a system of gestures and figures than to articulated language. However, it is the altered view of theory and representation that has persisted and had its most potent impact during the emergence of the early Modern movement.

### The Twentieth Century

Art critic Kenneth Clark uses Cézanne to represent the pivotal shift from a traditional, mimetic representation based in nature to the nonfigurative work of the Modern artists.[34] Clark acknowledges that Cézanne himself was not at all trying to work outside of nature and the primary realm. To the contrary, Cézanne was inspired to such an extent by nature that he wanted to discover a more profound way of expressing his "feeling" for a scene. He felt it appropriate to override the direct optical appearance of nature in favor of temperament. The same could also

apply to Piet Mondrian's early tree studies, which show a progressive transformation from appearance to essence.[35] [FIG. 11]

Also, in the work of artist Paul Klee, nature as image was displaced for a more profound look at its mythological and spiritual content. Wassily Kandinsky and Oskar Schlemmer were also particularly interested in the spiritual content of color and form. Others were to replace visible nature altogether, as in the abstract, formal inquiries of Kazimir Malevich or Mondrian. Here, the aesthetic object was solely the medium of expression and its specific technique of production. The new autonomy of the aesthetic sphere gave it license to become its own project.

The ascendancy of formalist aesthetics developed during the early-twentieth century. Retinal and sensory beauty were increasingly espoused as the primary role of art in the writings of this period. From art historian Konrad

FIG. 12 — The composition shows the primacy of formal inquiry.
Shape, color, transparency, visual balance, and optical dynamics form the primary
"idea content." *Composition QVIII*, by Lázló Moholy-Nagy, 1922;
Museum des 20. Jahrhunderts, Vienna

Fiedler's theory of "pure visibility" and "opacity," to the writings of philosopher Benedetto Croce or art historian Heinrich Wölfflin, developed the nonfigurative movement in art. Designer August Endell, a member of the German Art Nouveau, proclaimed:

> We are not only at the beginning of a new stylistic phase, but at the same time
> on the threshold of the development of a completely new art. An art with forms
> which signify nothing.[36]

In the early-twentieth century it was no longer required that art be imitative of nature or symbolic in its mediation between the mutable and the eternal. Instead, autonomous and self-referential form emerged as something "pure" that could be articulated within the limits of its own medium. If the specific realm of music was tone and rhythm, then that of the plastic arts was primarily form and color. [FIG. 12]

The power of this autonomous aestheticism has worked to pervade all art ever since. Modern art and modern landscape architecture were to evolve an aesthetic where form alone could motivate the content. No longer did form have to express or convey an idea, as an icon or figure. It was now possible for form itself to be the content. Whereas traditional art, understood as mimesis, represented an idea outside itself, pure form referred only to itself, thereby severing any mimetic relations. Pure form, or *gestaltung*, was therefore autonomous; self-referential, and self-generated.

Of course, this is not to say that such works had no meaning. The ground of meaning is in perception; and thus such works, once perceived, could be interpreted and could affect the way one sees the world thereafter. This was, and still is, the powerfully transformative value of autonomous and abstract art.

All of this new spirit had a profound effect on architecture. When the Bauhaus was formed, new inquiries were launched into the nature of pure form and geometrical space. Symbolic representation and even the notion of "essence" were radically displaced. A garden, or an artifact, no longer had to embody any values: It did not have to look like anything. It no longer had to directly express, signify, or recall any aspect of nature, tradition, or idea. Mimetically and symbolically it could be empty.

"Space" became the supreme concept—space as autonomous sets of Cartesian coordinates, floating infinitely, without context or place. "Space," crystalline product of the Enlightenment, was put forth as a substitute for the continuity of lived experience. The fascination with this new syntax of movement, spatial planes, volumes, geometries, and new materials prevailed and developed in the formalist experiments of the time. In landscape, such experiments were conducted in gardens by architect Gabriel Guevrekian, or to a lesser extent by landscape architect Fletcher Steele. This abstract method of work was later developed in various ways by landscape architects such as Garrett Eckbo, Dan Kiley, Roberto Burle Marx, Luis Barragán, and Lawrence Halprin. Perhaps Halprin was to be the sole practitioner in the group to continue a reference to nature itself through designs that both evoke and abstract natural forms and processes. [FIG. 13]

Early Modernism was, in particular ways noted above, an outcome of the Enlightenment project. Tradition and continuity were radically replaced by doctrines of "purism," originality, and novelty. Rationalization, aestheticization, and historicism evolved in a way that formed the basis for how a specialized

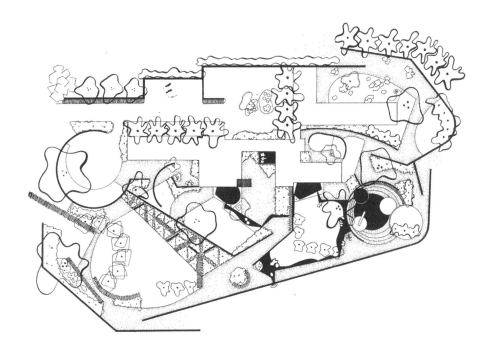

**FIG. 13 — Plan for the Burden Garden, by Garrett Eckbo, Westchester County, New York, 1945**

Courtesy Garrett Eckbo Collection, Environmental Design Archives, University of California, Berkeley

subculture of "experts" determined what was tasteful and beautiful and what was to be built. Theory today is merely an extrapolation of this. Whether it is used to explain why something exists or should be (positivism) or is used to provide the necessary know-how for the production of desirable work (normative methodology), theory today is clearly not that of theory in the classical sense. While theory was originally reconciliatory and afforded a collective participation in cosmic meaning, today it is aggressive, serving only as an instrument of autonomy, control, authority, and legitimacy.[37]

### Landscape and Theory Today—A Critique

From eighteenth-century landscape aesthetics to the social pragmatism and eclecticism of the nineteenth century, through the purist aesthetics of the early modern movement to the excessive positivism of the postwar era, the theoretical foundations of our contemporary profession have evolved directly from modern scientific thinking. They are simply extrapolated from a narrowly focused, one-sided, and contradictory doctrine with which we still live. On the one hand, there is an excessive technological school, based either in positivist problem-solving or in ecological mechanics and management. On the other hand, there is an equally excessive aesthetic school, based on personal combinations of historicist and formalist doctrines. Herein exists a separated and ambiguous relation between art, aesthetics, ecology, and history.

With this division, is it really so difficult to understand how many perceive landscape architecture as a mere service commodity trivialized to beautification and entertainment? This approach has produced landscapes that are efficient, practical for the user, and aesthetically pleasing, yet often strangely empty, without depth, mystery, or qualities of anything other than functional. In much of contemporary practice, a technological "ecology" replaces poetic dwelling; an overly aestheticized attitude displaces the power of symbolic content; parodic historicism replaces history and tradition; nostalgic regionalism opposes contemporary modernity; a fundamentalist "nature" movement displaces art and cultural representation; and the uncritical dogmatism of different camps replaces critical dialogue.

Theory's original mediatory role between the human and the divine, the immediate and the eternal, appears to have ended.[38] Theory today has been functionalized into a set of operational rules and procedures of primarily technological character: design methodologies, typologies, linguistic rules of formalism, functionalism, behavioralism, and so on. The result is that, for us as human beings, the mythical, metaphoric depth of the natural and cultural worlds has been neutralized, subject now to instrumentation and control.

At the beginning of this essay, I made a distinction between technique and motivation and stated that a landscape may well survive blemishes of craft, but that it will rarely survive a creative stillbirth. Today, stillborn landscapes are produced en masse around the globe. In the topography of pure reason, homogenous and without hiding places, the enigmatic encounter with things and places is flattened, without depth or horizon, devoid of imagination or greater meaning.

### Conclusion

Originally, artistic and architectural intentionality was transcendental, necessarily symbolic. Symbols effectively relate the finite and mutable to the immutable and eternal, lived reality to ideas. Symbolization is thus the most fundamental operation constituting meaning for human existence. As an operation, it belongs primarily to the realm of metaphor and poetics, not to objective reasoning and algebraic equations. The difficulty is that symbolic and poetic intentions are too often trivialized or rendered naive in a prosaic world where pragmatic values of efficiency and usefulness are predominant.

Landscape architecture has always stood in a privileged position in society, creating symbolic settings for cultural ritual and discourse. As a great mediator between nature and culture, landscape architecture has a profound role to play in the reconstitution of meaning and value in our modern cities and communities. It is not just a case of "greening" or providing "open space," but more a project of uplifting the human spirit and structuring deep forms of experiences and shared values. Such a project cannot exist outside the *a priori* of the human body and its engagement with the world. Landscape architectural theory ought therefore to find its basis less in prescriptive methodology and formulaic technique than in the realm of perception, the phenomenological, and the cultural imagination.

> Eternally chained only one single fragment of the whole, man himself grew
> to be only a fragment…Instead of imprinting humanity upon his nature,
> he becomes merely the imprint of his occupation.
> —Friedrich Schiller, *On the Aesthetic Education of Man* (1795, translated
>     1909–1914)

NOTES

**1**    This essay is closely allied to the work of others, to whom I am indebted. Similar
         arguments and discussion can be found in Dalibor Vesely, *Architecture and Continuity*
         (London: Architectural Association, 1981), Alberto Péréz-Gomez, *Architecture and the
         Crisis of Modern Science* (Cambridge, MA: MIT Press, 1983), and Hans-Georg Gadamer,
         *Reason in the Age of Science* (Cambridge, MA: MIT Press, 1981). I am particularly
         grateful for references and lengthy discussion provided by David Leatherbarrow and
         Laurie Olin.

**2**    See E. Grassi, *Kunst and Mythos* (Hamburg: Rowohlt, 1957), Jacques Ellul, *The
         Technological Society* (New York: Random House, 1964), and Dalibor Vesely,
         "Architecture and the Conflict of Representation," *AA Files 8* (London: Architectural
         Association, 1984).

**3**    See Maurice Merleau-Ponty, Introduction to *The Phenomenology of Perception*
         (Evanston, IL: Northwestern University Press, 1971); Edmund Husserl, *The Crisis of
         European Sciences and Transcendental Phenomenology*, translated by D. Carr
         (Evanston, IL: Northwestern University Press, 1970), and Alfred Schutz, *Structures of the
         Lifeworld* (Evanston, IL: Northwestern University Press, 1973).

**4**    I am indebted to David Leatherbarrow for this account. Also see Péréz-Gomez,
         *Architecture and the Crisis of Modern Science*.

**5**    David Leatherbarrow, "The end of theory," unpublished manuscript, 1989.

**6**    In this way, matter was "informed" by idea, and the artist thus performed a role
         analogous to that of God in creating the universe. See Erwin Panofsky, *Idea: A Concept
         in Art Theory*, translated by Joseph Peake (New York: Harper and Row, 1974), 40; and
         Rudolf Wittkower, *Architectural Principles in the Age of Humanism* (New York: Random
         House, 1962).

**7**    Alan Colquhoun, *Essays in Architectural Criticism* (Cambridge, MA: MIT Press, 1981), 13.

**8**    See Peter Carl, *Themes I: Architecture and Continuity* (London: Architectural
         Association, 1983).

**9**    See Anne-Marie Schimmel, "The Celestial Garden in Islam," *The Islamic Garden*, edited
         by Elizabeth MacDougal and Richard Ettinghausen (Washington, D.C.: Dumbarton Oaks
         and the Trustees of Harvard University, 1975).

**10**   See Wittkower, *Architectural Principles in the Age of Humanism*.

**11**   See David Coffin, *The Italian Garden* (Washington, D.C.: Dumbarton Oaks and the
         Trustee of the Harvard University, 1972).

**12**   In J. Kepler, *Harmonics Mundi IV, I* (1619), quoted by W. Pauli, "The Influence of
         Archetypal Ideals on the Scientific Theories of Kepler," in C. Jung and W. Pauli,
         *The Interpretation of Nature and the Psyche* (London: Routledge and K. Paul, 1955).

**13**   In Kepler, *Mysterium Cosmographicum* (Tubingen, 1956), quoted by Werner
         Heisenberg, *The Physicists' Conception of Nature* (Westport, CT: Greenwood
         Press, 1970).

**14**   Vesely, "Architecture and the Conflict of Representation," 22.

**15**   See Péréz-Gomez, *Architecture and the Crisis of Modern Science*.

**16**   In Edmund Husserl, *The Crisis of European Sciences and Transcendental
         Phenomenology,* trans. D. Carr (Evanston, IL: Northwestern University Press, 1970),
         21–60.

**17**   Jürgen Habermas, "Modernity—An Incomplete Project," in *The Anti-Aesthetic*, ed. Hal
         Foster (Port Townsend, WA: Bay Press, 1983), 16.

**18**   Michel Foucault, *The Archaeology of Knowledge* (New York: Pantheon Books, 1972).

**19**   Francis Bacon, *The Wisdom of the Ancients and the New Atlantis* (London:
         Cassell, 1900).

**20**   Péréz-Gomez, *Architecture and the Crisis of Modern Science*.

21  Vesely, "Architecture and the Conflict of Representation," 24. *Ars inveniendi* implies the "art" of uncovering truth through mathematics.

22  Rene Descartes, *Oeuvres* (11 volumes), eds. Adam and Tannery (Paris: L. Cerf, 1974).

23  See Karsten Harries, *Meaning and Modern Art* (Evanston, IL: Northwestern University Press, 1968), 24.

24  For a discussion on historicism, the reader is referred to writings of Alan Colquhoun, especially "Modern Architecture and Historicity," in *Essays in Architectural Criticism*, and "Three Kinds of Historicism," in *Modernity and the Classical Tradition* (Cambridge, MA: MIT Press, 1989).

25  Harries, *Meaning and Modern Art*, 26.

26  Péréz-Gomez, *Architecture and the Crisis of Modern Science*, 175.

27  William Chambers, *A Dissertation on Oriental Gardening* (London: W. Griffin, 1772).

28  See John Dixon Hunt and Peter Willis, *The Genius of the Place: The English Landscape Garden, 1620–1820* (London: Paul Elek Ltd, 1975).

29  For an account of how stage design permeated the early English Landscape School, see S. Lang, "The Genesis of the English Landscape Garden," in *The Picturesque Garden and Its Influence Outside the British Isles*, ed. N. Pevsner (Washington, D.C.: Dumbarton Oaks and the Trustees of Harvard University, 1974). Also see John Dixon Hunt, *Garden and Grove: The Italian Renaissance Garden in the English Imagination* (Princeton, NJ: Princeton University Press, 1987).

30  Quoted by Marcia Allentuck, "Sir Uvedale Price and the Picturesque Garden: The Evidence of the Coleorton Papers," in *The Picturesque Garden and Its Influence Outside the British Isles*, ed. N. Pevsner (1974).

31  For an interesting discussion on this reversal of picture and copy, see Rosalind Krauss, "The Originality of the Avant-Garde," in *The Originality of the Avant-Garde and other Modernist Myths* (Cambridge, MA: MIT Press, 1986).

32  Quoted in J.C. Loudon, *The Landscape Gardening and Landscape Architecture of the Late Humphrey Repton, Esq.* (London: Longman and Co, 1840).

33  Ibid., 164.

34  See Kenneth Clark, "The Return to Order" and "Epilogue," in *Landscape into Art* (New York: Harper and Row, 1984).

35  Essence, according to Immanuel Kant's *Critique of Pure Reason*, published in 1781, refers to something existent, but as it exists outside our knowledge, that which occurs when there is no direct human perception of it; that is, what it is in essence as opposed to appearance.

36  In August Endell, "The Beauty of Form and Decorative Art," in *Form and Function*, T. Benton and C. Benton, (London: Crosby Lockwood Staples, 1975).

37  The emancipation of techne from poiesis coincided with the origin of modern science (technology) and modern aesthetics. Whereas techne was once subordinate to poiesis, used only to inform the symbolic representation, they are now separate. The contemporary dominance of technology over the poetic perpetuates the primacy of the immanent and the material over transcendence and imagination.

38  See Leatherbarrow, "The end of theory."

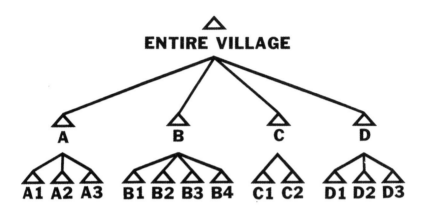

A1 contains requirements 7, 53, 57, 59, 60, 72, 125, 126, 128.
A2 contains requirements 31, 34, 36, 52, 54, 80, 94, 106, 136.
A3 contains requirements 37, 38, 50, 55, 77, 91, 103.
B1 contains requirements 39, 40, 41, 44, 51, 118, 127, 131, 138.
B2 contains requirements 30, 35, 46, 47, 61, 97, 98.

FIG. 1 — The structure of a design problem and the treelike hierarchy of logical
problem solving, from Christopher Alexander, *Notes on the Synthesis of Form,*
(Cambridge, MA: Harvard University Press, 1964), 151.

# THREE TYRANNIES OF
# CONTEMPORARY THEORY

Those who have always avoided the labor of the concept say they are tired of debates about theories, that one should get down to the thing itself, to the texts. This kind of talk is the symptom of a scientific crisis marked by the disjuncture of…theory and the practice of interpretation.
—Peter Burger, *Theory of the Avant-Garde* (1984)

For, if without prophecy there is no hope, then without memory there can be no communication.
—Colin Rowe, *Collage City* (1978)

The social and cultural dimensions of our postmodern condition have been explored by many over the past two decades, but the primary characteristic of the postmodern can be traced back through the whole modern era to the enlightenment shift during the eighteenth century.[1] Since that radical break with tradition, our culture has been caught in a period of transition. "Too late for the gods and too early for Being" according to Heidegger, a dislocated culture works toward a new time of consciousness, "learning anew to be human."[2] Faith has been superseded by reason in a world now governed primarily by the logic of modern technology and global economics. Heidegger refers to the resulting human condition as a "loss of nearness" or a loss of intimacy between humans and their environment as well as between people and their communities.[3] Clearly much of our built environment today reflects this estrangement and is perpetuated by most contemporary attitudes toward theory and practice in landscape

*Originally published in:* Landscape Journal 10/2 (Fall 1991): 159–61. © 1991 Regents of the University of Wisconsin. Reproduced with permission.

architecture and the related arts. This essay explores this condition by looking at the role of theory in landscape architecture and its ability to address some of the existential problems of our times.[4]

The objectifying logic of technology has emerged as a dominant force in our world during the past two hundred years. It has enabled societies to control the external world in the interests of efficiency and production; while at the same time it has displaced the movement of tradition (because of its progressivist position) and suppressed the poetries of art (because of its ideology of optimization). Many humanists have consequently attributed much of society's ills to the alienating effects of technology and capitalism, arguing for the need to transcend the reductionism of techno-economic thinking prior to the realization of a more humane built environment.[5] Indeed it could be argued that the primary problem of survival for the developed cultures of today is less a techno-biological one than it is an aesthetic and moral one.[6]

Traditionally, cultural products (as found historically in literature, painting, music, building, or landscape architecture) represent an infinitely rich array of interpretative gestures and figurative embodiments that have attempted in various ways to critically reconcile the historical with the contemporary, the eternal with the moment, the universal with the specific. Today, however, we find it increasingly difficult to manage this relationship. Many fail to appreciate the role that landscape architecture plays in the constitution and embodiment of culture, forgetful of the designed landscape's symbolic and revelatory powers, especially with regard to collective memory, cultural orientation, and continuity. It is not unfair to say that contemporary theory and practice have all but lost their metaphysical and mythopoetic dimensions, promoting a landscape architecture of primarily prosaic and technical construction.[7] After all, imaginative and poetic intentions are often rendered naive in a scientific world, where pragmatic values of efficiency and optimization are often considered more "real."[8]

Theory today is therefore quite different from *theoria*, the original Greek formulation of theory.[9] Whereas theoria was mediative and reflective and was derived from the primary realm of human experience and perception, modern theory has largely become an instrument of certainty and control, founded upon autonomous principles of external origin. The predominance of instrumental techniques and rational methods in an anthropocentric world is what has most characterized modern thinking. While the scientific attitude has led to a multitude of accomplishments in modern science, it has also underlain the emergence of a largely disembodied culture struggling to find meaning and continuity in community, environment, and time. For many, ours is a landscape of estrangement.

How might landscape architectural theory rebuild an "existential ground," a topography of critical continuity, of memory and invention, orientation and direction? To find answers, we must first explore and challenge three predominant approaches toward contemporary theory, each of which has a tendency to degenerate into a self-limiting tyranny of control and closure.

The first approach is *positivism:* a dogmatic, empirical approach that believes a logical synthesis will follow from a comprehensive and objective fact structure. The second is the use of *paradigms:* a belief that problems may be solved by looking to universal models for solutions and methods. The third is the *avant-garde:* a movement of intentional subversion, where the quest for originality spurs on an endless series of experimental reactions. In different ways, each approach derives from modern techno-scientific thinking, perpetuating an excessively "hard" world in which culture and the landscape imagination remains difficult to reconcile, or to figure.[10]

### Positivism

Positivism involves the explicit description and explanation of the factual phenomena with which it deals. Positive statements are assertions about reality as tested by scientific method, and that can withstand detailed and objective scrutiny. One part of positivism is *substantive theory,* or the science of the concrete. This aspect is concerned with identifying, explaining, and understanding the tangible phenomena with which it works. The purpose is to provide an objective and analytical knowledge base prior to any action. Another part of positivism is *procedural theory,* which is concerned with the scientific description and explanation of design processes. Combined, both parts constitute a *methodological theory* that strives to describe the world and account for actions taken in it.[11] The primacy of logical and objective reasoning in modern positivism has consequently led to the illusion of humankind's infinite capacity to explain, control, and put to work the forces of nature.

One of the positions taken by positivism in landscape architecture and planning is that no action may be taken, or any change initiated, until all the factual data have been collected. Teams of experts are assembled to work together in gathering the most complete and accurate data sets. This inductive procedure continues with the returns finally mapped, quantified, and tabulated. Rates of growth are then projected, predominant futures defined, and likely developments plotted. This is certainly true of modern "systems theory" and a variety of other methodological processes, especially in planning. One has only to plow through the complex matrices of architect Christopher Alexander's *Notes on the Synthesis of Form* (1964) or to look at the exhaustive collection of data involved

in Ian McHarg's suitability analyses to see the laborious nature of such an enterprise. Resembling pieces of electronic circuitry, formless diagrams, and maps
and charts are produced to show the rationale of the process, accounting for and
legitimizing the logical outcome. [FIG. 1]

Herein lies the tyranny, for it is assumed that factual data alone will auto-
matically lead to a logical and credible synthesis.[12] The data themselves are privileged as the source and destiny of the project and are often represented through
such a well-packaged techno-iconography that one wonders if an automaton
might be programmed to produce them. The final product never seems to be
quite so significant as the process.

The failing of extreme positivist approaches to design is that they validate
their theory in the realm of the objective and effectively suppress or exclude any
sort of imaginative vision or speculative free will. Subsequently the positivist's
quest for an empirically accountable resolution predicates the future as a "natural" extrapolation of the present status quo. Architectural historian Colin Rowe
has written:

> Not at all preoccupied with invention, their practical object is to disclose the
> immanent, to assist a particular condition (presumed to be latent) to "discover"
> itself; and, anxious to avoid the least possible imposition, their practice could be
> said to derive from a never too precisely formulated theory—that of maximum
> non-intervention. (Let us do nothing to inhibit the creative unrolling of time).[13]

The irony in such dogma is the failure to recognize or address the value-
impregnated quality of all observation. The experiment and the appropriate
fact gathering are produced under the assumption that the essence of factual
reality—nature—is mathematical. Instrumental thinking can take into account
only those facts that are susceptible to current mathematical and scientific
understanding, to the exclusion of those other aspects of the world that provide
us with the greater part of sensuous experience. What "facts" are selected and
used are those that support the hypothesis. As a consequence, "contemporary
thought is now endangered by the picture drawn by science," wrote theoretical
physicist Werner Heisenberg. "This danger lies in the fact that the picture is now
regarded as an exhaustive account of nature itself, so that science forgets that in
its study of nature it is merely studying its own picture."[14]

Further, facts, even if they could be found to be irrefutable and bias-free,
are inevitably overtaken by time—a consequence that will often undermine the
"all-accommodating" plan, rendering its original basis null and void.[15] Consider
the case of the Isle of Dogs at the London Docklands, planned as an "Economic

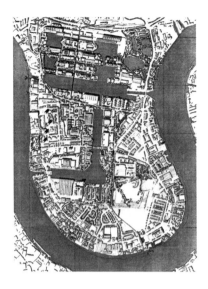

FIG. 2—Concept Plan for Isle
of Dogs, London Docklands,
1982, from *Isle of Dogs: A Guide
to Design and Development*
(London Docklands Development
Corporation, 1982)

© Greater London Authority (GLA) and GLA
Land and Property

Enterprise Zone" during the early 1980s. Architect Michael Wilford's penetrating critique of the planning process gone awry elucidates the failings of a "rational" design methodology supported by reams of analytical data and augmented only by populist vignettes in seductive marketing brochures.[16]

While the resulting plan at the Isle of Dogs was infinitely flexible and accommodating—as was demanded by the Thatcherite regime—it lacked strong formal and physical characteristics. An example of the "new pragmatism" in urban design, this "weak" form of flexibility was subsequently abused by the private and economic interests of those who bought into it, effectively destroying any possibility for a cohesive and stimulating public realm. The result is an urban landscape of "free for all" developer projects that relate very little, if at all, to one another. [FIG. 2]. In terms of scale and experiential coherence, the Isle of Dogs appears ad hoc and lacks any clear spatial vision or *idea.* Wilford describes the plan as "simplistic. It does not express either an exemplary image, or mood of confidence or credibility. It is a highly innocent diagram…based on caution, modesty, and the least possible imposition."[17]

Other built landscapes that result from the positivist attitude seem equally impoverished and uninspiring. They are usually mathematically efficient and economically profitable, while the poetries of place have been blindly erased. Built and planted over in universal fashion, the hygienic image is empty and inoffensive. Think of the sterility of Milton Keynes, much of the London Docklands, or many American shopping malls and suburban developments. Cleansed of memory and consciousness, these deserts of quantitative reasoning form a strip-like cortege of anaesthetized landscapes (however much used they may be by mass culture).

To extrapolate a future from an illusory, albeit quantitative, fact structure is highly dubious. If metaphysics, poetry, myth, and interpretive imagination are excluded from any synopsis of the real, then any outcome must be considered incomplete, if not completely erroneous. The existential world cannot be reduced to mathematical formulae imposed by techno-economic logic. This cybernetic attitude is anathema to anybody who knows the world to be as wonderfully enigmatic as it is, charged with mystery and infinite value. Yet how difficult is it for many of us today to imagine there being anything more to the world, or to a landscape, than its value as a measurable resource—with practical, economic, and aesthetic "performance metrics."[18]

### Paradigms

Another approach toward theory is that of the paradigm. A paradigm represents a lens through which a group of practitioners share a view of history and nature so as to be able to proceed in a stable, coherent manner. Physicist Thomas Kuhn defines paradigms as "universally recognized scientific achievements that for a time provide model problems and solutions to a community of practitioners."[19] Practice interprets the world and works within it using its paradigm. A paradigm is therefore a means by which a community can determine a sense of common identity, establish some form of socialization, and practice in a consistent and productive way. By following the rules and precepts of a particular paradigm and working methodically with its models, one can move toward an assured solution.

A paradigm works for a community because it sorts out fundamentals, providing a shared basis for focused and detailed work. It provides the models and methods by which complex problems may be comprehended and solved. However, a paradigm will only continue to work for as long as it can account for a particular situation. When anomalies do occur, paradigms become subject to modification and, ultimately, replacement by a new paradigm. Kuhn traces such "paradigm shifts" in astronomy and physics, beginning with Aristotle and Ptolemy, through the Copernican revolution in the thirteenth century, on to Kepler, Newton, Lavoisier, and Einstein. Landscape architecture also has a chronology of paradigmatic phases and subsequent shifts, such as the break from Classicism to Romanticism in England during the beginning of the eighteenth century; or the break from a nineteenth- and twentieth-century anthropocentric dominance of nature to a form of ecological integration between human systems and the environment during more recent years.

A new paradigm will carry with it attendant principles, methodologies, and models. In landscape architecture these are represented by new treatises, manifestos, journals, and executed works. To solve a problem, one must first turn to the principles underlying precedent solutions. As a landscape architect confronted with a particular site and program, one might use a paradigmatic "model solution." The task then would be to adapt or transform the model to fit the peculiarities of the specific problem. Over a long period of time this process of application, adaptation, and transformation can refine and enrich the paradigm, making it fuller.

Here a distinction needs to be made, because the term *paradigm* can legitimately be understood in two entirely different ways. First, it can stand for an *ideology:* a complete constellation of beliefs, values, and general laws as shared by a particular community—a way of looking at the world. Second, it can refer to *exemplary models,* particular forms, or "types," which represent the ideology *applied.*[20] Further elaboration of this distinction follows.

### Paradigms as ideologies

Ideological paradigms establish theoretical frameworks within a particular philosophy. In this sense, formalism, historicism, ecologism, or poststructuralism are paradigmatic. Positivism and the avant-garde are also ideological paradigms; that is, they are belief systems with laws and values necessary for coherent practice. We cannot escape this form of paradigm, nor should we want to if it is appropriate and working well.

However, while such paradigms are inevitable, they are always only partial, unable to account for every aspect of reality. A paradigm represents only one way of looking at things and often constructs such a compelling world that it becomes almost impossible to see the worlds of others. While there may be several "schools of thought," each developing its own paradigm, there is little chance of dialogue between them because each has its own specific languages, codes, and norms. At their worst, ideological paradigms can produce such blinkered research and practice as to become rigid and insular, inevitably closing in on themselves and degenerating into dogma. Consider the previous case of positivism, for example; or the deterioration of Modernism and subsequent emergence of Postmodernism in reaction to that.

### Paradigms as models

The second sense of the term *paradigm* is more problematic and has been the one most used by architects and landscape architects over the years.[21] This is the notion of paradigm as a very specific "type," or an exemplary formal model

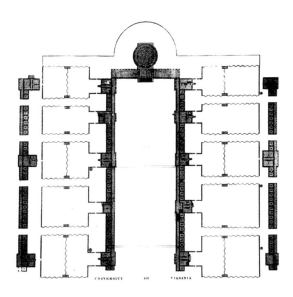

FIG. 3— Thomas Jefferson's plan of the University of Virginia, engraving by
Peter Maverick after a drawing by John Neilson, 1825

Courtesy Special Collections, University of Virginia Library, Charlottesville, Virginia, Accession #6552 and 6552-a

that represents an ideology applied. For example, Thomas Jefferson's University of Virginia (1822) may be considered as an applied model of Classical principles, appropriated from a specific work and applied to campus planning. [FIG. 3] Alternatively, from the world of Deconstructivists, one might look to the Wexner Center for the Arts (1988) at Ohio State University, by Peter Eisenman and Laurie Olin, as an applied example of decentering and scaling. In turn, these works themselves become paradigmatic models of spatial and social ideologies, available now for replication or transformation.

The early architectural treatises of Alberti and Palladio were written using paradigmatic models. Landscape treatises by Andre Mollet, Dezallier d'Argenville, Humphry Repton, and Andrew Jackson Downing also provided models that embodied the applied principles of a coherent landscape architecture. Presented like advice, a series of axioms, rules, and techniques were described in order for a "successful" landscape to be built.

For example, in Downing's *Treatise on the Theory and Practice of Landscape Gardening*, published in 1841, the purpose of the book was stated at the beginning. People who wished to embellish their grounds needed only to consult the book for "some leading principles, with the knowledge of which they would find it comparatively easy to produce delightful and satisfactory results."[22]

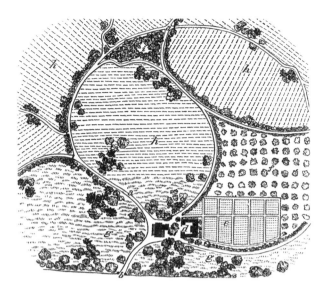

**FIG. 4**— A prototype plan for a picturesque farm (*ferme ornée*), by Andrew Jackson Downing,
in A *Treatise on the Theory and Practice of Landscape Gardening*, 1841

Following Repton's lead, Downing devoted a major part of the book to making a distinction between the "Beautiful" and the "Picturesque." The Beautiful was described as being "graceful…flowing…curvaceous…verdant…and placid," while the Picturesque was described as "striking…irregular…rough… and tumultuous." The paintings of Claude Lorrain were used as models of the Beautiful, while those of Salvator Rosa represented the Picturesque. One of Downing's "rules" was that the two styles should not be mixed, proclaiming that one should "always endeavor to heighten, or to make that single expression predominate; it should, clearly, either aim at the Beautiful or at the Picturesque."[23] Sketches, planting plans, massing diagrams, and layout plans were used as models to illustrate the application of either style. [FIG. 4]

Herein lies part of the problem with paradigmatic thinking in the arts; by the time Downing wrote his *Treatise*, the original ideological and intellectual fervor that initially produced the English Landscape School had degenerated. The philosophy had become illusory; only the *image* persisted. When the ideological content of the original model dissolves, the empty form becomes nothing more than an icon for past cultures and their ideals. This is the danger of paradigmatic models, or "types"—they persist long after the philosophical basis has been forgotten. Form lingers, replacing content.

This accounts for part of our difficulty today, where much of practice looks primarily at the formal image of certain models without understanding their origins or traditions. This consumption of signs merely perpetuates the excesses of aestheticism and historicism, exemplary models being reduced to "stencils" for easy reproduction as fashion and taste desire.

Two contemporary advocates of the typological approach in architectural and urban design are Leon Krier and Rob Krier.[24] For the Kriers, exemplary type is a de facto form, something invariable and not open to radical transformation. They understand architectural form to be external to historical evolution, with eternal and immutable laws. The Kriers' taxonomy of "types" and "design rules" is based on confined interpretations of Classical models and the nineteenth-century writings of the town planner Camillo Sitte.[25] Today's New Urbanists continue a practice of urban design and planning drawn from a catalog of principles, forms, and types.

While there is much good sense and aesthetic quality in some of the New Urbanists' work (Seaside comes to mind), one must be wary of an underlying nostalgia that effectively nullifies the movement of creativity and cultural change. The progressive nature of art stands still when an absolutist historicism is substituted for genuine history. To extrapolate a future from models of a pre-enlightenment past is to ignore all that has happened in between. How can we possibly say that Pablo Picasso, Willem de Kooning, or Marcel Duchamp have had no effect on us, not to mention the specific contributions to landscape architecture by Frederick Law Olmsted, Garrett Eckbo, Ian McHarg, Lawrence Halprin, Roberto Burle Marx, Robert Smithson, or James Turrell? And what of our investigations into the galaxies, or at the opposite scale into the very structure of genes, challenging our conceptions of space and time? Our paradigms of nature and landscape continually change. To work outside this dynamic continuum is a naive prescription, counteractive to the movement of historical time and negligent of what it means to be "modern." To recall historian Mircea Eliade: "Living in conformity with the archetypes amounted to respecting the 'law'...through the repetition of paradigmatic gestures, archaic man succeeded in annulling time."[26]

Not all typologists are as absolutist as the Kriers, however. Alan Colquhoun has explained how there have been two predominant views of history, one absolutist and the other relativist. The relativist view understands history as a series of closed epochs, each with identifiable beginnings and ends relative to culture and time.[27] An outcome of the creation of historicism and historiography during the Enlightenment, it is the way most landscape architectural history classes are presented—as a *chronology* of styles, forms, and types peculiar to a particular period. Typology for the relativist does not consist of "eternal" forms, but of forms and ideas belonging to stylistic "periods."

Rowe and Colquhoun both argue that the relativist view has produced two primary positions: one looking back, as in historicism, the other looking forward, as in futurism. In the former, history runs the risk of being reduced to what can be seen. Formal styles become signs for the "higher" ideals of previous cultures and can be appropriated in any combination. As we have seen in the Postmodernism of the previous two decades, this neoconservative view has tended to impoverish and trivialize an authentic sense of tradition. The problem here is stated poignantly by Goethe, who wrote in 1794:

> All dilettantes are plagiarizers. They sap the life out of and destroy all that is original and beautiful in language and thought by repeating it, imitating it, and filling up their own void with it. Thus, more and more, language becomes filled with pillaged phrases and forms that no longer say anything; one can read entire books that have a beautiful style and contain nothing at all.[28]

If the product of the positivists is a program devoid of form, then that of the rational typologists is a form devoid of program.[29]

In the progressivist view, by contrast, history runs the risk of being turned away from altogether. Instead of looking to paradigms of the past, the futurist looks to a radical invention of both social program and formal relationships. That is, by turning away from tradition and history, looking instead to a utopian future, the progressivists believe that they are actually being true to the relativity of their own time. This is in fact the basis of Modernism and underlies the tendencies of the avant-garde.

## The Avant-Garde

From Vitruvius to Quatremère de Quincy, from Repton and Downing to Alexander and McHarg, theory has primarily been the elaboration of rules and procedures for production. The avant-garde, however, can be characterized as a movement to resist the stability afforded by such precepts, actively avoiding any affiliation to tradition and convention. Its proponents believe that their work must be constantly made afresh, and they find creative adrenaline in risk, novelty, and polemical experiment. The rejection of rules and limits is an intentional attempt to create rupture, announced in the dictum: "Make it new!" [**FIG. 5**]

Our present time can be understood as the result of successive avant-garde movements—an outcome of the relativizing of history. Tired of historicist eclecticism and wanting instead to celebrate the advances of modernization, the early

**FIG. 5 — "The Art Critic," by Raoul Hausmann, 1919–1920**
Courtesy Tate Gallery, London © 2013 Artists Rights Society (ARS), New York / ADAGP, Paris

avant-gardists looked boldly into the future and, in so doing, believed they were being faithful to the *spirit* of history: Art could best fulfill its historical destiny by turning away from tradition and expressing instead the peculiarities of its own time. To be modern meant to be new, and to be new meant that one had to be original.

In the arts this view rejected the traditional bases of art, especially the traditions of *mimesis*—the notion that an artwork refer to an idea outside itself, as in mimetic representation.[30] Instead, Konrad Fiedler and others talked of the "opacity" of a work of art, where art need only refer to its own making.[31] As societal modernization stormed ahead, the early avant-garde sought refuge in this newfound autonomy. Thereafter followed Futurism, Purism, Constructivism, and a host of other movements. Polemical manifestos (usually to the political left) announced the end of classical notions of beauty and harmony and rejected the traditional idea that nature be the supreme metaphor for all art. The work of Kazimir Malevich, Vladimir Tatlin, El Lissitzky, and Yakov

FIG. 6 — Garden at the Villa of the Vicomte de Noailles, by Gabriel Guevrekian, Hyères, France, 1926
Courtesy André Lurçat, Terrasses et Jardins (Paris: Editions d'Art Charles Moreau, 1929)

Chernikov displayed the formal and nonrepresentational nature of these early experiments, completely unforeseen in any of the preceding art movements. In addition, the nonfigurative works of Mondrian and Kandinsky explored how the pure qualities of color and shape alone might be seen to have their own integrity and meaning. Georges Braque and Picasso developed the languages of Cubism and collage, privileging everyday materials. Duchamp went even further, reacting to the new formalism by proposing a completely "anti-retinal" art, an art where the pleasure was to be found in the "playfulness" of purely mental concepts. For the early avant-garde, therefore, the media of expression itself and the techniques of production became the aesthetic object, leading the critic Clement Greenberg to define such a movement as "autonomous," "self-referential," and "self-generating."[32]

In the early 1920s a few gardens that appeared in France sought to give expression in landscape architecture to the new ideas expressed in modern art. The landscape architect Andre Vera criticized historical approaches to garden design—especially those of Le Nôtre—as early as 1912, and his writing clearly influenced the architects Robert Mallet-Stevens and Gabriel Guevrekian.[33] Guevrekian's Jardin d'eau et de Lumiere, built at the Paris Exposition des Arts Decoratifs in 1925, was a striking triangular composition of stepped pools and terraces. Some were tilted and planted with colored flowers and grasses ranging from light pink to crimson. In the center was a sphere of stained glass and mirror, which would periodically flash brilliant light across the surfaces of the garden. His garden at Hyères was equally radical. [FIG. 6] Here, a chessboard of terraces, some planted in vibrant colors, others finished in concrete and mosaic, were tiered and rose toward the apex of a walled triangle. Saw-toothed beds of plants zigzagged up each of the walls. Both gardens were unprecedented at the time, reflecting Guevrekian's spirited exploration of cubist composition and simultaneity and the use of new materials.

Fletcher Steele wrote enthusiastically about Guevrekian and other French landscape architects in an essay entitled "New Pioneering in Garden Design," published in *Landscape Architecture* (1930). Thereafter, landscape architects such as Eckbo, Thomas Church, and Burle Marx ambitiously explored new ways of using materials, plants, and color in the forming of geometrical space. This modernist "tradition" continues today in the work of Martha Schwartz, the early work of George Hargreaves, or many of the new French-school landscape architects such as Michel Desvigne, and shows how in fact the avant-garde has now become normalized and encoded within its own tradition. Greenberg described this inevitable stabilization, explaining how the "function" of avant-gardist work is in fact to become paradigmatic within the traditional "laws" of a particular discipline. "The essence of Modernism," he wrote, "lies in the use of the characteristic methods of a discipline itself, not in order to subvert it, but to entrench it more firmly in its area of competence."[34] The notion that a reactionary act of rupture can provide a "fresh break" that later settles into a more paradigmatic disciplinary structure is still the primary value of avant-garde research.

For example, Bernard Tschumi's early theoretical work, before the Parc de la Villette, clearly transgressed the norms of architecture (and landscape architecture) by importing all sorts of ideas considered out of bounds.[35] The synthesis of architecture with such diverse territories as the montage techniques in cinematography, the manifesto writing of the futurists, the texts of James Joyce, the underworld eroticism of Georges Bataille, the psychoanalyticism of Jacques Lacan, the semiology of Roland Barthes, or the philosophy of Foucault and Derrida was achieved for Tschumi (after at least ten years of theoretical development) in his 1982 winning competition entry for the Parc de la Villette in Paris. The interesting thing here is that the park was thought by many to be

FIG. 7 —Parc de la Villette, by Bernard Tschumi, Paris, France, Photograph by Guillaume Bauviere, 2012

"avant-garde," meaning that it was fresh and original, and yet, despite what is said about it, it actually looks like early-twentieth-century Constructivism. Indeed, the work of the early-twentieth century formed much of Tschumi's preoccupation and research for more than ten years. One could say the same of Schwartz's work: It is not really that new or original, but represents a continuation of the avant-garde, and perhaps even nostalgia for the same. Although Tschumi and Schwartz may have stepped outside the traditional limits of their professions, they are still treading familiar ground to anyone acquainted with the effervescent age of the early-twentieth century. [FIG. 7]

An evolutionary avant-garde is clearly something different from an avant-garde of endless rupture. There is a distinction between the strategies of transgression and those of subversion. Transgression aims to construct theory from both within and outside the limits of one's discipline. It involves a creative resetting of limits and may, indirectly, lead to the institution of a new paradigm. "Transgression opens the door into what lies beyond the limits usually observed, but it maintains those limits just the same," wrote Bataille. "Transgression is complementary to the profane world, exceeding its limits but not destroying it."[36] To venture to the limits is to uncover the loose ends, the misfits. These are perhaps the anomalies of a paradigm that the blinkered specialist fails to see. To step into such a catalytic region requires a gutsy probing; it is an unpredictable searching that is not without danger or risk. "An artist might advance specifically to get lost, and to intoxicate himself with dizzying syntaxes; seeking odd intersections of meaning, strange corridors of history, unexpected echoes, unknown humors, or voids of knowledge," wrote Robert Smithson, but he warns that "this quest is risky, full of bottomless fictions and endless architectures."[37]

In this sense the work of the avant-garde can be provocative, if not productive. The danger lies in what author Peter Burger has referred to as the "neo-avant-garde," or the subversive:

> The neo-avant-garde institutionalizes the *avant-garde as art*, and thus negates genuinely avant-gardist intentions…It is the status of their products, not the consciousness artists have of their activity, that defines the social effects of works. Neo-avant-gardist art is autonomous art in the full sense of the term, which means that it negates the avant-gardist intention of returning art to the praxis of life.[38]

Burger goes on to describe how this cynical disregard of convention and everyday virtues "merely represents the deep-solitude of an individual's will to make a statement" and remains outside the norms and codes of a larger social group. This subversive attitude is most prevalent when the avant-garde enters its most radical phase. Here, the avant-gardists construct a particularly acute attack on whatever it is they are against, while failing to present any positive alternative or remedial vision. This nihilistic attitude is apparent in much of the writing of Friedrich Nietzsche and Derrida, as in their progeny, the deconstructivists.

Without hope of truth or transcendence, the deconstructivists launch a massive assault on the bases of meaning and stability in the world, seeking instead to maintain the irreconcilable contradiction of our times.[39] As philosopher Jean-François Lyotard has proclaimed:

> We have paid a high enough price for the nostalgia of the whole….Let us wage a war on totality; let us be witnesses to the unpresentable; let us activate the differences and save the honor of the same.[40]

The language here is vehemently resistant to completion, stability, and holism (utopia). A new syntax, based around the prefixes de-, dis-, and trans-, forms the core of the deconstructivists' vocabulary. Consider the language used by Eisenman and Tschumi: "decentering…deconstruction…dislocation…dissociation…transference…fragmentation…fracturing" and so on. As in psychoanalysis, the fragments of meaning by which the world may be understood

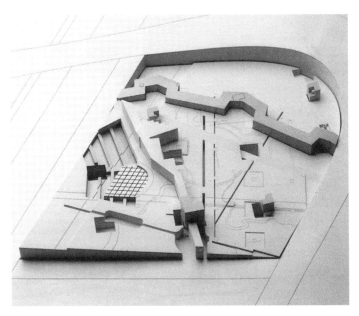

FIG. 8 — Several "texts" or overlapped layers are scaled, overlaid, and displaced, favoring an irreducible multiplicity of readings. "Choral Works," by Eisenman Architects and Jacques Derrida, for Parc de la Villette competition

Courtesy Eisenman Architects

are assembled in displaced and purposefully unresolved combinations. Through techniques such as collage, montage, scaling, superposition, and grafting, the sheer heterogeneity of our postmodern times is multiplied in an "intertextual field." Such a field, without limits, knows of no single center, no single logic, and no single order. As with nature, it is irreducible. [FIG. 8]

While one might be curious, if not completely seduced, by some of the creative strategies used in deconstruction, some disquieting questions remain: What of the future and the lived continuity of culture? The deconstructivists would probably answer that to structure such a vision is impossibly singular and utopian in what is now a heterogeneous and ever-changing world. However, their counterstrategies only work to embody the chaos of our time—something that is ironically traditional by virtue of the recourse to representation. Just because one might "deconstruct" a landscape in order to see it afresh does not necessarily mean that it has to *appear* fragmented and disorienting.

### The Tyrannies

The three attitudes discussed above represent the bulk of our approaches toward theory and practice in contemporary landscape architecture, even though it is fair to say that landscape architecture has generally been conservative in both its usage and contribution to such developments. This may have left the discipline with a certain innocence, insulated from the errors of excessive intellectualization, but it has also led to an uncritical and unsophisticated dogmatism. In our search for a theory and language specific to landscape architecture, we must first realize how the predominance of methodological problem solving, systems theory, ecologism, typologies, historicism, formalism, behavioralism, and so forth are all variants of the three attitudes outlined above.

While each approach is complex and not without some value for landscape architecture, these theories generally operate *outside* the full complexity of the existential realm and tend to reduce and close as humankind continues to demand absolute certainty and control. The modern emphasis on objective and pragmatic reasoning has promoted a view of life that is more about the efficiency of means and ends, methods and techniques over questions of existence and being—the question "why" displaced by "what" and "how."

### Tradition and Hermeneutics

On what grounds may we discover an alternative, especially one pertaining to landscape architecture? The answer can be found in the articulation of a *critical* (that is, nondogmatic) and *interpretive* attitude toward history, culture, tradition, nature, and art, the basis of which lies in three working assumptions.

First, the world is not omniscient, as modern technology might have us believe. Luminous and opaque, the lifeworld does not fit neatly into any one viewpoint. In an indeterminate, poetic world resistant to full capture, the disclosure of one aspect necessarily conceals another. In any understanding there is simultaneously light and shadow, giving and withdrawing. This means that all previous understanding is not in itself wrong, untrue, or without value, even though it may have long been discarded. Nietzsche has written:

> That which we now call the world is the result of a number of errors and fantasies, which came about gradually in the overall development of organic beings, fusing with one another, and now handed down to us as a collected treasure: for the *value* of our humanity rests upon it.[41]

Nietzsche's aphorism concludes that the history of the cultural world is nothing more than pure idea, a *projection* recorded in the products of culture (language, music, artifacts, gardens).[42] If humans could look beneath the historical process to witness pure nature, they might be amused by how the world seemed to be so much, indeed everything, "but that in fact it is empty, that is,

FIG. 9 — The painting depicts the role of imagination in disclosing hidden aspects of our world.
*Dalí at the Age of Six, When he Thought he was a Girl, Lifting the Skin of the Water to see
a Dog Sleeping in the Shade of the Sea*, by Salvador Dali, 1950

Comte Francois de Vallombreuse Collection, Paris

empty of meaning."[43] Meaning is thus "sedimented" by culture through art and language; it is not already "given."

By extension, therefore, "truths" are only relative concepts, subject to shift and change. "The world for us has become infinite," wrote Nietzsche, "meaning that we cannot refuse it the possibility to lend itself to an infinity of interpretations."[44] Hence, the world known in one way is always interpretable in another.

Interpretation is therefore different from the way productive theories operate. For example, interpretation is always in response to a particular situation, replete with specific sets of circumstances.[45] While much of today's theory is derived from a scientific approach—which tends to produce an ideal from a hypothetical or artificial arrangement—interpretation is always situated within particular contexts and must respond flexibly to the specific circumstances within which the interpreter operates. In *Truth and Method* (1960), Hans-Georg Gadamer states "what makes modern scholarship scientific is precisely the fact that it objectifies tradition and methodically eliminates the influence of the interpreter and his time on understanding."[46] The very idea of a situation means that we do not stand outside it, but rather that we inhabit it. We "dwell" in situations.[47]

Moreover, because interpretation is situated and circumstantial, it never presumes to be anything more than interpretative and partial. Interpretation recognizes its own incompleteness, working with smaller units of inquiry as opposed to grand utopian models or holistic schemata. Gadamer has written that interpretation is "only an attempt, plausible and fruitful, but never completely definitive. Interpretation is always on the way."[48] Unable to presume certainty, a situational and interpretative approach to theory and practice defers singular understanding and remains ever open to the world. [FIG. 9]

The second working assumption is that primary knowledge is that which comes from direct experience. We live in a corporeal and phenomenal world, amongst real things, in specific places, and it is only through the perception of this primary realm—rocks, rivers, solar cycles, seasonal change, human encounters, and so on—that different cultures have understood and found access to the ideal.[49] Humans make perception out of things perceived.[50]

Traditionally the arts have sought to unveil and make explicit the ideal (the invisible) through an interpretation of this phenomenal world. In this way the most inspired landscape architecture has provided humankind with a sense of meaningful belonging and orientation while transcending earthly limitations—think of the very concept of "garden" or "place," for example. Through physical embodiment, culture has been able to perceive the enigma of existence and nature, otherwise confused in the mutable reality of everyday life.

FIG. 10 — The photograph of a Japanese water edge detail depicts a poetic
and tactile use of various materials; the innate qualities of which can only be
properly understood through sensual and bodily appropriation.

Photograph by Norman Carver, Kyoto Gosho, Japan

The medium of ideation—and subsequent embodiment—in landscape architecture is the landscape itself. This not only encompasses the physical materials and natural processes that constitute landscape, but also includes the codes and languages through which landscape is culturally understood. The landscape is therefore the *setting* of our lives, the sensual-intellectual perception of which constitutes meaning and value. By extension, things and places can be properly understood only through nearness and intimacy, through bodily participation. [FIG. 10] A theory and practice that simultaneously emerges from and engages in this realm of perception is therefore qualitatively different from the application of a priori conceptual orders, which are analogous to mathematical logic or rational planning and always *precede* action. It is only through the actual undertaking of perception based work—imaginary drawings, models, artifacts, and the actual building of landscapes—that the landscape architect can best find access to the cinematic richness of landscape space and time. Only through the temporal and phenomenal processes of doing and making can revelation occur. Indeed, the quest becomes a dangerous *personal* task involving self-discovery and self-possession—a personal task because the primary source of creativity is rounded in the tactile experience of making, *techne-poiesis*, crucial for any significant ideation.[51] Thus one works toward a landscape of embodied thought—a built "topos" of mind.

The third working assumption is that "tradition" does not refer to some vague recollection of the past, frozen and inaccessible, but refers instead to the creative and processual power of which we are an integral part. Gadamer describes tradition as a "happening"; a continual unfolding of human endeavor, which might best be understood as humankind's equivalent to nature. Both are eventful phenomena, equally resistant to objectification and rational dissection and too fluid for the confines of formalization or repetition.

Tradition is therefore a dynamic artifact, a result of human work and the accumulation of ideas. In constituting culture, tradition is continuously being worked toward. Any intervention today, whether of personal or historical accident, can inevitably become a Formative ingredient in later movements.[52] Of course, the previously discussed "tyrannies" are obviously a part of this inheritance. Our rationality, as with our modes of abstraction, is part of our modern condition and will inevitably form the basis for any future work. To simply reject or work outside such a context would be both naive and irresponsible, running the risk of an impossible nostalgia on the one hand or a perverse isolationism on the other.

With the phenomenon of tradition so defined, it becomes possible to imagine an approach toward theory that critically engages the archaeology of previous accomplishments while also projecting into the future. Hence, a responsible and critical theory might be one that would seek to reconcile previous cosmologies with those of our own time, attempting to find new joints of meaning between our ancestry and our Future.

By extension, this task relates to what Paul Ricoeur has defined as a central problem in contemporary culture; that is, "how to become modern and to return to sources; how to revive an old, dormant civilization and take part in universal civilization."[53] The call for a relinking of modern culture to its vital heritages demands a remapping of our history and tradition, in which landscape architecture has a significant part to play. The objective is to devise new meanings (futures) from a critical and yet imaginative reinterpretation of our tradition (past), thereby transcending the superficiality of pictorial image and historical style. For example, Picasso's painting was in fact a critical interpretation of the history of Western art and, at certain moments, of primitive art.

The engaging of tradition is therefore a reconciliatory practice, equally able to distance itself from the enlightenment myth of progress (positivism and the modernist avant-garde) on the one side, and from regressive conservative impulses (historicism) on the other. Kenneth Frampton has defined such a position as a "critical *arrière-garde*"—a removal from both the "optimization of advanced technology and the ever-present tendency to regress into nostalgic historicism, or the glibly decorative."[54]

## Hermeneutics

These three working assumptions—situational interpretation, the primacy of perception, and the "happening" of tradition—form the basis of hermeneutics: a theory of understanding and interpretation.[55] Named after the god Hermes, known to be the mediator between gods and mortals, hermeneutics developed as a means of practical translation, first of difficult religious texts and later of complex ethical and legal issues. As a transposition of Aristotelian practical and political philosophy, hermeneutics was practiced in order to serve the *polis*, or the common good, reconciling universal "laws" with the particular circumstances at hand. Like theoria, it reflected the social significance of its work and was related to an existential function.

Today, hermeneutics' field of application is composed of all those situations in which we encounter meanings that are not immediately understandable but require interpretive effort.[56] It attempts to integrate bodies of knowledge through finding "places" of commonality and agreement. Furthermore, because hermeneutics is an intuitive-practical form of reasoning, it gives strength and validity to those bodies of knowledge—the experiences of art, landscape, poetry, and philosophy, for example—that cannot be verified by the methodological standards of science.

Thus hermeneutics differs from the approaches to theory described earlier in that it is primarily a contemplative and mediative practice, as opposed to an analytical and calculative "system" (positivism). It is also ontological and circumstantial rather than methodological and universal (paradigms). And it continually unfolds within a process of tradition, as opposed to the discontinuity of endless provocation and novelty (the avant-garde).

Hermeneutics is able to perform its difficult mandate primarily through the use of rhetoric and metaphor. Both are essentially bonding mechanisms whereby meanings once considered disparate or antithetical can be joined to find commonality—connections between art and science, theory and practice, or humans and nature, for example. In addition to joining, metaphors also extrapolate new meaning and usage to old figures, thereby disclosing hidden and latent relationships. The deployment of metaphor is therefore both a reconciliatory and innovative practice. In cultivating traditions from within, hermeneutics enables a *recognition*: a knowing of things anew.

Much of the difficulty in contemporary landscape architecture lies in such recoding and transformation. How might seemingly disparate and banal meanings in the landscape discover new life and usage, renewing an art form while also maintaining its tradition? That is, how can we make the ordinariness of everyday situations into something imaginative or fresh, pertinent to our time but not estranged from tradition?

Part of the answer lies in Gadamer's statement that "the heart of the hermeneutical problem is that the one and same tradition must again and again be understood in a different way," and that in landscape architecture this tradition may be said to consist of situations.[57] "Situation" is an existential term referring to our being in the world. As Dalibor Vesely writes:

> Situations are the receptacles of experience and of those events which sediment in them a meaning not just as survivals or residues but as an invitation to a sequel, the necessity of a future. Situations endow experience with durable dimensions, in relation to which a whole series of other experiences will acquire meaning…The richness of situations depend on the reverberations of meaning through the depths of their history.[58]

Human situations such as birth, death, love, healing—or on a different level, public encounters, friendship, learning, discussion, and so on—are what have constituted culture since its conception.[59] They are based in a profoundly human mythology that is pregnant with forgotten and latent meanings. Landscapes and buildings have traditionally formed the settings for these situations, framing and symbolizing their content. Highly situated events are thereby embodied and presented as the ultimate frame of reference for any future meaning.[60] Inevitably there is a correspondence between the setting and the situation, a dialogue that not only pertains to the moment but also relates to an ongoing conversation between past and future. A hermeneutical landscape architecture is therefore something that is based on situated experience, placed both within space and time as well as in tradition, and is as equally about resurgence or renewal as it is about invention.

In describing hermeneutics and art, literary critic George Steiner wrote that all serious works of art are "critical acts" that embody "an expository reflection on, a value judgment of, the inheritance and context to which they pertain."[61] The previous accomplishments of culture—landscapes, buildings, paintings, literature, and so on—therefore provide a remarkable resource in terms of reflecting on and relating to our present situation.[62] Any such judgment is, however, an imaginative task—not something that can be prescribed by equation or formal coding—and demands that any interpretation occur through working from within, as opposed to conceptual, logical reasoning from without.

### The Hermeneutic Landscape

The landscape is itself a text that is open to interpretation and transformation. It is also a highly situated phenomenon in terms of space, time, and tradition, and exists as both the ground and geography of our heritage and change. Landscape is distinguished from wilderness in that it is land that has been modified by humans. But it is more than this. Landscape is not only a physical phenomenon, but is also a cultural schema, a conceptual filter through which our relationships to wilderness and nature can be understood.

It is the well-formed world of occupied places as opposed to the world outside of that—the unplaced place. In other words, prior to language, "landscape" is a phenomenon beyond immediate comprehension; it is not until we choose a prospect and map what we see, marking some aspects, ignoring others, that the landscape acquires meaning.[63] Such interventions include paintings, poems, myths, and literature, in addition to buildings and other interventions upon the land. These works are the encodings that set and frame human situations. They are the posts that map out a "landscape."

As time passes, this marked landscape weathers, ever subject to the contingencies of nature. Other points of view are chosen as circumstances change and new ways of marking are overlaid upon the old, producing collaged and weathered overlays. Residua in this topographic palimpsest provide loci for the remembrance, renewal, and transfiguration of a culture's relationship to the land. Such are the familiar and unexpected places of authentic dwelling.

As a man-made projection, landscape is both text and site, partly clarifying the world and our place within it. The textual landscape is thus a hermeneutic medium. Landscape architecture might therefore be thought of as the practice of escaping and rescaping our relationship to nature and the "other" through the construction of built worlds. In the desire to reflect both on our modern context and on our inheritance, landscape architecture might practice a hermeneutical plotting of the landscape—a plotting that is as much political and strategic as it is relational and physical. The landscape architect as plotter is simultaneously critic, geographer, communicator, and maker, digging to uncover mute and latent possibilities in the lived landscape. With every "projection" there might follow a rebirth: the artifact of culture and the enigma of nature rendered fuller with every pass.[64] To plot, to map, to dig, to set: Are these not the fundamental traditions of landscape architecture?

FIG. 11 — Barragán was able to reset traditional activities within modern settings that evoke past accomplishments. There is neither simulation of the past nor any radical break from it, but rather there is an "assimilation" or absorbance of the old into the new and the new into the old. The Plaza and Garden of the Trough, by Luis Barragán, Las Arboledas, Mexico, 1950

As a partial attempt to exemplify such an approach, one might consider the work of Luis Barragán, especially El Pedregal (1945–1950), in the volcanic region of Mexico; or the ranch and stables at San Cristobal (1968); or many of his numerous small chapels and gardens. [FIG. 11] The built order is truly original and abstract, derived from the tenets of early Modernism, but the spaces are still rooted in the continuity of Barragán's culture, becoming meaningful to a larger culture through their appeal to primordial experiences we as human beings all share. The cultural archetypes are inexhaustibly reformulated with a religious passion—walls, steps, gates, paths, seats, and so on are the elements of both memory and prophecy, providing "places" for the collective orientation and perpetuation of culture. The serenity of enclosure and setting; the poetic accommodation of ritual and cultural situation; the sensual control of body placement and motion so as to arouse expectation and intrigue; the surrealistic quality of composition and arrangement; the hierarchical control of space, light, and tactile experience all embody the possibility of a lived continuity within a forward-probing culture recalling its heritage.

### Conclusion

A hermeneutic approach to landscape architectural theory might better provide an ontology grounded in the continuity of culture, as opposed to an ideology of blinkered reconstruction on the one hand, or of abstract destructive freedom on the other. What is sought is "a dialogue between culture in its present form and those possibilities forgotten or dormant in the depths of its tradition, alive in memories, in literature, in philosophy."[65] Such dialogue demands that one view the history of human endeavor as a deep repository of meaning, wherein certain profoundly human situations continually recur and are embodied in an infinitely rich variety of ways. This quarry of human consciousness might thereby provide the very source of our work, recalling the past while also disclosing new possibilities for a future that transcends the given present. Rather than a mimesis of nature, there might be a mimesis of culture, a mimesis of "exemplary situations"—that which humanity has already made, including landscapes.[66] Philosopher Maurice Merleau-Ponty talks of "the fecundity of the products of culture which continue to have value after their appearance and which open a field of investigations in which they perpetually come to life."[67]

So it is in the most inspired moments in landscape architecture, although we should remember that nature herself always enters into the contract to eventually supersede the encodings of humankind. Indeed, nature's infinite complexity will in itself continue to challenge landscape situations and metaphors, demanding hermeneutical reflection through the (re)building of critical landscapes—landscapes that do not stand still but continue to be revisited and transformed through time. Through the building of such landscapes we may well be able to mine the illimitable resources of both culture and nature, bringing modern dwelling toward a greater significance with its present and restoring a sense of wholeness, continuity, and meaning to our lived relations with the landscape.[68]

To forge a landscape as a hermeneutic locus of both divination and restoration, prophecy and memory, is to help figure and orient the collective consciousness of a modern culture inevitably caught in transition.

NOTES

1   See Jürgen Habermas, "Modernity—An Incomplete Project," in *The Anti-Aesthetic*, ed. Hal Foster (Port Townsend, WA: Bay Press, 1983); Jean-Francois Lyotard, *The Postmodern Condition—A Report on Knowledge* (Minneapolis: University of Minnesota Press, 1984); Andreas Huyssen, *After the Great Divide* (Indianapolis: Indiana University Press, 1986). Originally theory, or *theoria*, afforded a complete cosmology, understood and participated in by an entire culture. Gardens and artifacts were conceived as figurative representations of the theoretical world. Today we no longer understand theory in this classical sense. Instead, in our desire to participate in the exigencies of production, we tend to see theory as part of design "method"—a technical theory, procedural know-how. The projection of techno-scientific models onto reality has fundamentally altered the original transcendental sense of theory, displacing poetics and imagination for prescription and efficiency. In this way art and landscape can be visually beautiful, of course, but only seldom may they be understood as profound forms of knowledge.

2   Martin Heidegger, *Basic Writings* (New York: Harper and Row, 1977), 37; George Steiner, *Real Presences* (Chicago: University of Chicago Press, 1990), 2.

3   Heidegger, *Basic Writings*.

4   What is often referred to as a contemporary "crisis" of meaning and value was foreseen and described during the earlier twentieth century by Edmund Husserl, *The Crisis of European Sciences and Transcendental Phenomenology*, trans. D. Carr (Evanston, IL: Northwestern University Press, 1970). By "crisis," of course, one refers to the moment when one is not sure whether a problem may be solved or not, a time of both anxiety and hope.

5   See Husserl, *The Crisis of European Sciences*; Heidegger, *Basic Writings*; Alberto Péréz-Gomez, *Architecture and the Crisis of Modern Science* (Cambridge, MA: MIT Press, 1983).

6   Lyotard, *The Postmodern Condition*.

7   See Péréz-Gomez, *Architecture and the Crisis of Modern Science*. This tendency to think of theory as objective methodology and technique differs from the traditional conceptions of theory. Unlike the "abstractness," or autonomy, of modern theory's foundations, traditional theory was based in the *Lebenswelt*. See Alfred Schutz and T. Luckman, *The Structures of the Lifeworld* (Evanston, IL: Northwestern University Press, 1973).

8   Péréz-Gomez, *Architecture and the Crisis of Modern Science*.

9   Refer to David Leatherbarrow, "Book Review of *On the Art of Building in Ten Books*," *Journal of Architectural Education* 43/2 (1990): 51–53 and James Corner, "Sounding the Depths—Origins, Theory, and Representation," *Landscape Journal* 9/1 (1990):

60–78. *Theoria* was the original Greek formulation of theory. It emerged as a way to comprehend observed phenomena in the natural world, especially in relation to holy practices. Practice was understood as a theoretical form of reconciliation between humans and their being in the world.

10    By "hard" I mean that the world has become so clear, especially in empirical terms, that it has lost much of its enigma and mystery. For many the world has become impenetrable and unyielding—a cold and neutral entity devoid of wonder. This makes it very difficult for a culture to "figure itself." *To figure* is a term used in rhetoric, meaning "to form figuratively," especially through the use of metaphors. We do this as humans so as to be able to imagine and understand our human condition (to figure out). This is largely accomplished through the quest of making, or giving form to ideas (figuring through figuration).

11    Jon Lang, *Creating Architectural Theory* (New York: Van Nostrand Reinhold, 1987).

12    Colin Rowe, *Collage City* (Cambridge, MA: MIT Press, 1978).

13    Rowe, *Collage City*, 12.

14    Werner Heisenberg, *The Physicist's Conception of Nature* (Westport, CT: Greenwood Press, 1970).

15    Rowe, *Collage City*.

16    Michael Wilford, "Off to the Races, or Going to the Dogs?" *Urbanism: AD Profile 51* (London: Architectural Design, 1984).

17    Ibid., 15.

18    It is interesting to compare modern views of "nature" to those of the ancient Greeks, who understood the world through a more holistic concept called *physis*. Physis represented the total sum of being and existence. There was no separation between humans, nature, and gods. The rationality of techno-science, however, has now produced a world of separation—humans and their technologies are dominant, while the world of nature is subjugated. See Martin Heidegger, *The Question Concerning Technology* (New York: Harper Torchbooks, 1977).

19    Thomas Kuhn, *The Structure of Scientific Revolutions* (Second edition, Chicago: University of Chicago Press, 1970), viii.

20    Kuhn, *The Structure of Scientific Revolutions*, 176–91. Note that within the full scope of a paradigm, theory refers to something much more limited in function and structure. Kuhn prefers the notion of a paradigm as being similar to a "disciplinary matrix" (pp. 176–91), within which there are (1) a host of symbolic generalizations (laws), (2) particular metaphors and analogies (language), (3) values, and (4) model exemplars.

21    That is to say, models and exemplars have formed the greater part of our education. They are concrete, tangible forms representing solutions to problems under certain paradigmatic conditions. For a discipline so focused on spatial-visual structures, this will most likely remain a fundamental part of our education and practice.

22    Andrew Jackson Downing, *A Treatise on the Theory and Practice of Landscape Gardening* (New York: Orange Judd Company, 1841), vi.

23    Ibid., 30.

24    See Leon Krier, *Houses, Palaces, Cities: Architectural Design Special Profile*, n. 54 (London: Architectural Design, AD Editions, 1984); Robert Krier, *Architectural Composition* (New York: Rizzoli, 1988). The Kriers belong to a group called the neorationalists, who advocate an approach that seeks to provide an entire spatial typology across the social spectrum, as in an inventory or classification.

25    See Camillo Sitte, *The Art of Building Cities According to Artistic Principles*, trans. George R. Collins and Christiane Craseman Collins (New York: Random House, 1965).

26   Mircea Eliade, *Cosmos and History* (New York: Harper, 1959). It is important to distinguish between *archetype* as a "situation" or idea, and *type* as specific form or pattern. Archetypes are human situations that persist across time and space, like "archaic remnants" (Jung). They are not bound to form or image and can be represented or interpreted in many ways. Alan Colquhoun ("Modern Architecture and Historicity," in *Essays in Architectural Criticism*, Cambridge, MA: MIT Press and Oppositions Books, 1981) makes a distinction here between type as "archetype" and type as a very specific form. He says: "In the first sense, type has a genetic connotation: it is the essence that has been stamped on the original version which each subsequent form will recall. In the second sense, type merely has the connotation of a de facto form" (p. 15).

27   See Alan Colquhoun, *Essays in Architectural Criticism* and *Modernity and the Classical Tradition* (Cambridge, MA: MIT Press, 1989). According to Colquhoun, history, and therefore paradigmatic "types," may be viewed in one of two ways. Colquhoun (*Essays in Architectural Criticism*, 11–15) defines the first view as "culturalist," wherein history is an immutable repository of eternal values "with a myth of origins and a belief in a golden age in which those values were manifest in a pure form." Here, architectural form is something external to historical evolution, replete with universal and unchanging laws. In the second view, history is understood as a series of distinct epochs, each with its "own self-justificatory system of values." Here, the view is that all sociocultural phenomena are historically determined and are therefore relative. Colquhoun describes the first as a "normative" view of history, based on an idealized, exemplary past and which is therefore absolutist. The second he defines as a relativist view, where cultures and forms are relative to space, time, and cultural circumstance.

28   Johanne Wolfgang Goethe, *Werke*, vol. 47 (1794), 313. Quoted in Peter Burger, *Theory of the Avant-Garde*, trans. Michael E. Shaw (Minneapolis: University of Minnesota Press, 1984).

29   Rowe, *Collage City*.

30   Traditional art was understood as a mimesis of the primary reality of the phenomenal world given to perception. It was a representation of an idea outside itself, as opposed to modernist art, which sought to defer representation and refer only to its own making. See Clement Greenberg, "Modernist Painting," *Art and Literature* 4 (Spring 1965), 193–201, and Burger, *Theory of the Avant-Garde*.

31   See Colquhoun, *Modernity and the Classical Tradition* and Philippe Junod, *Transparence et Opaciti* (Lausanne: L'Age d'Homme, 1976).

32   Greenberg, "Modernist Painting."

33   Andre Vera, *Le nouveau jardin* (Paris: Emile Paul, 1912), iii–v.

34   Greenberg, "Modernist Painting," 194.

35   See Bernard Tschumi, "Architecture and Transgression," *Oppositions* 7 (Cambridge, MA: MIT Press and Oppositions Books, 1979) and *Questions of Space: Lectures on Architecture* (London: Architectural Association, 1990).

36   Georges Bataille, *Eroticism*, trans. Mary Dalwood (London: Boyars, 1987).

37   Robert Smithson, *Writings* (New York: New York University Press, 1979), 67.

38   Burger, *Theory of the Avant-Garde*, 58.

39   Deconstruction, a radical form of Poststructuralism evolved in literary criticism during the past twenty years. As a philosophy, deconstruction has been most fully developed by Jacques Derrida. In the architectural arts one may refer to Bernard Tschumi, Peter Eisenman, or Daniel Libeskind.

40   Lyotard, *The Postmodern Condition*, 82.

41 Friedrich Nietzsche, *Human, All Too Human*, trans. Marion Faber (Lincoln: University of Nebraska Press, 1984), 24.

42 "Because for thousands of years we have been looking at the world with moral, aesthetic, and religious claims; with blind inclination, passion, or fear; and have indulged ourselves fully in the bad habits of illogical thought, this world has become so strangely colorful, frightful, profound, soulful; it has acquired color, but we have been the painters." Ibid.

43 Ibid., 25.

44 Ibid.

45 See Robert Irwin, *Being and Circumstance: Notes toward a Conditional Art*, ed. Lawrence Weschler (Larkspur Landing, CA: Lapis Press with Pace Gallery, 1985); David Leatherbarrow, "Review of Thought and Place," *Journal of Architectural Education* 43/2 (1988): 51–53.

46 Hans-Georg Gadamer, *Truth and Method* (New York: Seabury Press, 1975), 333.

47 See Dalibor Vesely, "On the Relevance of Phenomenology," in *Form, Being Absence: Pratt Journal of Architecture* 2 (New York: Rizzoli, 1988), 59–62.

48 Hans-Georg Gadamer, *Reason in the Age of Science* (Cambridge, MA: MIT Press, 1981), 88.

49 The "primary structure" is the mutable and finite realm, which is "given" to sensory perception. This world of phenomena forms the realm of our existence. Perception is our primary form of knowing and does not exist without our a priori of the body's structure and its engagement with the world. The body is the locus of all existential formulations, and the mind is that which is capable of finding secondary meaning within the phenomenal. Maurice Merleau-Ponty, *Phenomenology of Perception* (London: Routledge and Kegan Paul, 1962).

50 Ibid.

51 *Techne-poiesis* was the original union between technique and knowledge; thus the phrase "embodied making." Traditionally, architects had to make in order to learn their *metier*. Logical-conceptual theories could not be substitutes for the traditional apprenticeship. Techne was originally the dimension of revelatory knowledge (revealing truth) and poiesis the dimension of creativity and symbolic representation (making). This unity was dissolved during the seventeenth century, when techne became a body of instrumental-productive knowledge (technology) and poiesis became the work of modern aesthetics.

52 Tradition can be likened to a geological continuity into which we are all embedded, our contemporary times being the outcome of a complex historical stratigraphy complete with rift and slippage. The "geological" metaphor is used frequently by contemporary philosophers and critics such as Jacques Derrida and Michel Foucault in *The Archaeology of Knowledge* (New York: Pantheon Books, 1972), especially when describing the ebbs and flows of historical production.

53 Paul Ricoeur, *History and Truth*, trans. Charles A. Kelbey (Evanston, IL: Northwestern University Press, 1961), 267–77.

54 Kenneth Frampton, "Towards a Critical Regionalism," in *The Anti-Aesthetic*, ed. Hal Foster (Port Townsend, WA: Bay Press, 1983), 20.

55 Hermeneutics is a theory of understanding and interpretation. It relates to textual exegesis (interpretation and explanation) and to the more general problems of meaning and language. Hermeneutics necessarily involves reflection and cannot be reduced to rule-governed technique or method. Interpreters are not passive observers, but bring with themselves certain ideas and knowledge that necessarily enter into the interpretation (i.e., an inevitable prejudice or bias). Interpreters can

only interpret with respect to their own particular situations and circumstances. As time, place, and circumstance vary, so too do arguments. As Gadamer (*Truth and Method*, 258) states, there is a "placing of oneself within a process of tradition." Among hermeneutics' contemporary advocates are Paul Ricoeur (see *The Conflict of Interpretation*, Evanston, IL: Northwestern University Press, 1974) and Hans-Georg Gadamer (see *Truth and Method*; *Philosophical Hermeneutics*, Berkeley: University of California Press, 1976; *Reason in the Age of Science*, Cambridge, MA: MIT Press, 1981).

**56**   The renewed interest in hermeneutics is in response to much of twentieth-century philosophy. In general, contemporary philosophy has been concerned with overcoming the alienation of the "subject" from a world reduced to "objects." Husserl (*The Crisis of European Sciences*) largely initiated this concern by expressing a desire to "gain access to the prereflective givenness of things in a way that would not be distorted by theories or anticipatory ideas of any kind" (Gadamer, *Philosophical Hermeneutics,* xiii). The movement to recover that which precedes theoretical objectification seeks to "situate" consciousness within the realm of lived experience (phenomenology). It therefore attempts to escape the methodologies that pervade modern thought by discovering nonobjectifying modes of disclosure.

**57**   Gadamer, *Truth and Method*, 278.

**58**   Dalibor Vesely, *Architecture and Continuity* (London: Architectural Association, 1983), 9.

**59**   Ibid.

**60**   Embodiment and setting must not be confused with "type" or model. Type is only the result of an eidetic abstraction (imaginary ideal of history) and is therefore only partial or secondary. The primary reality of meaning is grounded in experience and cannot be substituted for intellectualized "certainties." Vesely writes: "The typicality of experience in contrast to a type is a historically evolved phenomenon which cannot be understood by reference to form only. It is an embodied meaning which always precedes a particular form. Reading for instance, is essential to any vision of a library, but always transcends it" ["Architecture and the Conflict of Representation," *AA FILES* 8 (London: Architectural Association, 1984), 9].

**61**   Steiner, *Real Presences*, 11.

**62**   Vesely writes: "It is the miraculous power of tradition to mediate between different experiences and their different forms of embodiment that enables us to open the horizon of our present situation to the depths of history and to establish a dialogue with realities that are apparently mute or dead." See "Architecture and the Conflict of Representation," 8.

**63**   By "marking" I mean to suggest the whole spectrum of ways in which different people signify their relationship to the land. More often than not, these signs are physically constructed, but this need not always be the case, as in the aboriginal songlines, for example.

**64**   I borrow this analogy from David Leatherbarrow, "Book Review of *On the Art of Building in Ten Books*."

**65**   Dalibor Vesely, "Architecture and the Conflict of Representation," 12.

**66**   See Vesely, "Architecture and the Conflict of Representation," 12, and Péréz-Gomez, "Abstraction in Modern Architecture," *Via* 9 (Cambridge, MA: MIT Press and the University of Pennsylvania Press, 1988). Vesely writes: "The nature of exemplary situation is similar to the nature of the phenomena described in different terminology as institution, deep structure, paradigm, archetype, or archetypal image…the street, the garden, the house, and of course the town itself…the exemplary situation can be cultivated, reinterpreted, and transcended, but never completely replaced.

This is the essence but also the limit of the traditional process of interpretation, known in its Classical form as *mimesis*." "Architecture and the Conflict of Representation," 11–12.

67 Maurice Merleau-Ponty goes on to say that "the productions of the past, which are the data of our time, themselves once went beyond anterior productions towards a future which we are, and in this sense called for (among others) the metamorphosis which we impose upon them" in *Signs* (Evanston, IL: Northwestern University Press, 1964), 59.

68 The terms "wholeness" and "continuity" are not meant to imply a view of culture as something monolithic, but rather are meant to suggest two things. First, there appear to be certain archetypal situations, or acts, that still hold across a number of cultures, even though their specific forms vary significantly. There are certain primordial experiences we as humans all share. Second, wholeness and continuity can apply to one particular culture or to a number of cultures. Difference, contamination, collision, and diversity may in fact be maintained, celebrated, or embodied. Indeed, such tension may be the very foundation of cultural wholeness and continuity. Wholeness depends upon a highly articulated richness and diversity of cultural life, situation, and setting.

FIG. 1 — This image captures the sense of landscape as a large environmental milieu that can no longer exclude or ignore the metropolis as part of its emergent and dynamic condition. Satellite photograph of Florida by the American Landsat satellite, with the city of Miami to the right meeting the Everglades to the left.

Courtesy MDA Information Systems/Science Source (E09233)

# RECOVERING LANDSCAPE AS A CRITICAL CULTURAL PRACTICE

From a postmodern perspective, landscape seems less like a palimpsest whose "real" or "authentic" meanings can somehow be recovered with the correct techniques, theories, or ideologies, than a thickening text displayed on the word processor screen whose meaning can be created, extended, altered, elaborated, and finally obliterated by the merest touch of a button.

—Denis Cosgrove and Stephen Daniels, *The Iconography of Landscape* (1988)

Building on the growing critical foundation for landscape architectural theory and practice, this essay addresses two primary developments: first, the apparent recovery of landscape, or its reappearance in the cultural sphere after years of relative neglect and indifference; and, second, the revisions of the very nature of landscape itself, rethinking what landscape actually is—or might yet become—as both idea and artifact. [FIG. 1] In the first case, recollection, in the second, invention. In both, landscape is understood as an ongoing project, an enterprising venture that enriches the cultural world through creative effort and imagination.

Underlying my aim is the belief that landscape has the capacity to critically engage the metaphysical and political programs that operate in a given society, that landscape architecture is not simply a reflection of culture but more an active instrument in the shaping of modern culture.[1] Landscape reshapes the world not only because of its physical and experiential characteristics but also because of its eidetic content, its capacity to contain and express ideas and so engage the mind. Moreover, because of its bigness—in both scale and scope—landscape serves

*Originally published in: James Corner, ed.* Recovering Landscape: Essays in Contemporary Landscape *(New York: Princeton Architectural Press, 1999): 1–26. Reproduced with permission.*

as a metaphor for inclusive multiplicity and pluralism, as in a kind of synthetic "overview" that enables differences to play themselves out. In these terms, landscape may still embrace naturalistic and phenomenological experience but its full efficacy is extended to that of a synthetic and strategic art form, one that aligns diverse and competing forces (social constituencies, political desires, ecological processes, program demands, etc.) into newly liberating and interactive alliances.

Understandably, the skeptical reader may find the above claims a little optimistic, too overreaching. Landscape probably appears to the general public too benign or passive ever to assume active and strategic roles in contemporary affairs. Certainly the attention being paid to landscape today assumes more the character of sentimental recollection—with attendant demands for either the re-creation or preservation of past landscapes—than of visionary or ambitious projects. A combination of nostalgia and consumerism drives this desire while suppressing ambitions to experiment and invent.

This image of inertia is intensified if one compares landscape to the innovative efficacy surrounding modern-day economics, information, media technologies, and corporate and political initiatives. In a globalized context of rapid and expedient production, landscape must appear an antiquated medium and its design a fringe activity sustained through the eccentric passions of a handful of romantics and gentle nature-lovers. Consequently, as an image that evokes a virtuous and benevolent nature, landscape is typically viewed as the soothing antithesis to the placeless frenzy of technological urban life; few would share the view that the contemporary metropolis can be construed as a landscape or find it easy to imagine landscapes other than the pastoral and the gardenesque. In this sense, it is understandably difficult for many to imagine landscape as an innovative medium, one that might somehow dislocate the most conventional and regressive aspects of society while at the same time reorganizing these elements in the most liberating and life-enriching way.

Owing to the aforementioned prevalence of conservative attitudes toward landscape, there is a concomitant loss of will or desire to forge new landscapes—a suspicion, perhaps, of past state regimes and modernist utopias, or simply a sign of a culture seeking escape from the difficulties of the present in the idealized images of the past. While Europe and the United States have developed superb national agencies and trusts for the preservation of landscapes, no equally strong institution is dedicated to cultivating the future. In those places where visionary and exciting work is taking place—the Netherlands, France, and Spain, for instance—there is an underlying public and political will to both nurture and support inventive urban and landscape design, and to see these activities as fundamental to both a healthy economy and a vibrant culture.

The difficulty of advancing landscape is not only an issue of sentimentality and conservatism; it is further hindered by a growing contingent that believes landscape concerns ought to be directed solely toward the stewardship of the natural world. The extreme proponents of this view protest that culturally ambitious landscape projects are largely irrelevant in the face of environmental problems—that is, of course, unless such projects are solely focused on biotic restoration and habitat diversification. A culturally ambitious landscape architecture that does not revolve around ecological concerns is often construed by environmentalists as belonging to the domain of elitist and intellectual art practices rather than to the more practical aspects of healing the earth. This view holds great sway at a sociopolitical level, of course, for in a world whose population continues to grow while its resources diminish, ecological expertise is especially timely and relevant. As with the rise of heritage groups, there is today no shortage of national and regional agencies dedicated to environmental improvement and research, and thankfully and rightly so. But here too, the culturally innovative aspects of landscape architecture are often overlooked or even suppressed as emphasis is placed on more technical procedures aimed at the restoration of an essentially cultureless natural world.

This last phrase is, of course, a telling contradiction in terms; while there may well be phenomena that escape culture, I doubt that the "ecology" and "nature" sought by environmental groups are as culture-free as they might argue. Owing to the inevitable imaging that enframes and represents nature to a given society, the possibilities of a cultureless nature necessarily remain absolutely unknown and unimaginable. Unfortunately, environmental advocates continue to attend to an objectifiable nature that they believe remains external to culture. In so doing, they fail to consider the profound consequences of the world's *constructedness*—its schematization as a cultural idea and, therefore, its subjugation. In mistakenly conceiving of the environment and its many effects and maladies as being outside and not within the cultural world, environmentalists tend only to repair and perhaps forestall damage while cultural ways of being and acting in the world (which lie at the very root of environmental problems in the first place) remain relatively unchanged. As with stitching up wounds to the skin that are only recurring symptoms of some larger failing, the continual patching over of problems is a well-intentioned and praiseworthy effort but one that fails to adequately address their source. While we ought to be thankful for the good work and increased visibility of both preservation and environmental groups, organized and funded at regional and national levels, the lack of any power or group aimed toward the cultivation of landscape as an innovative cultural agent is unfortunate; such forces are much needed.[2]

## Landscape Agency

Recovering landscape requires focus on projects that serve as means to critically intervene in cultural habit and convention. The emphasis shifts from landscape as a product of culture to landscape as an agent producing and enriching culture. *Landscape* as noun (as object or scene) is quieted in order to emphasize *landscape* as verb (as process or activity). Here, it is less the formal characteristics of landscape that are described than it is the formative effects of landscape in time. The focus is upon the agency of landscape (how it works and what it does) rather than upon its simple appearance.

When the making of landscape is considered in terms of developmental process, the resulting project may assume any number of formal characteristics, depending on local circumstances and situations. Whether a particular project is naturalistic, rectilinear, curvilinear, formal, or informal is irrelevant; what matters is how the form and geometry of a project make sense with regard to the specific issues it is trying to address and the effects it is trying to precipitate. Thus, recovering landscape is less a matter of appearances and aesthetic categories than an issue of strategic instrumentality.[3] Form is still important, but less as appearance and more as an efficacious disposition of parts. The concern is less for finding a new formal or aesthetic style than for increasing the scope of the landscape project in a broader cultural milieu.

## The Landscape Idea

The power of the landscape idea must not be underestimated or severed from physical *space*.[4] Landscape is both a spatial milieu and cultural image. As such, the construction of landscape space is inseparable from particular ways of seeing and acting. In this sense, landscape is an ongoing medium of exchange, a medium that is embedded and evolved within the imaginative and material practices of different societies at different times. Over time, landscapes accrue layers with every new representation, and these inevitably thicken and enrich the range of interpretations and possibilities.[5]

Furthermore, the landscape idea is neither universally shared nor manifested in the same way across cultures and times; its meaning and value, together with its physical and formal characteristics, are not fixed. To assume that every society shares an American, English, or French view of landscape, or even that other societies possess any version of landscape at all, is to wrongly impose on other cultures one's own image. Indeed, there have been societies and times wherein the notion of landscape simply did not exist. Even in European history, landscape is a relatively recent development. As Kenneth Clark observed:

Until fairly recent times men looked at nature as an assemblage of isolated objects, without connecting [them] into a unified scene...It was [not until] the early sixteenth century that the first "pure" landscape was painted [and thus conceived].[6]

Moreover, it is clear that Eastern conceptions of landscape differ significantly from those of the West, which have traditionally been more scenic and stylized. And, as architecture scholar Stanislaus Fung has pointed out, there is an important aspect of mutuality and inclusion to Chinese ideas of landscape as distinct from the binary dualism characteristic of Western conceptions.[7] But whatever the precise origin, coding, and intensity of the lens, the landscape idea arises as an eidetic filter through which different cultures view their woods, mountains, waters, and fields, and gain a sense of social identity.

Consequently, whereas every society has historically been aware of an *environment*, that same physical seeing has not always been elevated to the level of landscape, which, as an explicit thematic genre, is intentionally set in the foreground in cultural imagery, art, and literature. Even the most modest of these representations indicates a fairly mature development of the landscape idea because they are products that arise subsequent to the act of conceiving a landscape. As Denis Cosgrove is right to remind us, "Landscape is already artifice in the moment of its beholding, long before it becomes the subject of pictorial representation."[8] It is precisely because landscape is construed in an eidetic and subjective way that it cannot be equated with nature or environment. As geographer Augustin Berque wrote:

> Landscape is not the environment. The environment is the factual aspect of a milieu: that is, of the relationship that links a society with space and with nature. Landscape is the sensible aspect of that relationship. It thus relies on a collective form of subjectivity...To suppose that every society possesses an awareness of landscape is simply to ascribe to other cultures our own sensibility.[9]

Thus, to historian John Stilgoe's oft-quoted definition that "the antithesis of wilderness is landscape, the land shaped by men," we might add that such shaping is as much imaginary (encoded in language, myth, maps, paintings, film, and other representations) as it is physical (made and represented as material space).[10] Indeed, wilderness itself has today become so widely available (in images, legally protected preserves of land, and tourist sites) that this once forbidding and strictly "unknowable" territory is now entirely consumed as preconceived landscape, packaged as much in pictures and literature as in topographical fact.

Wilderness is a socially constructed idea, a landscape, even though it appears wholly "natural." Thoreau recognized the profound existential aspects of this irony when he wrote, "It is in vain to dream of a wildness distant from ourselves. There is none such. It is the bog in our brain and bowels, the primitive vigor of Nature, that inspires our dreams."[11]

Changing ideas of nature, wilderness, and landscape continue to inform the physical practices of design and building, and these, in turn, further transform and enrich cultural ideas. "A landscape park may be more palpable but no more real, nor less imaginary, than a landscape painting or poem," write Cosgrove and cultural geographer Stephen Daniels, and these various representations each affect and alter one another.[12] The popular use of a polished copper mirror in eighteenth-century England, for instance, allowed a viewer to appreciate a particular scene as if it were painted by Claude Lorrain; the distance from it was doubled, in effect, as it was not the actual landscape scenery in front of the viewer that was the object of attention but its reflection in a tinted, beveled mirror and its subsequent allusion to a particular genre of painting. Indeed, an essential precondition for popular appreciation of picturesque landscape during the eighteenth century was prior knowledge of pictures—the landscape simply did not "appear" until it had been first presented through painting.[13] Similarly, the acquisition of "good taste" in landscape appreciation was not granted through education alone but through social background and occupation. Consequently, eighteenth-century developments in European landscape equated images of landscape with wealth, high culture, and power, an equation that was encoded not only in garden art but also in painting, literature, and poetry. Landscape, as in the French *paysage*, carries with it to this day a sense of nationhood and cultural identity, an image that is also reflected in the use of the English term "country" to indicate both nation and *that which is not the city*.

These instances point to landscape's inextricable bond with cultural ideas and images; it is thus a gross reduction to consider landscape simply as a scenic object, a subjugated resource, or a scientistic ecosystem. To consider landscape in solely visual, formal, ecological, or economic terms fails to embrace the complex richness of association and social structures that are inherent to it. From a specifically landscape architectural point of view, it is crucial to understand how cultural ideas condition construction and how construction, in turn, conditions the play of landscape ideas in a larger cultural imagination. The implications of reciprocity between ways of seeing and ways of acting are immense and point toward the means by which the landscape project may be critically revised and reformulated. With regard to design, how one maps, draws, conceptualizes, imagines, and projects inevitably conditions what is built and what effects that construction may exercise in time.

Techniques of representation are central to any critical act in design. If it is true that there can be no concept of landscape without prior imaging (and not just perspective but also maps, plans, and other modes of representation), then innovations in image projection are necessary for the virtual to be both conceived and actualized.

### Landscape in the Twentieth Century

It is perhaps inevitable that the landscape project will wax and wane with time. The degree to which the life of a particular view of landscape remains with a given society historically has been subject to periods of great cultural significance—as in eighteenth- and nineteenth-century Europe—and decline—as in much of the twentieth century, during which landscape has been largely neglected by progressive art movements and modernist culture in general, with the significant exception of the land-art experiments by artists such as Robert Smithson, Michael Heizer, and Richard Long.[14] Apart from these few works, the landscape idea throughout much of this century has come mostly in the form of picturesque, rural scenery, whether for nostalgic, consumerist purposes or in the service of environmentalist agendas.

As is widely prevalent in painting, film, communications media, and tourist marketing campaigns, contemporary representations of landscape typically invoke idealized images of countryside devoid of modern technology, urbanization, and change. Laura Ashley, Ralph Lauren, and various automobile corporations are obvious examples in this regard, but so too are the preservation and heritage groups that use pastoral, premodern images to promote their goals. Landscape is presented as a place of escape from the ills of the present and anxieties about the future. This cycle of sentimental aestheticization compounds the difficulty of forging a critical and fresh landscape. Instead, the tendency today is to treat landscape as a giant commodity. The built result in much of Europe and the United States is typically not only of experientially deadening effect—your local corporate park, theme park, or the new housing development down "the lane" or along the "winding way," for instance—but also of a depressing cultural atrophy whereby all hope for the future is replaced by too high a regard for past accomplishments. The subsequent re-creations of previous worlds might not offend anyone were it not for their absolute absence of hope and invention; that they might also conceal and compensate for some of the more problematic aspects of modern life ought to be further cause for skeptical reflection. For all of their apparently innocent effect, landscapes without portent sound a death knell for any form of—and perhaps desire for—a truly modern and enterprising landscape.

Whether one has romantic or radical ends in mind, however, to hope for a recovery of landscape requires looking beyond the confines of strictly professional interests to see how pervasively (and persuasively) *cultural* the landscape phenomenon actually is. As earlier described, the practice of building landscapes will only become more marginal and irrelevant in the face of time if the culturally critical dimensions of the craft are forgotten or ignored. Making landscapes entails cultural vision that cannot be reduced to formal or ecological procedures. Thus, it is important to speak as much to the rise in popular demand for and interest in landscape (in gardening, tourism, education, and outdoor recreation, for example) as to the resurgence of intellectual critiques and practices of landscape (particularly within the architectural arts, but also within geography, film, and literature).

Such a multidisciplinary perspective is crucial for any understanding of the contemporary landscape phenomenon, not least because the shifting of ideas across disciplines has traditionally affected design practice, modes of representation, and the way the built environment looks. Consider the effects of painting on the subsequent landscape architectural work of eighteenth-century Europe, especially England, for instance, or the evolution of twentieth-century ecology and its impact on current planning and design practices.[15] The influence of contemporary film and communications media on landscape appreciation has yet to be fully studied, but I suspect it is immense, especially in American popular culture.

These effects go both ways, of course, for the building of new landscapes and their subsequent representation in art can also affect the evolution, value, and meaning of larger landscape ideas as well as other cultural practices. Central Park, for example, helped to solidify an urban community's view of itself and its relation to the natural world, just as the rectilinear surveying, delineation, and settlement of America's heartland, with its relentless, nonhierarchical grid pattern, helped to make manifest a collective ideal of equity, freedom, and accessibility.[16]

The reciprocal interactions between the built and the imaginary is what lies at the center of landscape architecture's creativity and contribution to culture. The field embraces significantly more than regressive, sentimental views of "nature" and "countryside" might lead one to believe, and its creative potential far outreaches that of the service professional offering ameliorative services after the land developers have done their damage. The largely domestic practices of modern-day "landscaping" simply fail to take the leap into the more interventionist ground of cultural and artistic production.[17] Just as it is simplistic to consider landscape lightly, as if it were merely a fashionable term or an expendable luxury, it is equally negligent to underestimate the transforming effect landscape practices exert on environmental, cultural, and ideological affairs.

### The Dark Side of Landscape

The term *recovery* implies that something once lost, devalued, forgotten, or misplaced has been found again, retrieved, and brought forward with renewed vitality. Also implied are repossession, taking control, and the regaining of health and normalcy, as in a rightful return. Such meanings have been associated with land disputes and the marking of territory since antiquity. Recovery carries with it, therefore, an inevitable double connotation. On the one side, optimism and hope are attached to the reemergence of a precious cultural treasure—one looks toward new and exhilarating prospects. On the other side, recovery implies a degree of sentimentality (nostalgia) and power (possession), both of which are inextricably interrelated with regard to landscape and point toward a more insidious side of landscape formation. This condition was described by John Barrell as landscape's "dark side," a moral darkness that derives from landscape being used by power interests to veil and perpetuate their effects.[18] Such coercion of landscape's cultural sway points again to the distinction between environment and landscape, the latter assuming a subjective and rhetorical significance. As critic Raymond Williams remarked, "A working country is hardly ever a landscape," a claim echoed by Jean-François Lyotard: "To have a feeling for landscape, you have to lose your feeling of place."[19] Both these statements draw attention to the difference between working country as habituated place and landscape as objectified scene. In the former, the subjects are fully immersed within their milieu, active and distracted; in the latter, they are placed at a distance, passive and gazing. As a distancing device, landscape can be used (or deployed) by those in power to conceal, consolidate, and represent certain interests (whether of the aristocracy, the state, or corporate sector). Landscape is particularly effective in this regard because it so beautifully conceals its artifice, "naturalizing" or rendering invisible its construction and effects in time. This condition led Lyotard to conclude that "it is not estrangement that procures landscape. It is the other way around. And the estrangement that landscape procures…is absolute."[20]

Perhaps it is now possible to appreciate more fully Clark's observation that "in those times when the human spirit seems to have burned most brightly the painting [and, thus, the concept] of landscape for its own sake did not exist and was unthinkable."[21] Clark is referring to landscape's estranged and estranging characteristic, the recovery of which marks a somewhat ominous and difficult time—a period where landscape is used more to mask or compensate for failings rather than to assume a newly emancipating and transformative role. As W. J. T. Mitchell has written:

> We have known since Ruskin that the appreciation of landscape as an aesthetic object cannot be an occasion for complacency or untroubled contemplation; rather, it must be the focus of a historical, political, and (yes) aesthetic alertness to the violence and evil written on the land, projected there by the gazing eye. We have known since Turner—perhaps since Milton—that the violence of this evil eye is inextricably connected with imperialism and nationalism. What we know now is that landscape itself is the medium by which this evil is veiled and naturalized.[22]

This might be an excessive characterization, but it serves to remind the reader that landscape is not necessarily to the benefit of all in society, that its apparent innocence and idealism can often mask hidden agendas and conceal social inequities and ongoing ecological destruction. Inasmuch as landscape objectifies the world—in the form of "scenery," "resource," or "ecosystem," for example—it sets up hierarchical orders among social groups, and among humans and nature more generally. One is always an "outsider" as far as the beholding of manufactured landscape goes, for to be "inside" entails the evaporation of land-scape into everyday place or milieu. It is in this deeper sense that landscape as place and milieu may provide a more substantial image than that of the distanced scenic veil, for the structures of place help a community to establish collective identity and meaning. This is the constructive aspect of landscape, its capacity to enrich the cultural imagination and provide a basis for rootedness and connection, for home and belonging.[23]

For landscape to be recovered, attention must be paid to both insider and outsider perspectives, the inside view allowing for a deeper, socially informed, material sense of place and being, the outside view for a broader range of possibilities to be invoked beyond those of the known and the everyday. The former view grounds a project in the social practices and physical conditions of a locality while the latter brings a new and broader range of ideas to bear upon the site. Landscape architect Christophe Girot characterizes this distinction as the "intuitive" (the unalienated inside sense) and the "empirical" (the synoptic, factual analysis). This formulation echoes Berque's call for a new synthesis of environmental "facts" and landscape "sensibilities."[24]

### Recovering Landscape

As already inferred, landscape is not given but made and remade; it is an inheritance that demands to be recovered, cultivated, and projected toward new ends. A topic of particular importance to landscape architecture with regard to such theories of recovery is the specificity of site. Landscape architecture has traditionally sought to recover sites and places, employing site phenomena as generative devices for new forms and programs. In recent years, the recovery of sites has not only assumed mnemonic and temporal significance but also biological importance, as lost or impoverished ecologies are restored and diversified. Thus, the reclaiming of sites might be measured in three ways: first, in terms of the retrieval of memory and the cultural enrichment of place and time; second, in terms of social program and utility, as new uses and activities are developed; and, third, in terms of ecological diversification and succession. In this threefold way, the inventive traditions of landscape architecture actively renew the significance of those cultural and natural processes that undergird the richness of all life on earth.

Following the failures of universal and utopian trends in late modernist architectural and urban planning and design, the attention paid to landscape and site is gaining increased currency today. A significant reason for this relates to the abovementioned failing of planning and design approaches that ignored local characteristics and values. Landscape is instead seen as a means to resist the homogenization of the environment while also heightening local attributes and a collective sense of place. As geographer David Lowenthal describes, the presence of the past offers a "sense of completion, of stability, of permanence" in resistance to the rapid pace of contemporary life.[25] As such, landscape has assumed increased popular value as a symbolic image, a picture laden with signs that lends cultural uniqueness, stability, and value to a particular place or region. Of course, as earlier noted, there are more creative reasons to reclaim sites and places than the merely nostalgic and compensatory—reasons that see invention as an essential ingredient of reclamation, engendering new kinds of landscape for public enjoyment and use.

A second aspect of recovering landscape concerns ecology and environment. Landscape is often equated with the expression of ecological phenomena. These expressions are found not only in preserved natural vistas but, more significantly, in the regional and global ecosystems depicted in aerial photography and satellite imaging-perspectives. The remarkable images of Earth revealed through the windows of the first space flights allowed the idea of nature in landscape to escape the boundaries of the scenic frame. Suddenly, landscape became planetary, embracing and expressing the interrelational tenets of ecology.

The effects of local events on regional, continental, and global ecologies was made emphatically clear, as the fluidity of water, air, and even movements of the earth's crust were revealed for all to see.

Increased satellite imaging, combined with massive media coverage of natural disasters and the rise of environmental activist groups, has increased public awareness of and concern for environmental issues. These range in scale from local problems of waste, pollution, and decreased diversity of habitat to global trends of ozone depiction, deforestation, extinction of species, nuclear waste, and resource depletion. In each case, landscape provides the idea around which such concerns are made visible and subsequently contested and engaged.

In the environmental sphere, the idea of landscape plays a double role, however. On the one side, landscape provides the most visible expression and measure of environmental atrophy—it is both victim and indicator—whereas, on the other side, it provides the ideal, arcadian image of a profoundly green, harmonious world, a world both lost and desired again. Consequently, as already described, landscape exists as a sign of the good and virtuous, a figure that is both victimized by technological evils and appropriated by competing interests. As a simulacrum of environment, landscape has been fought over in recent years by advocates of radically divergent and competing ecologies (from the resourcists and preservationists to the deep ecologists and ecofeminists).[26] Here, the equation of landscape with nature not only reveals the ideological and subjective essence of both terms but also their inevitable irreconcilability. As earlier described, those who continue to assert unreflective, sentimental ideas of nature and landscape simply suppress cultural experimentation and the development of alternative modes of landscape practice. Clearly, an ecology of human creativity—as exemplified in adaptive, cosmographic, and artistic practices—has yet to be developed in resistance to an increasingly uncritical, scientistic ecology that refers to an increasingly abstract "environment."[27]

A third phenomenon surrounding landscape's recovery is the massive process of deindustrialization that has accompanied the shift toward global communication and service economies. These changes have stressed both urban centers and rural areas, perhaps even collapsing their differences.[28] As a consequence, new demands have been placed on land-use planning and the accommodation of multiple, often irreconcilable conflicts. Huge and complex postindustrial sectors of cities have presented new challenges for landscape architects and urban designers in the past few years.

Any innovative response to these developments will most likely come from a creative appreciation for how today's space and time are phenomena radically different from their historical antecedents. We are surrounded by a space-time landscape of electronic media, images, internets, information superhighways, transglobal commutes, and rapid exchange of materials both visible and invisible. It is a world of infinite communication.[29] Everything is now available and immediate, without delay or distance. The geographical coordinates of one's place in the world are no longer simply spatial but deeply folded into the processes of speed and exchange. Authors as divergent as J. B. Jackson and Jean Baudrillard have shown how the modern landscape—at least in America—is no longer one of place, hierarchy, and center but one of transience, mobility, circulation, and exchange.[30]

Associated with topics of site, environment, and new technologies are a number of other factors that have promoted landscape in recent years. The unprecedented rise in recreation and tourism during the postwar years, for instance, precipitated not only a renewed interest in landscape but also—for capitalists, hedonists, and sentimentalists at least—a renewed value. At the level of both consumer (public demand) and producer (regional economic development interests), landscape is increasingly sought for its unique and intrinsic characteristics—its scenery, history, and ecology. Whether as theme park, wilderness area, or scenic drive, landscape has become a huge, exotic attraction unto itself, a place of entertainment, fantasy, escape, and refuge.[31]

Another factor in landscape's recovery is the emergence of land art since the 1970s. This continues to draw attention to landscape, this time as visceral and elemental art form. Here, landscape is both the venue (site) and material (medium) of artistic expression. Bound into the passage of time and natural process, the uniqueness of site and material circumstances makes landscape a more engaging and ephemeral phenomenon than that of distant scenery or pictures. In the hands of artists such as Smithson, Heizer, Walter De Maria, Christo, Robert Morris, Herbert Bayer, and James Turrell, landscape is less a scene for contemplation and more a shifting, material field of natural processes engaged through motion and time.

Art critic Rosalind Krauss's essay, "Sculpture in the Expanded Field," provides a seminal moment in landscape architecture, revising traditional disciplinary distinctions among sculpture, architecture, and landscape.[32] Various intellectual activities have since further challenged the modernist negation of landscape and nature, criticizing the dominant forces of technology and expansionism over the voices of marginalized others (the feminist critique in particular, but also environmentalist and social critiques).[33] Together, these activities have precipitated an increase in intellectual and artistic reflection on landscape, even to the point of demanding new forms of landscape comprehension, design, and typology. As a consequence, the landscape recovered here is less that of the art historian, the descriptive analyst, or even the speculative hermeneutician, and more the physical ground itself. Here, both the site and materiality of landscape provides an experimental laboratory, a cultural testing ground to be directly engaged and experienced.

These physical and conceptual bases of landscape led to a resurgence of interest in landscape topics in leading architecture schools during the 1980s.[34] Since then, renewed interest in topography, site, ecology, and geography has emerged more generally in design schools. It was not long ago that architects drew the plans and elevations of their buildings without topographic features, trees, and larger horizons. Today, at least in the better schools of architecture, place and context permeate not only drawings and models but also the conceptual and material formation of the projects themselves. At their best, building projects are conceived less in terms of isolated objects and more as site-specific constructs that are intimately bound into larger contexts and processes.

The significance of the landscape context for the architectural and environmental arts lies not only in the deeply sensuous and experiential dimensions of the land but also its semiotic, ecological, and political content. Thus landscape can no longer be considered solely as decoration around the base of buildings; rather, it has come to assume deeper roles of contextualization, heightening experiences, and embedding time and nature in the built world.[35] It is increasingly recognized that landscape harbors a profound environmental and existential promise for architecture and urbanism, provoking new forms of experience, meaning, and value. The still-emerging architectural conception of landscape, then, is less that of scenery, greenery, wilderness, and arcadia and more that of a pervasive milieu, a rich imbroglio of ecological, experiential, poetic, and expressively living dimensions.[36]

During the past few years, architects have produced a remarkable array of drawings and projects in which landscape figures prominently and in unusual forms: the remarkable graphic suprematism of Zaha Hadid's drawings and paintings, for example, with imploded fragments of building matter settling uneasily into immense hillsides and regionally scaled infrastructures; the astonishing work of Rem Koolhaas and the Office for Metropolitan Architecture, wherein new syntheses of building, landscape, and region are formed in every project, big and small; the folded, single-surface ground planes of Peter Eisenman (many with Laurie Olin), which mark a similar recasting of territorial distinctions—both in disciplinary and geographical terms—to that of Koolhaas, but differing by more textual references to site than to program.

Perhaps the single most significant project in terms of forging a new architecture of the landscape was Tschumi's Parc de la Villette in Paris, 1983–1990.[37]

FIG. 2 — Eastern Scheldt Storm Surge Barrier as coastal bird
plateau, by West 8 Urban Design and Landscape Architecture, Zeeland,
Netherlands, 1992

Photograph by Hans Werlemann

His park controversially reversed the traditional role of nature in the city, bringing the density, congestion, and richness of the city to the park. Similar urban
design projects in Paris, Barcelona, Stuttgart, and Lille have also promoted
landscape as a means of injecting social and institutional vibrancy into the city.
For smaller-scale architects as diverse as Álvaro Siza, Enric Miralles, Antoine
Predock, Glenn Murcutt, and Georges Descombes, a formative attitude toward
site and landscape deeply informs design and construction, albeit in markedly
different ways.

　　While architects have gathered renewed interest in landscape topics, professional landscape architects have not been without voice and effect. In the
United States, contemporary landscape architecture's contribution to the revitalization of landscape and urban public space has perhaps been most graphically demonstrated in the work of Peter Walker and Martha Schwartz, both of
whom continue to relentlessly promote the visual and formal aspects of modernist landscape design.[38] At the other end of the spectrum, recent advances in
creative habitat restoration and environmentally sensitive planning by practices
such as Andropogon and Jones & Jones have promoted renewed public consciousness about the land while constructing more ecologically adaptive modes
of settlement.

The tension between "artistic" and "ecological" approaches to landscape formation has perhaps been most effectively bridged in the remarkably plastic and complex work of George Hargreaves. Drawing inspiration from the great earthwork artists while applying technical and scientific knowledge, Hargreaves has built a range of large and surreal environments atop landfills, old dredgings, and along once polluted, flood-prone rivers.[39] The nearest equivalent of Hargreaves in Europe is Peter Latz, who, with astonishing ingenuity and restraint, has recently completed a new park amid the ruins of an enormous smelting factory in Duisburg, Germany.[40] The park is designed to clean and recycle the water, soil, and material of the site over time. Both Latz and Hargreaves demonstrate not only the effort to revitalize the derelict and polluted lands that surround the fringes of so many European and American cities but also to bridge the gap between artistic expression and ecological technique.

The striking visual geometries of Adriaan Geuze and his Rotterdam-based practice, West 8, provide vast new landscapes for the people of the Netherlands. Recovered in Geuze's work is the unequivocal constructedness of the Dutch landscape, its ecology, and its agency in advancing a modern society and affording new forms of public space. The ecological and programmatic ingenuity that Geuze brings to these projects elevates them to a level of significance beyond that of empty, graphic formalism. The stripes of cockle and mussel shells in the Schelpen Project, for example, are both a source of food and a field of camouflage and sighting strips for coastal birds; similarly, the huge planting strategy at Schipol Airport, with its incorporation of beehives, clover beds, and drainage ways, demonstrates a commitment to the formation of self-regulating ecosystems. [FIG. 2]

Examples abound; my point is to show how landscape has been seized by creative professionals in recent years as a critical and exciting medium of cultural expression and transformation. Yet there is still much to be done. The need to experiment, to devise more sophisticated modes of notation and representation, and to practice with greater critical foresight and cultural knowledge clearly must underlie any future revitalization of the field.[41]

As we enter the new millennium, dramatic changes in the world are putting forward challenges and possibilities for the landscape architectural arts. Ranging from the planning of new regions and infrastructures to the design of parks, gardens, maps, and journeys, the onus is on those who practice in topographical affairs to seize the opportunity and place landscape squarely in the foreground of cultural and political life. Designers and artists have a more actively engaging and interventionist role in the recovery of landscape than do those who are preoccupied with historical description, informational analysis, or consumerist development of land and, because of this, new ambitions, techniques, and desires must guide the education and practice of landscape architects.[42] In this sense, what is being recovered is not the landscape of scenes and objects but the landscape of ideas, operations, and cultural significance. It is about the simple planting of seeds within the wilds of the landscape imagination, hopefully propagating a field more diverse and enabling than ever before.

NOTES

1    See W. J. T. Mitchell, ed., *Landscape and Power* (Chicago: University of Chicago Press, 1994); and James Corner, "Critical Thinking and Landscape Architecture," *Landscape Journal* 10/2 (Fall 1991), 159–62.

2    See James Corner, "Ecology and Landscape as Agents of Creativity," in *Ecological Design and Planning*, eds. George Thompson and Frederick Steiner (New York: John Wiley & Sons, 1997), 80–108.

3    A useful reference with regard to landscape strategy is Francois Jullien, *The Propensity of Things: A History of Efficacy in China*, trans. Janet Lloyd (New York: Urzone, 1995). See also Michael Speaks, "It's Out There: The Formal Limits of the American Avant-Garde," *Architectural Design Profile 133: Hypersurface Architecture* (1988): 26–31.

4    On the relationship between spatial formations of landscape and the cultural imagination, see Denis Cosgrove, *Social Formation and Symbolic Landscape* (1984; reprint, Madison: University of Wisconsin Press, 1998); and Denis Cosgrove and Stephen Daniels, eds, *The Iconography of Landscape* (Cambridge: Cambridge University Press, 1988). Also of interest is Simon Schama, *Landscape and Memory* (New Haven, CT: Yale University Press, 1995); Robert Pogue Harrison, *Forests* (Chicago: University of Chicago Press, 1992); and David Matless, *Landscape and Englishness* (London: Reaktion, 1998).

5    On "thickness" and interpretation, see Clifford Geertz, "Thick Description," in *The Interpretation of Cultures* (New York: Basic Books, 1973), 3–30. Also see James Corner, "Three Tyrannies of Contemporary Theory and the Alternative of Hermeneutics," *Landscape Journal* 10/1 (Fall 1991), 115–33.

6    Kenneth Clark, "Landscape Painting," in *The Oxford Companion to Art*, ed. Harold Osborne (Oxford: Oxford University Press, 1970). See also Kenneth Clark, *Landscape into Art* (1949; reprint, New York: Harper and Row, 1984).

7    See Stanislaus Fung, "Mutuality and the Cultures of Landscape Architecture," in *Recovering Landscape*, ed. James Corner, (New York: Princeton Architectural Press, 1999), 141–51.

8    Cosgrove, *Social Formation and Symbolic Landscape*, 16. See also D. W. Meinig, "The Beholding Eye," in *The Interpretation of Ordinary Landscapes*, ed. D. W. Meinig (Oxford: Oxford University Press, 1979), 33–48.

9    Augustin Berque, "Beyond the Modern Landscape," *AA FILES 25* (Summer 1993), 33.

10   John Stilgoe, *Common Landscape of America, 1580–1845* (New Haven, CT: Yale University Press, 1982), 12. On the complexity of landscape as representation, see Denis Cosgrove, *The Palladian Landscape* (State College: Pennsylvania State University Press, 1993); and James Duncan and David Ley, eds, *Place/Culture/Representation* (London: Routledge, 1993).

11   Henry David Thoreau, *Journal* (August 30, 1856), quoted in *Landscape and Memory*, 578.

**12** Cosgrove and Daniels, *Social Formation and Symbolic Landscape*, 1.

**13** See Norman Bryson, *Vision and Painting: The Logic of the Gaze* (New Haven, CT: Yale University Press, 1988), 42–44, for a discussion of painting in relation to the "true" landscape. See also James Corner, "Representation and Landscape," *Word and Image* 8/3 (July–Sept 1992), 258–60.

**14** See John Beardsley, *Earthworks and Beyond: Contemporary Art in the Landscape*, 3rd ed. (New York: Abbeville Press, 1998); and Gilles Tiberghien, *Land Art* (New York: Princeton Architectura1 Press, 1995).

**15** See Ann Bermingham, *Landscape as Ideology: The English Rustic Tradition, 1740–1860* (Berkeley: University of California Press, 1986); and Rosalind Krauss, "The Originality of the Avant-Garde," *The Originality of the Avant-Garde and Other Modernist Myths* (Cambridge, MA: MIT Press, 1985), 151–70; See Ian McHarg, *Design with Nature* (1969; reprint, New York: John Wiley & Sons, 1992), and George Thompson and Frederick Steiner, eds, *Ecological Design and Planning* (New York: John Wiley & Sons, 1997).

**16** See J.B. Jackson, "The Accessible Landscape," in *A Sense of Place, A Sense of Time* (New Haven, CT: Yale University Press, 1994), 3–10; and James Corner and Alex MacLean, *Taking Measures Across the American Landscape* (New Haven, CT: Yale University Press, 1996).

**17** On the philosophical implications of this failure, see Peter Carl, "Natura-Morte," in *Modulus 20,* ed. Wendy Redfield Lathrop (Charlottesville: University of Virginia School of Architecture and New York: Princeton Architectural Press, 1991), 27–70.

**18** John Barrell, *The Dark Side of the Landscape: The Rural Poor in English Painting, 1730–1840* (Cambridge: Cambridge University Press, 1980). See also W. J. T. Mitchell, "Imperial Landscape," in *Landscape and Power*, 5–34.

**19** Raymond Williams, *The City and the Country* (Oxford: Oxford University, Press, 1973), 36; Jean-François Lyotard, *The Inhuman*, trans. Geoffrey Bennington and Rachel Bowlby (Stanford, CA: Stanford University Press, 1991), 189.

**20** Lyotard, *The Inhuman*, 190.

**21** Clark, *Landscape into Art*, viii.

**22** Mitchell, *Landscape and Power*, 29–30.

**23** See Cosgrove, *Social Formation and Symbolic Landscape.*

**24** See C. Girot, "Four Trace Concepts in Landscape Architecture," in *Recovering Landscape*, 59–67. And Augustin Berque, "Beyond the Modern Landscape." See also Augustin Berque, *Mediance: De Milieux en Paysages* (Montpellier-Paris: Redus-Documentation Francoise, 1990).

**25** See David Lowenthal, *The Past is a Foreign Country* (Cambridge: Cambridge University Press, 1985).

**26** For a useful discussion of competing environmental viewpoints, see Max Oelschlaeger, *The Idea of Wilderness* (New Haven, CT: Yale University Press, 1991), 281–319; and Michael Zimmerman et al, eds, *Environmental Philosophy* (Englewood Cliffs, NJ: Prentice-Hall, 1993).

**27** See Corner, "Ecology and Landscape."

**28** See Peter Rowe, *Making a Middle Landscape* (Cambridge, MA: MIT Press, 1991); Joel Garreau, *Edge Cities: Life on the New Frontier* (New York: Doubleday, 1991); Deyan Sudjik, *The 100 Mile City* (New York: Harcourt Brace, 1992); David Harvey, *The Condition of Postmodernity* (Cambridge, MA: Blackwell, 1989), and *Justice, Nature, and the Geography of Distance* (Cambridge, MA: Blackwell, 1996).

**29** See Christine Boyer, *Cybercities* (New York: Princeton Architectural Press, 1996); and William J. Mitchell, *City of Bits* (Cambridge, MA: MIT Press, 1996). Further philosophical reflection on the consequences of modern time and speed can be found in Paul Virilio, *The Aesthetics of Disappearance* (New York: Semiotext(e),

Columbia University, 1991); and Gianni Vattimo, *The Transparent Society* (Baltimore, MD: Johns Hopkins University Press, 1992).

30    See Jackson, *Sense of Place*; and Jean Baudrillard, *America*, trans. Chris Turner (London: Verso, 1988).

31    See Alexander Wilson, *The Culture of Nature: North American Landscape from Disney to the Exxon Valdez* (Cambridge, MA: Blackwell, 1992).

32    Rosalind Krauss, "Sculpture in the Expanded Field," in *The Anti-Aesthetic*, ed. Hal Foster (Port Townsend, WA: Bay Press, 1983), 31–42.

33    See Elizabeth K. Meyer, "Landscape Architecture as Modern Other and Postmodern Ground," in *Ecological Design and Planning*. Also see E. A. Grosz, "Feminist Theory and the Challenge to Knowledge," *Women's Studies International Forum* 10 (1987): 475–80; and Zimmerman et al, *Environmental Philosophy*.

34    This was particularly the case with the Architectural Association School of Architecture in London, where people such as Rem Koolhaas, Bernard Tschumi, and Zaha Hadid developed a distinct interest in large-scale projects that invoked landscape themes during the early 1980s. Later, Peter Salter, Peter Wilson, Jeanne Sillett, and Peter Beard developed other approaches to landscape, drawing more from geography and ecology.

35    See Marc Treib, "Nature Recalled," in *Recovering Landscape*, 29–43.

36    Anne Whiston Spirn's *The Granite Garden* (New York: Basic Books, 1984) was one of the first books to argue for a synthesis of architecture, landscape, and city. Since then, others have described more animate and synthetic versions of the living city; see, for instance, Sanford Kwinter, "Landscapes of Change: Boccioni's Stati d'animo as a General Theory of Models," *Assemblage* 19 (1992), 50–65; and Lars Lerup, "Stim and Dross: Rethinking the Metropolis," *Assemblage* 25 (1994), 82–100. Significantly, both Kwinter and Lerup draw from Henri Bergson's much earlier *Creative Evolution*, trans. Arthur Mitchell (1911; reprint, Lanham, MD: University Press of America, 1983).

37    See Bernard Tschumi, *Cinegramme Folie: le Parc de la Villette* (New York: Princeton Architectural Press, 1987); and, for an interesting discussion on this, see Bernard Tschumi, Christophe Girot, and Ernest Pascucci, "Looking Back at Parc de la Villette," *Documents* 4/5 (Spring 1994): 23–56.

38    See Peter Walker, *Peter Walker: Minimalist Gardens* (Washington, D.C.: Spacemaker Press, 1997); and Heidi Landecker, ed., *Martha Schwartz: Transfiguration of the Commonplace* (Washington, D.C.: Spacemaker Press, 1997).

39    See *Process Architecture* 128: *Hargreaves—Landscape Works* (January 1996).

40    See Peter Latz, "Emscher Park, Duisburg," in *Transforming Landscape*, ed. Michael Spens (London: Academy Editions, 1996), 54–61; and Peter Beard, "Life in the Ruins," *Blueprint* (July 1996), 28–37.

41    See James Corner, "The Agency of Mapping," in *Mappings*, ed. Denis Cosgrove (London: Reaktion, 1999), 212–52.

42    On the search for the "new," see Jeffrey Kipnis, "Towards a New Architecture," in Greg Lynn, ed, *Architectural Design Profile* 102: *Folding in Architecture* (1993), 41–49.

Part Two

—

# REPRESENTATION
# AND
# CREATIVITY

FIG. 1 —*Citrus Grove with Sprinkler Irrigation*, by Alex S. MacLean, Blythe, California, 1996

© Alex S. MacLean / Landslides Aerial Photography

FIG. 2 —*New Highway Ramps with Construction Markings*, by Alex S. MacLean, Charlestown,
Massachusetts, 1996 © Alex S. MacLean / Landslides Aerial Photography

# AERIAL REPRESENTATION:

## IRONY AND CONTRADICTION IN AN AGE
## OF PRECISION

### Aerial Representation and the Making of Landscape

In a small book entitled *Aircraft*, published in 1935, Le Corbusier reflects upon new insights of the earth and human settlement as afforded by the view from the air. In describing how this new synoptic vision suggests an alternative attitude toward the planning and design of cities and regions, he writes: "It is as an architect and town planner—and therefore as a man essentially occupied with the welfare of his species—that I let myself be carried off on the wings of an airplane, make use of the bird's-eye view, of the view from the air." Aloft, "the eye now sees in substance what the mind could only subjectively conceive; [the view from the air] is a new function added to our senses; it is a new standard of measurement; it is the basis of a new sensation. Man will make use of it to conceive new aims. Cities will arise out of their ashes."[1]

From above, some of humankind's most extensive measures are revealed with detached and analytical clarity. [FIGS. 1 + 2] More than the mere aesthetic of flight, this ability to see and conceive large regions from the air, with rational and comprehensive understanding, is what first inspired Le Corbusier and other Modernist planners. Subsequently, throughout the twentieth century, the aerial representation of land is less significant for its scenographic perspective than for its instrumental utility in the modernization of the earth's surface. In other words, the aerial view has not only captured the imaginations of people around the planet but has also emerged as a powerful tool in the planning and shaping of regions.

*Originally published in: James Corner and Alex MacLean,* Taking Measures Across the American Landscape *(New Haven, CT: Yale University Press, 1996), 15–19, 25–37.* © *1996 Yale University Press. Reproduced with permission.*

FIG. 3 — Ridges of old beach deposits from the receding edge of an ancient lake drift counter to the geometry of the survey grid. *Remnant Beach Ridges Across the Grid*, by Alex S. MacLean, Reynolds, **North Dakota, 1996** © Alex S. MacLean / Landslides Aerial Photography

With synoptic rationality, the aerial view continues to inform and promote systematic planning of land across large, regional scales. Such planning methodology is described in Ian McHarg's seminal book *Design with Nature*, published in 1969, just after the first moon landing.[2] McHarg, widely credited as the pioneer of ecological landscape planning, opens his treatise with an *Apollo* photograph of the planet Earth, eerily alone in a great, empty universe. He supports his arguments and methods with additional satellite and remote-sensing views, aerial photographs, bird's-eye perspectives, and analytical maps and plans. Lavishly illustrated is an immense global project, conceived synoptically from above and promoting a rational planning of the land, if not actually aspiring to inventory and guide development across the entire planet. Whereas McHarg, like other environmentalists, occasionally portrays humankind as an enormous "planetary disease" (an image of scarring the earth's surface at a scale that would be unbelievable were it not for evidence provided by the aerial view), it is, ironically, the same humankind and its technology (aerial and otherwise) that he and other planners cite as the heroic arbiter and measure of all things. Paradoxically, the view from above induces both humility and a sense of omnipotent power.

Founded upon rational and technological instrumentality, the optimistic belief in social and economic progress has characterized American settlement and cultural life since the eighteenth century. The United States is predicated upon capitalist and entrepreneurial practices, wherein hard work and ingenuity will typically lead to profit and gain. The aerial view, with its analytical scope, is both a logical consequence and agent in this utopian scheme, a relationship that is especially reflected in the U.S. Rectangular Survey System devised in the late 1700s. [FIG. 3] Although the aerial photograph was obviously not available to the early surveyors of the United States, an aerial sensibility—expressed in Baroque, bird's-eye panoramic drawings, maps, and plans—nonetheless pervaded the rational construing, surveying, and colonizing of lands west of the Alleghenies. The endless rectilinearity of the United States survey was imposed maplike, as if from above, with little or no regard for local variations in topography and ecology. The same attitude toward controlling the land from above continues today, for example, in the massive engineering projects that dominate entire river systems and span many physiographic regions or in the large-scale planning of transportation and communication infrastructure.

Many of these modern works would have been unimaginable—or at least unrealizable—without both the factual and imaginative dimensions provided by the first aerial representations of this century. Currently, advances in satellite imaging with its capacity to record changes in the chemical composition of the biosphere, to represent global weather situations, and to correlate data with computerized geographic information systems—reflect just how sophisticated this synoptic view has become. It is a view that affects not only the cultural imagination but also the actions that human societies take, especially with regard to new policies and practices aimed toward regional and global ecology.

The power of the aerial image lies less in its descriptive capacity—compelling as that is—than in its *conditioning* of how one sees and acts within the built environment. Like other instruments and methods of representation, the aerial view reflects *and* constructs the world; it has enormous landscape agency, in real and imaginary ways. This point is evidenced in the fact that different people at different times see the same world in radically different ways; it is not the world that changes but the ways and means of seeing and acting. Description and projection entail taking a particular point of view—both spatial and rhetorical—that not only reflects a given reality but also produces one. Furthermore, as scholars and critics have recognized, the inescapable assumption of a viewpoint in representation is never neutral or without agency and effect; representation provides neither a mirror reflection of things nor a simple and objective inventory.[3] Instead, representations are projections, renderings of reality that are drawn from and thrown onto the world. Moreover, the history of painting, literature, and cartography has shown us that a mirror copy of the world—or a description that is so precise and truthful as to be identical to the object it describes is simply an impossible illusion and that the ontological presence of the representation itself is unavoidable.[4]

Consider the role of maps, for example, which, like aerial photographs or paintings, are documents that are not remotely like the land itself; they are flat, unidimensional, and densely coded with all sorts of signs and hieroglyphs. To read a map, one must be trained in cartographic conventions. But maps are not exactly incongruous with the land either, for they accurately reflect certain (selected) characteristics of it. Moreover, maps would have little meaning and utility without the prior condition of the land itself. Similarly, spatial and topographic awareness of a landscape would likely be limited and ambiguous without the prior knowledge of a map. Maps make visible what is otherwise invisible.

A number of geographers and cultural historians have described how maps are necessarily selective in content and can never exhaust the full range of interpretative meanings inherent to the experience of land, even though maps often lead readers to believe that they are looking at complete, objective descriptions of the land.[5] The fictional and incomplete characteristics of maps are often masked by the appearance of measured objectivity, as too are the effects that maps have upon people's future actions. Moreover, not only are these fictions the result of particular methods of construction (and, thus, only one outcome of many possible schemata), but they are also biased with regard to what is shown and what is not. Interpretation, after all, is never value-neutral, no matter how sincere the claims of impartiality. There is no innocent eye; reality is always read and written with prejudice, and maps are therefore susceptible to ideology and the abuse of power.[6] Powerfully effective symbolic and semantic effects of representation are found in the propaganda maps of Nazi Germany, for example, which presented geographical territories and figures in ways that were topographically incorrect in order to promote and control the nationalist imagination.[7] In less ominous ways, the maps of national parks, tourist areas, and commercial districts also precipitate forms of perception that serve the interests of those who commissioned the map. Similarly—in ways that are spatial, symbolic, and susceptible to misuse—the new aerial representations of the twentieth century have effected a new awareness of regional and global ecologies, instigated the planning and large-scale settlement of land, and colored the imaginations of millions of people who now live and act upon the planet.[8]

Changes in cultural practices and modes of understanding may precede or follow from innovations in representation. The development of pictorial perspective during the sixteenth century, for example, profoundly influenced the depiction of space as well as its subsequent design and construction, as infinitely extended lines radiated across the landscape and opened up the inward-looking enclosures of the medieval period. The gardens at Versailles exemplify perspectival practice, embodying a shift in spatial and aesthetic sensibility and at the same time symbolizing the new regal powers of seventeenth-century France together with the development of Enlightenment science.

For many artists, it is the inventive capacity of representation that enables them to provoke new and alternative ways of seeing the world. Similarly, the products of geographers, cartographers, historians, scientists, and writers enrich the cultural imagination and condition how and what actions are taken in the world. Black holes, DNA, the Bermuda Triangle, the equator, the desert, all these, like many other found places, are revelatory descriptions and constructions of reality. They are ideas. In turn, each of these new representations of the world becomes subject to the scrutiny of others, to be either corroborated and built upon or disagreed with and overturned. Further interpretations, instigated by and overlaid upon previous representations, shift and enrich a shared cultural reality with the passage of time. One might view with skepticism, then, those who claim to act upon the land with absolute confidence and certainty (as might the "master planner," for example), because such actions and measures are always predicated upon a particular fiction, a representation that is not only ideologically loaded but also subject to shift and revision over time. The enrichment of cultural life is predicated upon the continuing critical development of new modes of representation and interpretation, including that of the aerial view.

Consider the walks taken by Richard Long, for example. These are first plotted as straight lines derived from an autonomous quantitative/geometric logic drawn across various maps. The subsequent walk along the line in the actual landscape reveals a series of unexpected collusions between map, land, and event, with each informing and challenging one another afresh.[9] An indifferent form of measured precision toward the dissection of map and land opens up a trajectory of completely unforeseen possibilities and events.

The hope of the "Taking Measures" project is that the intersection of document, method, and practice—of representation and inhabitation—will be evident in the photographs and map drawings, and that these illustrations will suggest alternative modes of seeing and acting upon America's evolving topography. We attempt to describe and to project upon the radically fictional nature of the American landscape, to quarry as well as to contribute to the accumulated layers of aerial representation and their agency of transformation. Perhaps our ultimate aspiration is that this work might provoke others who practice upon the land to see and act with a more critical, synoptic eye in the cultivation of future landscapes.

### Irony and Contradiction in an Age of Precision

On the surface, America is a carefully measured landscape of survey lines, rectangular fields, irrigated circles, highways, railroads, dams, levees, canals, revetments, pipelines, power plants, ports, military zones, and other such constructions. All are efficiently laid out with ingenious indifference to the land, crossing desert, forest, plain, marsh, and mountain with a cool, detached, and rational logic. These highly planned geometrical constructions are literally measures that have been taken across the American landscape in order to ensure a productive human occupation of the earth and its resources. Many of these measures possess dimensions precise yet fantastic, and they have constructed what is perhaps the closest approximation of utopia yet achieved by humankind. The United States has emerged over the past two centuries as a remarkably democratic and powerful nation, a land in which practically everything has become available and anything is now possible. In philosopher Jean Baudrillard's *America* (1988): "Everything here is real and pragmatic, and yet it is all the stuff of dreams too…America is utopia made actual."[10] What appear to be some of the most prosaic and banal measures in the modern landscape (roads, transmission lines, and survey lines, for example) actually provide a "hyperreality" of exhilarating and emancipating opportunity—a place of desire and hope.

The paradox is not only of a dream reality, however. America is also a land of violence, indifference, and estrangement. Misfortune, stress, and fear are commonplace, symptoms of a "dis-measure," or a radical inequity and incongruity between things that comes as much from the land as from social conflict. Meteorological and geological disasters seem to occur with the same scale of indifference as do crime, greed, and hate, for example. For all the generous provision that America's measures yield, the land remains a challenging domain, a vulgar sprawl where many often feel disoriented and fearful. This America is a placeless space wherein all values are neutralized and all measures voided of meaning and hope. Here is utopia's absolute antithesis, a dystopia of dreadful dimension.

There is, then, an inevitable ambivalence to modern life in America. Although the measures of American life liberate people from the confines of nature and ideological tyranny, and grant access and opportunity to almost everyone, the same measures have also proven to be inadequate and even onerous, especially in their indifference to ecological and social relationships. In spite of providing wealth, freedom, hope, and potential for millions of people, modern measures have been largely ineffective in alleviating alienation, meaninglessness, pollution, and waste. It would appear that for every determination and provision of technological measure, there follows a peculiar excess or deficiency, as if everything becomes at once overly specific and overly simplistic. Consider the immense hydro-engineering projects in the West, for example. Enormous dams, power plants, canals, and irrigation systems have made an arid landscape productive and home to millions of people; yet the long-term effects of salt and silt accumulation, loss of habitat diversity, and increased population demands commit this otherwise creative system to failure. [FIG. 4]

The failure of modern measures is not only environmental and economic but also social and ethical. For many people today, modern reality appears fragmented, temporary, and without great purpose. Within such a flux of discontinuity (both spatial and temporal), all that seems to matter is an eternal present, the here and now, with scant memory of what has gone before and little enthusiasm, hope, or responsibility for the future. Of course, that so many continue to find America utterly fascinating and liberating to live in (myself included) only compounds this extraordinary aporia, lending to it a good dose of irony. As expressed in the air-conditioned casinos and fountains of Las Vegas; in the irrigated lawns across the arid deserts of Arizona and southern California; on the congested freeways and interchanges; in the ubiquitous gas stations and parking

FIG. 4 — The spring snowmelts of the Colorado watershed, high in the Rocky Mountains, cause
the torrential flows of water that have formed the great canyons of Utah and Arizona.
Today, this great water volume is controlled by a series of huge concrete dams that store the
water in enormous lakes. Once-raging river ravines and deep valleys are now filled with
passive water reservoirs, and the mouth of the great Colorado has been reduced to a trickle.
*Glen Canyon Dam*, by Alex S. MacLean, Colorado River, Arizona, 1996

© Alex S. MacLean / Landslides Aerial Photography; Citations: Marc Reisner,
*Cadillac Desert* (New York: Viking Penguin, 1986); Philip L. Fradkin, *A River No More* (New York: Knopf, 1981);
Norris Hundley, *Water and West: The Colorado River Compact and the Politics of Water
in the American West* (Berkeley: University of California Press, 1975)

lots; in the volume and diversity of foodstuffs grown on synthetically managed fields east, west, and central; or in the sprawling cities with their tall, corporate towers, peripheral ghettos, and green, bucolic suburbs, American life is extremely vibrant, exciting, productive, accessible, and desirable; yet at the same time it is all so strangely bland, entropic, and meaningless.[11] This double-edged paradox belongs uniquely to modern America, where heterogeneous and fragmented characteristics stand in stark contrast to the various holistic structures of traditional societies and the more harmonizing role of measure in structuring their worlds.

### Traditional Measures

Traditional measures possessed two characteristics that are no longer a part of modern convention. The first was the capacity of measure to relate the everyday world to the infinite and invisible dimensions of the universe, whether the movement of the planets, the rhythm of the seasons, or the actions of heavenly deities. For Plato, the definition of the good and the beautiful belonged to measure, appropriateness, and harmony. Ancient geometry, in particular, embodied cosmic order, symbolizing an ideal wholeness of relationship between the activities of people on earth while revealing the supreme order and perfection of the divine and universal. Nature and art were not antithetical but together revealed a wholesome and unified order.[12] Moreover, nature was understood as the ultimate source of beauty and held priority in the cosmography of many ancient cultures. Art and measure simply revealed the perfection of natural order and the supremacy of cosmic law, a unity that was also understood (in a different way) by Native American cultures such as the Hopi and the Anasazi and embodied in their cosmographic construction of space.

The second characteristic of traditional measure was its development through the relationship of the human body to physical activities and materials. In medieval Ukraine, for example, farmers would speak of a "day of field," referring to the area of land that they could physically sow or harvest in one day.[13] Obviously, the actual area would vary according to the lay of the land and the physical capacity of the individual farmer. Similarly, in early France, an *arpent* represented the area that a farmer could plow in one day using two oxen. Again, this measure, like other highly local and socially derived measures, varied greatly depending on circumstance. Fields along the west coast of Ireland, for example, were traditionally sized according to the distance a farmer was able to carry stones removed from the topsoil, a measure recorded today in the spacing between stone walls. These spacings and markings across the land, as with the farmer's calloused hands and crooked back, are visible measures of occupational circumstance; they are evolved forms of expression, the results of physical negotiation with the land, the elements, and the contingencies of a given situation.

Traditional units of measure therefore derived from the interrelationship of labor, body, and site. Tailors measured cloth using "arms" along its length and "hands" across its width, for example. Horses, too, were so many "hands" high, though this measure was not used with other animals. Similarly, a place a "stone's throw away" was not equal to one that was at "shouting distance." The sources of traditional measures were the concrete experiences of everyday life. Such measures were situated in the specific and were not necessarily applicable to other circumstances; they signified the value of a particular quantity along with its situational quality. An acre or a hectare, by contrast, quantifies an area into a standard unit but speaks not of its qualitative value or its circumstances of being.

The practical and place-specific nature of traditional measure, together with its idealized, cosmographic import via geometry, meant that the traditional world was generally conceived of as an organic whole, lending a representational and socially interactive unity to life (demonstrated by the Hopi and Chacoan examples). [FIGS. 5 + 6] Both the phenomenal and imaginative dimensions of reality were structured through these earlier uses of measure and geometry. Owing to the capacity of traditional measure to imbue practical life with symbolic meaning, such measures made coherent the relationships between people, place, activity, morality, and beauty.

### Modern Measures

The socially and symbolically derived coherency of traditional measure began to change during the scientific revolution of the seventeenth century. Following the radical developments put forth by Galileo, Francis Bacon, Isaac Newton, and René Descartes, measure assumed an increasingly autonomous and self-referential place in human knowledge, becoming less and less connected to experiential and culturally situated origins. The Enlightenment philosophers severed, or abstracted, the world from the subject in order to dissect it for empirical study. The sterility and isotropic constancy of the modern laboratory ensured that things could be studied in isolation, without external interference. Thereafter, the world came to consist of an array of quantifiable and manipulable objects arranged in homogeneous and absolute space. No longer were things qualified by their relation to a specific subject, place, or situation; instead, the various "parts" of reality were objectified and rendered neutral. Consequently, measure developed into a radically autonomous practice, related not to the phenomenal

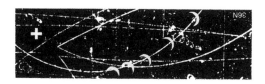

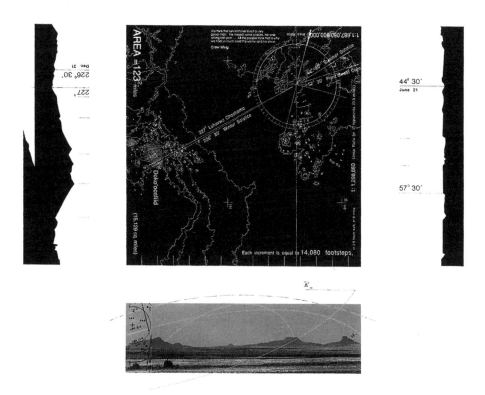

FIG. 5 — Hopi time is constructed by the track of the sun across the dramatically marked horizon.
As the sun rises and sets in a more extreme location along the horizon each day, and turns
back at times of solstice, the Hopi use the geological calibrations across the distant landscape
as a timepiece, a calendar to predict times for planting, harvest, and religious ceremony.
The solstices are the most important times of observation for the Hopi, as the sun's movement slows
and rests for a few days prior to returning along the horizon and bringing in the new season.
If the sun were to stay too long at its "winter house," a long, cold winter followed by spring frosts
might delay planting and damage young crops; whereas if it failed to stay long enough
in its "summer house," the growing season might be too short for a good harvest. Measured
with anticipation and hope, the track of the sun along the horizon constructs the varying
rhythms of time. *Hopi Horizon Calendar*, by James Corner, 1996

Citations: Leo William Simmons, ed., *Sun Chief: The Autobiography of a Hopi Indian* (New Haven, CT:
Yale University Press, 1972); J. McKim Malville and Claudia Putnam, *Prehistoric Astronomy in the Southwest*
(Boulder, CO: Johnson, 1991); Michael Zeilik, "Keeping the Sacred and Planting Calendar:
Archaeolastronomy in the Pueblo Southwest," in Anthony F. Aveni, ed., *World Archaeolastronomy*
(Cambridge: Cambridge University Press, 1989), 143–166.

FIG. 6 —*Pueblo Bonito, Chaco Canyon, New Mexico*, by James Corner, 1996

and interactive world but to things as solitary and inert objects. This splitting of the objective from the subjective established, for the first time, a detached distance between the human and phenomenal worlds, enabling humankind to assume a position of supremacy and mastery over nature. Thus, the synoptic perspective of modern technology promoted detached forms of surveillance that enabled an unprecedented belief in the human ability to control the natural world and forge ahead with the building of utopia. Furthermore, the potential for interrelatedness between diverse things was broken (or at least suppressed) and is marked today in a number of incommensurate situations, such as the polarity between the "rationalism" of the engineer and the "sensibility" of the artist, between the instrumentality of technology and the phenomenology of dwelling, or between the life of the universe and the life of the individual.

Consider the modern period's definition of the meter, which was originally devised in France in 1799 as a unit equal to 1/40,000,000 of the earth's meridian.[14] Later, from 1889 to 1960, a single bar of platinum and iridium alloy was kept in a Parisian assay office as an internationally binding standard for the meter. To reduce the tolerance of inaccuracy, the meter has since been defined as "a length equal to 1,650,763.37 wave lengths of the orange light emitted by the Krypton atom of mass 86 in vacuo," a convention that was specified in the isotropic, dehumanized space of the laboratory.[15] Thus, unlike the significant measures of the past, modern measures emerged as the outcome of technocratic convention; they have no greater social or cosmographic significance than the mathematical and international need for universal standards.

Unwittingly, the Enlightenment philosophers heralded a new technological era in which the universal application of measure was to become the ultimate instrument of human dominion, with the consequence that the world was reduced to a neutral stock of resources made available for profit and gain. This blinkered, detached form of measure is obviously significantly different from the qualitative, concrete, and symbolic types of traditional measure, yet these autonomous forms of measure underlie much of the development of the American landscape during the past two centuries and continue to pervade cultural reasoning today. This brief account of modern measure is neither so clean-cut nor nihilistic in modern-day America, however. America is more of a paradox than it is a sterile, mute, and easily dissected object. Although modern measure has pervaded the making of the American landscape, it has, at the same time, exposed a richness inherent to technology when situated in the cultural context of the United States. Consider the case of Thomas Jefferson, who is credited with the early planning of the Public Land Survey System.

For Jefferson, measure was not only of technological and instrumental value but also of moral and social worth. Beginning in his youth, Jefferson was constantly engaged with measuring, surveying, and mapmaking. As evidenced in the interiors at Monticello, he surrounded himself with all sorts of measuring instruments—compasses, rulers, scales, sighting lenses, barometers, tripods, microscopes, tables, charts, transects, and the like. These allowed him to pursue his fascination with observing natural phenomena, especially the weather, the passage of the seasons, the forces of the environment, gardening, farming, and botany. In particular, he was interested in observing and recording their measurable characteristics, from which he derived numbers, patterns, laws, and rhythms. These measured findings were of great practical import, enabling him to invent and order things in a rational, accessible manner.

Jefferson was just as interested in modest everyday events as he was in national affairs and politics. One of his favorite vegetables, for example, was the pea, and he went to great lengths to study the cultivation and growth habits of this epicurean delight. He wrote: "[On February 20th] I sowed a bed of forwardest and a bed of midling peas. 500 of these peas weighed 3 oz...about 2,500 fill a pint; [March 19th]...both beds of peas up...April 24th: forwardest of peas come to table...Here, our first peas [are the] cheapest, pleasantest, and most wholesome part of comfortable living."[16] This busy and important man took the time to plant, cultivate, observe, measure, and savor the delights of such a minor vegetable! But, in so doing, Jefferson finds that the quantitative and analytical aspects of measure enable and support "the most wholesome part of comfortable living." Although he is, of course, relating wholesome living to the refined cultivation of the pea, he is, by extension, also invoking what is good and beautiful in human dwelling. Through modesty, restraint, and measured discipline, immeasurable delights are made possible. With neither waste nor excess, a harmonious relationship among a man, the vegetable world, and the graces of civilized dining could be structured through the rigors of modern measure. Numeracy, activity, and value are here linked in a form of purposeful and creative reciprocity.

Further, there are always moral and aesthetic judgments embodied within dimensions, quantities, and proportions for Jefferson. In criticizing the Capital at Williamsburg, for example, he wrote: "The Capital is a light and airy structure, with a portico in front of two orders, the lower of which, being Doric, is tolerably just in its proportions and ornaments, save only that the intercolonnations are too large. The upper is Ionic, much too small for that on which it is mounted and its ornaments not proper to the order, nor proportioned within themselves. It is crowned with a pediment which is too high for its span."[17] For Jefferson, what was "just" and "proper" was a matter not only of dimensional exactitude but also of aesthetic and social propriety. He inherited this understanding from the European tradition and put it into practice in the siting and architecture of his home at Monticello.

In conceiving of the Public Land Survey System, Jefferson was most concerned with making land available, efficiently and equitably, for purchase and ownership by individuals. During a number of debates on the procedures for the division, marking, and sale of land, Jefferson had a guiding imperative: that "as few as possible shall be without at least a little portion of land."[18] This vision was later worked into the Land Ordinance Act of 1785 and then revised as the Land Act of 1796, which was when the survey really began (the procedure having been altered from that first proposed by Jefferson, which used a different dimensioning system and did not account for the converging of north-south lines).[19] The measuring and demarcation of the American landscape was therefore less about dominion and possession than it was about the democratic and orderly sale of land and its subsequent settlement. Any person could own a piece of the American dream and share in its bounty.

The unit by which land was to be divided was called a Gunter's Chain, a standard surveyor's chain used in England that consisted of 4 perches—or rods—each 16 feet long, making a chain equal to 66 feet. This unit proved useful because 10 square chains define an acre, and 640 acres fit into a square mile. Using repetitive survey procedures, the entire country was thereby marked according to a rectilinear grid following the lines of latitude and longitude. [FIG. 7]

To regulate the sale of land and avoid wholesale purchasing of large areas by land speculators, the government devised a system of division organized around thirty-six-square mile "townships," defined by a square whose sides measured six miles, which was believed to be a reasonable distance for horse and wagon to get to market and back. These townships were in turn divided into thirty-six parcels measuring one square mile, called "sections." Sections were numbered in what was called "boustrophedonic order" (or as the plow follows the ox), a curious appropriation of a traditional procedure by such a modern and rational scheme.[20] The sixteenth lot was typically reserved for community institutions and schools. Later, in order to make smaller parcels available to more people, sections were divided; first, into half sections, then quarter sections, then half-quarter and quarter-quarter sections. This latter unit is forty acres and was legislated in to effect in 1836, and it remains the plot that is most evident in Midwestern states today.

The Survey was itself a measure to ensure efficient, equitable, and secure occupancy by free and hard-working people. Expressed in the form and pattern

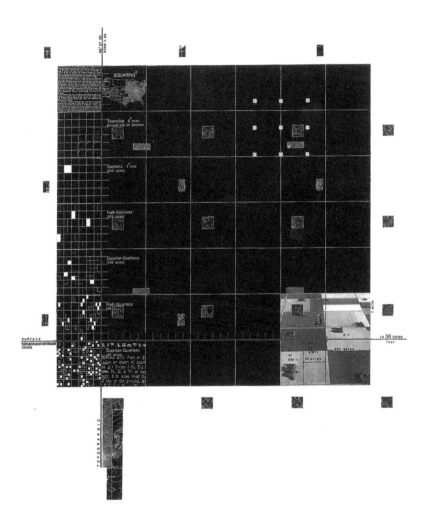

FIG. 7 — To provide more people with the opportunity to purchase land, sections of the
National Land Survey were later subdivided into half sections, quarter sections,
and half-quarter sections, which is the forty-acre parcel most evident in the Midwest today.
Section lines became roads and smaller plots of land were delineated and marked by posts
and fences. *The Survey Landscape*, by James Corner, 1996

of this geometrical, rectangular system is a major social imperative, one that reflects democratic and socially just proportion more than dominion and control.

This latter, autocratic view is perhaps understandable only in the context of the apparent indifference of those conducting the survey to local variations in topography, hydrology, and soils. One consequence of this bureaucratic inflexibility was that townships and individual lots sometimes significantly differed in quality from neighboring plats. Moreover, the configuration and size of a piece of land were not necessarily the most appropriate given the ecosystem of a particular region (the drumlin and Finger Lakes region of upper New York state, for example) or particular types of occupancy (American Indians could make no sense or use of the grid, and hillside farmers found the rectilinear property lines too awkward for plowing their sloped fields efficiently).

The French method of land division on the American continent was, by contrast, more responsive to its physiographic context. Most settlement by the French occurred along river floodplains (especially great arterial rivers such as the Mississippi and the St. Lawrence) owing to their interest in using these trade corridors to ship goods (especially furs) back to Europe during the seventeenth and early-eighteenth centuries. In response to the meandering nature of the river and the need of settlers to have their own access to the river frontage, straight lines were drawn perpendicularly to the river's edge to delineate property parcels, or long lots. Each long lot had a river frontage of two to three arpents (384 to 576 feet) and was typically ten times as long as its width.[21] Because each occupant had access to the river, the fertile floodplain soils, and the higher protected land at the end of the lot, they all shared the benefits and dangers of settling along the river. Such adjustment of land division to physiographic and programmatic circumstance was, of course, common to other forms of settlement (such as New England villages and hillside towns) prior to the development of the more direct and regularized procedures of the Public Land Survey System.

### Qualitative Determination

Questions of survey, inventory, number, size, scale, spacing, and interval continue to surface in the present-day planning and design of land. How these spatial determinations are made, however, is not so easy to answer. How does one know, in fact, the correctness and propriety of a particular spatial or material judgment? From where do these measures derive? More often than not, it appears that certain technical standards, as documented in manuals and technical guidebooks, serve as the benchmark for contemporary dimensioning and apportioning. Some land planners speak of "determinants," or quantifiable factors, that lead logically to certain measures and solutions. In fact, the modern production of environments by engineering and landscape architectural professionals is becoming increasingly standardized owing to the capacity of computers to store and manipulate all of the "determinant variables" and "prototypical solutions" for a given problem. The material world is subsequently spaced and organized according to some standardized specification that is usually required by warranty or legal code. To build anything less would be irresponsible with respect to the "health, safety, and welfare" of the "public" (whoever that constituency actually is), and to do anything more would be gratuitous (at least according to the often anonymous makers of these rule books).

Moreover, there is little uncertainty as to the success of these norms; they are at least sufficient for most situations. The result, of course, is a ubiquitous and standardized built environment, one that looks the same in New York as it does in Anchorage or Albuquerque. The experience and challenge of spatial discovery are consequently impoverished, with differences blended into the lowest common denominator and finally eradicated. Every place, regardless of special characteristics, begins to look and feel alike—neutralized and bland.

Fortunately, there are some aspects of the environment that, as yet, have not been subject to the rigor (mortis) of standardization. For example, some of the best landscape architects I know have expressed anxiety when making spatial and programmatic determinations in design. One struggles over the spacing of a grove of poplar trees in a particular place: should they be fifteen, eighteen, or twenty feet on center? Another never seems confident that the slope of a hill should be graded one in four (the ratio of the vertical fall to the horizontal dimension); perhaps it should be one in five, one in six, or even one in eight. Others take pains over the dimensions of a wall or step, sizing them differently every time owing to the uniqueness of a given situation. Each of these designers struggles with standards and norms because each has his or her own sense of how something ought to be in a particular circumstance, especially with regard to dynamics of growth, erosion, and processes of time. They decide how big or how small a designed element should be, without a ruler in hand or a particular program in mind. They decide that a certain material is too warm or too cold without thermometer or reference to radiant temperature. Instead, these spatial and material determinations are qualitatively negotiated; they are the outcome of informed experience and the "feeling out" of those phenomena believed to be most appropriate given the circumstances. Consequently, their designs are impossible to replicate elsewhere without their becoming somehow unfitting or improper. Informed by judgments about what is correct for a given situation, the measures taken by these designers are best approximations rather than certainties. They derive from a culturally grounded form of accuracy, a qualitative precision that is quite different from that of the techno-mathematical. Like Michelangelo's "false truths" (those artistic representations that appear to be more correct in feeling and in truth of spirit than the "true falsehoods" of empirical quantification), such intuitive determinations of measure are always peculiar to and right for their contextual circumstance.[22] Through their inventive fitting, such measures might also be understood in terms of metaphor in that their span reaches to join and produce something new.

What we may learn from this sense of qualitative precision is that quantities, limits, spacings, and tolerances are always situated within a complex milieu of social, moral, and aesthetic implications. To cite Derrida: "We appear to ourselves only through an experience of spacing.... What happens through [this spacing] both constructs and instructs [who we are]."[23] To gauge and space the world is not only to reflect upon the nature of human existence on earth but also to construct a relationship among people, community, and environment. By extension, to exercise "good measure" in everyday life is to practice what feels right and proper, with precision, economy, and grace. Measured correctness, then, is less of dimensional, mathematical exactitude than it is of moral propriety and precision of judgment—attributes that are culturally acquired and practiced within given circumstances; they cannot be practiced using the codes and conventions of standards and norms alone. As such, measure guides interpretation and action in ways that are as much qualitative and situated as they are quantitative and universal. This is more a practical form of knowledge than a strictly theoretical mode of knowing. The present-day incongruity between these two conditions—the instrumental, calculative, objective, standardized, and formulaic, on the one hand, and the sensual, poetic, subjective, and contingent, on the other—characterizes the aporia of measure in late-twentieth-century America. Neither position (the traditional or the modern) should be privileged over the other but, rather, both need to be brought into a greater form of reciprocity.

### The Reconciliatory Function of Measure

In a short, beautiful essay entitled "...Poetically Man Dwells...," Martin Heidegger reflects upon the essential nature of measure. Drawing from the poetry of Friedrich Hölderlin, Heidegger proclaims that "the taking of measure is what is poetic in dwelling."[24] He later turns this phrase around to read: "In poetry there takes place what all measuring is in the ground of its being."[25]

How are we to understand this elusive claim? Perhaps one must live in the poetic before any clear understanding is possible. The musician or the poet may not find such a claim elusive, perhaps appreciating the fact that Heidegger cannot be more explicit in grounding these assertions than through analogical reasoning. Almost certainly, he is not speaking of the quantitative and the instrumental here; after all, the dimensions and weights of the material world have been measured over and over again, from the scale of the solar system to that of the genetic code, and yet all of these data ultimately remain prosaic and flat. Moreover, sophisticated legislative and concrete measures have been taken across the surface of the earth, and well beyond. Perhaps at no other time have so many varied and complex measures been taken than during the twentieth century, and yet is it really possible to say that Americans "dwell poetically" today? Has there developed an authentic level of reciprocity among individuals, social communities, and the natural world? Whereas poetry and art are readily available to modern culture, this provision does not seem to be sufficient evidence of a "poetic society." In fact, if homelessness, pollution, waste, withdrawal, and general estrangement are to serve as guides, the dwelling of modern culture is altogether unpoetic, brutally real and entropic. Ironically, these same social conditions have also been subject to enormous efforts of measurement by government and scientific agencies, to little avail. Heidegger, too, recognizes these characteristics of modern life. In fact, he suggests that "our unpoetic dwelling, [our] incapacity to take the measure, derives from a curious excess of frantic measuring and calculating."[26] This excess is likened to the person who cannot see simply because he sees too much—a situation that is exemplified in the way measures of techno-economic exigency tend to overspecify and oversimplify at the same time, dominating and rendering trivial other forms of seeing and acting in the modern world. The result is atrophy in the health and diversity of the biosphere and of culture, characteristic of late-twentieth-century life. As documented by natural and social scientists alike, this deterioration has aesthetic and experiential effects (as evidenced in the increased homogeneity and impoverished state of the environment), together with ecological and ethical implications (such as the anthropocentric will to power over all others and the diminishing of alterity and difference).

Clearly, the measure taking of which Heidegger and the poets speak differs from the purely calculative and instrumental. It is a measure taking that is about the "letting appear" of what is right and fitting in human existence. This reconciliation of opposites is what is revealed by the poetic measure, the metaphor. Such measures are good and beautiful in their spanning and joining of differences, connecting things to make possible more wholesome forms of existence. As philosopher Albert Hofstadter comments: "Man's measure is not a quantity that can be calculated. Only man's being itself can tell what its measure is, by the fiery test of the living encounter of the human self with reality. Human measure is to be sought in the quantity of our belonging—in the magnitude, direction, and degree of our being with the other as with our own."[27] The kind of inter-connectivity spoken of here is one of relationship, a spatiotemporal mode of being among others in circumstantial and reciprocal ways. Measures as meta-phors might therefore be said to increase the world's being, further diversifying and enriching one thing's life among a multitude of others, which is ultimately of both ecological and social value.[28]

A further understanding of this reconciliatory function of measure need not be obscure or theoretical, for people practice good and just measure in daily life. When one enters into a conversation, participates in a dance, or sits to eat with friends, a sense of what constitutes appropriate behavior and response prevails. In philosophical terms, this self-awareness of measure is called "practical wis-dom": one is conscious of the quantities, properties, and limits of one's being within a particular circumstance, and is aware of how to extend and foster kin-ship with others.[29] By extending oneself with due measure (which is what ensues in any conversation or dance), one overcomes separation and distance to con-struct relationship and dialogue. These social measures unite self with other. With respect to the earth, such relationships are the foundations for culturally wholesome forms of cultivation and dwelling; they structure a spatial and ethical "fittingness" between the natural and social worlds that is neither excessive nor wasteful. [FIG. 8]

Obviously, humility and temperance pervade such an ethic. Measured behavior, for example, implies a sense of restraint and awareness of one's mea-sure with respect to another. As defined by Hofstadter: "Temperance is the keeping to due measure and proportion in the things that concern us—appetites, desires, aspirations, and claims; by our temperance we stay within the bounds of what belongs to us; we do not exceed the measures assigned to us by the nature of our being."[30] When one does exceed these limits ("by mete and bound") there typically follows a sense of separation and lostness characterized by such condi-tions as loneliness, addiction, obsession, schizophrenia, madness, alienation, and social withdrawal.

Here, then, lies the heart of the aporia of modern measure, with all of its irony and contradiction. In an age of precision and advanced technological resources, people are at once both closer to and more estranged from the earth and one another. On the one hand, standard and universal measures—each mathematically precise beyond any perceptible tolerance of magnitude—have fostered global cooperation and mutual understanding, thereby diminishing the threat of despotic tyranny and misrepresentation while providing new and advanced forms of medicine, communication, and technology. On the other hand, both the uniqueness and relatedness of things and places are objectified

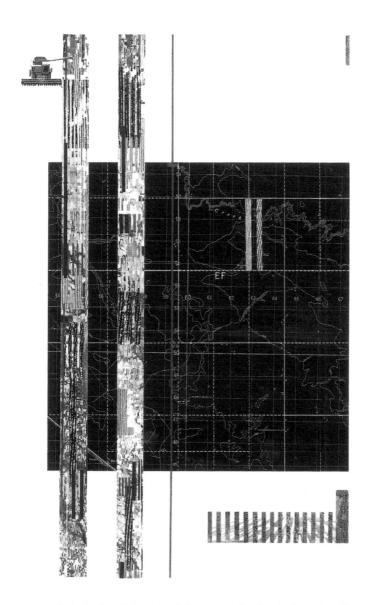

FIG. 8 — In the Northern Plains, strips of wheat run north and south, alternating with strips that lie fallow in order to accumulate precious water in these arid, windswept prairies. Sometimes a mile long and only 140 feet wide, the planted strips protect the exposed fallow soil from the drying and erosion effects of strong winds that blow from the west. The ridge and furrow of plow lines mirror this orientation with seed being sown in the protected and damper troughs. The width of each band derives from a carefully gauged degree of effective wind-shelter length for the fallow strips, in combination with the dimension of harvester headers. *Dry-Farming Strip*, by James Corner, 1996

and diminished through modern measures, promoting forms of homogeneity and alienation. Just as overspecification and oversimplification are the results of modern measure, so too are freedom and constraint, accessibility and estrangement. Could not this same dichotomy apply to American society and its landscape, wherein all that is generous, extending, and creative is both enabled and constrained by a universal, autonomous system? Certainly this is what lends irony to the "hydraulic society" of the Southwest, for example.[31]

Of course, the reverse of this situation is that the abstract systems of technology are both resisted and absorbed by prevailing social, cultural, and natural realities. Technological measure itself has no home; it is autonomous and freewheeling. Yet, when applied, it must always touch down somewhere at some time and must therefore become engaged with the wild forces of place and time. Here, the system will inevitably yield, further thickening and evolving the quarry of cultural and biological life.[32] For example, for all of its assumed monotony, the U.S. Rectangular Survey System is incredibly rich and diverse when experienced firsthand; the land, the passages of time, and the peculiarities of subsequent settlements have resisted and absorbed the ideality of the rational and repetitive scheme—a scheme that, in fact, facilitated fair and accessible opportunity for democratic settlement and land ownership.[33] Although there are places where lines do not quite meet up, where roads are not straight or true, where property lines take strange and irregular turns, and where the rectilinear order breaks down, it is the system that bends—albeit unwittingly. Everyday life upon the land has evolved a rich and delirious landscape, a complex imbroglio of farmsteads, diners, gas stations, crop dusters, motels, floods, tornadoes, baseball, cornfields, towns, hillsides, plains, conversations, arguments, dances, sunrise, snow, and drought. This same richness, accrued through a kind of inevitable errancy, might also describe other technological constructions upon the land. Biosphere 2, in Arizona, for example, is a completely sealed and self-sustaining environment, a mathematically modeled container that continues to fail owing to its incapacity to allow for human desire, error, mischief, and change. Similarly, many large-scale urban planning projects have failed in the twentieth century precisely because of this suppression of the volatile, complex, and unnavigable, forces of the inevitably promiscuous city. The techniques and measures of contemporary urban planning are simply incongruent to their object. As shown in the highly controlled environment of Biosphere 2, life cannot be created in the laboratory.

Revealed across the American landscape is the absurd and magnificent ingenuity of a people enmeshed with and yet remote from their land. [FIG. 9] Future work upon this ambiguously precise landscape might require a fresh approach

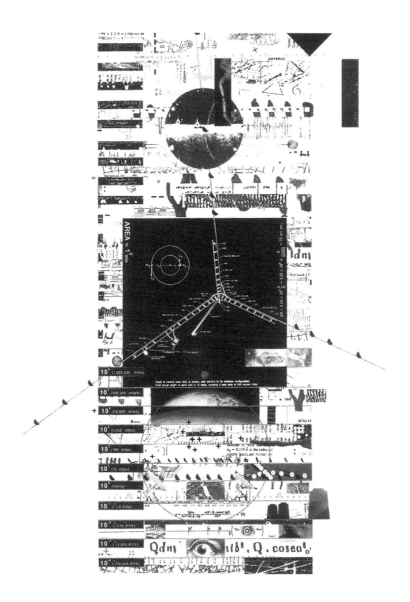

FIG. 9 — Sited on the high mountain plains of St. Augustine, Magdalena in New Mexico is the Very Large Array Radio Telescope (V.L.A.). As in ancient times, the angels of the heavens are revealed as constructed angles upon the ground, measured in the alternative spacing of these beacons along the horizon. In this still landscape, the micro-exactitude of modern instruments increasingly encompasses the full magnitude of the galaxies; nano-microns on earth become scaled-down mirror measures of light-years across space. *V.L.A.: Powers of Ten I*, by James Corner, 1996

Citation: Philip Morrison and Phylis Morrison, and the Office of Ray Eames, *Powers of Ten* (New York: Scientific American Books, 1982)

toward how measure is deployed in landscape and urban planning and design. More imaginative practices of measure and geometry than those of the calculative and instrumental must first be developed if we are to construct a landscape that is truly fitting with more robust forms of social and ecological life. Such an understanding may be predicated upon the metaphor of measure—its capacity to tie precision and objective reason to subjectivity and the imagination, and its powerful ability to span and join across distance and time. In this approach, landscape and nature might shed their status as external objects, as things possessed by quantitative measure, and emerge as active agents in the unfolding of life and in the relating of one to another. As with genes and ideas, such actants would be as playful and indeterminate as they would be precisely structured. Only then might the taking of measure assume further dimensions to those of either the traditional or the modern—dimensions of the precisely errant and the systematically bewildering.[34]

NOTES

1    Le Corbusier, *Aircraft: The New Vision* (1935; reprint, New York: Universe, 1988), 5, 96.

2    Ian McHarg, *Design with Nature*, Second ed. (New York: Wiley, 1992).

3    James Duncan and David Ley, eds., *Place/Culture/Representation* (London: Routledge, 1993); Denis Cosgrove and Stephen Daniels, eds., *The Iconography of Landscape* (Cambridge: Cambridge University Press, 1988); Svetlana Alpers, *The Art of Describing: Dutch Art in the Seventeenth Century* (Chicago: University of Chicago Press, 1983); D. W. Meinig, "The Beholding Eye," in *The Interpretation of Ordinary Landscapes*, ed. D. W. Meinig (New York: Oxford University Press, 1979), 33–48.

4    E. H. Gombrich, *Art and Illusion: A Study in the Psychology of Pictorial Representation* (Princeton, NJ: Princeton University Press, 1961); Jonathan Crary, *Techniques of the Observer: On Vision and Modernity in the Nineteenth Century* (Cambridge, MA: MIT Press, 1990); Kenneth Clark, *Landscape into Art* (New York: Harper and Row, 1976); Hans-Georg Gadamer, *Truth and Method*, Second revised edition, trans. J. Weinsheimer and D. G. Marshall (New York: Crossroads, 1990).

5    J. B. Harley, "Maps, Knowledge, and Power," in *The Iconography of Landscape*, 277–312; Trevor J. Barnes and James Duncan, eds ., *Writing Worlds: Discourse, Text, and Metaphor in the Representation of Landscape* (London: Routledge, 1992).

6    Denis Wood, *The Power of Maps* (London: Guilford Press, 1992).

7    John Pickles, "Text, Hermeneutics, and Propaganda Maps," in *Writing Worlds*, 193–230; W. J. T. Mitchell, ed., *Landscape and Power* (Chicago: University of Chicago Press, 1994).

8    For a remarkable example of satellite images conjoined with maps and environmental inventories, see National Geographic Society, *Atlas of North America: Space-Age Portrait of a Continent* (Washington, D.C.: National Geographic Society, 1985).

9    Richard Long, *Walking in Circles* (London: Southbank Centre, 1991); Rudolf Herman Fuchs, *Richard Long* (London: Thames and Hudson; New York: Solomon R. Guggenheim Museum, 1986).

10   Jean Baudrillard, *America*, trans. Chris Turner (London: Verso, 1988), 28.

11    Alexis de Tocqueville, *Democracy in America,* trans. George Lawrence, eds. J.P. Mayer and Max Lerner (New York: Harper and Row, 1966); Claude Lefort, *Democracy and Political Theory*, trans. David Macey (Minneapolis: University of Minnesota Press, 1988).

12    See, e.g., Hans-Georg Gadamer, *The Relevance of the Beautiful and Other Essays,* trans. Nicolas Water, ed. Robert Bernasconi (Cambridge: Cambridge University Press, 1986).

13    Witold Kula, *Measures and Men,* trans. R. Szreter (Princeton, NJ: Princeton University Press, 1986), 29–30.

14    Ibid, 120.

15    Ibid; See also Adrien Favre, *Les origins du systeme metrique* (Paris: Presses Universitaires de France, 1931).

16    Edwin Morris Betts, ed. *Thomas Jefferson's Garden Book, 1766–1824* (Philadelphia: American Philosophical Society, 1944), 4–5.

17    Thomas Jefferson, *Notes on the State of Virginia* (1785); quoted in Ralph E. Griswold and Frederick D. Nichols, *Thomas Jefferson: Landscape Architect* (Charlottesville: University of Virginia Press, 1978), 4.

18    Quoted in Hildegard Binder Johnson, *Order upon the Land: The U.S. Rectangular Survey and the Upper Mississippi County* (New York: Oxford University Press, 1976), 39.

19    Ibid, 40–49.

20    Ibid, 77.

21    John Fraser Hart, *The Look of the Land* (Englewood Cliffs, NJ: Prentice-Hall, 1975), 48–49; John Francis McDermott, *The French in the Mississippi Valley* (Urbana: University of Illinois Press, 1965).

22    David Leatherbarrow, "Qualitative Proportions and Elastic Geometry," in *The Roots of Architectural Invention: Site, Enclosure, Materials* (Cambridge: Cambridge University Press, 1993), 107–19.

23    Jacques Derrida, "Point de folie—maintenant l'architecture," in Bernard Tschumi, *La casa vide: La villette* (London: Architectural Association, 1986), 7.

24    Martin Heidegger, "…Poetically Man Dwells…," in *Poetry, Language, Thought,* trans. Albert Hofstadter (New York: Harper and Row, 1971), 221.

25    Ibid.

26    Ibid, 228.

27    Albert Hofstadter, *Agony and Epitaph: Man, His Art, and His Poetry,* (New York: George Braziller, 1970), 2.

28    Karston Harries, "The Many Uses of Metaphor," in *On Metaphor,* ed. Sheldon Sacks (Chicago: University of Chicago Press, 1978), 165-72.

29    Hofstadter, *Agony and Epitaph* (New York: George Braziller, 1970), 1–5; Werner Marx, *Is There a Measure on Earth?* trans. by Thomas J. Nenon and Reginald Lilly (Chicago: University of Chicago Press, 1987).

30    Hofstadter, *Agony and Epitaph*, 254.

31    See Marc Reisner, *Cadillac Desert* (New York: Viking Penguin, 1986); Philip L. Fradkin, *A River No More: The Colorado River and the West* (Tuscon: University of Arizona Press, 1984); Worster, *Rivers of Empire*. In discussing the hydro-engineering projects along the Colorado River, Reisner recognizes the paradox of these measures, referring to them as "a uniquely productive, creative vandalism" (p. 503).

32    Gianni Vattimo, "Utopia, Counter-utopia, Irony," in *The Transparent Society,* trans. David Webb (Baltimore: Johns Hopkins University Press, 1992), 76–88.

33   Johnson, *Order Upon the Land,* 239–42; Michael Conzen, ed., *The Making of the American Landscape* (London: Harper and Collins, 1990).

34   Interestingly perhaps, these last phrases echo those of the surrealists (like André Breton or Max Ernst), who were struggling, in their own way, with the increasing objectification of the world and the primacy of the rational over other modes of thought and action. See also, Kevin Kelly, *Out of Control: The New Biology of Machines, Social Systems, and the Economic World* (Reading, MA: Addison-Wesley, 1994).

FIG. 1 — The experience of landscape space is never simply an aesthetic one, but is more deeply experienced as a lived-within topological field, or as a highly situated network of relationships and associations that is perhaps best represented as a geographical map of collagic dimensions. *Geography Pages*, by Emmet Gowin, 1974

Reproduced with permission, courtesy of Emmet Gowin and Pace/McGill, New York

# DRAWING AND MAKING IN THE
# LANDSCAPE MEDIUM

A central characteristic of the often ambiguous term "landscape" is that it is first a schema, a representation, a way of seeing the external world, and, based on one's point of view, such schemata vary significantly. Geographers and painters see the land in different ways, as do developers and environmentalists.[1] If asked to draw the landscape, each party would no doubt produce a wholesome variety of graphic models and representations, reflecting their own peculiar mode of (re)cognition. Drawings might range from a cartographer's map, to an ecologist's transect, to an artist's perspective rendering. A poet might prefer words and tropes to visual images when describing a landscape. Collectively, each of these texts would "draw out" of an existing landscape a particular description, or analytique, as seen through a specific conceptual lens, and would subsequently alter or transform the meaning of that landscape. [FIG. 1] Landscapes are thus the inevitable result of cultural interpretation and the accumulation of representational sediments over time; they are thereby made distinct from "wildernesses" as they are culturally constructed, or layered.[2]

From a landscape architectural point of view, a major aspect of landscape is that it is not only a phenomenon of analysis, but is more significantly something to be *made*, or designed. The landscape architect is very much interested in physically manipulating the land to reflect and express human ideas about nature and dwelling therein. After all, landscape architecture is not simply an ameliorative or restorative practice, but is more precisely a figurative and representational art, providing culture with a sense of existential orientation through the construction of a built symbolic environment. Like any text, landscape architecture is conceptual, schematizing nature and humankind's place within it, but at the same time it differs from other landscape representations in that it operates through and within the medium of landscape itself. In other words, the actual lived landscape is the medium of both construal and construction; the representation is not only encoded in various related textual media, such as literature or painting, but is more significantly embodied in the constructed landscape. As such, landscape architectural drawing—a textual medium that is secondary to the actual landscape—can never be simply and alone a case of reflection and analysis; it is more fundamentally an eidetic and *generative* activity, one where the drawing acts as a producing agent or ideational catalyst.[3]

The relationship of drawing to the production of built landscapes remains, however, obscure. Indeed, this obscurity is made all the more difficult to understand when one stops to reflect on just why drawings have become so extensive and prevalent in the making of landscapes: Do drawings not seem particularly abstract phenomena when compared with the phenomena of landscape? [FIG. 2] This peculiarity is made all the more apparent when one compares drawing in landscape architectural production with other modes of artistic endeavor, such as painting or sculpture. It is not insignificant that many painters and sculptors often admit to not knowing where they are going with their work when they first begin. Instead, the work "unfolds" as the artist is personally engaged with the medium and the possibilities that emerge from the work. Invariably, the fine artist's most focused attention is on the making, the touching, and holding of the same worked artifact that will become the final piece.[4] During the time of engagement there occurs a spontaneity of feeling and expression arising both from a reactive response to the medium and from an imaginative source deep within. Here, the body and the imaginal are joined, inextricably involved with one another in a concentrated and creative, yet unselfconscious, unity. The making is itself a dialogue, a perceptive conversation between the medium and the imagination that cannot be intellectualized or thought of external to experience.[5] The ancient Greeks knew this; an important connotation of *poiesis,* meaning to create or to make, is that only through the sentient perception of tactile and creative activity—the actual *work* of making—can discovery and revelation occur, the longed-for "moment" of disclosure. As Heidegger has recognized, the hidden "truth" of things, their essence or *aletheia,* is something brought forth through human agency.[6]

The difficulty in landscape architecture, however, is that the actual work of building and construction is usually done by people other than the landscape architect. The instrumentality of modern construction procedures leaves little room for emotive or tactile involvement. Unlike the painter, the musician,

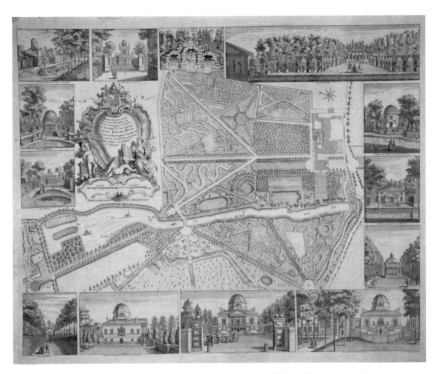

FIG. 2 — Landscape architectural engravings are inevitably bound into the production and reception of landscapes. They can affect the meaning of a given landscape depending upon when they were produced (before, during, or after construction); the convention of their presentation (plan, section, perspective); and their mode of expression (vibrant, quiet, dynamic, ethereal, pictorial, etc.). In essence, the engraving remains an integral part of the landscape architectural project, often making visible what is invisible and encoding a cultural screen, or lens, for interpretation. Engraved plan and views of Chiswick, by J. Rocque, Middlesex, England, 1736

Courtesy British Library

the sculptor, or the traditional gardener, the landscape architect rarely has the opportunity to significantly touch and mold the landscape medium as it plays out in response to intervention. Although landscapists ultimately make places out of plants, earth, water, stone, and light, they are caught at a peculiar distance from these same elements, working instead with a completely different medium, an intermediary and translatory medium that we call drawing. Creative access to the actual landscape is therefore remote and indirect, masked by a two-dimensional screen.

This problem of distance and indirectness is further complicated by the apparent disparity or incongruity between drawing and landscape. While the preliminary sketch bears an obvious and similar relationship to the work of painting and sculpture, a drawing, any drawing, is radically dissimilar from the medium that constitutes the lived landscape. The disparity between the phenomenon of drawing and that of the landscape means that there is often a discrepancy between what is represented and what gets built. It is significant—but not necessarily disadvantageous—that the nature and embodied meanings of drawings and landscapes belong to different worlds, as do their modes of experience.

Drawing in landscape architectural design is also different from the art of the landscape painter. In a brilliant essay called "Translations from Drawing to Building" (1986), architect Robin Evans has described how architectural design drawing differs from other pictorial arts in that it is not done after the subject, but prior to it, that is, prior to building and construction.[7] Landscape architectural drawing is not so much an outcome of reflection on a preexisting reality as it is productive of a reality that will later emerge. The built landscape must be determined in advance, and will exist after the drawing, not before it.

Therefore, as a preface to the argument that follows, it is possible to state that the difficulties of drawing, with respect to landscape architectural production, lie primarily in three characteristics: (1) the designer's indirect and detached, or remote, access to the landscape medium; (2) the incongruity of drawing with respect to its subject—its abstractness with respect to actual landscape experience; and (3) the anterior, prevenient function of the drawing—its generative role. Paradoxically, it is these same three characteristics that make such drawing enigmatic, in both a negative and a positive sense. On the one hand, the drawing can be an impotent imposter, an impossible analog, dangerously reductive and misused; whereas, on the other hand, drawing holds the possibility of forming a field of revelation, prompting one to figure previously unforeseen landscapes of richer and more meaningful dimensions.

The following essay further pursues the relationships that drawing has to the production of built landscapes, especially as it pertains to the apparent incongruity between the medium that is drawing and the medium that constitutes landscape. The first part of the discussion examines the medium of landscape and the second explores that of drawing. The remainder of the essay focuses upon the interface of drawing and landscape, highlighting the paradoxical and enigmatic aspects of drawing, and further explicating the mechanisms through which drawing best fulfills its role in the imaginative construing and constructing of built landscapes. After all, it is no small issue to suggest that the primary difficulty in achieving an artful and non-trivial landscape architecture lies within the limits of human imagination and speculative vision—the ability to "see," to see differently, and to see how things might be otherwise.

## The Medium of Landscape

The landscape is primarily a medium that is irreducibly rich in sensual and phenomenological terms. Traditionally, the landscape has provided a great experiential quarry from which a variety of ideas and metaphors have inspired artistic and cultural attitudes toward nature since antiquity. As a medium of symbolic representation, the landscape and its constitutive elements—stones, plants, water, earth, and sky, when artfully composed—have provided humans with some of the most sacred and powerful places of embodied meaning. Nothing, and certainly not a picture, can replace or equal the direct and bodily experience of such places. In particular, there are three phenomena unique to the medium of landscape and the experience of the same that evade reproduction in other art forms and pose the greatest difficulty for landscape architectural drawing. These may be tentatively called landscape spatiality, landscape temporality, and landscape materiality.

### Spatiality in Landscape

Unlike paintings or novels, there is very little opportunity to wander or turn away from the experience of landscape. Spatially, it is all-enveloping and surrounds us, flooded with light and atmosphere. Irreducible, the landscape controls our experience extensively: it permeates our memories and consciousness, and enframes our daily lives.

Not only does the landscape surround us, but it does so in a limitless way. Its scale is big. Scale refers to both size and measurement, but more directly it denotes the relative size of something, the relative extent or degree. When people normally speak of landscape scale, they are referring to its bigness, its enormity relative to themselves. The limitless immensity of the landscape is felt to be spacious, sweeping, vast, enveloping, and engaging of the subject. Scale engages not because it is an object—something external—but rather because it is a phenomenon that penetrates our imaginary consciousness. Philosopher Gaston Bachelard has written of this experience, distinguishing the "immediate immensity" of the world, the apparent limitlessness of the great forests and oceans, from the "inner immensity" of the human imagination, the inner space of the self, infinite and luminous. Bachelard has speculated that the vast world of external nature invokes a primal response within the subject, calming the soul and distilling a paradoxical though comforting sense of "intimate immensity" with the world. A dream space of infinite magnitude opens, wherein vast thought and imaginative extension are reciprocally engaged with the spatial corporeality of landscape.[8] Landscape scale not only envelops the body but also the imagination and the spirit.

This all-enveloping nature of landscape space, its overriding bigness and sheer sense of scale, and its inevitable correspondence with the poetic imagination are peculiar to the landscape medium. The full plenitude of landscape spatial experience cannot be represented without alteration or reduction: it can neither be drawn, for it is not in essence pictorial, nor can it be quantified, without gross simplification, for it is not all-measurable.

Furthermore, landscape space is a highly situated phenomenon, literally bound into geographical places and topographies. The spatial interrelationships of the cultural and natural patterns that constitute a particular landscape mean that places are interwoven as a densely contextual and cumulative weave. Every place is unique and special, nested within a particular topos, or "topography." For the ancient Greeks, *topos* referred to a tangible place that immediately brought to mind a variety of associations. Places, like things, conjure up a wealth of images and ideas; we place topics and rhetorical arguments as much as we do topography and space. We always find ourselves inextricably caught up with and bound into places. Our knowledge and experience of space is therefore more ontological, or "lived," than it is mathematical or Cartesian. Heidegger recognized the situatedness of space when he wrote:

> Space is in essence that for which room has been made, that which is let into its bounds. That for which room is made is always granted and hence is joined, that is, gathered, by virtue of a location...*Accordingly, spaces receive their being from locations and not from "space."* [9]

Locations "gather" and interconnect phenomena; they "admit and install" relationships to become "places." "Space is not the setting (real or logical) in which things are arranged, but the means whereby the position of things become possible," wrote Maurice Merleau-Ponty, describing how space is the "universal power" that enables things to be connected, and is fully dependent on the subject's ability to experience and move through it. [10] As such, each of us "spaces" the world around us. Through spacing we orient ourselves and construct our geographical being. [11]

Spacing also implies a conceptual ability to "think across" space. As Heidegger has shown, thinking can "persist through" distance and time to anything or place. [12] When one moves through landscape space, that person is going "somewhere," he/she has a destination, and, in a phenomenological sense, part of the individual is already there, occupying, thinking, pervading.

The subject in the landscape is therefore a fully enveloped and integral part of spatial and phenomenological relations. The experience of landscape space is never simply and alone an aesthetic one but is more deeply experienced as a lived-upon topological field, a highly situated network of relationships and associations that is perhaps best represented as a geographical map of collagic dimensions. The topo-ontological experience of landscape space obviously challenges the spatial instrumentality of Cartesian geometry and algebraic measurement that is so prevalent in most contemporary representations of space. The Cartesian coordinates that constitute purely technical projection drawing neither originate nor end in earthly space—they are not situated in place but float in an abstract frame of analytic-mathematic relations.

### Temporality in Landscape

Meaning, as embodied in landscape, is also experienced temporally. There is a duration of experience, a serial and unfolding flow of befores and afters. Just as a landscape cannot spatially be reduced to a single point of view, it cannot be frozen as a single moment in time. The geography of a place becomes known to us through an accumulation of fragments, detours, and incidents that sediment meaning, "adding up" over time. Where, when, and how one experiences a landscape precipitates any meaning that is derived from it.

Moreover, as Merleau-Ponty has identified, there are no events without someone to which they happen. He has written:

> Time is not a real process, not an actual succession that I am content to record. It arises from my relation to things...Let us not say that time is a "datum of consciousness;" let us be more precise and say that consciousness deploys or constitutes time.[13]

The disclosure of meaning in a given landscape can only occur when the subject is present, moving through it, open to sensation and experience. This phenomenological observation not only means that one's comprehension of landscape is bound to a particular time and conditions of experience, but also to a particular cultural view. Such are the periods that constitute history. We today "see" Versailles differently from the seventeenth-century courtiers and festivalgoers, for example.

Temporality in landscape experience is further complicated by the movement of the body itself, a phenomenon we call kinesthesias. When moving across landscape space there is not only a dynamic flow of perceptions derived from external sources, but there is also the muscular and nervous movement of the body itself through space and time.[14] One may run, stroll, dance, or ramble across, down, or along a landscape, changing relational meanings through the pace and nature of bodily movement. This is further complicated by the fact that moving bodies in the landscape are often in a distracted state, the individual paying little, if any, concentrated attention to their immediate environment. We rarely pay such conscious and sensorial devotion to landscape space as we do to a painting or an object. Rather, as critic Walter Benjamin has recognized, the meaning derived from landscape and architectural space is received "by a collectivity in a state of distraction," slowly appreciating its symbolic environment through "habitual appropriation," or through everyday use and activity.[15] The experience of landscape takes time, and results from an accumulation of often-distracted events and everyday encounters.

A third aspect of temporality in landscape distinguishes it from buildings and other spatial art forms: Landscape is a living biome that is subject to flux and change by natural processes operating over time. The dynamic action of erosion, deposition, and the effects of growth and weather continually transform the structure and pattern of the shifting landscape. The same landscape may be experienced in radically different ways when it is in flood, engulfed in fog, covered with snow, or burning with fire, meaning that the qualities of space, light, texture, and ambience are ever subject to change. Not only does this dynamism challenge the art and intentionality of landscape architectural meaning (because of the impermanence of a medium caught in flux), but it also makes it difficult, if not impossible, to represent and experience it externally, as through a drawing, for example.

### Substance and Materiality in Landscape

The landscape is further complicated because it is a concrete and substantial medium, composed of elemental matter. Matter is the raw, brutish stuff from which things are made. It is what constitutes material properties, making them perceptible to our senses. Materiality is the quality of being material and is best understood through the tactile and bodily perception of things, senses distinct from any form of secondary or objective deduction.

The tactile not only includes surface phenomena, such as roughness and smoothness, stickiness, and silkiness, but also substantial phenomena such as density and viscosity, elasticity and plasticity, hardness and rigidity. Materials in the landscape radiate a host of sensory stimuli that are deeply registered by the sentient body: the aroma of material; the feeling of humidity or dampness; the intensity of light, dark, heat, and cold. Different woods burn in different ways. They give off varying flame patterns—some crackle, some hiss, their embers may glow, sparkle, or smoke. As living trees, the same woods are known to us in significantly different ways. In the pine stand the wind whispers and whistles; in the gnarled oak forest it broods and wallows; in the aspen grove it rustles. Things and places become known to us because of what they impart to our senses through the very organization of their sensible aspects. The significance of anything encircles and permeates tangible matter.

Today's fascination with the visual image, the pictorial, makes it all the more important to recall how the greater part of landscape experience belongs to the sensorium of the tactile, the poetries of material and touch. A bogland, for example, can be quite monotonous or uninteresting visually, but it can be appreciated in a completely different way through bodily and tactile experience—the muttering squelch and lisp of water underfoot; the springy return of the spongy ground; the dampness of cold, gray, windless air; the peaceful softness of it all. Obviously, drawing is as limited here as it is in the realms of space and time. While a drawing can perhaps signify qualities, it cannot reproduce or represent the actual qualitative experience of materials that constitute the tactile landscape.

Thus, the phenomenological qualities of landscape space, time, and material present insurmountable difficulties for drawing and representation. First, the flatness and framing of the graphic presentation fails to capture the all-enveloping quality and sheer scale of landscape space. What is presented is a picture, a flat frontality approached from a distance as an object. Second, the drawing is autonomous, equally at home in a gallery or book. It is not situated, as are places and locations, and remains unaltered when estranged from the complexity of life situations. Third, the drawing is static and immediate, meaning that it is quickly decoded as the eye scans the image from a totalizing and singular point of view. Landscape experience, meanwhile, is received in moments, glances, and accidental detours, kinesthetically unfolding through rambling and habitual encounters over time. Fourth, a drawing is made of its own materials—it has its own substance, and is therefore unable to reproduce and actualize the sensuous and tactile experience of the corporeal landscape, even though a drawing may oftentimes possess the power to make humans more cognizant of a landscape's attributes. Fifth, and perhaps most significantly, the drawing is experienced optically, with rapt and full attention being paid to the image, whereas landscape is so much more, experienced as much if not more through the body than the eye. The subject in the landscape is a fully enveloped and integral part of spatial, temporal, and material relations, and nothing can reproduce the meaning that comes from this lived experience, no matter how accurate or skillful is the representation in other mediums.[16]

**The Medium of Drawing: Projection, Notation, and Representation**

The phenomenology of landscape experience eludes drawing to such a point that one might feel the need to end the discussion at this point, perhaps doubting or at best wondering how drawings can relate to the landscape at all. Yet useful and imaginative relationships have evolved over the centuries (no matter how partial or indirect these may at first seem). Landscape and architectural drawing can be discussed as three quite distinct and separate types. We shall call them projection, notation, and representation.

Projection

Projection has to do with *direct analogies* between drawing and construction, and includes the plan, the elevation, the section, the axonometric, and, in a lesser way, the perspective. In *Natural History* (AD 77–79), naturalist Pliny the Elder offered one myth of the origin of drawing when he told of the story of Dibutades tracing the shadow of her departing lover on the wall.[17] Evans has beautifully compared David Allan's painting of Pliny's tale, entitled *The Origin of Painting* (1773), with the architect Frederich Schinkel's painting of the same title, done in 1830.[18] In both, light rays project the shadow of a figure onto the flat wall and constitute a traced outline, which may be called a "projection." A shape is projected through space to be captured on a flat picture plane. Evans has described how, in Allan's depiction, the projected drawing was the outcome of a single-point light source casting the shadow of the seated lover onto a refined interior wall, whereas in Schinkel's painting—a man better known as an architect than a painter—the drawing was the result of solar illumination (and therefore the result of parallel projection), casting the shadow of a figure onto an uncut stone. [FIG. 3] For the architect, therefore, the projection drawing serves as a precedent to artifice, acting as a template of transfer from figure to cut-stone, or more precisely, from idea to built artifice.

The projection drawing is thus directly analogous to construction. One constructs a drawing as one does a building. Both are "projects." A drawing that surveys and measures an existing landscape is a literal projection of that topography onto the picture plane. On the other hand, a drawing that proposes a new and as yet unrealized landscape acts as the mediator between the designer's vision, or ideational project, and the actual construction of that project on the site. The survey drawing is projected from the ground, whereas the construction drawing is projected onto the ground. Both types of drawing are demonstrative as they reveal otherwise hidden aspects of the building or landscape. A plan, or a map, for example, makes visible an aerial topography that is otherwise inaccessible.

FIG. 3 — Schinkel's painting shows the projection of a shadow onto uncut stone. The shadow trace then becomes a template for the cutting of the stone, which represents the beginning of artifice, the "construction" of civilization. The idea of projection is therefore bound into mimesis and unites both the symbolic and the instrumental representations. K. F. Schinkel, *Die Erfindung der Zeichenkunst (The Origin of Painting)*, 1830. Gouache. 26 × 29 cm

Courtesy Von der Heydt—Museum Wuppertal (Inv. Nr. G 0184)

For Vitruvius, the parts of a construction were arranged according to the "ideas of disposition," which were constituted in three ways: *ichnographia*, the plan; *orthographia*, the elevation; and *scaenographia*, the sectional profile.[19] These drawings embodied in themselves the "ideas" necessary for architectural translation and construction. Thus, the plan drawing literally demonstrates the layout and organization on the ground, akin to the marking and pegging out of a foundation; the elevation drawing demonstrates the raising and construction of a vertical face, akin to scaffolding; the section or profile-cut demonstrates the details and relations between parts; and the sectional linear perspective allows for the optical correction of proportion and scale.[20] [FIG. 4]

The Vitruvian "ideas" were less graphic conventions than conceptual strategies analogous to the reality of execution. Another projection, which is more peculiar to landscape and gardens, is the planometric, probably first devised by the Ancient Egyptians and developed during Medieval times. Here, the vertical elements of a building or garden are "laid down," as in elevation, over the plan. This "double" projection embodies both the maplike topography of landscape terrain, as seen from above, and the frontal, or elevational, composition as seen by the standing subject, and it demonstrates to the gardener the layout and distribution of the various plant forms as well as the relationships between

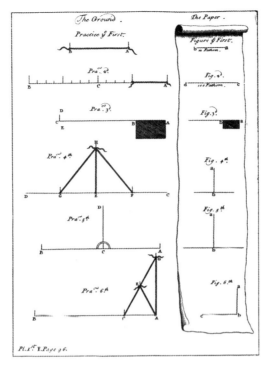

FIG. 4 — Illustration showing the translation of lines on paper to lines on the ground,
from John James, *The Theory and Practice of Gardening*, 1712

the parts. [FIG. 5] Unlike buildings, which are raised volumetrically as floors, walls, and roofs, the constructing of a landscape is much akin to the workings of the planometric, emphasizing both the ground plane and the frontal identities simultaneously.

Translator Daniele Barbaro, commenting on Vitruvius's Treatise in 1569, believed the projection geometries of plan, section, and elevation to be superior to perspective, making a clear distinction between "ideas" and "expression on the paper."[21] Projective drawings are neither a picture nor a neutral set of information, rather they embody in themselves architectural ideas through co-similar and complimentary projections that are ontologically conceived as being analogous to the symbolic intentions of the built work itself. This practical relationship has largely been forgotten today, displaced by a more instrumental and descriptive use of projective geometry. Alberto Pérez-Gomez has described how, during most of the seventeenth century, architects could still distinguish between ontological drawing and illusionary drawing, i.e., between "practical" drawing and artificial perspective. Describing the degeneration of eidetic

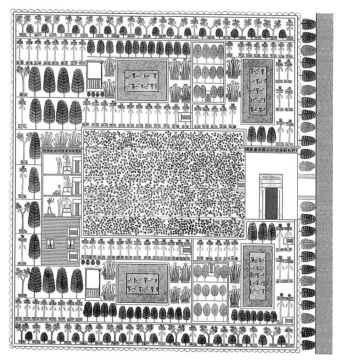

FIG. 5 — Planometric drawing of a garden, eighteenth-dynasty Thebes, painting from wall remains, by Ippolito Rosselini in *Monumenti dell' Egitto e della Nubia*, 1832–1840

projective drawing into the functional and systematic methodology developed at the École Polytechnique in Paris, Péréz-Gomez has written:

> The original architectural "ideas" were transformed into universal projections that could then, and only then, be perceived as reductions of buildings, creating the illusion of drawing as a neutral tool that communicates unambiguous information like scientific prose.[22]

In other words, the power of demonstrative drawing lies in the fact that it is open to interpretation, both prior to and after the built construct. Such drawing is an integral part of the whole artistic "project," making visible what is hidden and prompting one to understand something at a higher level. One attribute of William Kent's oeuvre of drawings, for example, or of Bernard Tschumi's portfolio for the Parc de la Villette, is that the images significantly affect the way one sees and understands the landscape to which they refer. Never is drawing merely a mute and instrumental document. However, the purely procedural techniques of modern-day projection drawings tend to alienate both designer and builder from a synesthetic and hermeneutical mode of making and knowing. From the eighteenth-century pattern books of Batty Langley, replete with a menu of geometrical templates for garden layout and design, to the current-day wide acceptance of "graphic standards" and glossaries of forms and "types," projective drawing has degenerated into a prescriptive recipe for relatively harmless, but thoughtless and trivial production. The contemporary belief that drawings are either objective communicative devices (instrumental construction drawings) or illustrations (facile presentation drawings) significantly misunderstands the traditional symbolic and ontological basis of projection.[23]

### Notation

Some systems of standard projection belong to a family of drawing called notation. Notation systems seek to *identify* the parts of a schema, enabling them to be reproduced, enacted, or performed. They include itinerary schedules, piano scores, and dance notations. Measured plans, sections, elevations, and written specifications are also notational, as their main purpose is to specify the essential properties of a particular work in order for it to be translated with minimum ambiguity. In *Languages of Art*, philosopher Nelson Goodman has written that notation schemes must employ a symbol system that is "syntactically differentiated within unambiguous and finite parameters."[24] Notations are therefore strictly denotative constructs rather than connotative ones. Statistician Edward Tufte has remarked that "Design strategies for recording dance movements encompass many...display techniques: small multiples, close text-figure integration, parallel sequences, details and panorama, a polyphony of layering and separation, data compression into content-focused dimensions, and avoidance of redundancy."[25] The unambiguous nature of the notation is an attempt to avoid connotative or subjective misinterpretation—even though the playing of a musical score, for example, is still open to interpretation by the musician. Obviously, the quest for strictly denotative objectivity remains a fundamental principle for notational work, but, at the same time, we cannot forget that interpretative semiosis remains an inevitable part of notational reading, even though the tolerance of variation may be small.

Notation systems in landscape architectural design are not only useful for their communicative and translatory status, but also because they enable one to consider the simultaneity of different layers of experience, including movement and time. Theorist Rudolf Laban, for example, developed a system of dance notation called Labanotation, which precisely choreographs the movement of the body through time and space, enabling dancers to enact a particular performance.²⁶ [FIG. 6] It successfully challenges the view that complex motion is too difficult a subject matter for notational articulation through a layered deployment of abstract symbols and encodings. Lawrence Halprin has also devised notational scores to design and coordinate fountain displays, as well as to consider the disposition and experience of elements along a particular route or sequence. Halprin also developed a method of "scoring" that enabled group participation in decision making and planning. The complicated, but highly active, score itself becomes a performed piece as the creative process is graphically played out.²⁷ Apart from Halprin, however, notational developments specific to landscape architecture have been few and far between, and yet the analogous qualities of landscape to narrative, dance, theater, or film, suggest that notations would be a promising area of research. One might begin by studying the theatrical scores developed by painter László Moholy-Nagy or the film storyboards of director Sergei Eisenstein, who effectively separated the various layers of cinematic experience in order to coordinate the movements of the camera with the playing of the soundtrack, the dimming and brightening of light, and the timing of editing and cutting. Eisenstein called the intersection of the various layers "correspondences," explaining how the full meaning embodied in the film would be a result of their simultaneous correspondence—an overlay known as montage.²⁸ Tschumi adopted a similar strategy, layering spatial, temporal, and material phenomena into a notational sequence for a "cinematic path" at the Parc de la Villette. The notation successfully plays down visual aspects of the experience while highlighting programmatic and spatial ones. [FIG. 7]

Such notations afford a coded matrix upon which to design narratives of time and space, enabling one to orchestrate the simultaneity of spatial, temporal, and tactile experience. However, these syntactically complicated graphics remain limited because of the need for specialist reading to decode the complex score and understand it as experience. How many of us can actually hear the music when we read a piano score, or experience a movie sequence from looking at a storyboard? On the other hand, notations cannot, nor should they necessarily try to, portray or depict experience; their function is simply to identify the parts that constitute it.

### Representation

Unlike projection and notation, representational drawings aim to *re-present* a given landscape or building, seeking to elicit the same experiential effects but in a different medium—to give the same effects again.²⁹ Pictorial perspective is therefore a representation in this sense as it depicts the depth and spatiality of a scene at eye level from a certain vantage point. An accurate perspective structure,

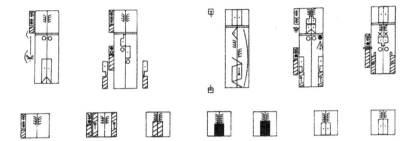

FIG. 6 — The dance score is read vertically with the right and left sides of the body represented on each side of the vertical timeline. The numerous marks and figures on this labanotation detail are the encodings for particular body parts and related dance gestures.

From Albrecht Knust, *Dictionary of Kinetography Laban (Labanotation)*, (Plymouth: Estover, 1979)

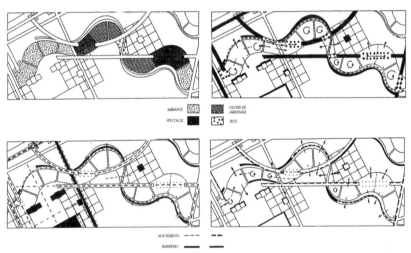

PRINCIPES DE MONTAGE DES DIFFÉRENTS CADRAGES DE LA PROMENADE CINÉMATIQUE

FIG. 7 — These drawings coordinate a plan delineation with a notational coding scheme, orchestrating a variety of experiences along the "cinematic path" at the Parc de la Villette. "Cinematic path notations," by Bernard Tschumi

From Bernard Tschumi, *Cinégramme folie: Le Parc de la Villette* (New York: Princeton Architectural Press, 1987) © Bernard Tschumi

with carefully observed and applied chiaroscuro, texture, and color, will closely resemble and imitate a particular scene, as if drawn on a pane of glass positioned between the viewing subject and the landscape. John Constable, for example, strove to capture in his painting the "truth" of a scene, recording the landscape before his eyes with an almost scientific precision and discipline. [FIG. 8] With equal if not more emphasis on chiaroscuro than perspective, Constable's "naturalistic" school of painting sought to make a canvas as perfect an imitation as possible, accurately recording a retinal, almost photographic, impression. Constable's genius lay in his ability to surpass formulaic and technical approaches to painting, such as the "Claude-glass" (a polished copper mirror that made a scene appear more as it might in a canvas by the seventeenth-century painter Claude), and in his skill at transcending the rigidity of methodical schemata and technique, especially with regard to the innate attributes of oil paint on canvas. The lively one-to-one correspondence between scene and picture, unimpeded by cultural codes of vision, was the aspiration and success of Constable's "art of truth."[30]

However, the realism of direct imitation poses problems for landscape architectural design. Let us not forget how landscape architectural drawings precede the subject matter, unlike Constable's, which were derived from a preexisting subject. Therefore, to draw a "scene" that is yet to be built is to reverse the direction of artistic production. Whereas a painter's picture is a representation of a scene as perceived, a landscape architectural picture is a representation of a scene imagined, and, in turn, the built landscape becomes a representation of that picture. Rosalind Krauss, in her essay in "The Originality of the Avant-garde," has explained how the Picturesque paintings of Salvator Rosa, Claude Lorrain, and William Gilpin were conceived as pictorial "copies" of nature, formulaic, and therefore reproducible, which actually preceded how the "original," the landscape, was subsequently seen and understood. Gilpin, for example, wrote extensively about how to look at a landscape scene and observe the "effects" of foreground, distance, perspective, and "roughness." In describing this, Krauss has written: "'the priorness and repetition of pictures [were] necessary to the singularity of the Picturesque," and the understanding and meaning derived from a particular landscape was "made possible only by a prior example"—a picture.[31] Krauss is describing how pictures can affect the reception and understanding of a landscape, the basis of the Picturesque, but pictures can also work to affect the production and management of landscapes. Andrew Wyeth's paintings, for example, have helped the aristocracy of Chester and Delaware Counties, Pennsylvania, form a regional landscape aesthetic, which they (indirectly) employ to control the design and management of their estates.[32]

FIG. 8 — Constable's search for the "truth" of a scene, the retinal copy, was most developed
through his astute observation of the "chiaroscuro of nature" and its subsequent rendering
with pigment so as to make the paint and the canvas transparent to the actual scene.
*Dedham Vale*, by John Constable, 1828. Oil on canvas. 145 × 122 cm

Courtesy National Galleries of Scotland, Edinburgh

Furthermore, pictures can also be used to literally transform a landscape physically. *The Red Books* of Humphry Repton, for example, show the beautification of a series of rural landscapes through the use of "before and after" paintings of specific scenes. The logic of the picture plane determines the landscape composition, subtracting and adding earth, water, and vegetation to an existing "inferior" view. Both the existing and proposed views are compared or overlaid so that one might understand the precise nature of the transformation. [FIGS. 9 + 10] Of course, many eighteenth-century landscapes were laid out as an arrangement and disposition of scenes. One might stroll through such a landscape catching glimpses and then fully composed views of scenes evocative of contemporary paintings. The moving bodies of the visitors themselves would often provide the action necessary to complement the scene, now backdrop.[33] The problem, however, with scenographic approaches to landscape architectural design is that they demand that the subject's primary mode of attention be visual and participatory. Vision is, of course, only one part of landscape experience; rarely is one's full attention devoted to the aesthetics of sight. Landscape perception is more fully the result of an accumulation of incident, impression and detour, more like a rambling and unpredictable sequence of events than a contrived picture show. Reduced to a scene, the pictorial landscape is often conceived in a manner remote from both the laws of its own constituency (the effects of time and ecological flows of energy, for example) and from the experiencing subject (aspects of distraction and the tactile, for example). The danger of pictorial representation lies in the designer making "pictures" as opposed to "landscapes," scenes and visual compositions based upon the illusionary logic of the picture plane, rather than upon the sensual arrangement of landscape form, replete with a fullness of spatial, temporal, and material qualities.[34]

However, there are other types of representation, which are perhaps better able to articulate a greater sense of experience than the singularity of perspectival pictures. These representations deploy graphic signs and symbols, which are rich with connotative value, unlike the strictly denotative symbol systems used in notational drawing. Expression in representation works because of the way in which semantically rich symbols (marks, gestures, shapes, colors) can be related to metaphoric labels, figures that disclose an infinite network of associated meanings due to what Goodman has called their "semantic density."[35] The experience of inference and association in art is called *synesthesia*, which means the splashing over of impressions from one sense mode to another. For example, Kandinsky illustrated how shape and color, purely visual phenomena, could be juxtaposed so as "to weep," "to shout," or to "kill each other." We speak of "loud colors," "bright sounds," or "cold light."[36] It is the signifying capacity

FIG. 9 — "Water at Wentworth, Yorkshire," by Humphry Repton,
From *Observations on the Theory and Practice of Landscape Gardening*, 1805

FIG. 10 — "Water at Wentworth, Yorkshire," by Humphry Repton,
From *Observations on the Theory and Practice of Landscape Gardening*, 1805

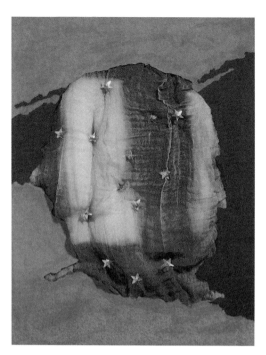

FIG. 11 — *Genre Allegory (George Washington)*, by Marcel Duchamp, 1943,
Cardboard, iodine, gauze, nails, gilt-metal stars, 53.2 × 40.5 cm
Courtesy Musée National d'Art Moderne, Paris © Succession
Marcel Duchamp / ADAGP, Paris / Artists Rights Society (ARS), New York 2013

of a semantically rich representation that speaks to us, as in Duchamp's powerful *Genre Allegory (George Washington)* (1943), wherein the iodine-soaked bandages pinned to a canvas' with military stars ironically recall a rather disordered American flag and also silhouette the distinctive facial profile of Washington. [FIG. 11] While such highly suggestive works are clearly visual, they are not images. That is, they do not directly resemble the optical image of things, the *imago*, or the retinal specter, but rather they point to the *idea* that underlies things. In other words, the *cause* of a particular effect is shown. We may call this the archetypal essence of things: that which persists through any number of forms and appearances, and which remains ever open to new interpretations. Drawing of this sort is therefore re-presentational; that is, it does not simply represent a world already in existence, a quantity we already know, but rather it tries to re-present the world in ways previously unforeseen, thereby making the old appear new and the banal appear fresh. The fact that drawing in landscape architectural design precedes a built reality means that it might also have first to transform a society's vision about landscape, perhaps playing less on the picture and more on the phenomenological enigmas inherent in the landscape itself. To understand representation as (de)sign—as portent or harbinger—one must first learn to forget the scenic surface of the image and think behind it, beneath it, around it.[37]

### The Misuse of Drawing

Projections, notations, and representations are all, though in differing ways, indirect, abstract, incongruous, and anterior in relation to the landscape medium. These qualities have led to two major misconceptions about the value and action of drawing in contemporary design.[38] The first misuse occurs when emphasis is placed on the drawing itself, as if the drawing is the artistic and prized artifact. In this camp, the seductive qualities of drawing promote a detached and personal preoccupation with it, whereupon the drawing is overprivileged as an art form unto itself. It is commonplace today to see autonomous and self-referential drawings as the bearers of effect and the focus of attention. Such works are eminently consumable, affording a visual feast for those with the appetite, while remaining ineffectual with regard to the actual production and experience of landscape. The wide availability of images and their mass dissemination has prompted architect John Whiteman to write:

> First, in critical magazines, architecture becomes its own market, both producing and consuming its own images. Second, the ideology and impulses which then surround architectural drawing no longer aim toward the production of architectural experience, but instead lead to images that can only be picturesque in their hidden drive to be available for distribution.[39]

The second misuse of drawing is a reaction against the former. This party is suspicious of any meaning a drawing may hold beyond that of the strictly instrumental. Consequently, the potential richness of drawing is suppressed through a reductive and overly technical practice. Here, the emphasis is on the mute language of objective, denotative systems (plans, sections, isometrics). An outcome of the eighteenth century, this scientific view of drawing is widely practiced today owing to the emphasis on rational methodology in the design professions and building trades.[40] Moreover, as Whiteman has argued, the instrumental use of drawing has continued to gain greater currency because of the effects of modern criticism, which, like drawing, usually has its greatest impact prior to construction, but relies on the drawing, rather than the built artifact, to make its judgments—judgments made not only by professional peers but also by clients and other interest groups that can influence precisely what gets built. As Whiteman has pointed out, the problem lies in the fact that modern criticism seeks objectivity and remains suspicious of alternative symbolic systems of interpretation.[41] Subsequently:

> We get scared of the artistic power of architecture and distrust our capacity to notate and represent artistic intentions to ourselves. We are made nervous by the possibility that a commitment in symbolic form might be rendered naive. So we turn aside from a way of architecture which can reshape things to make meanings immediate and present to us. Instead we run to ideas and conceptions which seem to have automatic justification for us.[42]

Both the mystical "artist" and the pragmatic "technician" effectively sever any authentic dialogue the drawing may have with built experience and the material world, significantly misunderstanding the function of drawing in landscape architectural production. The frequent discrepancies between what is represented and what gets built means that there is often a rift or translatory failure between drawing and building. In effect, the landscape medium becomes "contaminated" by drawing; that is to say, the innate richness of the landscape itself is suppressed or suffocated by another medium, which is either excessively privileged or significantly undervalued.

The source of this dichotomy lies in the fact that both the excessive and repressive uses of drawing are linked to drawing's apparent incongruity, or indirectness, in relation to landscape architecture; one camp revels in drawing's abstractness, while the other is repelled by the same level of abstraction.[43] On the one side are those who insist on an irreducible expressiveness, on the other are those insisting on an objective "realism." As Evans has observed:

> The two options, one emphasizing the corporeal properties of things made, the other concentrating on the disembodied qualities in the drawing, are diametrically opposed: in the one corner, involvement, substantiality, tangibility, presence, immediacy, direct action; in the other, disengagement, obliqueness, abstraction, mediation, and action at a distance.[44]

However, neither camp recognizes that landscape architectural drawing gains its potency precisely from its directness of application to landscape, on the one hand, *and* its disengaged, abstract qualities on the other. After all, it is just as erroneous to suggest that the designer's free imagination is the source of inventive form as it is to discuss drawing as the sole generator of formal creation. Rather, both play off one another, as in an engaging and probing conversation.

How else are the leaps and abridgements between ideas and their embodiment in form made?

Drawing is an eidetic medium, and to use it simply as a means to an end, or as a means of self-indulgence in the name of "artistic expression," is irresponsible with respect to the real work of landscape architecture. This suggests a difference between drawings used merely as tools of composition and communication, and drawings that act as vehicles of creativity.[45] The emphasis shifts from drawing as image to drawing as *work* or process, a creative act that is somehow analogous to the actual construing and constructing of built landscapes.[46]

### The Metaphoricity of Drawing

This essay began by describing drawing as a translatory medium, which enabled the figuration of an imaginary *idea* into a visual/spatial corporeality embodied in the built fabric of the landscape. While the essay so far may have stressed the differences between the medium of drawing and the medium that constitutes the landscape, highlighting the limits of drawing in representing (and therefore designing for) landscape experience, there still remain properties of drawing that make it an extraordinarily powerful medium in relation to the production of landscapes. The dilemma of both the ethereal and instrumental drawing, so prevalent today, can be resolved when drawing is understood as the locus of reconciliation between construal and construction, or between the symbolic and instrumental representations.[47] For example, the original Vitruvian "ideas" as embodied in drawing suggest that drawings hold the possibility of being projective, notational, and representational at the same time. Neither images nor pictures, such drawings are analogical demonstrations of both construal and construction. They are the architecture, embodying the symbolic intentions of the building and demonstrating its construction.

A more significant type of drawing in landscape architectural design might arise from a twofold use of the graphic medium: one is the speculative function, and the other is the demonstrative function. In the first, drawing is used as a vehicle of creativity, and in the second, drawing is used as a vehicle of realization. Both types of drawing work by analogy and occur alongside one another simultaneously.

As a vehicle of creativity, drawing is a highly imaginative and speculative activity, entailing both spontaneity and reflection. It first involves the making of marks and the "seeing" of possibilities. Such work is both imaginal and theoretical, making images and recording spatial and tactile qualities through a process of association, akin to what was said earlier about Kandinsky and the power of synesthesia. For example, in the Chinese and Japanese technique of "flung ink" painting, originating as early as the fourteenth and fifteenth centuries, ink is first thrown onto the canvas in an energetically random manner to form a visual field. The painter then improvises through immediate response to the thrown image and begins to construct a landscape through the working of the brush. [FIG. 12] Painter Alexander Cozens developed a similar approach of responsive drawing during the eighteenth century in England. In such improvisational, rapid response work, the graphic field is deeply inhabited by all the visceral and imaginative capacities of the artist striving to see, to draw out, and to bring into being.

The flung ink (although it could be any graphic medium, some much richer such as tempera or oil paints) begins the process by opening up a synesthetic "field," a metaphorically suggestive realm that prompts an imaginative seeing. Leonardo da Vinci had once said that one first truly learns to see by allowing one's attention to become absorbed in streaks of dried spittle or the surface of an old stained wall until the imagination is able to distinguish an alternative world.[48] Seventeenth-century artists Johann König and Antonio Carracci used the suggestive fields of veined marbles and agates as the bases for highly imaginative paintings of landscapes and other representations. Figures and images were literally drawn out and metamorphosed from the surfaces of stones and minerals.[49] Similarly, the making of graphic and collage fields "irritate" the mental faculties to such a degree that fountains of possibilities emerge before the percipient; one becomes so engaged with the wealth of images that new worlds are disclosed, as if in a dream or hallucination. Like the luminous collages of Kurt Schwitters or Max Ernst, these fields of interpretation make impressions on the receptive mind and, in turn, the imagination impresses itself into the field. Fresh images might be conjured up as one "sees" things in new associations. As the Surrealists have already shown, the power of a psychically inhabited and synesthetic realm can reenchant the ordinary and make the everyday world magical once again.[50]

The tactics of appropriation, collage, abstraction, imaginative projection, and so on, are strategies used to prompt free association, providing liberatory mechanisms of construal. However, such work first requires that the drawing be theoretically and critically motivated by the maker. Collage, for example, is not a random and unfocused activity, but demands a highly disciplined and reflective mind. It is not simply a matter of "anything goes." Any creative transformation that results from human intellection will always entail special vocabularies, procedures, and modes of demonstration, specific to a particular theorem and motive. The game is complex, elusive, unsystematic, and ever subject to modification. It is important to remember that these types of drawing are only strategies; their primary work is in critical response to something. They are neither automatic divination screens, yielding up ideas of their own making, nor are

FIG. 12 — Process, work, duration, accident, flux: while landscape is the subject, equally so is the painter's own spontaneity and involvement with the brush. *Landscape*, by Sesshu, 1495, Ink on paper. 147.9 × 32.7 cm

Courtesy Tokyo National Museum, TNM Image Archives

they grounds of justification, falsely legitimizing the project simply because of their perceived magic. The function of abstraction in drawing is simply to discover new ground, to gain insight, not to obfuscate, nor to justify a project.

The difficulty in such drawing lies in distinguishing the culturally and architecturally relevant from the limits of personal fancy or those of more transient value. The percipient must be able to distinguish between weak, fanciful ideas, and the more potent images and symbolic structures relevant to landscape architectural experience. Ideas such as archetype, deep structure, and the constancy of the primary or typical human condition, belie the fact that there are universally significant situations peculiar to the human condition.[51] Essentially, a significant "seeing" is about recognition, and remains the outcome of productive and meaningful poetic activity. Drawing can best function in this capacity if two tenets are first upheld: first, drawings are eidetic phenomena, which work through symbols and analogs, not through likeness of representation. This point is illustrated by architect Marco Frascari, who equates graphic and constructed angles with "angels." In describing the journeys of the early Mediterranean sailors, Frascari has written:

> The imagining of angels, guiding essences, was a way of finding the angles necessary to determine the direction for reaching land safely. In architecture this traditional chiasma of angels and angles is recorded, in an oblique way, by Vitruvius. In his explanation or the planning of the angles of cities, Vitruvius cites as an example the Tower of Winds in Athens. This Hellenistic edifice incorporates both representations of the winds as figures of angels and as the angles of direction.[52]

Later, he concludes:

> The objects of architecture should not be given to public knowledge in a rigid, finished state, in their naked "as suchness." Rather, they should be presented as demonstrations in such a way that each angle should be dressed up as an angel.[53]

For Frascari then, the instrumental and the symbolic (or the visible and the invisible), are united through analogies between the signifier and the signified. The degree of reciprocity between both the signifier and the signified thus forms a second tenet of drawing. Whiteman has referred to this correspondence as a "qualitative precision" between the symbols used in representation and the ideas they embody in built landscape form. He has written:

[An understanding of the term qualitative precision] means admitting that the logics of formal manipulation cannot be purely autonomous, that judgments in architectural design are guided not by the autonomous reasons of form alone but rather by a coupled sense of the physical and the symbolized, the visible and the invisible.[54]

A more laconic and accurate form of drawing might best be realized by the individual with time and experience, as one can only properly understand the interrelationships between the symbolic and the material worlds more through sensible observation than by secondary constructs such as concepts and analytical matrices. However, the qualitative precision of angles and angels is not simply a case of observational clarity (which is something always susceptible to scientific prescription and duplication), but more properly derives from imaginative construal. The paradox inherent in the term "qualitative precision" is that accuracy of observation belongs not to scientific certainty but to the realm of myth and poetry wherein things make sense and ring true without necessarily being explicit or accountable. It is in this way that symbols retain their open-endedness and are subject to ever-richer association.

Speculation through drawing is, however, only part of drawings' full function with respect to landscape architectural production. A necessary complement lies in drawings' capacity to demonstrate intention and construction—the drawing as a vehicle of realization. This type of drawing goes beyond speculative fields (and the emergence of ideas), and instead it begins to demonstrate the project in practical terms. In describing the drawings of two contemporary architects, Carlo Scarpa and Mario Ridolfi, Frascari has written:

Scarpa works out his strata of architectural mediations on pieces of Bristol board with overlays of light pieces of tracing paper, using drafting and colored pencils, diluted inks and applying the painterly technique of *pentimenti*. Ridolfi utilizes layers of heavy tracing paper for his analogical thinking, employing a fountain pen, and editing the final drawing with a skillful use of scissors and transparent adhesive tape. Scarpa's and Ridolfi's drawings…are visual descriptions of processes that are not visible. They are conceived not to be read by the public, but to carry out a demonstration of intent. On the other hand, conventional working drawings are scientific tools for presenting a future reality within an appearance of continuous and uniform order; *they show a result, not the intent*.[55]

The dynamic drawings of Scarpa and Ridolfi are "productive representations of an eidetic process," the result of analogically working the medium of drawing with the medium of building.[56] Scarpa, for example, first scores his paper with a plan delineation of the particular site and its physical context. Layers are then added and subtracted orthographically, as if alternately building and partly demolishing foundations. [FIG. 13] Scales are shifted and overlaid as parts and details are played alongside the construal of the whole. The drawings are made neither for construction nor presentation, but rather for the disciplined work of the architect. Both the symbolic and instrumental representations are found in these ideational drawings, enabling the ideas to be translated into built form. The representation of space is not separated from the space of representation, just as the function of representation is not separated from the representation of function.

A common aspect of both the speculative and demonstrative drawing is that they each act as vehicles for creativity, as intermediary catalysts that are used to *generate* a landscape architectural project. Never are they merely descriptive on the one hand, nor decorative and fetishistic on the other. Rather, they both belong to a kind of work called *deixis*. In describing deixis, art historian Norman Bryson has explained how the term originally derives from *deikononei*, meaning "to show," to make evident, and that, in linguistics, the term *deictic* is applied to utterances that supply information regarding the source of the utterance. Deictic tenses are always compounds of the present, the here and now, and stand in contrast to aoristic tenses that are past and imperfect, and belong characteristically to the historian "reciting the events of the past impersonally and without reference to his/her own position."[57] In further describing deixis, Bryson has written:

> The wider class of deixis therefore includes all those particles and forms of speech where the utterance incorporates into itself information about its own spatial position relative to its content (here, there, near, far), and to its own relative temporality (yesterday, today, tomorrow, sooner, later, long ago). Deixis is utterance in carnal form and speaks back directly to the body of the speaker.[58]

In relationship to painting, Bryson has elaborated on deixis by discussing the making of Chinese and Japanese flung ink paintings. While landscape is clearly the focus of attention in these canvases, equally so is the spontaneous work of the brush in "real," or processual, time. Bryson has written:

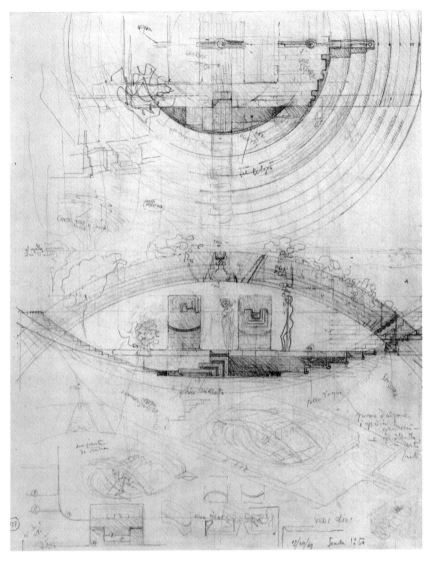

FIG. 13 — Plan and section of the "arcosolium" at Brion, by Carlo Scarpa, 1969,
Pencil and crayon on brownline copy, 50 × 40 cm

Courtesy Carlo Scarpa Archive, MAXXI Museum collection, the Italian State Museum of Architecture

The work of production is constantly displayed in the wake of its traces; in this tradition the body of labor is on constant display, just as it is judged in terms, which, in the West, would only apply to a *performing* art.[59]

The imaginal is both enacted and constructed in a radically temporal and dynamic sequence of painterly responses. The action of seeing and marking does not attempt to conceal its own evolvement, mistaken attempts and all. Instead, the paintings deictically play out and express their own construal, like a performance that maps out its own body. This is in contrast to "the image that suppresses deixis," the image that "has no interest in its own genesis or past, except to bury it in a palimpsest in which only the final versions show through above an interminable debris of revisions....[Here] the existence of the image in its own time, of duration, of practice, of the body, is negated by never referring the marks on canvas to their place in the vanished sequence of local aspirations."[60] The deictic drawing, meanwhile, records and traces its own evolution, and refers back to an entire corpus of prior thoughts, ideas, and associations. Deixis both marks and realizes the moment at which construal becomes construction.

Research into the development of projection, notation, and representation vis-à-vis the effective and artful construal, construction, and sustenance of built landscape form has still yet to occur in a vibrant and imaginative way.[61] This research might begin through an increased understanding of the mechanisms of analogy and metaphor in both speculative and demonstrative drawing. Analogical drawing looks for some form of interaction and dialogue between the symbolic realms of ideas and meaning and the structures of projection and embodiment. In this way, the drawing is an integral part of the landscape "project," holding within its deictic traces the symbolic and instrumental intentions of the scheme. Such drawings might not only tell us what things might be, but also what they are like, suggesting, without necessarily prescribing, quite specific settings and topologies. Plans, sections, notation scores, scale shifts, light and texture studies, and so on, are drawn alongside the speculative play of the collagic field, actively plotting landscape relationships between idea and construction. While the focus of attention shifts from normative modes of perception to a more liberating discovery of intertextuality between things, a precision of intent and demonstration thereof is still demanded. Analogical thinking is both intuitive and rational, and must play subjective sensibilities off and against systems of order and measure.[62]

Metaphorical/analogical drawing is thus radically different from analytical drawing, which is more instrumental and calculative than it is poetic and imaginative. The generative free play of metaphorical and deictic drawing, in dialogue with the discipline of notation and projection, is a critical and speculative practice that demonstrates the chiasm of a landscape's construal and construction. Rich with significance and interpretative ambiguity, landscape architectural drawing as a synesthetic and commutative medium might better afford a richer realization of ideas within the built environment. Such a drawing is less a finished "work of art," and even less a tool for communicating instrumental ideas, than it is itself a catalytic locale of inventive subterfuges for the making of poetic landscapes. In essence, the drawing is a plot, necessarily strategic, maplike, and acted upon.

NOTES

1   See Donald Meinig, ed., *The Interpretation of Ordinary Landscapes* (Oxford: Oxford University Press, 1979). See especially the essays by Meinig, "The Beholding Eye," 33–48; "Reading the Landscape: An appreciation of W. G. Hoskins and J.B. Jackson," 195–244; and Pierce Lewis, "Axioms for Reading the Landscape," 11–32.

2   Meinig, "The Beholding Eye" and Meinig, "Reading the Landscape," *The Interpretation of Ordinary Landscapes*, 195–244. See also Denis Cosgrove and Stephen Daniels, eds., *The Iconography of Landscape* (Cambridge: Cambridge University Press, 1988), 1–10; Denis Cosgrove, *Social Formation and the Symbolic Landscape* (Madison: University of Wisconsin Press, 1984), 13–38; and Max Oelschlaeger, *The Idea of Wilderness: from prehistory to the age of ecology* (New Haven, CT: Yale University Press, 1991).

3   By "eidetic" I mean that which pertains to the visual formation of ideas, or to the reciprocity between image and idea. That drawing is fundamentally about making images suggests that it might actually generate and transform ideas for the percipient rather than simply representing them.

4   See Robin Evans, "Translations from Drawing to Building," *AA Files* 12 (London: Architectural Association, 1986), 3–18.

5   See Maurice Merleau-Ponty, *The Primacy of Perception* (Evanston, IL: Northwestern University Press, 1964), especially chapters 2 and 5.

6   See Martin Heidegger, "The Origin of the Work of Art," *Poetry, Language, Thought*, trans. Albert Hofstadter (New York: Harper and Row, 1975), 17–87.

7   Evans, "Translations from Drawing to Building," 3–18.

8   Bachelard uses extracts from books by Baudelaire and Philippe Diolé to further explicate the idea of "intimate immensity." Bachelard quotes from Diolé describing "the magical operation that, in deep water, allows the diver to loosen the ordinary ties of time and space and make life resemble an obscure, inner poem....Neither in the desert nor on the bottom of the sea does one's spirit remain sealed and indivisible." Imaginative extension and all-surrounding limitlessness are poetic qualities of landscape, which enable us to dream. In the dark forest we may enter the closed and veiled forests of ourselves. In the open desert our own spirit may also be sensed as unbounded and infinite. See Gaston Bachelard, *The Poetics of Space* (Boston: Beacon Press, 1974), pp. 183–210.

9   Martin Heidegger, "Building, Dwelling, Thinking," 154.

10  See Maurice Merleau-Ponty, *Phenomenology of Perception*, trans. Colin Smith (London: Routledge and Kegan Paul, 1986), 243.

11  The notion of landscape spatiality being akin to a layered map of locations, or as situated places perceived through "spacing," can be related to Kevin Lynch's work in his book *The Image of the City*. The thesis of the book is that we know our built environment as a complex structure of nameable locations, as named loci of phenomena. Lynch's layers of analysis—"path, node, landmark, district, edge"—are collectively understood by ordinary citizens who mentally overlay them as a cognitive map—"something is over there in relation to this." Lynch's notion that a densely stratified landscape fabric, of enormous perceptual complexity, can actually be understood and translated into a spoken, written, or drawn "map" by most of its inhabitants, is in concurrence with Heidegger's insights into spatiality: the fact that space is situated, connected, spaced, named, and, most importantly, "thought through." Kevin Lynch, *The Image of the City* (Cambridge, MA: MIT Press, 1964). In relation to the concept of spacing, see Jacques Derrida, "Point de Folie Maintenant l'Architecture," in *AA Files* 12 (London: Architectural Association, 1986).

12  Heidegger, "Building, Dwelling, Thinking," 156.

13  Merleau-Ponty, *Phenomenology of Perception*, 412.

14  See J. J. Gibson, *The Ecological Approach to Visual Perception* (Boston: Houghton-Mifflin, 1979).

15  Walter Benjamin, *Illuminations*, ed. Hannah Arendt (New York: Schocken Books, 1969), 239.

16  See John Whiteman, "Criticism, Representation and Experience in Contemporary Architecture," *Harvard Architecture Review* 4 (New York: Rizzoli, 1985), 137–47.

17  Robert Rosenblum, "The Origin of Painting," *Art Bulletin* (Dec. 1957), 279–90.

18  Evans, "Translations from Drawing to Building," 6–7.

19  Vitruvius Pollio, *On Architecture*, from the Harleian manuscript 2767, and trans. Frank Granger, 2 vols. (Cambridge, MA: Harvard University Press, 1983), Vol. I, Bk. I, Ch. II, pp. 24–25. Also see Claudio Sgarbi, "Speculation on design and Finito," *VIA 9: Representation* (New York: Rizzoli for the University of Pennsylvania Press, 1988), 155–65.

20  See Kenneth Frampton, "The Anthropology of Construction," *Casabella* 251/2 (January 1986), 26–30. Also see Marco Frascari, "A New Angel/Angle in Architectural Research: The Idea of Demonstration," *Journal of Architectural Education* 44/1 (November 1990), 11–19.

21  Daniele Barbaro, *La Pratica della Perspettiva* (Sala Bolognese, 1980), 129–30. Referred to by Alberto Péréz-Gomez, "Architecture as Drawing," *Journal of Architectural Education* 36/2 (1982), 2–7.

22  Alberto Péréz-Gomez, "Architecture as Drawing," 3. Also see Alberto Péréz-Gomez, *Architecture and the Crisis of Modern Science* (Cambridge, MA: MIT Press, 1988), esp. Ch. IV.

23  See Péréz-Gomez and Frascari, "The Ideas of Demonstration," 12.

24  Nelson Goodman, *Languages of Art* (Cambridge: Hackett Publishing, 1964), 127–76.

25  Edward R. Tufte, *Envisioning Information* (Cheshire, CT: Graphics Press, 1990), 114.

26  See Ann Hutchinson Guest, *Dance Notation* (London: Dance Books, 1984). Also see Albrecht Knust, *Dictionary of Kinetography Laban* (Labanotation) (Estover, Plymouth, England: Macdonald and Evans, 1979).

27  See Lawrence Halprin, *RSVP Cycles* (New York: George Braziller, 1969).

28  See Sergei Eisenstein, *Film Sense*, ed. Jay Leyda (New York: Harcourt, Brace, Jovanovich, 1975), pp. 176–77.

29  See Arthur Danto, *The Transfiguration of the Commonplace* (Cambridge, MA: Harvard University Press, 1981), Ch. 6. Also see Nelson Goodman, *Language of Art*.

30  This is discussed by Norman Bryson in *Vision and Painting: The Logic of the Gaze* (New Haven, CT: Yale University Press, 1988), 43–44. Also see E. H. Gombrich, *Art and Illusion: A Study in the Psychology of Pictorial Representation* (Oxford: Phaidon, 1977), 29–34, 320–30.

31  Rosalind Krauss, *The Originality of the Avant-Garde and Other Modernist Myths* (Cambridge, MA: MIT Press, 1985), 166.

32  See Dan Rose, "The Brandywine: A Case Study of an Ecological Strategy," *Landscape Journal* 7/2 (Fall 1988), 128–33.

33  The development of landscape as a scene to be "completed" by the action of visitors was most evident in the landscape gardens by William Kent, especially at Rousham. See John Dixon Hunt, *William Kent, Landscape Garden Designer* (London: A. Zwemmer, 1987), 29–40, 60–69.

34  There are two problems with pictorial representation when making landscapes. The first is that the predominance of the picture plane remains an extremely remote aspect of landscape experience, emphasizing the visual over other modes of cognition. The second is that the drawn picture itself begins to accrue a certain value, inevitably ascending to the status of an aesthetic object, and subsequently playing all-too comfortably into the hands of modern criticism and the consumptive demand of glossy magazines and galleries. See Whiteman, "Criticism, Representation and Experience," 137–47.

35  Nelson Goodman, *Languages of Art*, iii.

36  See Wassily Kandinsky, *The Spirit of Art* (New York: Dover, 1977). Also see E. H. Gombrich, *Art and Illusion*, ch. XI. Gombrich also has described how figures, in addition to forms or colors, can be juxtaposed to create a new message. The "ideogram" of water alongside an eye might signify "to weep," a mouth and a dog might signify "to bark," and so on. The correspondence between matter and idea forms the basis for meaning.

37  See Robin Evans, "In Front of Lines That Leave Nothing Behind," *AA Files* 6 (London: Architectural Association, 1983), 96–98.

38  This division is most clearly identified and explained by Robin Evans, "Translations from Drawing to Building," 3–18.

39  Whiteman, "Criticism, Representation and Experience," 145.

40  See Alberto Péréz-Gomez, "Drawing and Architecture," 2–7.

41  Criticism has ascended to a primary role in the production of art works since the enlightenment. Its aim is to reflect on the underlying assumptions and premises that constitute a work. In our modern age, there is a deep suspicion that everything must be questioned if it is to be substantiated. It is a skeptical position, but one most prevalent in our work today.

42  Whiteman, "Criticism, Representation and Experience," 143.

43  This observation is derived from Robin Evans, "Translation from Drawing to Building," 5.

44  Ibid.

45  The term "drawing as a vehicle of creativity" is derived from Dalibor Vesely, "Drawing as a Vehicle of Creativity," *Scroope* 2 (Cambridge University School of Architecture, 1990), 13–17.

46  See Frascari, "The Ideas of Demonstration." One constructs both theoretical schemata as to things and plans. Construal is theoretical whereas construction is instrumental. Thus, "there is no construction without a construing, and no construing without a construction….The construing of a cosmological order is constructed in a Renaissance villa," 18. Frascari uses the word chiasm to mean "an exchange between the phenomenal body and the 'objective' body, between the perceiving and

perceived" (quoted from Merleau-Ponty, *The Visible and the Invisible* [Evanston, IL: Northwestern University Press, 1968], 215). Frascari's "angel/angle" trope is used to illustrate this union. Drawings are therefore the site, or locus, of both construal and construction.

47  Frascari, "The Ideas of Demonstration," 11–19. Also see Dalibor Vesely, "Architecture and the Conflict of Representation," *AA Files* 8 (London: Architectural Association, 1984), 21–38.

48  See A. Chastel, *Leonardo da Vinci par lui-meme* (Paris: Nagel, 1952).

49  See Jurgis Baitrusaitis, *Aberrations: An Essay in the Legend of Forms*, trans. Richard Miller (Cambridge, MA: MIT Press, 1989), 60–105.

50  For an account of the surrealist view toward the reenchantment of the world, see André Breton, "Artistic Genesis and the Perspective of Surrealism," *Painting and Surrealism* (New York: Harper and Row, 1972), 350–62.

51  See Vesely, "Drawing as Vehicle of Creativity," 13–17.

52  See Frascari, "The Ideas of Demonstration," 11.

53  Ibid, 17.

54  Whiteman, "Criticism, Representation and Experience," 147.

55  Marco Frascari, *Monsters of Architecture* (Lanham, MD: Rowman and Littlefield, 1991), 102.

56  Ibid, 104.

57  Bryson, *Vision and Painting*, 88.

58  Ibid.

59  Ibid, 92.

60  Ibid, 92.

61  While the preceding paragraphs have described drawings primarily in relationship to buildings, the same arguments still hold true for drawings vis-à-vis the design of landscapes, with minor modification. The landscape is a different phenomenon from building. It is experienced differently and the procedures for its construction are also different. Landscapes are also dynamic phenomena, living, growing, changing form, and eventually dying. Surely management plans and schedules seem integral parts of any landscape project, for example, demonstrating temporal as well as spatial intentions, and demonstrating practical techniques of stewardship.

62  For more on analogical drawing, see Dalibor Vesely, "Drawing as a Vehicle of Creativity," 13–17.

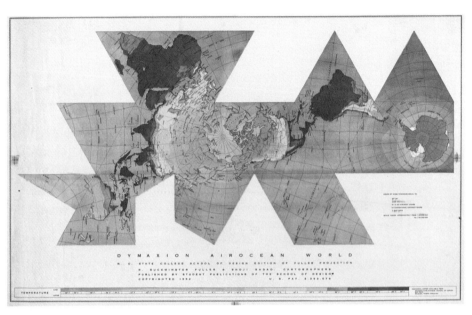

**FIG. 1 —** *Dymaxion Airocean World Map,* **by R. Buckminster Fuller and Shoji Sadao, 1954**

# THE AGENCY OF MAPPING:

## SPECULATION, CRITIQUE, AND INVENTION

Mapping is a fantastic cultural project, creating and building the world as much as measuring and describing it. Long affiliated with the planning and design of cities, landscapes and buildings, mapping is particularly instrumental in the construing and constructing of lived space. In this active sense the function of mapping is less to mirror reality than to engender the reshaping of the worlds in which people live. While there are countless examples of authoritarian, simplistic, erroneous, and coercive acts of mapping, with reductive effects upon both individuals and environments, focus in this essay is upon more optimistic revisions of mapping practices.[1] These revisions situate mapping as a collective enabling enterprise, a project that both reveals and realizes hidden potential. Hence, in describing the "agency" of mapping, I do not mean to invoke agendas of imperialist technocracy and control but rather to suggest ways in which mapping acts may emancipate potentials, enrich experiences, and diversify worlds. We have been adequately cautioned about mapping as a means of projecting power-knowledge, but what about mapping as a productive and liberating instrument, a world-enriching agent, especially in the design and planning arts?

As a creative practice, mapping precipitates its most productive effects through a finding that is also a founding; its agency lies in neither reproduction nor imposition but rather in uncovering realities previously unseen or unimagined, even across seemingly exhausted grounds. Thus, mapping unfolds potential; it re-makes territory over and over again, each time with new and diverse consequences. Not all maps accomplish this, however; some simply reproduce what is already known. These are more "tracings" than maps, delineating

---

*Originally published in: Denis Cosgrove, ed.* Mappings *(London: Reaktion Books, 1999): 188–225. Reproduced with permission.*

patterns but revealing nothing new. In describing and advocating more open-ended forms of creativity, Gilles Deleuze and Félix Guattari declare: "Make a map not a tracing!" They continue:

> What distinguishes the map from the tracing is that it is entirely oriented toward an experimentation in contact with the real. The map does not reproduce an unconscious closed in upon itself; it constructs the unconscious. It fosters connections between fields, the removal of blockages on bodies without organs, the maximum opening of bodies without organs onto a plane of consistency… The map has to do with performance, whereas the tracing always involves an "alleged competence."[2]

The distinction here is between mapping as equal to what is ("tracing") and mapping as equal to what is and to what is not yet. In other words, the unfolding agency of mapping is most effective when its capacity for description also sets the conditions for new eidetic and physical worlds to emerge. Unlike tracings, which propagate redundancies, mappings discover new worlds within past and present ones; they inaugurate new grounds upon the hidden traces of a living context. The capacity to reformulate what already exists is the important step. And what already exists is more than just the physical attributes of terrain (topography, rivers, roads, buildings) but includes also the various hidden forces that underlie the workings of a given place. These include natural processes, such as wind and sun; historical events and local stories; economic and legislative conditions; even political interests, regulatory mechanisms, and programmatic structures. Through rendering visible multiple and sometimes disparate field conditions, mapping allows for an understanding of terrain as only the surface expression of a complex and dynamic imbroglio of social and natural processes. In visualizing these interrelationships and interactions, mapping itself participates in any future unfoldings. Thus, given the increased complexity and contentiousness that surrounds landscape and urbanism today, creative advances in mapping promise designers and planners greater efficacy in intervening in spatial and social processes. Avoiding the failure of universalist approaches toward master planning and the imposition of state-controlled schemes, the unfolding agency of mapping may allow designers and planners not only to see certain possibilities in the complexity and contradiction of what already exists but also to *actualize* that potential. This instrumental function is particularly important in a world where it is becoming increasingly difficult to both *imagine* and actually to *create* anything outside of the normative.

### The Agency of Mapping

Mappings have agency because of the double-sided characteristic of all maps. First, their surfaces are directly *analogous* to actual ground condition; as horizontal planes, they record the surface of the earth as direct impressions. As in the casting of shadows, walks and sightings across land may be literally *projected* onto paper through a geometrical graticule of points and lines drawn by ruler and pen. Conversely, one can put one's finger on a map and trace out a particular route or itinerary, the map projecting a mental image into the spatial imagination. Because of this directness, maps are taken to be "true" and "objective" measures of the world, and are accorded a kind of benign neutrality. By contrast, the other side of this analogous characteristic is the inevitable *abstractness* of maps, the result of selection, omission, isolation, distance, and codification. "Map" crevices such as frame, scale, orientation, projection, indexing, and naming reveal artificial geographies that remain unavailable to human eyes. Maps present only one version of the earth's surface, an eidetic fiction constructed from factual observation. As both analogue and abstraction, then, the surface of the map functions like an operating table, a staging ground or a theater of operations upon which the mapper collects, combines, connects, marks, masks, relates, and generally explores. These surfaces are massive collection, sorting and transfer sites, great fields upon which real material conditions are isolated, indexed, and placed within an assortment of relational structures.

The analogous-abstract character of the map surface means that it is doubly projective: It both captures the projected elements off the ground and projects back a variety of effects through use. The strategic use of this double function has, of course, a long alliance with the history of mapping, and not only militaristically (*reconnaissances militaires*) but also ideologically.[3] Surprisingly, however, the strategic, constitutive, and inventive capacities of mapping are not widely recognized in the urban design and planning arts, even though cartography and planning have enjoyed a long and mutually influential relationship since the fifteenth century.[4] Throughout the twentieth century, mapping in design and planning has been undertaken conventionally as a quantitative and analytical survey of existing conditions made prior to the making of a new project. These survey maps are both spatial and statistical, inventorying a range of social, economic, ecological, and aesthetic conditions. As expertly produced, measured representations, maps are conventionally taken to be stable, accurate, indisputable mirrors of reality, providing the logical basis for future decision making as well as the means for later projecting a designed plan back onto the ground. It is generally assumed that if the survey is quantitative, objective, and rational, it is also true and neutral, thereby helping to legitimize and enact future plans and decisions.[5] Thus, mapping typically precedes planning because it is assumed that the map will objectively identify and make visible the terms around which a planning project may then be rationally developed, evaluated, and built.[6]

What remains overlooked in this sequence, however, is the fact that maps are highly artificial and fallible constructions, virtual abstractions that possess great force in terms of how people see and act. One of the reasons for this oversight derives from a prevalent tendency to view maps in terms of what they represent rather than what they do. As with art historical analyses of drawings and paintings, considerations of maps as a successive series of paradigmatic types and representations overlook the durational experiences and effects of mapping. That mappings are constructed from a set of internal instruments, codes, techniques, and conventions, and that the worlds they describe and project derive only from those aspects of reality that are susceptible to these techniques, are dimensions of mapping still barely understood by the contemporary planner. Instead, most designers and planners consider mapping a rather unimaginative, analytical practice, at least compared to the presumed "inventiveness" of the designing activities that occur after all the relevant maps have been made (often with the contents of the maps ignored or forgotten). An unfortunate consequence of these attitudes is that the various techniques and procedures of mapping have not been subjects of inquiry, research, or criticism. Instead, they have become codified, naturalized and taken for granted as institutional conventions. Thus, critical experimentation with new and alternative forms of mapping remains largely underdeveloped if not significantly repressed.[7] The "alleged competence" of the tracing effectively dominates the exploratory inventiveness integral to acts of mapping.

This indifference toward mapping is particularly puzzling when one considers that the very basis upon which projects are imagined and realized derives precisely from how maps are made. The conditions around which a project develops originate with what is selected and prioritized in the map; what is subsequently left aside or ignored; how the chosen material is schematized; indexed, and framed; and how the synthesis of the graphic field invokes semantic, symbolic, and instrumental content. Thus, the various cartographic procedures of selection, schematization, and synthesis make the map *already* a project in the making.[8] This is why mapping is never neutral, passive or without consequence; on the contrary, mapping is perhaps the most formative and creative act of any design process, first disclosing and then staging the conditions for the emergence of new realities.

In what follows, I discuss mapping as an active agent of cultural intervention. Because my interests lie in the various processes and effects of mapping

I am less concerned with what mapping *means* than with what it actually *does*. Thus, I am less interested in maps as finished artifacts than I am in mapping as a creative *activity*. It is in this participatory sense that I belie new and speculative techniques of mapping may generate new practices of creativity, practices that are expressed not in the invention of novel form but in the productive reformulation of what is already given. By showing the world in new ways, unexpected solutions and effects may emerge. However, given the importance of representational technique in the creative process, it is surprising that whilst there has been no shortage of new ideas and theories in design and planning there has been so little advancement and invention of those specific tools and techniques—including mapping—that are so crucial for the effective construal and construction of new worlds.[9]

### The Efficacy of Technique

A comparison between cartographer Gerardus Mercator's projection of the earth's surface and architect Buckminster Fuller's Dymaxion projection reveals radically different spatial and sociopolitical structures. [FIG. 1] The same planet, the same places, and yet significantly dissimilar relationships are revealed or, more precisely, constructed. The Mercator map stretches the surface of the globe without excision onto a flat surface, oriented "upward" to the north. The compass directions are made parallel, leading to gross distortions of land area and shape, especially as one moves toward the poles. The northern hemisphere dominates, with Greenland more than twice the size of Australia, even though the southern island is in fact greater than three times the land area of the northern. Needless to say, this view has well suited the self-image of Europeans and North Americans in an era of Western political hegemony. By contrast, Fuller's Dymaxion Airocean World Map of 1943 cuts the earth into triangular facets that are then unfolded as a flat polyhedron. [FIG. 2] Both the north and south poles are presented frontally and equally, with little distortion, although the typical viewer is at first likely to be disoriented by this unusual, poly-directional arrangement of countries. Only the graphic graticule of latitude and longitude allows the reader to comprehend the relative orientation of any one location.[10]

Interestingly, the Dymaxion structure can be unfolded and reoriented in any number of different ways, depending on the thematics of one's point of view. The polyhedral geometry provides a remarkably flexible and adaptive system wherein different locations and regions can be placed into significantly different sets of relationship. Precisely where the map is cut and folded determines how the parts are seen in relationship to each other, each time in radically altered, yet equally true, configurations. Potentially at least, each arrangement possesses

eserch

ymaxion

Also where subject matter is situated has a big effect on veiwers gaze and spatial understanding/ prejadice

**ONE CONTINENT**
Bottom of the Areonautical Ocean

**EAST BY STEAM TO THE ORIENT VIA SUEZ**

**ONE OCEAN**
Admiral Mahan named it.
The British discovered and used it.

**EAST BY SAIL—TO THE ORIENT VIA GOOD HOPE**
From the Spanish Main via the Piratical Indian Waters.
12,000-mile great circle route from New York to Australia.

**STRATOSPHERE STRATEGIC**
European triangle controls the altitude merry-go-round.

**NORTHWARD TO THE ORIENT AND NORTHWARD TO EUROPE**
Old and new worlds on either hand.
Russia overhead and McKinder's World Island trisected.

FIG. 2 — *Alternative Sectional Arrangements of the Airocean World Map,* by R. Buckminster Fuller, 1943

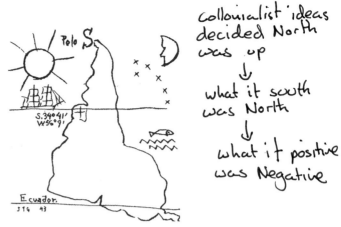

FIG. 3 —*Inverted Map of South America*, by Joaquin Torres-García, 1943
Courtesy Museo Torres García, Montevideo, Uruguay

great efficacy with regard to certain sociopolitical, strategic, and imaginative possibilities. Unlike the scientific objectivism that guides most modern cartographers, artists have been more conscious of the essentially fictional status of maps and the power they possess for construing and constructing worlds.[11] In the same year as Fuller's projection, the Uruguayan artist Joaquín Torres-García drew the *Inverted Map of South America* with a very distinct "S" at the top of the drawing. [FIG. 3] This remarkable image reminds us of the ways in which habitual conventions (in this case the unquestioned domination of north on top) condition spatial hierarchies and power relations. The convention of orienting the map to the north first arose early in the global and economic expansion of Northern Europe and in response to practices of navigation. But there are many instances of other societies at different times orienting their maps toward one of the other cardinal points, or making them circular without top and bottom (the Dymaxion map is perhaps one of the few modern instances where singular orientation is not a prerequisite). Maps of this sort are still legible and "correct" in their depiction of spatial relationship, but the reader must first learn the relevant mapping codes and conventions.

Another instance of critique and invention of the modern map is Brazilian artist Waltercio Caldas's *Japao*, of 1972.[12] Here, the artist is mapping a territory that is foreign, or "unimaginable" for many in the West. Rather than colonizing this territory through survey and inventory, typically Western techniques of power-knowledge, Caldas simply marks an otherwise empty map surface with very small inscriptions and numbers. These are contained by a very prominent, classical cartographic frame. There are no other outlines, shapes, or forms, just small type and a few scribbles. There is no scale, no identifiable marks, no graticule of orientation, just a square ink frame. In this stark, minimal carto-graphic field, Caldas presents an elusive geography, an open and indeterminate field of figures that returns terra incognita to an otherwise excessively mapped planet. The image is also a commentary on the cage-like power of the imperial-izing frame: the graphic square surrounds, captures, and holds its quarry, but at the same time its contents remain foreign, evasive, and autonomous. This blank, nonfigured space raises both anxiety and a certain promise—promise because its potential efficacy lies in the emancipation of its contents. The autonomous, abstract structure suggests how mystery and desire might be returned to a world of places and things that have been otherwise excessively classified and struc-tured. In Caldas's image, such places are liberated through precisely the same measures that first captured them.

Whereas certain artists have engaged creatively with cartographic tech-niques, planners and designers have been less ambitious.[13] Techniques of aerial-oblique and zenithal views—planimetry, ichnography, and triangu-lation—were most developed during the early-sixteenth century, and have since become the primary tools with which cities and landscapes are analyzed, planned, and constructed. Quantitative and thematic mapping techniques orig-inated with the Enlightenment enthusiasm for rational progress and social reform, and these were later complemented by various statistical, comparative, and "zoning" techniques during the late-nineteenth and early-twentieth cen-turies.[14] Some advances in these techniques have occurred over the past thirty years with the rise of satellite and remote-sensing capabilities, together with new computer technologies such as Geographic Information Systems (GIS), but in principle they remain unchanged. These techniques remain largely unques-tioned, conventional devices of inventory, quantitative analysis, and legitimiza-tion of future plans. Issues of selectivity, schematization, and synthesis remain generally oriented around the same conventions used a hundred years ago. With only a handful of exceptions, the relationship of maps to world making is sur-prisingly under-thought. The limitations of this condition are extremely unfor-tunate; as the late geographer J. B. Harley argues:

One effect of accelerated technological change—as manifest in digital cartogra-phy and geographical information systems—has been to strengthen its positiv-ist assumptions and [to breed] a new arrogance in geography about its supposed value as a mode of access to reality. If it is true that new fictions of factual repre-sentation are daily being foisted upon us, then the case for introducing a social

dimension into modern cartography is especially strong. Maps are too important to be left to cartographers alone.[15]

In what follows, I suggest ways in which the social, imaginative, and critical
dimensions of mapping may be reestablished in modern cartography, especially
in mapping for urban and landscape planning and design. First, I discuss three
points of clarification: the map's relationship to reality; the changing nature of
time-space relations; and an insistence on equality of importance amongst mapping actions (techniques), mapping effects (consequences), and maps themselves.
These will underpin my outline of a number of alternative mapping practices
that play actively constitutive roles in forging culture, space, and place.

### Maps and Reality

The Argentinian author Jorge Luis Borges's tale of a fully detailed and life-
sized map that eventually tore and weathered to shreds across the actual territory it covered is frequently quoted in essays on mapping.[16] Not only does the
tale beautifully capture the cartographic imagination, it goes to the heart of a
tension between reality and representation, between the territory and the map.
Equally referenced is English writer Lewis Carroll's tale, also of a life-sized map,
in *Sylvie and Bruno*, in this case folded and thus preventing it being unfolded
for practical application. The map was useless, allowing Carroll's character Mein
Herr to conclude, "so now we use the country itself, as its own map, and I assure
you it does nearly as well." In these two fables, not only is the map an inferior,
secondary representation of territory, but the more detailed and lifelike the map
strives to be, the more redundant or unnecessary it becomes. Unlike paintings or
photographs, which have the capacity to bear a direct resemblance to the things
they depict, maps must by necessity be abstract if they are to sustain meaning
and utility. And such abstraction, the bane of untrained map-readers, is not at all
a failing of maps but rather their virtue.

Jean Baudrillard reverses Borges's tale to make another point:

> Simulation is no longer that of a territory, a referential being or substance. It is
> the generation by models of a real without origin or reality: a hyper-real. The
> territory no longer precedes the map, nor survives it. Henceforth, it is the map
> that precedes the territory.[17]

Arguably, of course, the map *always* precedes the territory, in that space
only becomes territory through acts of bounding and making visible, which are
primary functions of mapping. But Baudrillard is going one step further here,

claiming that late-twentieth-century communication and information technologies have produced such a blurring of what is real and what is a representation that the two can no longer be distinguished. He inverts Borges's fable to proclaim, that "it is the real and not the map whose vestiges subsist here and there."[18] Here, Baudrillard is careful to explain that this reversal does not mean that the world is scarcely more than a vast simulacrum, but rather that the act of differentiating between the real and the representation is no longer meaningful.

The dissolution of difference between reality and representation can also be approached through studies of spatial perception and cognition, especially those of child psychologists such as Jean Piaget, Edith Cobb, and Donald Winnicott. Winnicott, for example, discusses the necessity of play for the maturing of psychological selfhood, describing how children relate to the external world of things and spaces in extremely fluid and labile ways. In discussing the importance of engagement and discovery through playing, he describes "transitional objects" as those that are so possessed by the imagination that they are neither fully part of the self nor explicitly external. Emphasizing the creativity afforded by play, Winnicott argues that the space of play must remain beyond the reach of the empiricist question, "Did you find that (in the world) or did you make it up?"[19] To distinguish so completely an external, a priori, "real world" from a constructed and participatory one would not only deny imagination but also be incongruent with humankind's innate capacity to structure reciprocal relationships with its surroundings.

If for Borges and Carroll the territory itself wins out over the map, and for Baudrillard the map has come to both precede and construct the territory, Winnicott points to the futility of trying to make any distinction between the two, or indeed to accord primacy to either. And, whereas Baudrillard writes about the dissolution of difference with regard to the world of contemporary culture and its various systems of production, and Winnicott is more concerned with psychological development in relation to the phenomenal world, both authors recognize the conflation of cultural invention with found nature.

Reality, then, as in concepts such as "landscape" or "space," is not something external and "given" for our apprehension; rather it is constituted, or "formed," through our participation with things: material objects, images, values, cultural codes, places, cognitive schemata, events, and maps. As the philosopher of science Jacob Bronowski pointedly observes, "there are no appearances to be photographed, no experiences to be copied, in which we do not take part. Science, like art, is not a copy of nature but a re-creation of her."[20] This mediated mode of being is more fully described by the philosopher Ernst Cassirer:

In truth…what we call the world of our perception is not simple, not given and self-evident from the outset, bur "is" only insofar as it has gone through certain basic theoretical acts by which it is apprehended and specified. This universal relationship is perhaps most evident in the intuitive form of our perceptual world, in its spatial form. The relations of "together," "separate," "side-by-side," are not just "given" along with our "simple" sensations, the sensuous matter that is order in space; they are a highly complex, thoroughly mediated product of empirical thought. When we attribute a certain size, position, and distance to things in space, we are not thereby expressing a simple datum of sensation but are situating the sensory data in a relationship and system, which proves ultimately to be nothing other than a relationship of pure judgment.[21]

The application of judgment, subjectively constituted, is precisely what makes a map more a project than a "mere" empirical description. The still widely held assumption that maps are mute, utilitarian tools of secondary significance to the *milieu* they represent, and lacking in power, agency, or effects beyond simple, objective description, is to grossly misconstrue their capacity for shaping reality. Both maps and territories are "thoroughly mediated products" and the nature of their exchange is far from neutral or uncomplicated.

I offer this sketch of maps and reality because it charts out what I think remains markedly under-thought (or, more precisely, *under-practiced*) in current cultural projects. The implications of a world derived more from cultural invention than from a preformed "nature" have barely begun to be explored, let alone accepted, at the level of cartographic practice. While contemporary scholars have begun to demonstrate how even the most objective descriptions of reality are culturally "situated," and that "nature" is perhaps the most situated yet shifting construction of all, few have dared to develop and practice techniques for realizing the potential offered by such an emancipated (even playful and promiscuous) world of constructions.

Whereas the architectural and planning arts ought to be leading such an exploration, they are still largely entrenched with the tools of thought passed down from Enlightenment and modernist paradigms: orthography, axonometry, perspective, maps as quantitative surveys and inventories, and plans as rational, self-contained ideals. Although these conventions are closely aligned with procedures of translation and construction, they are also technical instruments that enable the utopian renovation of huge tracts of urban fabric. Sites are treated either as blank areas (*tabulae rasae*) or as simple geometrical figures to be manipulated from high above. The synoptic "master plan" governs, while mapping, and all its potential for engaging and evolving local intricacy, is relegated to the relatively trivial role of marking location, inventorying resources and justifying future policies.

In recent years, however, much greater attention has been paid in the landscape and architectural arts to the specificity of site and context. Also, there has been a corresponding interest in developing more discreet and local modes of intervention as distinct from universal planning. Hence the resurgence of interest in mapping by a generation of young landscape architects, architects, and urban planners. For them, mapping refers to more than inventory and geometrical measure, and no presumption is made of innocence, neutrality, or inertia in its construction. Instead, the map is first employed as a *means* of "finding" and then "founding" new projects, effectively reworking what already exists. Thus the *processes* of mapping, together with their varied informational and semantic scope, are valued for both their revelatory and productive potential. Consequently, concepts of "site" are shifting from that of simply a geometrically defined parcel of land to that of a much larger and more active milieu.

Milieu is a French term that means "surroundings," "medium," and "middle": Milieu has neither beginning nor end, but is surrounded by other middles, in a field of connections, relationships, extensions, and potentials. In this sense, then, a grounded site, locally situated, invokes a host of "other" places, including all the maps, drawings, ideas, references, other worlds, and places that are invoked during the making of a project. "Site" today is a multiplicitous and complex affair, composing a potentially boundless field of phenomena, some palpable and some imaginary. In making visible what is otherwise hidden and inaccessible, maps provide a working table for identifying and reworking polyvalent conditions; their analogous, abstract surfaces enable the accumulation, organization, and restructuring of the various strata that comprise an ever-emerging milieu.

These ideas return us to the opening concern of this essay for the role of maps within the landscape and architectural imagination. For the landscape architect and urban planner, maps are sites for the imaging and projecting of alternative worlds. Thus maps are between the virtual and the real. Here, Winnicott's question, "Did you find that in the world or did you make it up?" denotes an irrelevant distinction. More important is how the map permits a kind of excavation (downward) and extension (outward) to expose, reveal, and construct latent possibilities within a greater milieu. The map "gathers" and "shows" things presently (and always) invisible, things which may appear incongruous or untimely but which may also harbor enormous potential for the unfolding of alternative events. In this regard, maps have very little to do with representation as depiction. After all, maps look nothing like their subject, not only because of their vantage point but also because they present all parts at once, with immediacy unavailable to the grounded individual. But more than this, the function of maps is not to depict but to enable, to precipitate a set of effects in time. Thus, mappings do not *represent geographies* or ideas; rather they *effect* their actualization.

Mapping is neither secondary nor representational but doubly operative: digging, finding, and exposing on the one hand, and relating, connecting, and structuring on the other. Through visual disclosure, mapping both sets up and puts into effect complex sets of relationship that remain to be more fully actualized. Thus mapping is not subsequent to, but prior to landscape and urban formations. In this sense, mapping is returned to its origins as a process of exploration, discovery, and enablement. This is a case of mapping to assert authority, stability, and control, and more one of searching, disclosing, and engendering new sets of possibility. Like a nomadic grazer, the exploratory mapper detours around the obvious so as to engage what remains hidden.

**Space and Time Today**
A creative view of mapping in the context of architectural, landscape, and urban production is rendered all the more relevant by the <u>changing nature of spatial and temporal structures in today's world</u>. Events occur with such speed and complexity that <u>nothing remains certain</u>. Large numbers live in a world where local economies and cultures are tightly bound into global ones, through which effects ripple with enormous velocity and consequence. Surrounded by media images and an excess of communication that makes the far seem near and the shocking merely normal, local cultures have become fully networked around the world. Air travel and other modes of rapid transportation have become so accessible that localities can be more closely connected to sites thousands of miles away than to their immediate surroundings. Today, structures of community life are shifting from spatial stability toward shifting, temporal coordination. Public life is now scheduled and allocated more by time than centered according to place, while the circulation of capital demands an ever more mobile and migratory workforce. Ten-mile linear cities are built in Southeast Asia in a matter of months, seemingly constructed out of nothing according to modes of agreement that are neither democratic nor authoritarian, merely expedient. And finally, perhaps, the near conquest of both the Genome and the Universe proclaim the end of earthly limits and coherence. Such fantastic play across the world's various surfaces is characterized not only by a fertile heterogeneity but also by conceptual elements coming loose from their traditional moorings. The boundaries

between different foundational realities have become so blurred, in fact, that it is practically impossible in a cyber world to distinguish between what is information and what is concrete, what is fact and what is fiction, what is space and what is time.

Mapping and contemporary spatial design techniques more generally have yet to find adequate ways to engage creatively with the dynamic and promiscuous character of time and space today. Most design and planning operations appear somewhat outmoded, overwhelmed, or incongruent in comparison to the rapidly metabolizing processes of urbanization and communication. In celebrating the urban freedoms and pleasures of Los Angeles, for example, the urbanist Reyner Banham goes to great lengths to explain the complex array of forces that led to the city's development, with planners and designers playing a distinctly minor role.[22] He questions whether or not Los Angeles would be as rich and modern a city if planners had exercised more of their authority—a point often made about London in comparison to Paris. While not everyone may share Banham's enthusiasm for the contemporary metropolis, his point is that new and productive forms of socialization and spatial arrangement are evolving without the aid, direction, or involvement of planners and designers. Moreover, Banham suggests that to assume this is a bad and negligent thing is to adopt a somewhat naive and insular, even elitist, position. This point is also argued by Rem Koolhaas in his discussion of "the generic city," or those identity-less areas that today comprise the bulk of the sprawling urban fabric where most people live. In criticizing a continued fascination of architects and planners with the "old identities" of traditional city centers such as Paris or Berlin, Koolhaas argues that there is a much more current and urgent urban condition that is being neglected. He argues that there might be certain virtues in these generic regions, such as their complete lack of memory or tradition that then liberates the urban planner from a whole series of conventional obligations, models, and assumptions. "The stronger identity, the more it imprisons, the more it resists expansion, interpretation, renewal, contradiction," he writes. "The generic city presents the final death of planning. Why? Not because it is unplanned…[but because] planning makes no difference whatsoever."[23]

Through such urbanists as Banham, Edward Soja, David Harvey, Koolhaas, and Bernard Tschumi, anthropologists such as Marc Augé, or philosophers such as Henri Lefebvre or Deleuze, it is becoming clearer to architects and planners that "space" is more complex and dynamic than previous formal models allowed. Ideas about spatiality are moving away from physical objects and forms toward the variety of territorial, political, and psychological social processes that flow through space. The *interrelationships* amongst things in space, as well as the *effects* that are produced through such dynamic interactions, are becoming of greater significance for intervening in urban landscapes than the solely compositional arrangement of objects and surfaces.

The experiences of space cannot be separated from the events that happen in it; space is situated, contingent, and differentiated. It is remade continuously every time it is encountered by different people, every time it is represented through another medium, every time its surroundings change, every time new affiliations are forged. Thus, as Harvey has argued, planners and architects have been misdirected in believing that new spatial structures alone would yield new patterns of socialization. The struggle for designers and planners, Harvey insists, lies not with spatial form and aesthetic appearances alone (the city as a thing) but with the advancement of more liberating processes and interactions in time (urbanization). Multiple processes of urbanization in time are what produce "a distinctive mix of spatialized permanences in relation to one another";[24] hence the urban project ought to be less about spatial determinism and more about reshaping those urbanization processes that are "fundamental to the construction of the things that contain them."[25]

Thus, in criticizing the formalism of both the modernist utopia and the sentimental, communitarian "new urbanism," Harvey argues that the dynamic multiplicity of urban processes cannot be contained within a singular, fixed spatial frame, especially when that frame neither derives from, nor itself redirects, those processes moving through it. He writes:

> The issue is not one of gazing into some crystal ball or imposing some classic form of utopian scheme in which a dead spatiality is made to rule over history and process. The problem is to enlist in the struggle to advance a more socially just and emancipatory mix of spatiotemporal production processes rather than to acquiesce to those imposed by finance capital, the World Bank, and the generally class-bound inequalities internalized within any system of uncontrolled capital accumulation.[26]

Harvey's point is that projecting new urban and regional futures must derive less from a utopia of form and more from a *utopia of process*—how things work, interact, and interrelate in space and time. Thus, the emphasis shifts from static object-space to the space-time of relational systems. And, it is here, in this complex and shifty milieu that *maps*, not *plans*, achieve a new instrumental significance.

## Mapping

"To plan a city is both to think the very plurality of the real and to make that way of thinking effective," writes Michel de Certeau: "it is to know how to articulate it and be able to do it."[27] Mapping is key here for it entails processes of gathering, working, reworking, assembling, relating, revealing, sifting, and speculating. In turn, these activities enable the inclusion of massive amounts of information that, when articulated, allow certain sets of possibility to become actual. In containing multiple modes of spatiotemporal description, mapping precipitates fresh insights and enables effective actions to be taken. Thus, mapping differs from "planning" in that it entails searching, finding, and folding complex and latent forces in the existing milieu rather than imposing a more or less idealized project from on high. Moreover, the synoptic imposition of the "plan" implies a consumption (or extinguishing) of contextual potential, wherein all that is available is subsumed into the making of the project. Mapping, by contrast, discloses, stages, and even adds potential for later acts and events to unfold. Whereas the plan leads to an end, the map provides a generative means, a suggestive vehicle that "points" but does not overly determine.

A particularly important aspect of mapping in this regard is the acknowledgment of the maker's own participation and engagement with the cartographic process. In studying the development of spatial perception in children, Piaget has written:

> Geometrical intuition is essentially active in character. It consists primarily of virtual actions, abridgements, or schemata of past, or anticipatory schemata of future actions, and if the action itself is inadequate, intuition breaks down.[28]

In describing the mental imaging of various relational processes, such as cutting, folding, rotating, and enlarging, Piaget writes:

> Spatial concepts can only effectively predict these results by becoming active themselves, by operating on physical objects, and not simply evoking memory images of them. To arrange objects mentally is not merely to imagine a series of things already set in order, nor even to imagine the action of arranging them. It means arranging the series just as positively and actively as if the action were physical.[29]

Actions precede conceptions; order is the outcome of the act of ordering. Thus, mapping precedes the map, to the degree that it cannot properly anticipate its final form. Cartographers Arthur Robinson and Barbara Bartz Petchenik claim that "in mapping, one objective is to discover (by seeing) meaningful physical and intellectual shape organizations in the milieu, structures that are likely to remain hidden until they have been mapped…plotting out or mapping is a method for searching for such meaningful designs."[30] In other words, there are some phenomena that can *only* achieve visibility through representation rather than through direct experience. Furthermore, mapping engenders new and meaningful relationships amongst otherwise disparate parts. The resultant relational structure is not something already "out there," but rather something constructed, bodied forth through the act of mapping. As the philosopher Brand Blanshard observes, "space is simply a relation of systematized outsideness, by itself neither sensible nor imaginable;" it is *created* in the process of mapping.[31]

### Mapping Operations

The operational structure of mapping might be schematized in three stages consisting of "fields," "extracts," and "plotting." The field is the continuous surface, the flat bed, the paper, or the table itself, schematically the analogical equivalent to the actual ground, albeit flat and scaled. The field is also the graphic *system* within which the extracts will later be organized. The system includes the frame, orientation, coordinates, scale, units of measure, and the graphic projection (oblique, zenithal, isometric, anamorphic, folded, etc.). The design and set up of the field is perhaps one of the most creative acts in mapping, for as a prior system of organization it will inevitably condition how and what observations are made and presented. Enlarging the frame, reducing the scale, shifting the projection, or combining one system with another are all actions that significantly affect what is seen and how these findings are organized. Obviously, a field that has multiple frameworks and entryways is likely to be more inclusive than a singular, closed system. Also, a field that breaks with convention is more likely to precipitate new findings than one that is more habitual and routine. And third, a field that is designed to be as nonhierarchical and inclusive as possible—more "neutral"—is likely to bring a greater range of conditions into play than a field of restrictive scope.

Extracts are the things that are then observed within a given milieu and drawn onto the graphic field. We call them extracts because they are always selected, isolated, and pulled out from their original seamlessness with other things; they are effectively "deterritorialized." They include objects but also other informational data: quantities, velocities, forces, and trajectories. Once detached they may be studied, manipulated, and networked with other figures in the field. As described above, different field systems will lead to different arrangements of the extracts, revealing alternative patterns and possibilities.

Plotting entails the "drawing out" of new and latent relationships that can be seen amongst the various extracts within the field. There are, of course, an infinite number of relationships that can be drawn depending upon one's criteria or agenda. Richard Long, for example, who has made an art form of walking, may plot a line upon a map to connect the highest to the lowest summit in sequential order, for example, revealing a latent structural line across a given terrain. Upon the same map, however, it is possible to plot a line that connects all south-facing aspects in sequential order from large to small areas, or to find a range of wet conditions that can then be set into relationship by plotting a comparative index of water characteristics. In addition to geometrical and spatial plotting, taxonomic, and genealogical procedures of relating, indexing, and naming can often be extremely productive in revealing latent structures. Such techniques may produce insights that are both utilitarian and metaphoric. In either case, plotting entails an active and creative interpretation of the map to reveal, construct, and engender latent sets of possibility. Plotting is *not* simply the indiscriminate listing and inventorying of conditions, as in a tracing, a table, or a chart, but rather a strategic and imaginative drawing out of relational structures. To plot is to track, to trace, to set-in-relation, to find, and to found. In this sense, plotting produces a "reterritorialization" of sites.

Thus we can identify three essential operations in mapping: first, the creation of a field, the setting of rules, and the establishment of a system; second, the extraction, isolation, or "deterritorialization" of parts and data; and third, the plotting, the drawing-out, the setting-up of relationships, or the "reterritorialization" of the parts. At each stage, choices and judgments are made, with the construing and constructing of the map alternating between processes of accumulation, disassembly, and reassembly. By virtue of the mapmaker's awareness of the innately rhetorical nature of the map's construction as well as of personal authorship and intent, these operations differ from the mute, empirical documentation of terrain so often assumed by cartographers.

We may now identify four thematic ways in which new practices of mapping are emerging in contemporary design and planning, each producing certain effects upon perceptions and practices of space. I label these techniques "drift," "layering," "gameboard," and "rhizome."

### Drift

The Situationists were a European group of artists and activists in the 1950s and 1960s. They aimed somehow to disrupt any form of what they took to be the dominant regime or capitalist power. Drawing from various Dadaist practices, and later influencing other conceptual art movements such as Fluxus and

Performance Art, the Situationists advocated a series of works that increased public consciousness and promoted direct action and systematic participation in everyday life. They were less interested in art objects and stylistic concerns than with the engaging life situations and social formations.[32]

Guy Debord, a key Situationist theorist, made a series of maps, or "psychogeographic guides," of Paris. These were made after Debord had walked aimlessly around the streets and alleys of the city. Recording these wanderings, Debord would cut up and reconfigure a standard Paris map as a series of turns and detours. The resultant map reflected subjective, street-level desires and perceptions rather than a synoptic totality of the city's fabric. [FIG. 4] More a form of cognitive mapping than mimetic description of the cityscape, Debord's maps located his own play and representation within the recessive nooks and crannies of everyday life. Such activity became known as the *dérive*, or the dreamlike drift through the city, mapping alternative itineraries and subverting dominant readings and authoritarian regimes.

What is interesting about the dérive is the way in which the contingent, the ephemeral, the vague, fugitive eventfulness of spatial experience becomes foregrounded in place of the dominant, ocular gaze. As de Certeau writes:

> The ordinary practitioners of the city live "down below," below the threshold at which visibility begins. They walk—an elementary form of this experience of the city: they are walkers. *Wandersmanner*, whose bodies follow the thicks and thins of an urban "text" they are able to write without being able to read it.[33]

The political and moral underpinnings of this view gesture toward the valorization of individual participation within a seemingly repressive apparatus of state or bureaucratic power. In describing the importance of such cognitive mapping in relation to urban space, literary critic Fredric Jameson writes:

> Disalienation in the traditional city…involves the practical reconquest of a sense of place and the construction or reconstruction of an articulated ensemble which can be retained in memory and which the individual subject can map and remap along the moments of mobile, alternative trajectories.[34]

If mapping had been traditionally assigned to the colonizing agency of survey and control, the Situationists were attempting to return the map to everyday life and to the unexplored, repressed topographies of the city. In this regard, Fluxus founder George Maciunas organized a series of "Free / Flux Tours" around Manhattan in 1976, which included an "Aleatoric Tour," a "Subterranean

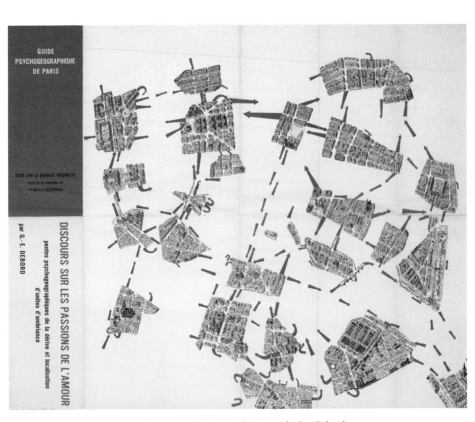

**FIG. 4** — *Discours sur les Passions de L'amour,* by Guy Debord, 1957

Courtesy RKD (Rijksbureau voor Kunsthistorische Documentatie / Netherlands Institute for Art History), The Hague

216     THE AGENCY OF MAPPING

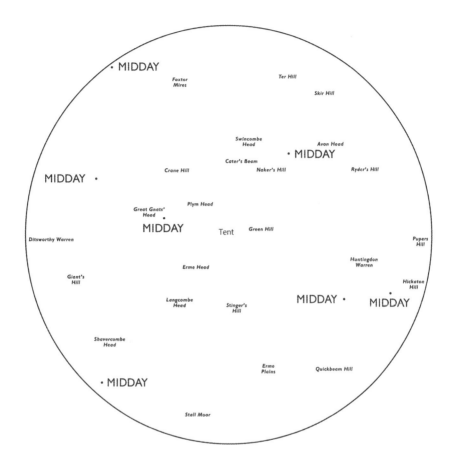

A SEVEN DAY CIRCLE OF GROUND

SEVEN DAYS WALKING WITHIN AN IMAGINARY CIRCLE 5½ MILES WIDE

DARTMOOR ENGLAND 1984

**FIG. 5 — *A Seven Day Circle of Ground,* by Richard Long, 1984**

Tour," an "Exotic Sites" itinerary, and an "All the Way Around and Back Again" trip. The art "object" here was the city itself, the map's role to facilitate alternative impressions of and interventions in the urban milieu. There are similar instances of such work—Daniel Buren's Seven Ballets in Manhattan, or Yoko Ono's urban "scores," for example—but the essential characteristic shared by all these projects is an ambition to contest and destabilize any fixed, dominant image of the city by incorporating the nomadic, transitive, and shifting character of urban experience into spatial representation.[35]

Although Long shares little of the political and strategic agenda of the Situationists, his systematic play with maps and landscapes is very much in the same vein as the dérive. Long works closely with maps in planning and then recording his walks.[36] [FIG. 5] Sometimes he will simply draw a straight line across a terrain and embark on the mission of walking it in actuality. The line may have a particular unit of measure (a mile, sixty minutes, or seven days) to which he will adhere, or it may assume a geometrical configuration such as a circle, a square, or a spiral, superimposed upon a variegated terrain. At other times, the line might follow a particular topographic condition, tracing the highest to the lowest point, following a lake edge, or bisecting human boundaries. He links together river beds, mountaintops, wind directions, left turns, dead ends or any number of other topographic itineraries in an effort both to experience the land through what is an "unusual" walk or journey and to trace upon it (albeit lightly, or even only in memory) an alternative gesture.

It is important to understand that the primacy of both Long's and the Situationists' use of maps belongs to their *performative* aspects, which is the way in which mapping directs and enacts a particular set of events; events that derive from a given milieu. But, of course, there are the recordings that come after the proceedings, and these are neither passive nor neutral in their effects either. In Long's *A Seven Day Circle of Ground—Seven Days Walking Within an Imaginary Circle 5 ½ Miles Wide* (1984), for example, the extremely selective choice of place names (spaced locationally) are brought into a unique associational relationship simply by the straightforward and laconic recording of the performance, recorded by the word "tent" and the array of seven "midday" points contained within a circular frame. The circle itself, like other lines and figures in Long's work, is not visible on the ground; it exercises its effect through its (arbitrary) delineation on the map. Like a frame or graticule, the circle is an imaginary figure that holds otherwise inchoate things in a field of relationship. This, in turn, points toward various alternative readings and actions that might then be exercised upon a particular landscape.

These various practices of "drift" use maps as instruments for establishing and aligning otherwise disparate, repressed, or unavailable topographies; they are "set ups" that both derive from and precipitate a series of interpretative and participatory acts. Their highly personal and constructive agency make them quite unlike the detached work of conventional mapmakers. They are openly cognitive, mental maps, rendering new images of space and relationship. Moreover, the drift permits a critique of contemporary circumstances, not from outside and above (as a master plan) but from participation *within* the very contours and fabric of political and institutional reality. The field, the extracts, and the plottings are played out not only upon the surface of the map but also upon the physical terrain itself, leaving an entire corpus of interventions and effects behind. Thus, drift discloses hidden topographies within ruling, dominant structures in an attempt to reterritorialize seemingly repressed or spent ground.[37]

### Layering

A relatively new development in the design of large-scale urban and landscape fabrics has been "layering." This involves the superimposition of various independent layers one upon the other to produce a heterogeneous and "thickened" surface. Tschumi and Koolhaas were amongst the first to develop layering strategies in design and planning in their respective proposals for the Parc de la Villette in Paris (1983).[38] Generally, these projects dismantle the programmatic and logistical aspects of the park into a series of layers, each of which is then considered independently from the other layers. [FIG. 6] There is an internal logic, content, and system of organization to each layer, depending on its function or intended purpose. The layers are not mappings of an existing site or context, but of the complexity of the intended program for the site. In both analyzing and synthesizing the enormously complex array of data and technical requirements surrounding the program for the new park, these mappings also array an enabling geometry. When these separate layers are overlaid together, a stratified amalgam of relationships amongst parts appears. The resulting structure is a complex fabric, without center, hierarchy, or single organizing principle. The composite field is instead one of multiple parts and elements, cohesive at one layer but disjunctive in relation to others. Such richness and complexity cannot be gained by the limited scope of the single master plan or the zoning plan, both of which group, prioritize, and isolate their component parts. Unlike the clear order of the compositional plan, the layering of independently structured conditions leads to a mosaic-like field of multiple orders, not unlike the combination of different colored paint delineations for the playing of games superimposed

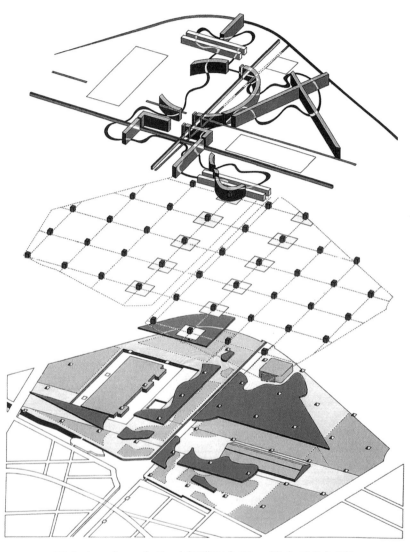

FIG. 6 — Layer diagram for Parc de la Villette, by Bernard Tschumi, Paris, 1982

© Bernard Tschumi

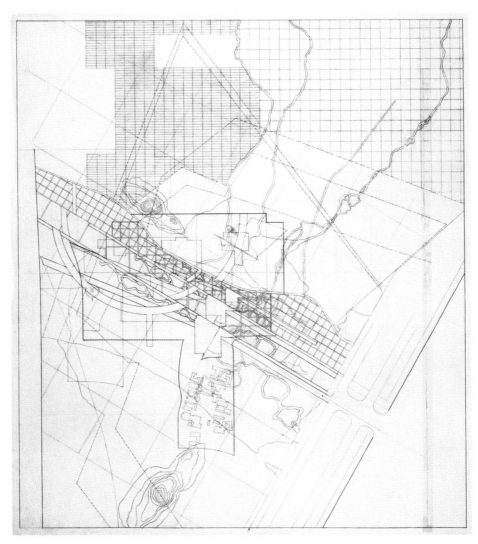

FIG. 7 — *University Art Museum, Long Beach: site plan*, by Peter Eisenman, 1986, pen, black ink and graphite on translucent paper, 105 × 101 cm

Courtesy Peter Eisenman fonds, Collection Centre Canadien d'Architecture/ Canadian Centre for Architecture, Montréal [DR1987:0859:302]

on a gymnasium floor. One layer becomes legible only through the lens of the game or rules of use that apply to it. But, of course, the possibility of "hybrid" games becomes possible here, too—not only may things occur simultaneously side by side, but they may also merge as a new event structure (as in many children's games where throwing, hitting, passing, and running are combined into a new system of play).

The same effects of multiplicity, montage, and hybridization are found in similar layering techniques used in some contemporary rock music genres. Several autonomous mixes may be simultaneously run together to develop a polyrhythmic and cross-cultural condition. The music escapes any single interpretation, as a range of cultural and genre sources come into radically new fields of combination. Caribbean rhythms are overlaid with country-western and techno-dance music, often producing a frenzied cacophony of associations and new possibilities. Significantly, this effect is performative, not representational; it engenders new possibilities out of old and does not simply array its extracts as a muted archaeology.

Another way one can characterize the multiplying functions of layering is in terms of indeterminacy. Unlike a traditional plan, the layered field remains open to any number of interpretations, uses, and transformations in time. Just as upon the gymnasium floor, almost anything can happen; the layered structure provides little restraint or imposition. Unlike traditional plans, maps share this open-ended characteristic. Maps are not prescriptive but infinitely promising. Thus, as constructed projects, mapping strategies propose organizational field-systems that both instigate and sustain a range of activities and interpretations in time.

Another architect who has worked with strata in the formation of projects is Peter Eisenman. In his proposal for a new Art Museum at the California State University, Long Beach, developed in collaboration with landscape architect Laurie Olin, a whole series of local maps are drawn upon and transformed into a new composite assembly.[39] [FIG. 7] In the resulting design, landscape and building are merged into one large fractured ground plane, evoking both the excavations typical of archaeological sites as well as the strata of historical and projective time that are often visible in maps but not on the ground.

In documenting the site, the designers found a number of significant historic moments: the Gold Rush settlement of California in 1849, the creation of the campus in 1949, and the anticipated "rediscovery" of the museum in 2049, two hundred years after its initial marking. Seven key "figures" emerge from this: "ranch," "campus," "fault lines," "land division grids," "river," "channel," and "coastline." An archival search through historical maps enables these primary figures to be identified and drawn out as discrete shapes. Each figure is considered a separate layer, and can be either shrunk, enlarged, or rotated according to the designer's syntactical code. "Scaling," for instance, is a significant step in Eisenman's work.[40] This involves the displacement, reduction/enlargement, and multiplication of prominent textual figures (forms derived from topographical maps) so as to remove any fixed or stable reading. The trace of the fault lines, for instance, is not intended to represent or even invoke a geological condition, but rather to produce a new, deterritorialized figure through extraction and scaling. In both defamiliarizing and systematizing the landscape through such a series of mapping operations, Eisenman eliminates the traditionally assumed causal relationship between form and intention while also avoiding the limitations of purely autonomous, self-referential procedures of composition. He argues that in manipulating mappings of the site and its larger milieu, the project can "evolve" a future form out of specific and unique local histories.

In tracing out several iterations of the scaled overlays, Eisenman searches for new analogic relationships; for example, amongst the "ranch," the "campus," and the "fault line." He finally settles on what he believes to be the most poignant composition of combination and relationship. As he says, "the overlapping registration of several maps...are combined in such a way that none of the notations takes precedence over any other, and so as to textualize coincidental overlaps by subjective interpretation."[41] The composite quarry reveals certain relationships that were never visible, as if the ground itself were now a constructed map, or text, albeit infinitely interpretable. Constructed fragments of information become "marks of intelligence, glimpses of the way the culture organized itself," writes Eisenman, continuing: "One recognizes in this project that architecture is about telling stories, and this stone text that is being written, this fiction, might tell a very different story about Long Beach than has ever been recorded before."[42] In other words, the way in which the narrative is assembled, the relating or registering of one thing to another, constructs a radically new fiction out of old facts.

Whereas Koolhaas and Tschumi's strategic layers are drawn from and anticipate future programs, Eisenman's layers are site and textual in origin. They are less intended to accommodate a variety of changing activities than they are to produce new formal arrangements. In both cases, however, the practice of superimposing otherwise independent layers of information is aimed toward the production of a constructed milieu that is heterogeneous and multiple in its effects. In other words, traditional notions of centering, bounding, imparting meaning, and asserting finish or completion are here banished in favor of more plural, open-ended "performances" of the project in time. In this context, mapping is no longer restricted to preliminary site surveys or data collection but rather extends generatively into the formation of the design itself, analytically transforming the originating referents into new figures and coordinates.

### Gameboard

A third thematic development of mapping in contemporary design practice, and one related to the notions of performance mentioned above, has been the projection of "gameboard" map structures. These are conceived as shared working surfaces upon which various competing constituencies are invited to meet to work out their differences. As a representation of contested territory, the map assumes an enabling or facilitating status for otherwise adversarial groups to try and find common ground while "playing out" various scenarios. Ideas of drift and layering are developed here as the former allows for personal engagement between mapper and constituents, while the latter permits the analytical separation of multiple issues and agendas.

Raoul Bunschoten is a London-based architect who has engaged with a number of complex and contentious urban regions in Europe, and has developed a number of innovative mapping techniques for working with such sites.[43] For Bunschoten, cities are dynamic and multiple; they comprise a vast range of "players" and "agents" whose "effects" flow through the system—continually reworking the variety of urban spaces in any given field. His approach is aimed first toward identifying and then redirecting the temporal play of these various forces. Consequently, urban design is practiced less as spatial composition and more as orchestrating the conditions around which processes in the city may be brought into relationship and "put into effect." Bunschoten calls this "stirring."

A key principle in Bunschoten's work is the idea of "proto-urban conditions." These are the range of potentially productive situations in a given milieu. But whereas the conventional planner's list of possibilities derive more from some overall governing authority, proto-urban conditions are "drawn out" from existing structures and potentials, and, thus, are already invested with local, emotive force. "Proto-urban conditions are like emotions in human beings," writes Bunschoten, "subliminal conditions that strongly affect physical states and behavior. These conditions form a metaphoric space in the city, a space that is in need of appropriate forms of expression."[44] In order to employ and operate these various conditions, they must first be made visible. Bunschoten accomplishes this by setting up a number of map frames, within which certain processes or conditions are graphically identified. He is careful to link the various cultural aspirations of each group to a physical space or

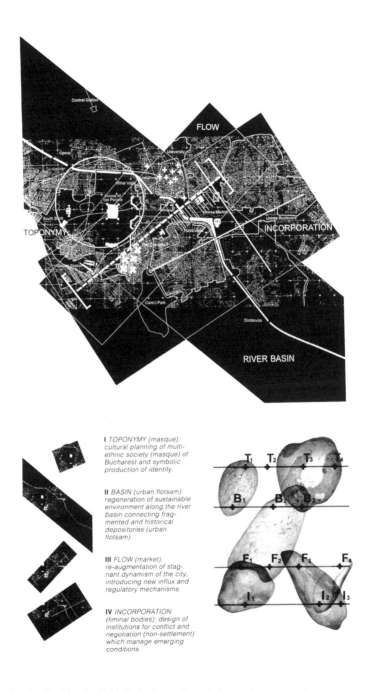

**I** *TOPONYMY (masque): cultural planning of multi-ethnic society (masque) of Bucharest and symbolic production of identity.*

**II** *BASIN (urban flotsam): regeneration of sustainable environment along the river basin connecting fragmented and historical depositories (urban flotsam).*

**III** *FLOW (market): re-augmentation of stagnant dynamism of the city, introducing new influx and regulatory mechanisms.*

**IV** *INCORPORATION (liminal bodies): design of institutions for conflict and negotiation (non-settlement) which manage emerging conditions.*

FIG. 8 — *Four Planning Fields for Bucharest, Romania*, by Raoul Bunschoten/CHORA, 1996

territory, distinguishing amongst "local authorities" who anchor conditions into specific institution or place, "actors" who participate with stated desires and "agents" who have the power and capacity to make things happen. Each frame permits the play of certain thematic conditions (preservation, ecology, economic development, or cultural memory, for instance), whilst the composite overlay of all of the frames more accurately conveys the plural and interacting nature of the urban theater.

In Bunschoten's proposal for Bucharest, Romania, the city is clearly mapped into the larger context of the Black Sea basin with respect to the various social, political, and physical changes that have affected the city's development. [FIG. 8] "In this way, the Black Sea is a large-scale object that relates to cultural identification," writes Bunschoten, "but, importantly, it is also virtually a 'dead sea,' a cause for international concern that engenders a kind of operational power and creates the possibility of linking global economy to urban planning propositions within the context of cultural and ecological planning."⁴⁵ In other words, through situating the city in its larger geographical and political-economic region—linking Bucharest with Russia, Central Asia, Western Europe, and the Middle East—Bunschoten develops a cartographic "stage" upon which various interests and agents can be identified and brought together for mutual benefit.

To clarify the process further, Bunschoten itemizes four fields: "toponymy" refers to the deployment of the colorful, cultural, and ethnic diversity that characterizes Bucharest; "basin" refers to the desire to regenerate the various ecologies and historical sites of the river basin; "flow" refers to both the regulatory mechanisms and the physical venues for market and economic exchange in the city; and "incorporation" refers to the specific design of new institutions and small-scale self-organizational forms that permit public negotiation. When the layers are superimposed, there are revealed a number of vertical correspondences, or "stepping stones," that are conceived by Bunschoten to permit decisions and actions on one plane to have effects upon the others. He writes:

> The overall aim of the project is to provide a cultural planning concept that acts as a model for interested parties in Bucharest. It is a rule-based plan for developing and advancing possible scenarios of urbanization, a type of game structure. The game suggests a mode of planning based on temporal structures that evolve independently and yet may intertwine with fruitful effects. This requires players, acting both in the city and at a distance. Both model and game are based on an understanding of as many different proto-urban conditions as possible.⁴⁶

The graphic map provides the gameboard for playing out a range of urban futures. Identified players and actors are brought together to try to work out complex urban issues within an open-ended generative structure. Diverse forms of negotiation are promoted as the survival strategies of each player unfold and become interwoven with others in reaction to changing interests and situations. Thus, the maps themselves are evolving structures, drawn and redrawn by the urban planner so as to permit the game to continue while also generating the necessary conditions for the emergence of an enterprising urbanity.

This tactical kind of mapping is not to be confused with the simple inventory and empirical presentation of resources. First, its data is not indiscriminately derived from the usual statistical and quantifiable sources and represented in the form of tracings; rather, data is knowingly selected and arrayed according to local knowledge of and direct participation within the field itself. These maps are informed by a kind of street-level ethnography that is often highly personalized and peculiar to places and individuals. In this way, the field-worker/mapper gains a remarkably detailed and socially colorful sense of local dynamics and desires. [47] Moreover, gameboard mapping is more purposefully active and rhetorical than the passivity and neutrality assumed by a GIS engineer. The gameboard mapper exercises shrewd judgment in designing the map structure, incorporating and engaging the various imaginations of all the relevant parties. In devising the map (constructing field frames, naming, indexing, graphic iconography, and so on), the designer "sets up" the gameboard in a very specific way, not in order to predetermine or prefigure the outcome but rather to instigate, support, and enable social forms of interaction, affiliation, and negotiation. And in this sense, once can see the similarity of Bunschoten's approach to the revitalization of urban fields to that of the Situationists. In neither case is it believed that a single authority, or a single directive, can ever really produce a rich form of urbanism. It is recognized instead that multiple *processes* of urbanization must be engaged and artfully, yet indeterminately, choreographed in relation to evolving and open-ended spatial formations.

### Rhizome

Open-ended and indeterminate characteristics can be likened to the process-form of the rhizome. "Unlike trees or their roots," write Deleuze and Guattari, "the rhizome connects any point to any other point...It has neither beginning nor end, but always a middle (*milieu*) from which it grows and overspills, [constituting] linear mulitiplicities."[48] In contrast to centric or treelike, hierarchical systems, the rhizome is acentric, nonhierarchical, and continually expanding across multiple terrains. "Rats are rhizomes. Burrows too, in all of their functions of shelter, supply, movement, evasion, and breakout."[49]

As mentioned earlier in this essay, Deleuze and Guattari draw an important distinction between "maps" and "tracings," describing the former as open, connectable, "experimentations with the real," and the latter as repetitive redundancies that "always come back to 'the same.'" Hence, tracings belong to hierarchical systems of order that ultimately limit any hope of innovation—"all of tree logic is a logic of tracing and reproduction."[50] By contrast, the infinitely open, rhizomatic nature of mapping affords many diverse entryways, exits, and "lines of flight," each of which allows for a plurality of readings, uses, and effects.

The significance of the rhizome for mapping is encapsulated in Deleuze and Guattari's belief that "the book" (and we might equally say the map, the city, or the landscape) "has no object. As an assemblage [it] has only itself, in connection with other assemblages and in relation to other bodies without organs." Thus, they conclude:

> We will never ask what a book means, as signifier or signified; we will not look
> for anything to understand in it. We will ask what it functions with, in connec-
> tion with what other things it does or does not transmit intensities, in which
> other multiplicities its own are inserted and metamorphosed, and with what
> other bodies it makes its own converge.[51]

This viewpoint privileges actions and effects over representation and meaning; the concern is for how things work and what they do. Moreover, there is an explicit interest here for new kinds of affiliate relationships and interconnections. The argument emphasizes probing practices of interpretation that extend previous products of culture (maps and landscapes, for instance) toward more diverse and interconnected fields of possibility, their "becoming" bodied forth through various acts of mapping and relating.

One especially important principle with regard to mapping as a rhizomatic (burrowing and extending) activity is what Deleuze and Guattari refer to as the "plane of consistency." While this assumes a rich and complex array of meanings for the authors, I shall summarize plane of consistency here as a surface that is both inclusive (even of things that may not normally fit or "belong" to any given scheme, including arbitrary "debris") and *structuring* of new and open-ended series of relationships. Obviously, if such a surface is both inclusive and structuring, the techniques and modes of representation must be both multiple and flexible. Several different graphic and notational systems have to come into play so that diverse and even "unmappable" aspects of a milieu are revealed.

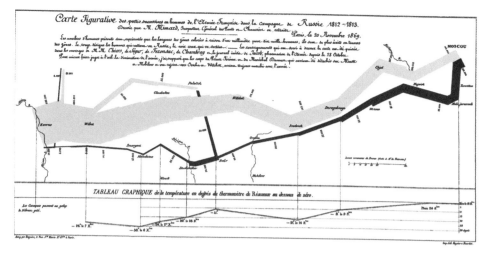

FIG. 9 — The width of the band is reduced as Napoleon's army shrinks while
moving across Russia. The lower black line indicates continued losses upon the retreat
back to Poland owing to a bitterly cold winter. *Carte figurative des pertes successives
en hommes de l'armée Francaise dans la campagne de Russie 1812-13*

From E. J. Marey, *La Méthode graphique,* by Charles Joseph Minard, 1885

All of this must be brought to bear on one plane, one fully inclusive, nondif-
ferentiated surface (as many architects are fond of saying, if one cannot see
it all right in front of one's eyes, as a visual synthesis, then one cannot properly formulate a proposition). The devised systems of collection and array cannot be closed; they must remain open, fostering endless chains of possibility
and insight. Rather than limiting reality, the rhizomatic map opens reality up
to a host of new and alternative possibilities. The process is not unlike working
with bits of arbitrarily found matter upon a dissecting table—a mode of work
integral to collage, and with all the similar experiences of discovery, revelation,
and pleasure. Unlike collage, however, which functions mostly connotatively
(by suggestion), mapping typically *systematizes* its material into more analytical and denotative schemas. Where mappings may become more inclusive and
suggestive, then, is less through collage, which works with fragments, and more
through a form of systematic montage, where multiple and independent layers
are incorporated as a synthetic composite.

A useful example of multiple and inclusive synthesis of complex information is the French engineer Charles Joseph Minard's narrative map of the fate
of Napoleon's army in Russia during the winter of 1812–13.[52] [FIG. 9] Moving
from the left on the Polish-Russian border, the thick band shows the size of the
army (422,000 men) in June 1812. Its width diminishes as the size of the army

is reduced through casualties. When the army reaches Moscow (to the east/right) in September there are only 100,000 men who must begin their retreat west through the winter months. The retreat line is in solid tone and can be read in conjunction with location and temperature readings. The army returned to Poland with a mere 10,000 survivors. Minard's graphic describes a complex and tragic human story in an enlightening and eloquent way. But more than telling a story, the map conditions how places on the land have come to exist in new relationships precisely through the vector of an event.

Minard's map very elegantly synthesizes a complex amalgam of facts and interrelationships (the size of the army, the locations and times of battle, vectors of movement, topography, place names, weather and temperature, and the passage of time). These events in time assume particular geometrical shape-forms, vectors, densities, and patterns of effect. It is no small feat to encode graphically complex and multivariate temporal events in direct relationship to geography, but even more impressive is how the mapping visually layers and embeds the network relationships amongst all of the variables. If the chart were to be animated in a computer program, its shape-forms would change significantly if any one of the many variables were altered. Thus the map depicts a *systemic* field of interrelationships; it is dynamic performance of interacting parts, mapping "shaping forces" as much as spatial terrain.[53] This is akin to what the Dutch urbanist Winy Maas calls a "datascape," which is a spatial visualization of otherwise invisible flows and forces that exercise enormous effects across terrain.[54]

At the same time, however, Minard's datascape is far from the rhizomatic plane of consistency outlined above because it is a closed system. It only depicts the facts that are relevant to its narrative theme, and it must therefore be read in a linear way. There is a clear intention of thematic communication in this map, together with a sequential, narrational reading, common to itinerary maps. The map offers clues for rhizomatic mappings because of its overlay and structural incorporation of different space-time systems of analysis, but at the same time it is not at all rhizomatic because of its focused content and single, linear reading. A more rhizomatic map would be much more multivariate and open. Indeed, such a map might not "represent" anyone thing at all; rather, it might simply array a complex combination of things that provides a framework for many different uses, readings, projections, and effects, rather like a thesaurus, without beginning, end, limit, or single meaning.

Of course, regular Ordnance Survey and United States Geological Survey (USGS) maps are "open" in the sense described above. They contain many different layers of information, with multiple entryways, diverse uses and applications, infinite routes and networks, and potentially endless surfaces of engagement. Long's drifts might be considered rhizomatic exploitations of these "neutral" planes. What these maps do not show, however, are time structures—local stories, histories, events, and issues on the one hand, and local processes such as capital flows or seasonal hydrological patterns on the other. In some of my own mappings of the larger, working American landscape, I have purposefully used and subverted the conventions of USGS maps, and incorporated into them other systems of notation that are intended to "open" and further "extend" the field.[55] In *Pivot Irrigators I*, for instance, the USGS map is cut as a circle without scale, place names, or geographical coordinates visible; the cropping and reframing effectively deterritorializes the map and its referent. [FIG. 10] Incorporated into this frame are other fragments of images such as underground aquifer maps—which are allied with the irrigation landscapes of the West—and infrared satellite photographs that capture the circular forms of different fields as temperature traces (the more recently irrigated fields coolest and therefore lightest). Satellites, too, use these temperature "fixes" to register their own location in space, and thus another circular construction is drawn to invoke both the planetary geometry of fixing location as well as the engineered geometry of the pivot irrigator field. Similarly, in *Windmill Topography*, the deterritorialized map is framed as an egg-like ellipse (the shape of both a turbine gear and a wind shadow) and combined with a topographical section that depicts the mountain range, air temperature, air-pressure, and wind velocity charts. Together, the composite parts of the map construct an ideographic, synesthetic image of the vast windmill territories east of Los Angeles while also arraying the various shaping forces and conditions that undergird the genesis of this still evolving landscape. There are similar mappings in this project: the poly-oriented and calendar maps of the Hopi, the multi-scaled maps of the Very Large Array radio telescope installation in New Mexico, or the various "field plots" of contour farming in the Midwest or dry strip farming across the northern plains. In each, the codes and conventions of the USGS maps (frame, scale, orientarion, color-separation, numerical coordinates, grid measures, and indexes) are co-opted, enhanced, and subverted. There is an attempt to represent and describe certain geographical conditions and processes of landscape formation whilst also to suggest new foundations for future work. In a sense, these mappings construct "planes of consistency" that present analytical information while also allowing for suggestive readings and projections. They "draw out" of common maps and landscapes certain figural and processual relationships that might occasion new landscapes. Admittedly, these mappings are not as open or rhizomatic as they might be, owing to their thematic focus, but their inclusion and incorporation (synthesis) of diverse kinds of information and possibility, as well as their utilization and

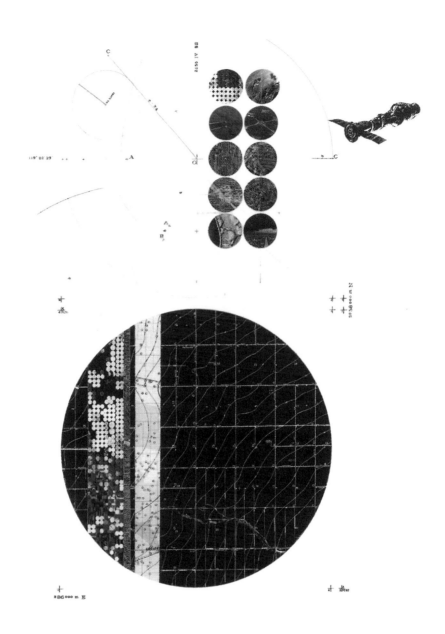

FIG. 10 — *Pivot Irrigators*, by James Corner, 1996

subversion of dominant conventions, illustrates two important ways in which mapping might move toward more polymorphous and creative ends. They are also suggestive of how temporal, systemic, performance networks can be rendered distinct from traditional cartographic concerns with static space.

Performance networks are multiple systems of interconnection, which liberate elements while also fostering nonhierarchical communication and relationship amongst otherwise disparate parts. "To network" means to work one's way into a field of opportunity, mapping the various players and sites whilst remaining an active a player in the field. Cities and landscapes are becoming increasingly dependent upon network spaces and processes; as urbanist Paul Virilio puts it:

> The essence of what we insist on calling urbanism is composed/decomposed by these transfer, transit, and transmission systems, these transport and transmigration networks whose immaterial configuration reiterates the cadastral organization and the building of monuments.[56]

In other words, the experience of spatial life today is as much immaterial as it is physical, as much bound into time and relational connections as it is to traditional notions of enclosure and "place." By extension, the principle of rhizomatic planes of consistency—together with the above-mentioned and closely allied themes of drift, dérive, layering, scaling, milieu, and gameboard structures—provides a useful model for mapping as a creative form of spatiotemporal practice in urban planning and design. In this way, we move away from urbanistic projects as authoritative master plans, concerned solely with the composition and order of static parts, toward practices of self-reflexive organization. Mapping as an extensive and rhizomatic set of field operations precipitates, unfolds, and supports hidden conditions, desires, and possibilities nested within a milieu. Here, the concern becomes less about the design of form and space *per se*, and more about engaging, accelerating, and networking interactions amongst forces in time. Instead of designing relatively closed systems of order, rhizomatic mappings provide an infinite series of connections, switches, relays, and circuits for activating matter and information. Hence *mapping*, as an open and inclusive process of disclosure and enablement, comes to replace the reduction of *planning*.

"All perceiving is also thinking, all reasoning is also intuition, all observation is also invention," wrote Rudolf Arnheim.[57] Moreover, these activities are not without effect; they have great force in shaping the world. It is in this intersubjective and active sense that mappings are not transparent, neutral, or passive devices of spatial measurement and description. They are instead extremely opaque, imaginative, operational instruments. Although drawn from measured observations in the world, mappings are neither depictions nor representations but mental constructs, *ideas* that enable and affect change. In describing and visualizing otherwise hidden facts, maps set the stage for future work. Mapping is always already a project in the making.

If maps are essentially subjective, interpretative, and fictional constructs of facts, constructs that influence decisions, actions, and cultural values generally, then why not embrace the profound efficacy of mapping in exploring and shaping new realities? Why not embrace the fact that the potentially infinite capacity of mapping to find and found new conditions might enable more socially engaging modes of exchange within larger *milieux*? The notion that mapping should be restricted to empirical data-sorting and array diminishes the profound social and orienting sway of the cartographic enterprise. And yet the power of "objective analysis" in building consensus and representing collective responsibility is not something to be abandoned for a free-form "subjectivity;" this would be both naive and ineffective. The power of maps resides in their facticity. The analytical measure of factual objectivity (and the credibility that it brings to collective discourse) is a characteristic of mapping that ought to be embraced, co-opted, and *used* as the means by which critical projects can be realized.[58] After all, it is the apparent rigor of objective analysis and logical argument that possesses the greatest efficacy in a pluralistic, democratic society. Analytical research through mapping enables the designer to *construct* an argument, to embed it within the dominant practices of a rational culture, and ultimately to turn those practices toward more productive and collective ends. In this sense, mapping is not the indiscriminate, blinkered accumulation and endless array of data, but rather an extremely shrewd and tactical enterprise, a practice of relational reasoning that intelligently unfolds new realities out of existing constraints, quantities, facts, and conditions.[59] The artistry lies in the use of the technique, in the way in which things are framed and set up. Through reformulating things differently, novel and inventive possibilities emerge. Thus, mapping innovates; it derives neither from logical possibility (projection) nor necessity (utility) but from logical force. The agency of mapping lies in its cunning exposure and engendering of new sets of possibility.[60]

This discussion of mapping also implies a parallel with contemporary practices in urban design and planning. The bureaucratic regime of city and landscape planning, with its traditional focus on objects and functions, has failed to embrace the full complexity and fluidity of urbanism, and of culture generally. This failing results in large measure from the inadequacy of techniques and instruments to imaginatively incorporate the rich interplay of processes that shape the world. In asserting authority and closure, current techniques have also failed to embrace the contingency, improvisation, error, and uncertainty that inevitably circulate in urbanism. Given the complex nature of late capitalist culture, together with the increased array of competing interest groups and forces, it is becoming ever more difficult for urban designers and planners to play a role in the development of cities and regions beyond scenographic or environmental amelioration. There is a kind of inertia and leveling of possibilities as it becomes politically impossible in a mass democracy to do anything out of the ordinary. While there is no shortage of theories and ideas for addressing this condition more critically, there has been very little development of new operational techniques for actualizing them. In other words, the difficulty today is less a crisis of *what* to do than of *how* to do anything at all. It is precisely at the strategic and rhetorical level of operation, then, that mappings hold great value.

Instances of drift, strata, gameboard, and rhizome represent only a handful of techniques that mapping practices might assume if they are to play more creative roles in design and planning, and in culture more generally. These techniques presupposed any number of variations and enhancements as issues of framing, scaling, orientation, projection, indexing, and coding become more flexible and open-ended, especially in the context of powerful new digital and animation media. As we are freed from the old limits of frame and boundary—preconditions for the survey and "colonization" of wilderness areas—the role of mapping will become less one of tracing and retracing already known worlds, and more one of inaugurating new worlds out of old. Instead of mapping as a means of appropriation, we might begin to see it as a means of emancipation and enablement, liberating phenomena and potential from the encasements of convention and habit. What remains unseen and unrealized across seemingly exhausted grounds becomes actualized anew with the liberating efficacy of creatively aligned cartographic procedures. Mapping may thus retain its original entrepreneurial and exploratory character, actualizing within its virtual spaces new territories and prospects out of pervasive yet dormant conditions.

NOTES

**1** On the coercive aspects of mapping, see Denis Wood, *The Power of Maps* (New York: Guilford Press, 1992); Mark Monmonier, *How to Lie with Maps* (Chicago: University of Chicago Press, 1991); and John Pickles, "Texts, Hermeneutics and Propaganda Maps," in *Writing Worlds*, eds. Trevor J. Barnes and James S. Duncan (London: Taylor & Francis, 1992), 193–230. On the technocratic and reductive force of mapping, see James C. Scott, *Seeing Like a State: Why Certain Schemes to Improve the Human Condition Have Failed* (New Haven, CT: Yale University Press, 1998), 1–83. On the more revelatory attributes of maps, see Stephen Hall, *Mapping the Next Millennium* (New York: Random House, 1992); and *Cartes et figures de La terre* (Paris: Centre Georges Pompidou, 1980), cat. no. 206.

**2** Gilles Deleuze and Felix Guattari, *A Thousand Plateaus: Capitalism and Schizophrenia*, trans. and foreword by Brian Massumi (Minneapolis: University of Minnesota Press, 1987), 12.

**3** See J.B. Harley, "Maps, Knowledge, and Power," in *The Iconography of Landscape*, eds. Denis Cosgrove and Stephen Daniels (Cambridge: Cambridge University Press, 1988), 277–312; J.B. Harley, "Deconstructing the Map," in *Writing Worlds*, 231–47; and Scott, *Seeing Like a State*, 38–76.

**4** See David Buisseret, *Envisioning the City: Six Studies in Urban Cartography* (Chicago: University of Chicago Press, 1998); and Ola Soderstrom, "Paper Cities: Visual Thinking in Urban Planning," *Ecumene* III/3 (1996), 249–81.

**5** See Anthony Giddens, "Living in a Post-Traditional Society," in *Reflexive Modernization: Politics, Tradition and Aesthetics in the Modern Social Order*, eds. Ulrich Beck, Anthony Giddens and Scott Lasch (Stanford, CA: Stanford University Press, 1994). Giddens likens "expert systems" to "abstract systems," wherein credibility and "truth" are accorded to certain abstract systems of representation precisely and only because they are constructed by experts. Similarly, much of mapping and planning goes unquestioned because of the apparent sophistication of their respective abstract systems, a sophistication that in itself is taken to be true and correct. See also Theodore M. Poner, *Trust in Numbers: The Pursuit of Objectivity in Science and Public Life* (Princeton, NJ: Princeton University Press, 1995). Porter demonstrates how "mechanical objectivity" shown in various abstract forms of representation is more effective in democratic bureaucracies than expert "judgment" or expert "opinion" because the latter are always still suspected of holding self-serving interests.

**6** See Scott, *Seeing Like a State*, 44–63; Peter Hall, *Cities of Tomorrow: An Intellectual History of Urban Planning and Design in the Twentieth Century* (Oxford: Blackwell Publishing, 1988); Soderstrom, "Paper Cities."

**7** See Soderstrom, "Paper Cities," 272–75. Soderstrom argues this point from the perspective of the institutionalized scientizing of planning methods that has occurred throughout the twentieth century, where objective, empirical procedures have become so ingrained in state bureaucracy and decision-making processes that fresh approaches toward urban issues remain intellectually repressed.

**8** See Rudolph Arnheim, *Visual Thinking* (Berkeley: University of California Press, 1970), 278. See also Arthur H. Robinson and Barbara Bartz Petchenik, *The Nature of Maps* (Chicago: University of Chicago Press, 1976), 1–22.

**9** See James Corner, "Eidetic Operations and New Landscapes," in *Recovering Landscape: Essays in Contemporary Landscape Architecture* (New York: Princeton Architectural Press, 1999) and "Representation and Landscape," *Word & Image* 8/3 (1992), 243–75.

10     See Roben Marks and R. Buckminster Fuller, *The Dymaxion World of Buckminster Fuller* (New York: Doubleday Anchor Books, 1973), 50–55, 148–63.

11     See Robert Storr, ed., *Mapping* (New York: Museum of Modern Art, 1994).

12     Ibid., 26.

13     There have been a few exceptions, but none has exerted a particularly strong influence upon design practice. Some of the more interesting explorations are summarized in Jane Harrison and David Turnbull, eds., *Games of Architecture: Architectural Design Profile* 66 (London: Academy Editions, 1996).

14     See Hall, *Cities of Tomorrow*; Soderstrom, "Paper Cities."

15     Harley, "Deconstructing the Map," 231.

16     Jorge Luis Borges, "Of Exactitude in Science" (1933), reprinted in *A Universal History of Infamy* (London: E. P. Dutton, 1975).

17     Jean Baudrillard, *Simulations* (New York: Semiotext(e), 1983), 2.

18     Ibid.

19     D. W. Winnicott, *Playing and Reality* (London: Routledge, 1971).

20     Jacob Bronowski, *Science and Human Values* (New York: Julian Messner, Inc, 1965).

21     Ernst Cassirer, *The Philosophy of Symbolic Forms*, vol. 2 (New Haven, CT: Yale University Press, 1955), 30; quoted in Robinson and Petchenik, *The Nature of Maps*, 7.

22     See Reyner Banham, *Los Angeles: The Architecture of Four Ecologies* (London: Penguin Books, 1973).

23     Rem Koolhaas and Bruce Mau, *S,M,L,XL* (New York: Monacelli Press, 1995), 1248.

24     David Harvey, *Justice, Nature, and the Geography of Difference* (Cambridge: Wiley-Blackwell, 1996), 419.

25     Ibid.

26     Ibid., 420.

27     Michel de Certeau, *The Practice of Everyday Life* (Berkeley: University of California Press, 1984), p. 94.

28     Jean Piaget and Bärbel Inhelder, *The Child's Conception of Space* (New York: Routledge, 1967), 452; quoted in Robinson and Petchenik, *The Nature of Maps*, 101.

29     Piaget and Inhelder, 454.

30     Robinson and Petchenik, *The Nature of Maps*, 74.

31     Brand Blanshard, *The Nature of Thought* (London: G. Allen & Unwin, 1948), 525; quoted in Robinson and Petchcnik, *The Nature of Maps*, 103.

32     See Ken Knabb, ed., *Situationist International Anthology* (Berkeley, CA: Bureau of Public Secrets, 1981); Cristel Hollevoet, Karen Jones and Tim Nye, eds., *The Power of the City; The City of Power* (New York: Whitney Museum of American Art, 1992).

33     De Certeau, *The Practice of Everyday Life*, p. 95; see also Cristel Hollevoet, "Wandering in the City," in Hollevoet et al, eds., *The Power of the City*, 25–55.

34     Fredric Jameson, *Postmodernism, or the Cultural Logic of Late Capitalism* (Durham, NC: Verso, 1991), 51.

35     See Hollevoet et al, eds., *The Power of the City*.

36     See Richard Long, *Richard Long* (Dusseldorf: Kunstsammlung Nordrhein-Westfalen, 1994); R. H. Fuchs, *Richard Long* (London: Thames & Hudson, 1986).

37     See de Certeau, *The Practice of Everyday Life*. This book is about how everyday "users" "operate," arguing for various modes of situated and tactical actions. Things such as "making do," "walking in the city," "reading as poaching," "diversionary practices," and "*détournement*" are cited as techniques by which dominant structures are resisted.

38     See Bernard Tschumi, *Cinegramme folie: Le Parc de La Villette* (Princeton, NJ: Princeton University Press, 1987); Bernard Tschumi, *Architecture and Disjunction* (Cambridge, MA: MIT Press, 1994), 171–259; Koolhaas, *S,M,L,XL*, 894–935.

39  See Jean-Francois Bedard, ed., *Cities of Artificial Excavation: The Work of Peter Eisenman, 1978–1988* (Montreal: Canadian Centre for Architecture, 1994), 130–85; Peter Eisenman, *Eisenman-amnesie: Architecture and Urbanism* (Tokyo: Architecture & Urbanism, 1988), 96–111.

40  See Jonathan Jova Marvel, ed., *Investigations in Architecture: Eisenman Studios at the GSD, 1983–1985* (Cambridge, MA: Harvard University Graduate School of Design, 1986).

41  Bedard, *Cities of Artificial Excavation*, 132.

42  Ibid.

43  See Raoul Bunschoten, *Urban Flotsam* (Rotterdam: CHORA Publishers, 1998); Raoul Bunschoten, "Proto-Urban Conditions and Urban Change," in Maggie Toy, ed., *Beyond the Revolution: The Architecture of Eastern Europe: Architectural Design Profile* 119 (London: Academy Editions, 1996), 17–21; Raoul Bunschoten, "Black Sea: Bucharest Stepping Stones," in Peter Davidson and Donald Bares, eds., *Architecture After Geometry: Architectural Design Profile 127* (London: Academy Editions, 1997), 82–91.

44  Bunschoten, "Proto-Urban Conditions," 17.

45  Bunschoten, "Black Sea," 82.

46  Ibid., 83.

47  See de Certeau, "Walking in the City," and "Spatial Stories," in *The Practice of Everyday Life*, 91–130; Scott, "Thin Simplifications and Practical Knowledge: Metis," in *Seeing Like a State*, 309–41.

48  Deleuze, *A Thousand Plateaus*, 6.

49  Ibid.

50  Ibid., 12.

51  Ibid., 4.

52  See Charles Joseph Minard, *Tableaux graphiques et cartes figuratives de M. Minard, 1845–1869*, Portfolio (Paris, 1869); E. J. Marey, *La methode graphique* (Paris: G. Masson, 1885); Arthur H. Robinson, "The Thematic Maps of Charles Joseph Minard," *Imago Mundi*, 21 (1967), 95–108; Tufte, *The Visual Display of Quantitative Information* (Cheshire, CT: Graphics Press, 1992), 40–41, 176–77.

53  See Greg Lynn, ed., *Folding in Architecture: Architectural Design Profile 102* (London: Academy Editions, 1983); Sanford Kwinter, "The Reinvention of Geometry," *Assemblage* 18 (1993), 83–85; Davidson and Bates, *Architecture After Geometry*.

54  See Winy Maas and Jacob van Rijs, *FARMAX: Excursions on Density* (Rotterdam: 010 Publishers, 1998); "Maas, van Rijs, de Vries, 1991–1997," *El Croquis* 86 (1998).

55  See James Corner and Alex MacLean, *Taking Measures Across the American Landscape* (New Haven, CT: Yale University Press, 1996).

56  Paul Virilio, *The Art of the Motor*, trans. Julie Rose (Minneapolis: University of Minnesota, 1995), 139.

57  Rudolf Arnheim, *Art and Visual Perception* (Berkeley: University of California Press, 1964), viii.

58  This "extension" of pervasive conditions toward new, more critical ends underlies in part some of the arguments made in Corner and MacLean, *Taking Measures*. Here, there is an attempt to view the mostly technocratic, utilitarian approaches that are assumed in shaping the larger American landscape as things that are potentially positive. Measure, in both its numerical and instrumental sense, is less criticized or replaced by some other concept than it is expanded and enriched. In design and planning terms, the suggestion here is to see logistical, technical, economic, and environmental constraints not as limits but as vehicles of creativity and efficacy. See also Stan Allen, "Artificial Ecologies," *El Croquis*, 86 (1998), 26–33 and note 5.

59  Much of the profession of architecture and planning today is concerned more and more with complex tasks of management and organization, especially of information. The forms of creativity suggested in this essay suggest a shift from a traditional emphasis in design upon forms of space to new, emergent emphasis upon creative forms of practice. The difficulty today lies less at the level of formal innovation and design talent but more at the level of operational innovation: how to set new and exciting things in motion given the general inertia that currently surrounds planning and design projects. See Beck, *Reflexive Modernization*; Allen, "Artificial Ecologies"; and Koolhaas, "Whatever Happened to Urbanism?" in *S,M,L,XL*, 961–71, and Corner "Eidetic Operations and New Landscapes."

60  See Jeffrey Kipnis, "Towards a New Architecture," in *Folding in Architecture,* 46–54; see also James Corner, "Landscape and Ecology as Agents of Creativity" in *Ecological Design and Planning,* eds. George F. Thompson and Frederick R. Steiner (New York: John Wiley, 1997), 80–108.

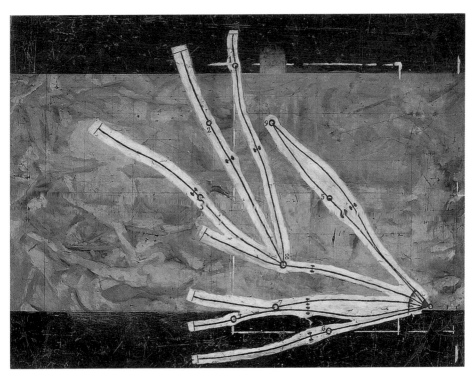

FIG. 1 — *Reseaux des stoppages (Network of Stoppages),* by Marcel Duchamp,
1914, Oil and pencil on canvas, 148.9 × 197.7 cm

# EIDETIC OPERATIONS AND
# NEW LANDSCAPES

Landscape and image are inseparable. Without image there is no such thing as landscape, only unmediated *environment*.[1] This distinction can be traced back to the Old English term *landskip*, which at first referred not to land but to a picture of it, as in the later, selectively framed representations of seventeenth-century Dutch *landschap* paintings. Soon after the appearance of this genre of painting, the scenic concept was applied to the land itself in the form of rural vistas, designed estates, and ornamental garden art. Indeed, the development of landscape architecture as a modern profession derives, in large measure, from an impulse to reshape areas of land according to *prior* imaging. Not only is a collective recognition of land as landscape made possible through exposure to prior images (a phenomenon central to both spectacle and tourist landscapes) but also the ability to intentionally construe and construct designed landscapes is enabled through various forms and activities of imaging.

Whereas imaging is central to forging landscape, the tendency of many contemporary landscape architects to assume that this prioritizes visual and formal qualities alone significantly limits the full eidetic scope of landscape creativity. I use the term *eidetic*—meaning "of a mental image"—to refer to a mental conception that may be picturable but may equally be acoustic, tactile, cognitive, or intuitive. Thus, unlike the purely retinal impression of pictures, eidetic images contain a broad range of ideas that invigorate human creativity. Consequently, how one "images" the world literally conditions how reality is both conceptualized and shaped. [FIG. 1] That representation exercises such agency and effect is

*Originally published in: James Corner, ed.* Recovering Landscape: Essays in Contemporary Landscape *(New York: Princeton Architectural Press, 1999): 153–69. Reproduced with permission.*

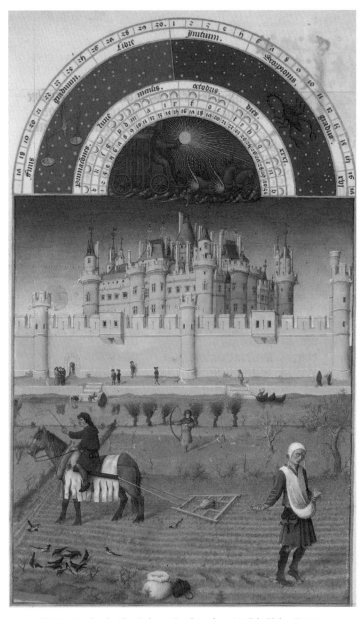

FIG. 2 — *October*, by The Limbourg Brothers, from *Les Très Riches Heures du Duc de Berry*, 1413–1416

Courtesy Musée Condé, Chantilly, France

precisely why images in design cannot properly be considered as mute or neutral depictions of existing and projected conditions of secondary significance to their object; on the contrary, eidetic images are much more active than this, prompting or participating in the shaping of new realities. Far from the assumed inertia of passive and objective representations, the paper surfaces and computer screens of design imaging are highly efficacious operational fields on which the theories and practices of landscape are produced.[2] Any recovery of landscape in contemporary culture is ultimately dependent on the development of new images and techniques of conceptualization.

However, there is another side of landscape that has significantly less to do with pictures, or even with any obvious *a priori* imaging. Both J.B. Jackson and John Stilgoe have documented the complexity of the term landscape and draw distinctions between art historical, representational versions and vernacular, geographical definitions.[3] They describe the Old German *landschaft* as actually preceding landskip and as referring not to scenery but to the environment of a working community, a setting comprising dwellings, pastures, meadows, and fields, and surrounded by unimproved forest or meadow. Moreover, as Stilgoe writes, "Like the Anglo-Saxon tithing and the Old French *vill*, the word meant more than an organization of space; it connoted too the inhabitants of the place and their obligations to one another and to the land."[4]

In other words, the meaning of landschaft composes a deep and intimate mode of relationship not only among buildings and fields but also among patterns of occupation, activity, and space, each often bound into calendrical time. [FIG. 2] In this sense, landschaft is related to the German *gemeinschaft*, which refers to those forms and ideas that structure society in general. Whereas the scenery of landschaft may be picturable (that is, to the degree that scenery is a valid or knowable concept in the deeply habituated landschaft), its deeper, existential aspects circle more socially cognitive, eidetic processes. Spatial, material, and ambient characteristics are still here, but their essence is not necessarily that of Cartesian objecthood; they are present in sometimes foggy and multiplicitous ways, structured but not immediately visible—structured, in fact, more through use and habit in time than through any prior schematization.[5]

Distinctions between the designed landscape and the more evolved, working landschaft are further elaborated in cultural geography. As Raymond Williams remarks, "A working country is hardly ever a landscape."[6] Here, Williams invokes the necessary detachment, contrivance, and focused attention necessary for the formation of landscape. Similarly, in distinguishing between "outsiders" and "insiders," Denis Cosgrove describes how:

The visible forms [of the land] and their harmonious integration to the eye, may indeed be a constituent part of people's relationship with the surroundings of their daily lives, but such considerations are subservient to other aspects of a working life with family and community. The composition of their landscape is much more integrated and inclusive with the diurnal course of life's events — with birth, death, festival, tragedy — all the occurrences that lock together human time and place. For the insider there is no clear separation of self from scene, subject from object.[7]

To the degree that everyday inhabitants experience landscape, they do so in a general state of distraction, and more through habit and use than through vision alone. Any eidetic image of place is bound into a greater phenomenal range of significance than vision or contemplation affords. By contrast, as Michel Foucault and others have argued over the past twenty-five years, visual regimes — such as perspective and aerial views — are extremely effective instruments of power, enabling mass surveillance, projection, and camouflage. Synoptic, radiating vision extends a gaze that makes the viewer the master of all prospects, a scopic regime of control, authority, distance, and cool instrumentality.[8] Much of the so-called postmodern critique is targeted at exposing the authoritarian and alienating characteristics of synoptic objectification, including master planning (aerial regimes) and scenography (oblique and perspectival regimes). Extended to landscape, this critique suggests that a too-narrow concern for landscape as object (whether as formal composition or as quantifiable resource) overlooks the ideological, estranging, and aestheticizing effects of detaching the subject from the complex realities of participating in the world. Here, I want to echo Heidegger's "loss of nearness" as well as modern culture's withdrawal into privacy, as foreseen by Nietzsche and Marx. Now, these remarks paint a perhaps too skeptical perspective that may be difficult for many to share. The scenic overlook, for example, is an apparently benign situation that presents a delightful view and transports one back into collective memory. That the scene itself displaces viewers, keeps them at a safe and uninvolved distance, and thus presents the landscape as little more than an aesthetic object of attention, escapes the attention of the gazing subject, as does the fact that the scenic moment literally transports viewers back in time, effectively decontextualizing them from the very real ills of the present.

Furthermore, the scenic landscape tends not only to displace the viewing subject in both space and time but also to displace the objects that it contains. As the geographer Jonathan Smith explains, the "durability" and autonomy of landscape causes its physical appearance to move further and further away from the agency and scene of its creation, and with this displacement "it loses the taint of intention and assumes the purity of nature."[9] In other words, because of the passage of time, landscape decontextualizes its artifactuality and takes on the appearance of something natural. Such enduring innocence may well herald great emancipating potential (as the landscape itself escapes the authority and control of its makers), but it also harbors a deceit that can be covertly appropriated by those who exercise power in society.

The preceding paragraphs simplify the case greatly, but it is not my purpose here to outline a further critique of scenography. I am more interested in drawing a distinction between landskip (landscape as contrivance, primarily visual and sometimes also iconic or significant) and landschaft (landscape as an occupied milieu, the effects and significance of which accrue through tactility, use, and engagement over time). Both terms connote images, but the latter comprises a fuller, more synesthetic, and less overtly picturable range than the former. Furthermore, the working landscape, forged collectively and according to more utilitarian demands than anything artistic or formal, has been more the traditional domain of descriptive analysis by historians and geographers than of speculation by landscape architects.[10]

In the working landschaft, performance and event assumes precedence over appearance and sign. The emphasis here shifts from object appearances to processes of formation, dynamics of occupancy, and the poetics of becoming. While these processes may be imaged, they are not necessarily susceptible to picturing. As with reading a book or listening to music, the shaping of images occurs mentally. Thus, if the role of the landscape architect is less to picture or represent these activities than it is to facilitate, instigate, and diversify their effects in time, then the development of more performative forms of imaging is fundamental to this task (see "Agency of Mapping," FIG. 9, 229). A move away from ameliorative and scenographic designs toward more comprehensive, experiential design borne from process and use necessitates a parallel shift from appearances and meanings to more prosaic concerns for how things work, what they do, how they interact, and what agency or effects they might exercise over time. A return to complex and instrumental landscape issues involves more organizational and strategic skills than those of formal composition per se, more programmatic and metrical practices than solely representational.[11] Under an operational rubric, issues such as program, event space, utility, economy, logistics, production, constraints, and desires become foregrounded, each turned through design toward newly productive and significant ends. This turning, as in *rhetorical turn* or the more interventionist *détournement*, is allied with the French term *dispositif*. This refers to the tactical but subtle and tempered disposition of parts (as in arrangement, complexion, management, and array). In setting up a well-disposed field, the designer stages the conditions necessary to precipitate a maximum range of opportunities in time, turning negatives and limits into positives and potentials.[12]

Although I am moving perhaps too quickly through this complex and important subject, I want to bring the question of image back into play, particularly the efficacy of imaging, or its agency in turning, forming, and enabling. While theorists and historians focus on the object or the idea, designers focus on the actual activities of creativity, with the "doing" and with the often bewildering effects of bodying forth things neither foreseen nor predetermined. The question, then, concerns not so much the kinds of images designers should work with but rather what kinds of imaging activities should be developed and advanced. I am referring here to the actual durational experience of mapping, drawing, modeling, and making as a generative sequence in creative thinking (see "Drawing and Making," FIG. 12, 186). This is where a clear distinction between imaging and picturing needs to be made.

W. J. T. Mitchell characterizes the distinction between picture and image as:

> The difference between a constructed concrete object (frame, support, materials, pigments, facture) and the virtual, phenomenal appearance that it provides for the beholder; the difference between a deliberate act of representation ("to *picture* or depict") and a less voluntary, perhaps even passive or automatic act ("to *image* or imagine"); the difference between a specific kind of visual representation (the "pictorial" image) and the whole realm of iconicity (verbal, acoustic, mental images).[13]

Mitchell describes this latter category as eidetic images, or:

> *Sensible forms*…which (according to Aristotle) emanate from objects and imprint themselves on the wax-like receptacles of our senses like a signet ring; the *fantasmata*, which are revived versions of those impressions called up by the imagination in the absence of the objects that originally stimulated them… those "appearances" which (in common parlance) intrude between ourselves and reality.[14]

Thus, Mitchell identifies five families of image: the graphic (as in the picture), the optical (as in the mirror), the perceptual (as in cognitive sense), the mental (as in dreams, memories, and ideas), and the verbal (as in description and metaphor). Of course, each is never independent of the other categories; the mixing of synesthetic senses and impressions is inevitable. Consequently, not all images are picturable, as in those mental ideas one "sees" but that bear no likeness to natural perception. One might speak here of an aesthetics of invisibility, a perception of essences. Speech, verbal description, gestures, and other rhetorical figures conjure up such otherwise invisible images, allowing one to see an idea. The ancient Greeks recognized the image aspect of ideas, as in the term *eidos*, which conjoins "idea" with "something seen." This is why imaging, understood as idea formation, is integral to the conception and practice of landscape. In landskip, the making of a picture participates in and makes what is to be pictured, whereas in landschaft the formation of synesthetic, cognitive images forges a collective sense of place and relationship evolved through work.

This latter phenomenon can be likened to a kind of mental map, or diagram, a spatio-organizational image that is not necessarily picturable but is nonetheless laconic and communicable. As with all maps, such an image produces an appearance that is otherwise not visible, even though it rings true and eventually naturalizes into accepted convention. Space by itself is neither sensible nor imaginable, but is instead created in the act of imaging. Such eidetic constructs effectively bind individuals to a collective and orient them within a larger milieu. Thus, as highly situated and subjectively constituted schemata, eidetic mappings lie at the core of shaping an invisible landscape, one that is more an unfolding spatiality than surface appearance, more poetic property than the delineation of immediate real estate. [**FIGS. 3 + 4**]

Now, what does all this mean for landscape architectural practice? First, it points to both the difficulties and potentials that underlie representational technique in design, especially those conventions—such as plan, perspective, and rendering—that have become so institutionalized and taken for granted that we fail to appreciate their force and efficacy in shaping things. Second, it points to the limits exercised by the pictorial impulse over other aspects of knowing and belonging, highlighting the difficulty of representing other dimensions of being. And third, it suggests a need to revise, enhance, and invent forms of representational technique that might engender more engaging landscapes than the still-life vignettes of many contemporary landscapes. Those techniques that might prove most useful in this regard may be called *eidetic operations*—specific ideational techniques for construing (imagining) and constructing (projecting) new landscapes. These are partly akin, though not identical, to what Marco Frascari calls "technographies," composite images of three essential relationships defined as:

  1) between a real architectural artifact and a reflected or projected image of it;
  2) between a real artifact and the instrumental image in the mind of someone

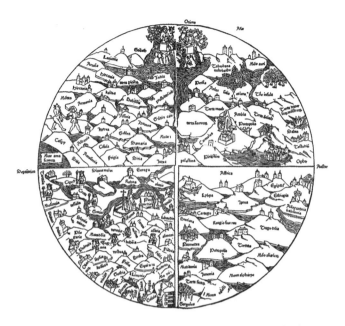

FIG. 3 — Mappemonde **Rudimentum Nivitiorum, 1473,** from *L'Atlas du Vicomte de Santarem*

Courtesy Bibliothèque Nationale, Paris

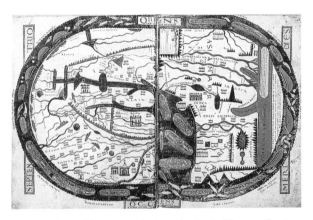

FIG. 4 — This ovoid mappemonde shows the classical three continents (Africa, Asia, and Europe) and depicts the still mysterious Australia as a crescent separated by a sea. In this figure is the caption: "Next to the three parts of the world, there is a fourth beyond the Ocean, toward the south and unknown to us because the sun is too strong. In these areas live the Antipods." *Beatus of Liebana from Saint-Sever,* c. eleventh century, from *Le commentaire sur l'Apocalypse,* 1823

Courtesy Bibliothèque Nationale, Paris

involved in a building trade related with its construction; and 3) between the instrumental image devised by the architect and the symbolic image that rests in the collective memory of a culture.[15]

Thus, explains Frascari, "technographies are enigmas that can only be solved in construction…images that are played in the world of construction but not necessarily explained."[16]

Designers need to more fully equip their arsenal of eidetic operations, in both the imaginative and efficacious senses of technographies. In reading analyses of image construction—whether E. H. Gombrich, Nelson Goodman, Rudolf Arnheim, Jean Piaget, Ernst Cassirer, Norman Bryson, or Mitchell, for instance—or in simply looking at the great works of art over the centuries—whether maps, paintings, collage, performance arts, or cinematic and digital media—I am struck by the range of types and forms of representation in comparison to the relatively small number of techniques used in the landscape, architectural, and planning arts. Imaging has a metaphoric agency in that the (mostly arbitrary) bringing together of two or more elements fosters a host of associative possibilities. When Picasso joins a bicycle handlebar to a down-turned seat, the new union is suggestive not only of a bull's head but also of a minotaur (as in part animal, part machine), an image that may be actualized by placing and using the assembly on a real bicycle. Similarly, such extension of association is achieved through the ideogram, or the pairing of two elements to produce a new image, a conception that is otherwise not picturable. This is exemplified, for instance, in Duchamp's *Genre Allegory (George Washington)* (1943), where iodine-stained gauze bandage, speckled with military stars, constitutes the profile silhouette of Washington and invokes a tattered American flag, if not the rupture of the American sense of nationhood (see "Drawing and Making," FIG. 11, 181). Such eidetic images are fundamental stimuli to creativity and invention; they do not represent the reality of an idea but rather inaugurate its possibility. By contrast, images in conventional design practice tend more toward the wholly technological, the strictly denotative, the explicit, and the immediately intelligible. I am more than well aware of the increasing preponderance of unintelligible, hermetic abstractions on the academic gallery and magazine circuits; however, a range of imaginative and demonstrative eidetic instruments greater than that the conventional practitioner currently employs must be developed if landscape and urbanism are to be recovered as significant contemporary practices. If landscape architects construct ideas, then the role of imaging in idea formation and projection needs to be better articulated than simply by opposing "artistic" renderings to "technical" working documents.

In other words, perhaps a key to understanding eidetic imaging in design is found in a kind of thinking that is neither instrumental nor representational but simultaneously both.

It should be emphasized that such innovations do not necessarily have to be radical and completely new; they may derive equally from a subtle realignment of the codes and conventions of some convention or technique. In an essay on architectural drawing, David Leatherbarrow has argued that the primary mode of eidetic imaging in building belongs to the orthographic views of plan and section: "The plan view presents a simultaneity that prosaic seeing never enjoys; the section offers a penetration that is strikingly detective. Each translates depth by concentrating the temporality of its eventual unfolding."[17] The fact that orthography enables architectural insight and ideation in such fundamental and yet inexhaustible ways makes it perhaps the most powerful tool of eidetic imaging for spatial design. In recent years, the superimposition of multiple and sometimes incongruent layers in plan and section has led to the generation of new possibilities. Rem Koolhaas, for instance, effectively altered traditional large-scale planning and diagramming from simply composing form and organizing program to completely *reformulating* form and program into freshly hybrid conditions. The dismantling and isolation of layers and elements in plan not only proposes a productive working method, akin to montage, but also focuses attention on the logic of *making* the landscape rather than on its appearance per se. Bernard Tschumi's work with notation and combinatory indexes further exemplifies the reworking of certain orthographic and choreographic conventions.

In a similar vein, contemporary urban designers (such as Koolhaas, MVRDV, and a-topos) have developed a series of techniques they call "datascapes." These are revisions of conventional analytical and quantitative maps and charts that both reveal and construct the shape-forms of forces and processes operating across a given site.[18] [FIG. 5] Not only are these imagings constructive and suggestive of new spatial formations but also they are so "objectively" constructed — derived from numbers, quantities, facts, and pure data — that they have great persuasive force in the hugely bureaucratic decision-making and management aspects of contemporary city design. Where they differ from the quantitative maps of conventional planning is in their imaging of data in knowingly rhetorical and generatively instrumental ways. They are designed not only to reveal the spatial effects of shaping forces (such as regulatory, zoning, legal, economic, and logistical rules and conditions) but also to construct an eidetic argument in space-time geometry. The artistry lies in the *use* of the technique, how things are framed and set up. There is no assumption of truth or positivist methodology; instead, the datascape planner reveals new possibilities latent in a given field

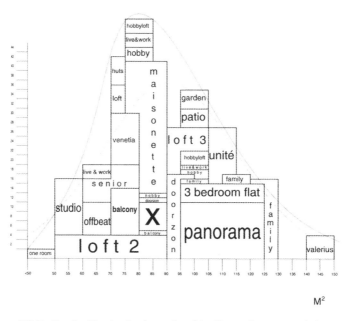

FIG. 5 — *Housing Silo*, showing the number of dwellings to the area occupied, by MVRDV, Amsterdam, 1996

simply by framing the issues differently. Unlike the assumed and passive neutrality of traditional data maps, datascapes reformulate given conditions in such a way as to produce novel and inventive solutions.

The revision of such fundamental imaging techniques as mapping, planning, diagramming, and sectioning effectively liberates the designer/planner from representation. In concentrating on how things work, how they go together, and how the project makes sense accords priority to the working of inhabited ground as opposed to the formalization of scenic landscapes[19]. Rather than a series of drawings that show what a finished project looks like or how all the different parts fit together, I am arguing for the thinking through a program — not a description — that outlines the performative dimensions of a project's unfolding. [FIGS. 6 + 7]

Hybridized and composite diagram techniques will allow even further advances in landscape formation because of their inclusive and instrumental capacity. Techniques such as layering and separation, for example, enable a multiplicity of issues to be included and incorporated into the development of a project. Composite montage is essentially an affiliative and productive technique, aimed not toward limitation and control but toward emancipation,

FIG. 6 — *Ideogram, Greenport Harborfront*, by James Corner, New York, 1996

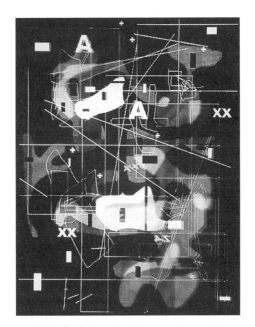

FIG. 7 — *Älsvjö Gameboard*, by James Corner, 1999

heterogeneity, and open-ended relations among parts. In particular, analytic and systematic operations can precipitate revelatory and rich effects. This point is as true for the dense sketches and notations inscribed and overlaid in the technical drawings of Carlo Scarpa, for instance, where multiple views and scales are developed as a sort of speculative yet systematic unfolding, as it is for the more strategic layer-diagrams by architects such as Koolhaas, Tschumi, and Eisenman. Whereas both these imaging types differ significantly in their formation and function, they share the same character of incorporating multiple levels of information; they avoid instantaneous disclosure and reduction. Moreover, composite techniques focus on the instrumental function of drawing with regard to production; they are efficacious rather than representational. In other words, through utilizing a variety of analytic and analogous imaging techniques, otherwise disparate parts can be brought into productive relationship, less as parts of a visual composition and more as *means* or agents.

Other composite imaging operations include ideograms, imagetexts, scorings, pictographs, indexes, samples, gameboards, cognitive tracings, and scalings. Imagetexts, in particular, are conspicuously absent and underdeveloped in the design arts. These are synthetic and dialectical composites of words and pictures that together contain and produce an array of striking and otherwise unpicturable images.[20] As cultural critic Mark Taylor describes, "The audio-visual trace of the word involves an inescapable materiality that can be thought only if it is figured."[21] Whereas most architectural and planning images combine words on drawings (as labels, keys, names, etc.), the sheer connotative power of this combination is rarely developed beyond what is, again, a merely descriptive function. And yet imagetexts by artists as divergent as William Blake, Richard Long, and Barbara Kruger, and by architects as divergent as Daniel Libeskind, Raoul Bunschoten, and Arakawa and Madeline Gins push the rhetorical and transfigurative force of synesthetic imaging in extremely suggestive ways.

The landscape imagination is a power of consciousness that transcends visualization. To continue to project landscapes as formal and pictorial objects is to reduce significantly the full scope of the landscape idea. If ideas are images projected into the political and cultural imagination in ways that guide societies as they try to manage change, then their absence can only precipitate social regression into memory (nostalgia), on the one hand, or complete deference to technology (rational expediency), on the other. How one generates and effectuates ideas is bound into a cunning fluency with imaging. Similarly, the future of landscape as a culturally significant practice is dependent on the capacity of its inventors to image the world in new ways and to body forth those images in richly phenomenal and efficacious terms.

NOTES

**1** To the degree that the term *environment* has assumed many meanings and values (as evidenced in the number and divergence of environmental philosophies), it is true to say that environment, too, in its various mediated forms, has become just as much a subjectively constituted and sensible idea *as landscape*. And, of course, here too lie the inevitable ideological strands inherent to any landscape formation. See Augustin Berque, "Beyond the Modern Landscape," *A.A. Files* 25 (Summer 1993), 33–37. See also Alain Roger, *Court traité du paysage* (Paris: Gallimard, 1997).

**2** I use the term *theories* here in the ancient Greek sense of *theoria*, meaning "to see."

**3** John Brinckerhoff Jackson, *Discovering the Vernacular Landscape* (New Haven, CT: Yale University Press, 1984), 1–8; John R. Stilgoe, *Common Landscape of America, 1580 to 1845* (New Haven, CT: Yale University Press, 1982), 12–29.

**4** Stilgoe, *Common Landscape of America*, 12.

**5** An important reference here is Maurice Merleau-Ponty, *Phenomenology of Perception*, trans. Colin Smith (London: Routledge and Kegan Paul, 1962), especially 3–63, and 207–98. See also Michel de Certeau, *The Practice of Everyday Life*, trans. Steven Rendell (Berkeley: University of California Press, 1988).

**6** Raymond Williams, *The City and the Country* (New York: Oxford University Press, 1973), 36.

**7** Denis Cosgrove, *Social Formation and the Symbolic Landscape* (1984; reprint, Madison: University of Wisconsin Press, 1998), 19.

**8** See Michel Foucault, *Discipline and Punish*, trans. Alan Sheridan (New York: Vintage Books, 1979); and Martin Jay, "Scopic Regimes of Modernity," in *Vision and Visuality*, ed. Hal Foster (Seattle: Bay Press, 1988), 3–23.

**9** Jonathan Smith, "The Lie That Blinds: Destabilizing the Text of Landscape," in *Place/Culture/Representation* (London: Routledge, 1993), 78–92.

**10** See John Stilgoe, J.B. Jackson, "A Literary Appreciation," in *Land Forum* 1 (Summer/Fall, 1997), 8–10.

**11** The term *metrical* is used here all its senses: numerical, spacing, instrumental, and poetic. See James Corner and Alex S. MacLean, *Taking Measures Across the American Landscape* (New Haven, CT: Yale University Press, 1996).

**12** See Francois Jullien, *The Propensity of Things: Toward a History of Efficacy in China*, trans. Janet Lloyd (New York: Zone Books, 1995).

**13** W. J. T. Mitchell, *Picture Theory* (Chicago: University of Chicago Press, 1994), 4 (n. 5).

**14** W. J. T. Mitchell, *Iconology: Image, Text, Ideology* (Chicago: University of Chicago Press, 1986), 10.

**15** Marco Frascari, "A New Angel/Angle in Architectural Research: The Ideas of Demonstration," in *Journal of Architectural Education* 44/1 (1990), 11–18; quote on 15.

**16** Frascari, "A New Angel/Angle," 16–17.

**17** David Leatherbarrow, "Showing What Otherwise Hides Itself," *Harvard Design Magazine* (Fall 1998), 50–55. See also James Corner, "Representation and Landscape," *Word & Image* 8/3 (July–Sept. 1992), 243–75.

**18** See interview with Winy Maas and essays by Stan Allen and Bart Lootsma in *El Croquis* 86: MVRDV (1997); and "Datascapes," in Winy Maas, Jacob Van Rijs, and Richard Koek, *FARMAX: Excursions on Density* (Rotterdam: 010 Publishers, 1998). See also James Corner, "The Agency of Mapping," in *Mappings*, ed. Denis Cosgrove (London: Reaktion, 1999), 212–58.

**19** See also Stan Allen, "Diagrams Matter," in *ANY23: Diagram Work* (Fall 1998), 16–19; Julia Czerniak, "Challenging the Pictorial: Recent Landscape Practice," in *Assemblage* 34 (1998), 110–20; and *Architectural Design Profiles 121: Games of Architecture* (May–June 1996).

20  This is a slightly narrowed definition. Mitchell, *Picture Theory*, extends the term to cinema, advertising, cartoons, and theater (for instance: "Artaud's emphasis on mute spectacle and Brecht's deployment of textual projections are not merely 'aesthetic' innovations but precisely motivated interventions in the semio-politics of the stage," 91). Also see Roland Barthes, *The Responsibility of Forms: Music, Art and Representation* (New York: Farrar, Straus and Giroux, 1985).

21  Mark C. Taylor and Esa Saarinen, *Imagologies: Media Philosophy* (London: Routledge, 1994).

FIG. 1 — *The Bewildered Planet (La planète confuse)*, by Max Ernst, 1942, Oil on canvas. 119 × 140 cm

# ECOLOGY AND LANDSCAPE AS
# AGENTS OF CREATIVITY

Unchanged within to see all changed without
Is a blank lot and hard to bear, no doubt.
—Samuel Taylor Coleridge, *The Works of Samuel Taylor Coleridge,*
  *Prose and Verse* (1845)

The existence of which we are most assured and which we know best is
unquestionably our own, for of every other object we have notions, which may
be considered external and superficial, whereas, of ourselves, our perception
is internal and profound. What, then, do we find?
—Henri Bergson, *Creative Evolution* (1944)

The processes of which ecology and creativity speak are fundamental to the
work of landscape architecture. Whether biological or imaginative, evolutionary
or metaphorical, such processes are active, dynamic, and complex, each tending
toward the increased differentiation, freedom, and richness of a diversely
interacting whole. There is no end, no grand scheme for these agents of change,
just a cumulative directionality toward further becoming. It is in this productive
and active sense that ecology and creativity speak not of fixed and rigid realities
but of movement, passage, genesis, and autonomy, of *propulsive life unfolding
in time.*

It is odd, then, that while ecology and creativity have each received increasing attention over the years, there remains ambiguity over their content and

Originally published in: George F. Thompson and Frederick R. Steiner, eds. Ecological
Design and Planning *(New York: John Wiley & Sons, 1997): 80–108. Reproduced with
permission.*

relationship toward one another, especially with respect to their agency in the evolving of life and consciousness. It is striking, for example, that the possibilities for a vibrant exchange between ecology, creativity, and the design of landscape have barely been recognized beyond mechanical and prescriptive methods. Moreover, landscape architecture's appropriation of ecology and creativity—and the manner in which they are understood and used—has rarely led to the production of work that is equal in effect and magnitude to the transformative phenomena these topics represent. Contemporary landscape architecture has drawn more from objectivist and instrumental models of ecology (the emotional rhetoric of some environmentalists notwithstanding), while design creativity has all too frequently been reduced to dimensions of environmental problem solving (know-how) and aesthetic appearance (scenery). This lack of inventiveness is both surprising and difficult for many landscape architects, especially those who originally entered the field believing that ecology and artistic creativity might together help develop new and alternative forms of landscape. This failing points to a relationship between ecology, creativity, and landscape that is either incongruous and impossible to reconcile or (and more likely) to a potential relationship that has not yet been developed—a potential that might inform more meaningful and imaginative cultural practices than the merely ameliorative, compensatory, aesthetic, or commodity-oriented.

My concern in this essay is to outline the grounds that are necessary for this potential to appear. I argue that ecology, creativity, and landscape architecture must be considered in terms other or greater than those of visual appearance, resource value, habitat structure, or instrumentality. Instead, these somewhat restrictive traditional views might be complemented by an understanding of how ecology, creativity, and landscape architecture are metaphorical and ideological representations; they are cultural images, or ideas. Far from being inactive, however, these ideas have profound agency in the world, effecting change in a variety of material, ideological, and experiential ways. These cultural ideas and practices interact with the nonhuman world in such a way as simultaneously to derive from them while being constitutive of nature, human dwelling, and the modes of relationship therein. What is important and significant here is how ecology and landscape architectural design might invent alternative forms of relationship between people, place, and cosmos. Thus, the landscape architectural project becomes more about the invention of new forms and programs than the merely corrective measures of restoration.

If one were to conceive of landscape architecture as an active agent in the play of evolutionary intervention, how would one have to construe ecology and creativity in design practice? In what ways would they have to be appropriated for landscape architecture to function as a significant evolutionary agent—one that might develop greater diversity and reciprocity between the cultural world and unmediated Nature? Of what would such a creative ecology consist?

### The Ecological Idea

Ecology has assumed a heightened level of significance in social and intellectual affairs during the past few decades. This emergence is due, in large part, to an increased awareness of local and global environmental decline, a view that continues to be shaped through vivid media coverage and well-organized ecological activism.[1] The lesson of ecology has been to show how all life upon the planet is so deeply bound into dynamic, complex, and indeterminate networks of relationships that to speak of nature as a linear mechanism, as if it were a great machine that can be either intrinsically or extrinsically controlled and repaired, is simply erroneous and reductive. The ecological view, with its emphasis on temporal, interactive processes, has been further reinforced by new scientific findings of nonlinearity, complexity, and chaos dynamics.

While ecology speaks of a "harmony of nature," writes ecologist Daniel Botkin, it is a harmony that is at the same time "discordant, created from the simultaneous movements of many tones, the combination of many processes flowing at the same time along various scales, leading not to a simple melody but to a symphony at some times harsh and at some times pleasing."[2] While the full measure of these and other emerging views of ecology remains to be realized, the idea of ecology has diversified to such a point that it can no longer be used with unambiguous clarity. Today, one may observe that "ecology" is appropriated as much by corporate and media industries as by environmentalists, land artists, or politicians. Although ecology has generally been understood as providing a scientific account of natural processes and their interrelationships, the fact that it also both describes and constructs various ideological positions to be taken with regard to nature points to a greater significance. Ecology is never ideologically (or imaginatively) neutral, despite claims of its objectivity. It is not without values, images, and effects. Instead, ecology is a social construction, one that can initiate, inform, and lend legitimacy to particular viewpoints (from "green politics" to nationalism to feminism, for example). Ecology constructs particular "ideas" in the imagination of its advocates; it conjures up particular ways of seeing and relating to Nature—views that range from the extremely rational to the most mystical and religious.

It is, therefore, necessary to distinguish two "natures": The first "nature" refers to the *concept* of nature, the cultural construction that enables a people to speak of and understand the natural world, and that is so bound into ecological language; the second "Nature" refers to the amorphous and unmediated flux that is the "actual" cosmos, that which always escapes or exceeds human understanding.

The development of the ecological idea of nature in the cultural imagination—how one conceives of, relates to, and intervenes in Nature—is a radically different kind of reflection than what is found in current instrumentalist (or problem solving) approaches toward ecology in landscape architectural design and planning, wherein "ecology," "nature," "landscape," and "environment" form the primary foci of attention, considered as separate from and external to culture. By "culture," I refer to more than just the behavioral and statistical characteristics of a human group (something that human ecology claims to describe), and to invoke, instead, the image of an unfolding and multivariate artifact, a dynamic entity constructed from the vocabularies, attitudes, customs, beliefs, social forms, and material characteristics of a particular society. Culture is a thick and active archaeology, akin to a deep field that is capable of further moral, intellectual, and social cultivation. Thus, people can only ever know what they have made (their language, representations, and artifacts). "Because for thousands of years we have been looking at the world with moral, aesthetic, and religious claims," writes Nietzsche, "with blind inclination, passion, or fear, and have indulged ourselves in the bad habits of illogical thought, this world has gradually *become* so strangely colorful, frightful, profound, soulful; it has acquired color but we have been the painters: the human intellect allowed appearance to appear, and projected its mistaken conceptions onto things."[3] For Nietzsche, the cultural world (like nature) is the result of an accumulation of "errors and fantasies," an accrual that is nothing less than "a treasure: for the *value* of our humanity rests upon it."[4] It is this dynamic, representational, and "erring" characteristic of culture, then, that descriptive and instrumentalist ecology fails to recognize, although it is itself a constituent part and product of the cultural milieu (and is, therefore, just as fictional). In other words, many landscape architects and planners who are advocates of ecological views often fail to understand how the metaphorical characteristics of ecology inform and construct particular realities. Moreover, the sheer diversity of ways in which different social groups represent, speak of experience, and relate to Nature embodies a richness—a treasure of fiction—that a strictly scientistic ecology (ironically) cannot embrace—nor even acknowledge—its own image within that richness.

### The Ambiguities of Ecology within Landscape Architecture

Ecology has been particularly influential in landscape architecture and planning, especially since the publication of Aldo Leopold's *A Sand County*

*Almanac* (1949), Rachel Carson's *Silent Spring* (1962), and Ian McHarg's *Design with Nature* (1969). Earlier American naturalists such as George Perkins Marsh, Henry David Thoreau, Ralph Waldo Emerson, John Muir, and, later, Lawrence Henderson had no doubt partly influenced some late–nineteenth- and early-twentieth-century landscape architects—most notably Frederick Law Olmsted, Charles Eliot, Jens Jensen, and Warren Manning. The cumulative result over the past century, but especially since the original Earth Day, has been the establishment of ecology as a central part of landscape architectural education and practice.

Whereas ecology has changed and enriched the field of landscape architecture substantially, it has also displaced some of landscape architecture's more traditional aspects and prompted a somewhat ambiguous and estranged disciplinary identity (the oft-asked question: "Is it art or science?"). A number of schools of landscape architecture, for example, now teach little visual art, design theory, or history, focusing instead upon natural science, environmental management, and techniques of ecological restoration. Although these aspects of landscape study are important, one cannot help but feel a concern for the loss of foundational traditions, especially landscape architecture's agency as a representational and productive art, as a *cultural* project. The subsequent polarization of art from science, planning from design, theory from practice, and the lack of critical reflection within "ecological design" circles are further symptoms of this forgetfulness. While the countertendency to privilege design and form at the exclusion of ecological ideas has proven to be retrogressive and productive of environments more like entertainment landscapes than significant places for dwelling, the appropriation of ecology within landscape architecture has yet to precipitate inventive and animistic forms of creativity. This failure is evidenced most embarrassingly in the prosaic and often trivial nature of much contemporary built work, whether it claims to be "ecological" in its design or not.

Moreover, it is ironic that the lively and spontaneous morphogenesis characteristics of evolutionary creation—the active life processes of which ecology speaks—are rarely paralleled in the modern landscape architect's limited capacity to transfigure and transmute.[5] This lack of imaginative depth and actual agency is compounded by often uncritical, reductive, and sometimes even exclusionary views of what is considered to be "natural." For example, the popular conception of ecological design as reconstructing "native" environments is not only founded upon illusory and contradictory ideas about a noncultural "nature," but also displays a remarkably nonecological intolerance of alternative viewpoints and processes of transmutation (terms such as *foreign* and *exotic* betray an exclusivity and privileging of the *natives*).

Given the increased marginalization of contemporary landscape architecture, it would seem promising for landscape architects to look to ecology less for techniques of description and prescription (and even less for its apparent legitimizing of images of "naturalness") and more for its ideational, representational, and material implications with respect to cultural process and evolutionary transformation. After all, as social ecologist John Clark argues, "The flowering of the human spirit and personality is a continuation of natural evolution. Liberation of the human imagination from the deadening effects of mechanization and commodification is one of the most pressing ecological issues."[6] It is ironic that the emancipation of human creativity through the imaginative appropriation of ecological ideas and metaphors has been largely neglected by contemporary landscape architects (and especially those who wave the flag of ecology), even though the deeper traditions of landscape architecture are founded upon such existential objectives. The garden, for example, was historically developed as a place of both connectivity *and* differentiation between people and the world of Nature. Here, the exchange that occurs through cultivation (of food, body, spirit, and physical and psychological relationship) literally unites and distinguishes human life and Nature. The persistent archetype of the garden portends an ecological consciousness that is simultaneously useful and symbolic, one that is rooted not in an external world of nature but within a particular culture's mode of relating to Nature. The same power of relationship is encoded not only in the construction of physical places, but also in maps, images, and other place-forming texts.

The difficulty for many landscape architects today lies in a forgetfulness of (and perhaps, too, a skepticism toward) the power that symbolic representation can have in forging cultural relationships, both between one another and between one and Nature. This loss of traditional focus is compounded, in part, by the privileging of scientistic ecology (utilized in highly rationalized descriptive and prescriptive ways) over phenomenological forms of ecological consciousness (which are all too often wrongly belittled by scientistic ecologists as having naive or trivial goals with respect to the massive techno-economic scale of the ecological "crisis"). The popular notion that subjectivity, poetry, and art are welcome in the private domains of the gallery or the library but are no match for the power of "rational" instrumentality in "solving" the real problems of the world is to understand these problems in terms that are somehow external to the world of symbolic communication and cultural values.[7] This use of ecology as a rational instrument in landscape architectural design and planning not only externalizes the "problem," but also promotes human domination over the nonhuman world—a world that is either rendered mute and inert or deified as a privileged domain over culture. This continual emphasis upon rational prowess—often at the exclusion of phenomenological wonderment, doubt, and humility—also fails to recognize the very minor degree to which the combined landscape architectural constructions around the world have affected the global environment, especially when compared to the scale of industrialization, deforestation, and toxic waste. In contrast, the impact that gardens, parks, and public spaces (and also maps, images, and words) have had on the formation of cultural and existential values has historically proven to be immeasurable. Landscape architecture's focus of concern simply can never be that of the external environment alone but must always entail profoundly cultural interests and ideas.

Clearly, the point remains that, although ecology has surfaced in modern landscape architectural discourse (as in public life in general), a culturally animate ecology—one that is distinct from a purely "scientistic" ecology—has yet to emerge. That such an urgent development might derive from, and contribute to, more animistic types of creativity than current frames of instrumentalism would allow points to a necessary dialogue between the scientific and artistic worlds. Such an emphasis asks that ecology inform and embrace those poetic activities that create meaningful relationships between people, place, and earth. An eco-imaginative landscape architecture would be creative insofar as it reveals, liberates, enriches, and diversifies both biological and cultural life. How, then, might the ecological idea precipitate imaginative and "world-enlarging" forms of creative endeavor? In turn, how might landscape architectural creativity (informed through its representational traditions) enrich and inform the ecological idea in the imagination and material practices of a people?

### Modernity and Environment

Prior to any further discussion of the above themes, it might be helpful to outline some of the central characteristics of modernity (the Western cultural paradigm that stems from development during the late-sixteenth century). To discuss the significance of ecology and creativity outside this context is to overlook their relationship within a larger cultural sphere. Of particular importance is an appreciation for how an all-pervasive belief in human "progress" underlies much of what is troublesome in our current age. The widespread faith in the capacity of technology to make a more perfect world in the future first arose during the sixteenth and seventeenth centuries, when new advances in science (from Copernicus, Galileo, and Descartes, to Newton and Bacon) and the rise of capitalist market economies inspired many Enlightenment intellectuals to assume that people could master nature. With progressive optimism, it was believed that all disease and poverty could be eradicated while material standards of living could be improved. The many successes of modern science during the past three hundred years (especially in medicine and communications) have continued to foster the expectation that further advances in technology will continue to solve all of humankind's problems. That this same science has also led to the development of "darker" technologies, such as nuclear weaponry and the production of toxic waste, has proven to be increasingly troubling. Similarly, more apparently benign experiments such as Biosphere 2, in Arizona, point to a future in which people might live in their own self-manufactured environments, in which the threats (and marvels) of nature are not allowed to intrude (or appear)—except, of course and inevitably, by accident.

Clearly, it is fair to observe that advances in technology and productivity have not led to an equivalent growth in either moral or ecological consciousness.[8] A corresponding decline of the sacred and the spiritual has only compounded the deterioration of ethical measures in society, especially in terms of establishing the limits for technological inventiveness. This detachment of cultural value from the autonomous, freewheeling development of a limitless technology is exacerbated by the rise of global, market-based economies, which are governed solely by the capitalist maxims of profit and gain, often at the expense of other people, nations, or lifeforms. In turn, the rise of a hierarchical and bureaucratic society—with dominant groups limiting the freedoms of others—has led to radical inequalities, cultural estrangements, and gross reductions in both the cultural and natural spheres. The subsequent loss of alterity and difference portends an increasingly homogeneous and impoverished lifeworld—one that might have the busy appearance of pluralism, but only as media image and rarely as a copresence of radically "other" realities. In sum, the belief in human progress and mastery over Nature, for all of its good intentions and successes, has at the same time promoted an often brutally mechanistic, materialistic, and impersonal world, a domain in which the potential creativity of both Nature and culture is diminished to dull equations of utility, production, commodity, and consumption.

The fallacies of progressivist and objectivist practices are sustained in large measure by another primary characteristic of the modern paradigm: The tendency to construct binary oppositions, as in the polarization of the human and social world from the natural world.[9] This dualism parallels the dichotomy between subject and object, wherein concepts such as "environment" are conceived as things that are external to humankind. The severing of reality into opposites is again an outcome of Enlightenment (particularly Cartesian) thinking, in which the objective and subjective worlds were absolutely distinguished and separated, and the incommensurability between the artists' "sensibility" and the scientists' "rationality" first arose. The tension within contemporary landscape architecture between the rational, analytical, and objective "planners" (who put such great emphasis upon a linear process of data accumulation, logical determinism, and large-scale engineering) and the emotional, intuitive, mystical "artists" (who put such great emphasis on subjectivity, emotive experience, and aesthetic appearance) is but one fallacious outcome of this larger, dualistic paradigm.[10]

Although it may be characterized as a "gentle" profession, landscape architecture remains caught within the techno-economic, progressivist, and dualistic characteristics of modernity. While modern landscape architecture's contribution to resource management, scenic preservation, zoological and commercial theme park design, and corporate image building has certainly lessened the damage done to the environment, its tendency to conceive and present the landscape as an object—whether aesthetically, ecologically, or instrumentally—has, at the same time, led to further devaluation of the environment in cultural terms (the landscape now qualified as resource, as commodity, as compensation, or as system). If landscape architecture is to concern itself with the "ecological crisis" and other difficulties of human life upon the earth, then it must recognize expeditiously how the root cause of environmental (and spiritual) decline is buried in the complex foundations of modern culture, particularly its political-economic practices, its social institutions, and the psychology and intolerance of much of its citizenry.

### Conservationist/Resourcist and Restorative Ecology

From within this modern cultural paradigm, two dominant streams of ecological practices of landscape architecture have emerged: One conservationist/resourcist, which espouses the view that further ecological information and knowledge will enable progressive kinds of management and control of ecosystems; and the other restorative, which espouses the view that ecological knowledge may be used to "heal" and reconstruct "natural systems."

In the conservationist/resourcist view of ecology, the landscape is composed of various resources that have particular value to people—such as forestry production, mining, agriculture, built development, recreation, and tourism. Scenery, too, is considered a resource, as are "heritage areas" and tracts of "wilderness," which are valued as a resource for "future human generations." Through the quantification of economic, ecological, and social values, strategies of landscape conservation are developed as "balances" between human needs and natural life. Ecological concepts provide the land-use manager and planner with rational (and apparently value-neutral) criteria for evaluating the "fit" between proposed land uses and environmental systems. The most popular technique for such evaluation of land is suitability analysis, developed by McHarg at the University of Pennsylvania during the 1960s. This ecological method allows for the quantification of the various parts that make up a particular ecosystem (or at least those parts that are susceptible to being quantified and mapped); measures the impact for various scenarios of development; and recommends the most appropriate, least disruptive land use.[11] The result is a systematic and rational accounting framework—a resource value matrix—for planning and managing development ("growth").

In his book *Nature's Economy* (1979), environmentalist Donald Worster recognizes that scientific ecology is used by the conservationist/planner solely to enable a "more careful management of…resources, to preserve the biotic capital while maximizing the income."[12] In criticizing this view, environmentalist author Neil Evernden argues that the use of ecology in resourcist planning is simply the means by which people may achieve "the maximum utilization of the earth as raw material in the support of one species…[even though] environmentalism has typically been a revolt against the presumption that this is indeed a suitable goal."[13] For all its good intentions, a major consequence of the resourcist project is the inevitable reduction of other lifeforms and processes of Nature's creation to objectified factors of utility—a devaluation that is often compounded by (and, also, constitutive of) an emotional detachment, or distance, between people and the earth. "In reducing the living world to ingredients that could be easily measured and graphed," observes Worster, "the ecologist was also in danger of removing all the residual emotional impediments to unrestrained development."[14] "To describe a tree as an oxygen-producing device or bog as a filtering agent is [a violence] that is debasing to being itself," writes Evernden.[15] Both Worster and Evernden conclude that resourcist views of ecology effectively neutralize the wonders of creation; that the objectivist, instrumental manner of manipulating the world leads only to the domestication of all that is genuinely wild, self-determining, and free. "In combating exploitation, [resourcist] environmentalists have [merely] tutored the developer in the art of careful exploitation," Evernden notes.[16] Through such practices, ecology simply promotes an analytic and detached instrumentality, one that facilitates an apparently "harmless" human control over an objectified and inert natural "reserve." In other words, progressivist ecology merely conditions a particular way of seeing that effectively severs the subject from the object. It is this culturally perpetuated relationship to landscape, this continual objectification, that prohibits a more empathetic reciprocity between people and the world. While Evernden's remarks may upset professional land planners whose practices are founded upon objective, ameliorative, and "rational" means, he points directly to the root source of continued environmental decline: *The will to manage and control something that is "out there," not within.*

The second approach toward ecology in landscape architecture is the restorative. Here, the emphasis is on the acquisition of technical knowledge and skill with respect to the physical reconstruction of landscapes or, at a larger scale, regional ecosystems. The belief is that the refinement of more ecologically sensitive techniques of land development will minimize damage to local and regional habitats. Ecology is employed by the restorationist to provide a scientific account of natural cycles and flows of energy, thereby explaining the network of interdependencies that comprise a particular ecosystem. Furthermore, ecology provides the restorationist with a palette of native and successional plant materials and planting patterns, allowing for the re-creation of a precultural, "naturalistic" landscape aesthetic. There is little room for cultural, social, and programmatic innovation in restorative work; the primary focus of attention is the natural world and the techniques necessary to recreate it (token gestures toward local heritage notwithstanding). Of course, as restoration is essentially an ideological project—derived from a particular cultural idea of "nature"—it can never escape its inherent cultural status. Unfortunately, restorationists are often as uncritical of this inescapable metaphoricity as they are unaware of the ease with which romantic, ideals of "nativeness" can degenerate into exclusionary and "purist" nationalistic attitudes (as most extremely evidenced in fascist Germany in the 1930s and 1940s).[17]

So despising of modern cultural life are some restorationists that a radically ecocentric ideology has emerged in one extreme wing of the environmentalist circle. Although the ecocentric impulse is rarely as fierce in landscape architecture as it can be in some environmental groups, there remains a strong sentiment that urbanity, art, and cultural life in general are grossly inferior to the life of unmediated Nature, a Nature that finds its finest, most creative expression in evolutionary history and wilderness areas (blind though these groups often are to the fact that such views of "untouched nature" are themselves cultural images). Modern dualism and hierarchy (this time, Nature over culture) are not overcome in the ecocentric model, but simply reinforced. It is a model (or an "ethic") that is seriously flawed in its often mystical, antirational, and romantic views of nature—views that privilege ideas of harmony, mutuality, interconnectedness, and stability, while overlooking equally natural phenomena such as competition, exclusion, exploitation, disease, and species extinction.

In both conservationist/resourcist and restorative/ecocentric practices, ecology remains entrenched within the same modern paradigm that many argue is the structural cause of environmental and social decline. Whereas one position utilizes ecology to facilitate further control over the human environment, the other uses it to provide rhetorical force to emotional feelings about the primacy of Nature and the errors of anthropocentricity. In both cases, only the symptoms of ecological distress are dealt with, while causal cultural foundations—the social structures that underlie dualism, alienation, domination, and estrangement—are ignored and unchanged, if not actually upheld. In their dualistic objectifying of the world, both ecological resourcism and restoration are ameliorative at best, and facilitating of exploitation and exclusionism at worst. Unwittingly, landscape architecture, like the multifaceted environmental movement generally, merely replicates and sustains the shortcomings of modernity. Whether the locus of environmental concern is nature or culture, the problem is the belief in a controlling instrumentality and a failure to recognize bioecological constructions as cultural "errors and fantasies"—as treasured fictions that have profound agency in the unfolding of lifeworlds.

### Radical Ecology

In response to the apparent failing of conventional frames of ecology and environmentalism, other, more radical ecological positions have emerged in recent years.[18] They are radical because their work focuses not on Nature but on the sphere of culture. They are also critical of progressivist ecology and its largely technocratic "solutions" to environmental "problems," believing them to be piecemeal approaches toward the manifestations—rather than the foundational social causes—of ecological distress. Philosophical critiques of anthropocentrism, biocentrism, rationalism, objectivism, patriarchism, dualism, hierarchy, moral rights, and ethics form the ground of the debate, with groups such as the "deep ecologists," the "ecofeminists," and the "social ecologists" at odds with one another over foundational principles. That these debates have occurred infrequently in landscape architectural discourse is profoundly unfortunate, as it will only be through a more sophisticated understanding of ecology—one that transcends its status as a descriptive and analytical natural science and recognizes its metaphoricity as a cultural construction—that ecology's significance for a more creative and meaningful landscape architecture might be realized.

Of the various radical ecologies, the one that appears to be of particular interest for landscape architecture is social ecology.[19] This approach targets the techno-economic aspects of the modern cultural paradigm and is especially critical of social practices of domination, commodification, and instrumentality. In the development of a "new liberatory project," social ecologists believe that the greatest potential for cultural reformation lies within the power of human imagination and creativity, although they insist as well on the parallel development of alternative social structures (political, institutional, ideological, ethical, and habitual) to those that sustain the modern paradigm.[20]

While social ecology seeks an "ethics of complementarity"—structured through a nonhierarchical politics of freedom, mutualism, and self-determination—its advocates are simultaneously aware of the difficulties of trying to promote change in cultural life without resorting to enforcement or dualism. Instead, some social ecologists believe that political, economic, and institutional change may best be effected less through instrumental means than through the reinvigoration of the cultural imagination. They call for a new kind of social "vision," a "new animism" in which human societies would see the world with new eyes—with wonderment, respect, and reverence. In social ecology, the ecological idea transcends its strictly scientific characteristics and assumes social, psychological, poetic, and imaginative dimensions. In shying away from solitary or mystical subjectivity, however, social ecology seeks to construct a dialectical synthesis between rational thought, spontaneous imagination, and spiritual development—moreover, social ecologists see their project as having an evolutionary and moral imperative. They believe that humanity has developed evolutionarily as "nature rendered self-conscious," as nature reflecting upon itself. It is, therefore, an ecological and moral responsibility for human creativity to, as poet Samuel Taylor Coleridge so beautifully wrote, "body forth the form of things unknown"; to promote a diversity of evolutionary pathways; and to foster an aesthetic appreciation and sense of responsibility toward the fecundity of Natural and cultural evolution.[21] "Evolution" here refers to a propulsive fecundity that is life itself, predicated upon spontaneity, chance, self-determination, and directionality toward the "actualization of potential."[22] For social ecologists, people must function as "moral agents," creatively intervening in the unfolding of evolution and the increasing of diversity, freedom, and self-reflexivity.[23]

The irony of this moral imperative is hauntingly rational, for, as philosopher Erazim Kohák writes: "If there is no God, then everything is not a creation, lovingly created and endowed with purpose and value by its creator. It can only be a cosmic accident, dead matter propelled by blind force, ordered by efficient causality. In such a context, a moral subject, living his life in terms of value and purpose, would indeed be an anomaly."[24] Kohák shows how civilization is simultaneously of Nature and yet radically different from it. It is within the space of this anomalous dialectic that further discussion of ecology and creativity as active agents in the unfolding of evolutionary time must lie, and from within which more critical and active practices of landscape architecture may emerge.

### Dialectical Ecology and Landscape

Human beings, by virtue of their ability to construct a reality through verbal and visual language, are radically different from the wild and indifferent flux that is nature, and different cultures at different times have, of course, related to the same "reality" in significantly dissimilar ways. Cultural "worlds" are composed of linguistic and imagistic structures; they are as much fictional as they are factual, as much symbolic as they are useful. As Nietzsche recognized: "To a world that is not our idea, the laws of numbers [and concepts] are completely inapplicable: they are valid in the human world."[25] The only nature that is real for us is constituted through the field of language. Without language there would be no place, only primal habitat; no dwelling, only subsistence. Moreover, not only does language ground and orient a culture, but it also facilitates moral reflection upon human existence and the existence of others.

The capacity of the human mind to comprehend and reflect upon the comprehensibility of the cosmos was "the most significant fact" of any for Aristotle, and this correspondence underlay the Greek formulation of the word *logos*, which referred to the "natural" symmetry of mind and Nature, and to the forging of that relation through language.[26] Of course, the word ecology carries with it the union of *oikos* with which allows it to be loosely translated as the "relations of home." In tracing this etymology, author Robert Pogue Harrison writes: "The word ecology names far more than the science that studies ecosystems; it names the universal manner of being in the world.... *We dwell not in nature but in the relation to nature. We do not inhabit the earth but inhabit the excess of the earth.*"[27] This relation—or network of relations—is something that people make; it is an excess (of which landscape architecture is a part) within which a culture dwells. As such, human dwelling is always an estranged construction, one that can be as destructive and parasitic as it can be reciprocal and symbiotic. This view is echoed by photographer Charles Bergman's claim: "Extinction...may always have been with us, but endangered species are a modern invention, a uniquely modern contribution to science and culture. They are one of the unhappy consequences of the way we have come to know animals, the dark side of our relation with nature."[28] Consequently, "even though it is the demise of earthly forests that elicit our concern," writes Evernden, "we must bear in mind that as culture-dwellers we do not so much live in forests of trees as much as in forests of words. And the source of the blight that afflicts the earth's forests must be sought in the word forests—that is, in the world we articulate, and which confirms us as agents of that earthly malaise."[29]

The realization that nature and culture are constructions, woven together as a network of relationships, has led some to argue that any development of

social behavior belongs to a critical revitalization of the powers of significa-
tion—to the poetics of worldmaking and transfiguration. Clark, for example,
writes of the need to "delve more deeply into those inseparable dimensions of
body and mind that dualism has so fatefully divided. As we explore such realities
as thought, idea, image, sign, symbol, signifier, and language on the one hand,
and feeling, emotion, disposition, instinct, passion, and desire on the other, the
interconnection between the two realms will become increasingly apparent."[30]
Evidently, the locus of such an enterprise is the liminal space between signifier
and signified, mind and matter, intellect, and body. People are caught, then, in
this place between recognizing themselves as part of Nature and being separate
from it. This double sense arises through the acknowledging of "otherness," or
the copresence of what is not of culture and what will always exceed cultural
definition. This is the wild in its most autonomous and unmediated form. As
a radical "other," the wild is unrepresentable, unnamable; and although it can
never be captured as a presence, it is at the same time not exactly nothing. The
poet Wallace Stevens perhaps best captures this sense in the last few lines of "The
Snow Man":

> For the listener who listens in the snow,
> And, nothing himself, beholds
> Nothing that is not there and the nothing that is.[31]

The nonabsent absence of the "other" escapes being seen or said, and yet
it remains the original source of all saying, the first inspiration. All people have
likely experienced this at one time or another, especially as young children star-
ing with wonder at the world, or, perhaps, during times of hallucination or of
religious and holy encounter.[32] Such "happenings," in turn, precipitate wonder, reflection, language, and ideas, enabling reality to "appear" (partially) and
be shared among members of a community. With time, the surrounding of this
(partial) reality with words and concepts attributes an everyday status to things,
a familiarity.

The difficulty arises when the wonderful original disappears behind an
excessively habitual, meaningless language—one in which the signifier has thickened to a "crust," denying the fullness of what is signified to present itself fully
as other. Such paralysis occurs when the habits and conventions of cultural sig-
nification become so prosaic, so hardened, so total as absolute presence, that one
can simply no longer see the self-contained mystery and potential of beings and
things in themselves. Banished, also, is the unruly wildness and freedom of the
nonhuman other—of what is, in fact, the very source of evolutionary life and

human creativity. One need only consider how the engineering of the gene—that last bastion of nonhuman, indeterminate, and wild freedom—is close to being fully mapped, colonized, and manipulated. Our modern-day "wilderness areas" are no refuge either, as they, too, have been charted, mapped, photographed, painted, managed, and "set aside" as a cultural resource. All of creation is apparently becoming less wild and more domesticated, possessed, inert, and drained of all that prompts wonderment and reflection. Habitual modes of knowing and speaking, when hardened and blinkered, simply exclude the otherness that is internal to things, denying them the possibility of becoming, of further emerging and fulfilling their potential. The contemporary denial of others is of consequence for both biological evolution as well as for the development of human consciousness and moral reflectivity.[33]

In evolutionary terms, the calcification of life occurs when transmutation slows or ceases, when life stops. In linguistic and cultural terms, this atrophy translates to the deadening of poetic metaphor, to the failure to recognize that metaphor and image are not secondary representations of a deeper, external truth, but are constitutive of a cultural reality and ever capable of inventing truth. This atrophy of the imagination has arisen in large part because of the predominance of empiricist and objective logic, inherited from the promotion of rationality during the Enlightenment. Here, one simply cannot see beyond "X is equal to what is." Creative development in both Natural evolution and the human imagination, however, entails the realization of potential—the bringing forth of latent and previously unknown events and meanings; in the creative process of becoming "X is equal to what is and what is not (yet)." The revitalization of wonderment and poetic value in human relations with Nature is, therefore, dependent on the ability to strip away the crust of habit and convention that prohibits fresh sight and relationship. One must get behind the veneer of language in order to discover aspects of the unknown within what is already familiar. Such transfiguration is a process of finding and then founding alternative worlds. I can think of no greater raison d'etre for the landscape architectural project.

In describing the capacity of human thought, George Steiner writes that "ours is the ability, the need, to gainsay or 'unsay' the world, to image it and speak it otherwise."[34] Through the *disappearance* of the distinct and separate form of things there is enabled the *appearance* of a radically new form of experience and knowing. One must first shed the conventional view that language merely describes an external, detached reality, and realize instead that both the signified field and the things signified are combined inextricably in mutually constitutive processes. Nature as an autonomous, free, irreducible, and animate "other" must be enabled to engage with, and have presence for, people, thereby continually challenging human concepts and ways of knowing. As Maurice Merleau-Ponty outlines: "It is essential for the thing and the world to present themselves as 'open,' to project us beyond their predetermined manifestations and constantly to promise us other things to see."[35] This view may entail as much terror and fear as it does harmony and mutuality (which, of course, was the idea of the Sublime in landscape and art during the eighteenth century, and which underlay theologian Rudolf Otto's ideas of the Holy in the twentieth century). Current attempts to control Nature, to leave it alone, or to conflate it with culture fail to recognize the inevitable anomalous dialectic of human existence.

The emancipation of both nature and the human imagination depends, therefore, first on the capacity to "unsay" the world and, second, on the ability to image it differently so that wonder might be brought into appearance. This transformation and enrichment of meaning belongs to the poetic—to the capacity of the visionary to change vocabularies and break convention so that hidden potentials are made actual. As scholar Joel Kovel recognizes: "We cannot collapse the human and Natural worlds one into the other, except as a wishful illusion. We have only the choice as to how Nature is to be signified: As an inert other, or as [the poet William] Blake fully expressed, an entity transfigured with spirit."[36] Culture evolves through metaphor and the release of more edifying relationships between things. Poetic transfiguration enables an unfolding of things previously unforeseen, raising people to a perception of the wonderful and the infinite. The aim is one of ever-increasing wholeness, richness, and fullness of differentiation and subjectivity.

The idea that the poetic language of images and likenesses can expand—both imaginatively and literally—the internal structures of the world underlies the writings of Gaston Bachelard, who believed that poetic image could be "a synthesizing force for human existence."[37] In warning against the studying of matter as an object (as in the scientific experiment), Bachelard insisted instead on the development of a deeply sensual knowledge of the world, derived from how one lives or experiences it. He spoke, also, of the "reverberancy" with which poetic images resonate with human feelings and imagination, describing their constitutive power in forging renewed relations between things. Through his description of "poetic reverie," Bachelard's work shows how the joining of substances with adjectives can derive from matter a spirit—a truth. Hence, one might speak of "humid fire," "milky water," or "night as nocturnal matter."

### Bewilderment, Wonder, and Indetermination

These ideas about imaginative renewal through fresh and resonant association were particularly well understood by the Surrealists. Artists such as André

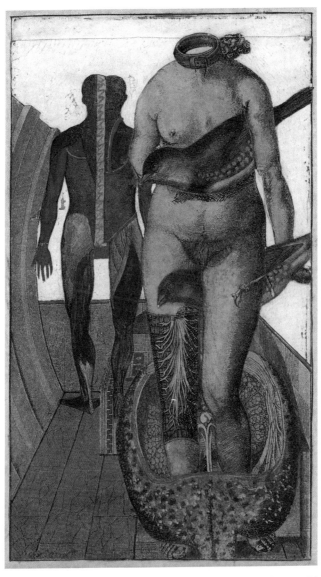

**FIG. 2** —*Speech of the Bird Woman*, by Max Ernst, 1920, Collage and gouache, 7¼ × 4¼ inches

Breton, Joan Miró, René Magritte, Yves Tanguy, and Max Ernst sought to find correspondences between Natural life and human life through the workings of the psyche and the imagination.[38] In Ernst's work, sun, sky, universe, earth, vegetable, animal, serpent, mineral, and human are woven together in ways that are both familiar and radically new. [FIGS. 1 + 2] They are uncanny in that their oddness, their strange and bewildering quality, prompts both wonder and imaginative recognition—they evoke *relationship*. The Cartesian dualities of people and Nature, matter and thought, subject and object, male and female are conflated into fantastic worlds of mutuality, paradox, and difference. In describing certain poetic procedures such as "overpainting," "frottage," and "loplop," Ernst insisted upon the "bewitching" of reason, taste, and objectivity. In fact, one of the key procedures in Surrealist transformation was "the exploitation of the fortuitous meeting of two distant realities on an inappropriate plane...or, to use a shorter term, *the cultivation of a systematic bewildering*."[39]

Bewilderment is simply a prerequisite for another form of seeing; it is an unsettled appearance that allows for the double presence of human and other. That the poet or the artist are the seers and makers of such works derives from the traditions of *mimesis* and *poesis*, activities that entail the actualization of potential, the bringing forth of something previously unknown, or even nonexistent. The development of techniques of collage and montage simply represents the deep (natural?) human desire to realize new and latent visions—new connections and possibilities for relationship between things.[40] Furthermore, the parallels between the vocabularies of ecology and collage are striking—terms such as *indeterminacy, inclusivity, overlay, rupture, simultaneity, stochastic event, instability, association, collusion*, and other morphological processes speak of an ever renewing "unity through diversity." Similarities between ecology and creative transmutation are indicative of an alternative kind of landscape architecture, one in which calcified conventions about how people live and relate to land, nature, and place are challenged and the multivariate wonders of life are once again released through invention.

These forms of ecological creativity would appear to follow from philosopher Henri Bergson's remark in *Creative Evolution* that "the role of life is to inject some *indetermination* into matter."[41] Bergson speaks of the infinite creativity of biological and imaginative *life*. In his refusal to reduce nature to a physical, "knowable" object he describes a need to liberate life so that its fullest potentials may come into appearance. Bergson's is a creative evolution of indeterminate unfolding, a process in which "matter is the deposit of life, the static residues of actions done, choices made in the past. Living memory is the past felt in the actualities of realities, of change."[42] Such an interrelational view

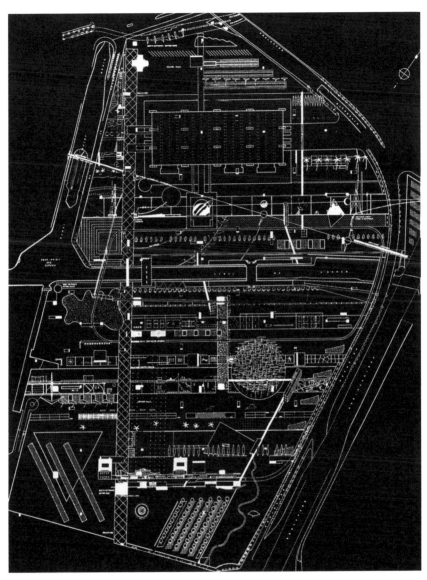

FIG. 3 — *Plan for the Parc de la Villette, Paris* (unbuilt proposal), by Rem Koolhaas/
Office for Metropolitan Architecture, 1982–1983

FIG. 4 — *Planometrie demonstration, Parc de la Villette,*
*Paris* (unbuilt proposal), drawing by Alex Wall, design by Rem Koolhaas/
Office for Metropolitan Architecture, 1982–1983

directs us toward more "heterotopic" kinds of activity and space than singular, "utopic" acts. Whereas heterotopia's ad hoc inclusivity and open-endedness portends a disturbing and bewildering prospect, it also systematically denies singularity, totality, determinacy, and hierarchy. As a "structured heterogeneity," such a complex field is neither chaotic nor ordered, but free and organic. Thus, a truly ecological landscape architecture might be less about the construction of finished and complete works, and more about the design of "processes," "strategies," "agencies," and "scaffoldings"—catalytic frameworks that might enable a diversity of relationships to create, emerge, network, interconnect, and differentiate.[43]

The aim for the design of these strategic grounds would be not to celebrate differentiation and pluralism in a representational way, but rather to construct enabling relationships between the freedoms of life (in terms of unpredictability, contingency, and change) and the presence of formal coherency and structural/material precision. This double aim underlies—in part—the work of Rem Koolhaas and is particularly well exemplified in his unbuilt proposal for the Parc de la Villette, in which the delineation and "equipping" of a "strategic field" with "social instruments" was planned to optimize physical, spatial, and material identity while allowing for an almost infinite range of programmatic events, combinations, improvisations, differentiations, and adjacencies.[44] [FIGS. 3 + 4] As architectural theorist Sanford Kwinter describes: "All of Koolhaas's recent work is *evolved*—rather than designed—within the hypermodern event—space of complex, sensitive, dynamical indeterminacy, and change.... [The design principles display] a very clear orientation toward evolutionary, time-based processes, dynamic geometric structurations—not structures per se, but forms that follow and fill the wake of concrete yet unpredeterminable events.... This is because, instead of designing artificial environments, [Koolhaas] deploys richly imbricated systems of interacting elements that set in motion rather artificial ecologies that, in turn, take on a genuine self-organizing life of their own."[45] The resultant "image" of such designs may not be one that is currently thought to be ecological in appearance (which, as I have argued, remains fallaciously bound up with ideas of untouched and native "nature"), but its strategic organicism—its deployment as an active agent, a metabolic urbanism—aspires to nothing less than the injection of indetermination, diversification, and freedom into both the social and Natural worlds—values that are surely central to any ecological, moral, and poetic notions about evolutionary and creative life. Other projects by Koolhaas, such as Yokohama Harbor, further demonstrate the oneiric lyricism of programmatic strategies that remain open-ended and promote new lifeforms and sets of events.

**Coda**

My purpose in this essay is to present a number of theoretical bases that might allow for a more animate appropriation of ecology in landscape architectural practice. These bases have little to do with the object-centered advocacy of Nature ("environment") or culture ("art") and point instead toward the highly interactive processes and relationships that are life itself—life as both a specific and autonomous system of networks, forces, combinations, unfoldings, events, and transformations. What is important in this view is how creative practices of ecology and landscape architecture construct—or, more precisely, enable—alternative forms of relationship and hybridization between people, place, material, and Earth. Echoing evolutionary principles, these enabling strategies function less as instruments and ameliorants and more as agents, as processes, as active imbroglios and ever emerging networks of potential. Obviously, I am speaking here of a landscape architecture that has yet to appear fully, one that is less preoccupied with ameliorative, stylistic, or pictorial concerns and more actively engaged with imaginative, enabling, and diversifying practices—practices of the wild.[46]

How may the pulsing flow and flux of wild life, its autonomous status as "other," and its reflective and moral sense be channeled, liberated, and expressed through an ecology and landscape of creative agents? The answers, I believe, lie within the powers of both Natural and cultural agencies in the evolving landscapes that precipitate (and are caught within) processes of indetermination and diversification; landscapes that engage, enable, diversify, trick, emancipate, and elude—put simply, landscapes that function as actants, as continual transformations and encounters that actively resist closure and representation.[47]

NOTES

1   Alex Wilson, *The Culture of Nature* (Cambridge, MA: Blackwell, 1992).

2   Daniel Botkin, *Discordant Harmonies: A New Ecology for the Twenty-First Century* (Oxford: Oxford University Press, 1990), 25.

3   Friedrich Nietzsche, *Human, All Too Human*, trans. by Marion Faber (Lincoln: University of Nebraska Press, 1984), 23–24.

4   Ibid., 24.

5   The relationship between biological, evolutionary processes and the human imagination is discussed beautifully in Edith Cobb, *The Ecology of Imagination in Childhood* (New York: Columbia University Press, 1977). Creativity and evolution is also implicit in Henri Bergson, *Creative Evolution*, trans. Arthur Mitchell (New York: Modern Library, 1944).

6   John Clark, "Social Ecology: Introduction," in *Environmental Philosophy*, eds. Michael Zimmerman et al (Englewood Cliffs, NJ: Prentice Hall, 1993), 351.

7   James Corner, "A Discourse on Theory II: Three Tyrannies of Contemporary Theory and the Alternative of Hermeneutics," *Landscape Journal* 10/2 (1991), 125–31.

8   Jurgen Habermas, "Modernity: An Incomplete Project," in *The Anti-Aesthetic,* ed. Hal Foster (Port Townsend, WA: Bay Press, 1983), 13–15; Peter Goin, *Humanature* (Austin: University of Texas Press, 1996).

9   Although the tendency to speak of a duality between nature and culture has persisted throughout modernity, the truth of this belief has been challenged by Bruno Latour in *We Have Never Been Modern* (Cambridge, MA: Harvard University Press, 1993), who argues that the social and natural worlds are inextricably interrelated. See, also, Elizabeth K. Meyer, "The Expanded Field of Landscape Architecture," in *Ecological Design and Planning,* eds. George Thompson and Frederick Steiner (New York: Wiley, 1997), 45–79.

10  James Corner, "A Discourse on Theory I: Sounding the Depths—Origins, Theory, and Representation." *Landscape Journal* 9/2 (1990), 60–78.

11  Ian McHarg, *Design with Nature* (Garden City, NY: Doubleday/Natural History Press, 1969).

12  Donald Worster, *Nature's Economy: The Roots of Ecology* (New York: Anchor Press, 1979), 315.

13  Neil Evernden, *The Social Creation of Nature* (Baltimore: Johns Hopkins University Press, 1993), 22.

14  Worster, *Nature's Economy,* 304.

15  Evernden, *The Social Creation of Nature,* 23.

16  Ibid.

17  Gert Groenig and Joachim Wolschke-Buhlman, "Some Notes on the Mania for Native Plants in Germany," *Landscape Journal* 11/2 (1992), 116–26; and "Response: If the Shoe Fits, Wear It!" *Landscape Journal* 13/1 (1994), 62–63; Kim Sorvig, "Natives and Nazis: An Imaginary Conspiracy in Ecological Design," *Landscape Journal* 13/1 (1994), 58–61; and J. MacKenzie, *The Empire of Nature* (Manchester: Manchester University Press, 1987).

18  Zimmerman et al, *Environmental Philosophy*; Carolyn Merchant, *Radical* Ecology (New York: Routledge, Chapman & Hall, 1992); Max Oelschlaeger, *The Idea of Wilderness: From Prehistory to the Age of Ecology* (New Haven, CT: Yale University Press, 1991), 281–319.

19  Zimmerman et al, *Environmental Philosophy,* 345–437.

20  Murray Bookchin, "What Is Social Ecology?" in *Environmental Philosophy* and *The Ecology of Freedom* (Montreal: Black Rose Books, 1991).

21  Samuel Taylor Coleridge, *The Works of Samuel Taylor Coleridge, Prose and Verse* (Philadelphia: Thomas Cowperthwait, 1845). Quoted in Cobb, *The Ecology of Imagination,* 15.

22  Bookchin, *The Philosophy of Social Ecology* (Montreal: Black Rose Books, 1990), 12–48.

23  For more on the idea of agency, see Donna Haraway, *Simians, Cyborgs, and Women: The Reinvention of Nature* (New York: Routledge, 1991); Latour, *We Have Never Been Modern;* and Dan Rose, *Active Ingredients* (Unpublished manuscript, University of Pennsylvania, 1994).

24  Erazim Kohak, *The Embers and the Stars* (Chicago: University of Chicago Press, 1984).

25  Nietzsche, *Human,* 27.

26  Janet Biehl, "Dialectics in the Ethics of Social Ecology," in *Environmental Philosophy,* 375.

27  Robert Pogue Harrison, *Forests: The Shadow of Civilization* (Chicago: University of Chicago Press, 1992), 201. Emphasis added.

28  Charles Bergman, *Wild Echoes* (New York: McGraw-Hill, 1990), 1–2.

29  Evernden, *The Social Creation of Nature,* 145–46.

30   Clark, "Social Ecology," 352.

31   Wallace Stevens, *Collected Poems* (New York: Knopf, 1981), 10.

32   Evernden, *The Social Creation of Nature*, 107–24; Cobb, *The Ecology of Imagination*, 30; Mark Taylor, *Tears* (Albany: State University of New York Press, 1990); and Paul Vanderbilt, *Between the Landscape and Its Other* (Baltimore: Johns Hopkins University Press, 1993).

33   Evernden, *The Social Creation of Nature*, 116–24; Oelschlaeger, *The Idea of Wilderness*, 320–53; and Bergman, *Wild Echoes*.

34   George Steiner, *George Steiner: A Reader* (Oxford: Oxford University Press, 1984), 398.

35   Maurice Merleau-Ponty, *The Phenomenology of Perception*, trans. Colin Smith (Suffolk, UK: Routledge and Kegan Paul, 1962), 384.

36   Joel Kovel, "The Marriage of Radical Ecologies," in *Environmental Philosophy*, 413–14.

37   Gaston Bachelard, *On Poetic Imagination and Reverie*, rev. ed. tran. Colette Gaudin (Dallas: Spring Publications, 1987), 107.

38   The importance of the psyche for how people relate to Nature is discussed most profoundly in C. G. Jung, *Synchronicity: An Acausal Connecting Principle*, trans. by R. Hull (Princeton, NJ: Princeton University Press, 1973). Of particular relevance is Jung's discussion of "synchronicity," and which, like Bachelard's ideas of "reverberation," describes correspondence between Natural life and human life, especially as apprehended in the unconscious imagination.

39   Werner Spies, *Max Ernst: Collages*, trans. John William Gabriel (New York: Harry N. Abrams, 1991), 43.

40   James Corner, "Representation and Landscape: Drawing and Making in the Landscape Medium," *Word and Image* 8/3 (1992), 265–75.

41   Bergson, *Creative Evolution*, 139.

42   Ibid., xiv.

43   Haraway, *Simians, Cyborgs, and Women*; Latour, *We Have Never Been Modern*; Rose, *Active Ingredients*.

44   Rem Koolhaas and Bruce Mau, *S, M, L, XL* (New York: Monacelli Press, 1995), 894–939; Jacques Lacan and Rem Koolhaas, *OMA* (Princeton, NJ: Princeton University Press, 1991), 86–95.

45   Sanford Kwinter, "OMA: The Reinvention of Geometry," *Assemblage* 18 (1993), 84–85. See, also, Koolhaas and Mau, *S, M, L, XL*.

46   Gary Snyder, *The Practice of the Wild* (Berkeley, CA: North Point Press, 1990).

47   James Corner, "Aqueous Agents: The (Re)Presentation of Water in the Work of George Hargreaves," *Process Architecture* 128 (1996), 46–61.

# Part Three

# LANDSCAPE URBANISM

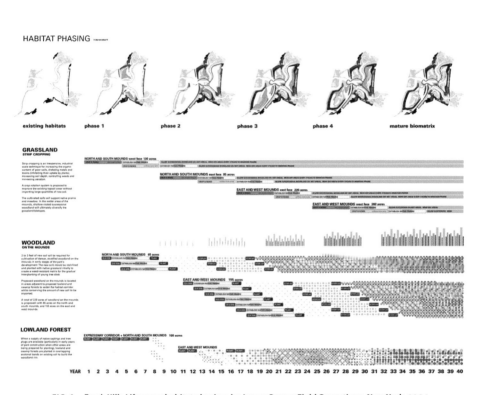

FIG. 1 — Fresh Kills Lifescape habitat phasing, by James Corner Field Operations, New York, 2004

# NOT UNLIKE LIFE ITSELF:
## LANDSCAPE STRATEGY NOW

The notion of "design intelligence," defined by architectural theorist Michael Speaks as "practices [that] allow for a greater degree of innovation because they encourage opportunism and risk-taking rather than problem solving," is pertinent to this particular moment and fundamental, I believe, to the advancement and larger cultural efficacy of landscape architecture, architecture, and urban design.[1] The idea of strategy, more generally, invokes the art of engagement, typically in battles, but also in any activity that requires careful positioning and intelligent, informed, coordinated actions to ensure success. However, to think solely in terms of ends is perhaps not accurate, for a good strategy remains dynamic and open and thereby assures its own longevity. [FIG.1] It is more conversational and engaging than it is confrontational or assertive. A good strategy is a highly organized plan (spatial, programmatic, or logistical) that is at the same time flexible and structurally capable of significant adaptation in response to changing circumstances. Too rigid a strategy will succumb to a surprise or to a logic other than that for which it was designed, and too loose a strategy will succumb to anything more complex, organized, or better coordinated.

Life scientists will tell you that a resilient system must be both robust and open. Such suppleness is essential for successful adaptation, which is in turn necessary for survival in an evolving open system. In order to grow and develop, life forms must both persist and change, their organizational structures sufficiently strong to withstand challenges while also flexible enough to morph and reorganize. These principles are as topical today in business and management as they are in biology and ecology, urbanism, and the design of public space. And,

---

*Originally published in: Harvard Design Magazine 21 (Fall 2004/Winter 2005): 32–34. Reproduced with permission.*

importantly, these principles describe not only pathways and processes but also specific forms of organization, specific arrangements, configurations, and relational structures that are essential for constructing both resilient and adaptive capacities. In this case, a "fitness landscape" is one best disposed toward and best adapted to certain conditions. It is both healthy (or physically fit) and synthetically symbiotic (or "fitting") because of its specific organizational and material form. Now, because architectural, landscape, and urban projects are inevitably formal (both geometrical and material), durational (subject to time and process), and complex (subject to multiple forces and relations) strategy is fundamental to contemporary design practices.

Moreover, the increased marginalization of design from public life—architecture and landscape are valued more as symbolic, aesthetic, or emblematic works rather than as modes of practice directed toward larger urban issues and social/public improvement—necessitates a stocktaking of the field, a revamping of professional orientation toward future practices. In an increasingly unregulated, dispersed, global, and pluralistic world, projects have become more complicated, more difficult to pull off, more difficult to maintain in quality. Without kings, autocratic presidents, singular corporate leaders, or similarly single-minded "clients with power and authority," it is very difficult to produce significantly innovative work, especially at a larger, urban scale. The kind of ad-hoc, inclusionist populism that passes as participatory public process today typically leads to dull projects, bland politics, and general cultural inertia. Now, not wanting to return to hierarchical societies and wanting instead to more fully, effectively, innovatively engage urban public life in the realization of complex projects, how exactly might one act professionally?

### Landscape, Ecology, and Propagation

Both landscape and ecology serve as useful strategic models for three primary reasons: 1) they accept the often messy and complex circumstances of the given site, replete with constraints, potentials, and realities, and they have developed techniques—mapping, diagramming, planning, imaging, arranging, and so on—for both representing and working with the seemingly unmanageable or inchoate complexities of the given; 2) they both address issues of large-scale spatial organization and relational structuring among parts, a structuring that remains open and dynamic, not fixed; and 3) they both deal with open-ended time, often viewing a project more in terms of cultivation, staging, and setting up certain conditions rather than obsessing on fixity, finish, and completeness. Landscape architects tend to view the specificity of a given site—its environment, culture, politics, and economies—as a program unto itself, a program that has an innate

FIG. 2 — Emergence Through Adaptive Management, Downsview Park, by James Corner Field Operations, Toronto, 2001

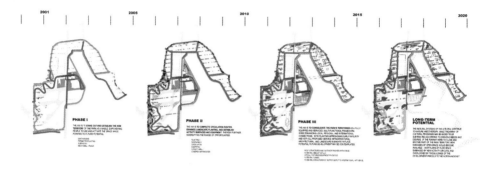

FIG. 3 — Downsview Park phasing, by James Corner Field Operations, Toronto, 2001

tendency or propensity with regard to future potentials. This is why practices of agriculture, silviculture, horticulture, and other techniques of adaptive management of material systems are so interesting and pertinent to urbanism.

Subsequently, once seeded, set up, or staged, ecological succession presents one site state that establishes the conditions for the next, which in turn overwrites the past and precipitates a future not necessarily in foreseeable or prescriptive ways. In a sense, the landscape project is less about static, fixed organizations than it is about "propagating organizations," provisional sets of structures that perform work to construct more of themselves in order to literally propagate more diverse and complex lifeworlds (described by biologist Stuart Kauffman). A single cell or unit working to produce a second copy from small building blocks is literally propagating not only an organization of material but also an organization of process, which goes on to gradually construct increasingly diverse sets of emergent forms. Self-constructing organization propagates and evolves — our globe is covered by propagating organizations — life and its consequences.

In design terms, landscapes and urban organizations set up the conditions for life to unfold and evolve. [FIGS. 2 + 3] Any landscape configuration has an inherent potential for future growth. Design strategy involves understanding that potentiality and shaping or deploying form in order to maximize effects. The notion of a propagating organization is totally enmeshed in unfolding the unlocked promise of real things over time. The evolution of circumstances and configuration opens new sets of possibility and effect, and hence the efficacy of the disposition.

### Dispositions: Materiality, Form, and Design

This brings me to my third point: Design practices that are contextually responsive, temporal and open-ended, adaptive and flexible, and ecologically strategic do not imply that formal, material precision is irrelevant. Proponents who argue for strategic modes of practice over formal, material practices, or even for a kind of objective naturalism over subjective creativity are misguided. First, as landscape architects, architects, and urban designers, we give physical shape and form to the world—geometry and material are fundamental. [FIG. 4] We draw from strategy and from various disciplines that deploy strategic and organizational thinking not to become master strategists per se but rather to find greater efficacy and potential for the physical reshaping of our world. Strategic technique—research, survey, mapping, projecting, decentralizing, bundling, networking, testing, shaping, sounding-out, and so on—are of enormous value to designers trying to expand the scope and efficacy of their work. At the same time, however, form, geometry, and material are precisely the physical media, the substrate if you will, through which any strategy plays itself out. In other words, there is no general strategy of battle, only a specific unfolding of battle as dictated or afforded by the specific contours and local conditions of a particular terrain.

Similarly, in designing pathways, corridors, patches, fields, matrices, meshworks, boundaries, surfaces, mats, membranes, sections, and joints—each configuration highly specific in dimension, material, and organization—we are constructing a dynamic expanding field, literally a machinic stage for the performance of life, for the propagation of more life, and for the emergence of novelty. In other words, arguments for staging uncertainty, for indeterminacy and open-endedness, for endless scenario gaming and datascaping—in fact anything to do with the whole notion of free flexibility and adaptation—do not make sense in a world without specific material form and precise design organizations.

The very performance of life is dependent upon a highly organized material matrix, a landscape ecology both robust and adaptable, strategic by virtue of

FIG. 4 — High Line planting overlay design study, by James Corner Field Operations
with Diller Scofidio + Renfro, New York, 2005

its material cunning in diversification and survival. Fluid, pliant fields—whether wetlands, cities, or economies—are able to absorb, transform, and exchange information with their surroundings. Their stability and robustness in handling and processing movement, difference and exchange derives from their organizational configuration, their positioning, their arrangement, and relational structuring: in sum, their "design intelligence."

NOTES

1   Michael Speaks, "Theory was interesting…but now we have work" *arq* 6/2, "perspective" (June 26, 2002).

# LAYERS OF FRESH KILLS **lifescape**

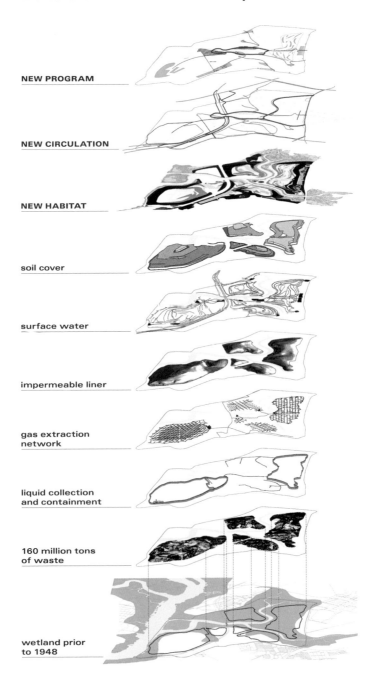

NEW PROGRAM

NEW CIRCULATION

NEW HABITAT

soil cover

surface water

impermeable liner

gas extraction
network

liquid collection
and containment

160 million tons
of waste

wetland prior
to 1948

FIG. 1 — Fresh Kills Lifescape site layers, by James Corner Field Operations, New York, 2004

# LANDSCAPE URBANISM

Landscape urbanism brings together two terms to suggest a new hybrid discipline. Not unlike the combination of biology and technology to spawn biotech, or of evolutionary science with business management to produce organizational dynamics, the merging of landscape with urbanism suggests an exciting field of new possibilities. Such possibilities range from the new high-tech eco-metropolis—"green cities" colored by vegetated roofs and working gardens, and sustained by solar panels, wind turbines, and stormwater wetlands—to examples of a more postindustrial "meta-urbanism"—replete with brutalist layers of concrete intersections flying over densely packed houses, distribution centers, and parking structures, collectively a "landscape" by virtue of its flattened accumulation of programs, textures, and flows. Contradictory perhaps, but definitions and examples of landscape urbanism may be drawn from the regionally scaled and carefully planned ecological greenways of Stuttgart to the tough, unplanned, market-driven "sprawl" of Los Angeles; from the exquisitely designed public spaces and streets of Barcelona to the densely layered unregulated spaces of Tokyo; from the infrastructural landscapes of roads, utility networks and hydrological systems of Phoenix to the symbolic representation of local identity undergirding cities as divergent as Las Vegas and Berlin; and from the reclamation of huge tracts of postindustrial land for new uses in Philadelphia to the planned erasure of underpopulated sectors of the city of Detroit. Each of these instances is valid and not necessarily exclusive of any of the others. Paradoxical and complex, landscape urbanism involves understanding the full mix of ingredients that compose a rich urban ecology.

*Originally published in: Mohsen Mostafavi and Ciro Najle, eds.* Landscape Urbanism: A Manual for the Machinic Landscape *(London: Architectural Association, 2003): 58–63. Reproduced with permission.*

As a complex amalgam, landscape urbanism is more than a singular image or style: it is an ethos, an attitude, a way of thinking and acting. In many ways it can be seen as a response to the failure of traditional urban design and planning to operate effectively in the contemporary city. The complexity of market-based real estate, community activism, environmental issues, and short-term political mindsets has made it all but impossible for the urban planner to do much more than facilitate commercial development plans. With a lighter touch, greater ambition, and more entrepreneurial techniques, landscape urbanism offers alternative approaches to urban practice. It marks a dissolution of old dualities such as nature-culture, and it dismantles classical notions of hierarchy, boundary, and center. Perhaps most importantly, it marks a productive attitude toward indeterminacy, open-endedness, intermixing, and cross-disciplinarity. Unlike the overly simplified view of the city as a static composition, with the planner as the figure in charge, landscape urbanism views the emergent metropolis as a thick, living mat of accumulated patches and layered systems, with no singular authority or control. Such a dynamic, open-ended matrix can never be operated upon with any certainty as to outcome and effect. It escapes design and, even more so, planning. The contemporary metropolis is out of control—and this is not a weakness but its strength.

In viewing the city as a living ecology, landscape urbanism offers neither remedies nor fixes. Instead its protagonists look for opportunities to simply engage the dynamics of the city on their own terms, to be a player, an agent continually looking for ways to make a difference. But beyond opportunism, a propensity for cross-disciplinarity, and an acceptance of—perhaps even a lust for—indeterminacy, what are some of the main characteristics of landscape urbanism as a practice? Here we can chart out five general themes:

### Horizontality

Many social and cultural theorists have described the perceived shift of social structures from vertical to horizontal during the latter part of the twentieth century. Global economies, television, communication, mass-mobility, and the increased autonomy of the individual are some of the factors undergirding a general transition from hierarchical, centric, authoritative organizations to polycentric, interconnected, expansive ones. A view across a city like Los Angeles makes this horizontal spread more palpable, animated by endless circuitries of movement and flow. From a landscape urbanist perspective, the emphasis now shifts from the one to the many, from objects to fields, from singularities to open-ended networks.

Horizontality maximizes opportunities for roaming, connecting, interrelating, assembling, and moving—all while allowing differences to comingle and proliferate. And so the structuring of the horizontal surface becomes a predominant concern for landscape urbanism, for the surface is the organizational substrate that collects, distributes, and condenses all the forces operating upon it. Land division, allocation, demarcation, and the construction of surfaces constitute the first act in staking out ground; the second is to establish services and pathways across the surface to support future programs; and the third is ensuring sufficient permeability to allow for future permutation, affiliation, and adaptation. These surface strategies permit the creation of more or less coherent fields that allow an almost infinite range of varied and flexible arrangements. As vast organizing fields that establish new conditions for future development, these horizontal matrices function as infrastructures.

### Infrastructures

Landscape urbanism implants new potential in a given field through the orchestration of infrastructural catalysts—infrastructures that perform and produce. In traditional landscape terms, such infrastructures might include earthwork grading, drainage, soil cultivation, vegetation establishment techniques, land management, and so on—the preparatory substrate that conditions ground for subsequent uses. In traditional urban planning terms, infrastructures might include roads, utilities, bridges, subways, and airports—the hidden systems that not only support but also instigate development. Codes, regulations and policies may also form part of the infrastructural milieu, as may many of the hidden forces, directions and regimes that work to shape development over time. The attention paid to the dynamic structures and processes that engender future development distinguishes landscape urbanism from more object-based ideas such as "cityscape," "infrascape," "green city," or any other such hybrid image that derives from an objectified notion of formal appearance.

Landscape urbanism deploys geometry, materials, and codes less to control composition or determine social program than to liberate future sets of possibility—cultural as well as logistical. It is an art of staging. And as such, it is an art that is concerned with spatial form and geometry less for stylistic or semiotic modes of expression and more for the effects that those forms and materials produce. [FIG. 1]

### Forms of Process

In comparing modernist formal determinism to the more recent rise of communitarian "new urbanism," David Harvey suggests that both these projects fail because of their presumption that spatial order can somehow control history and process.[1] He argues that the struggle for designers and planners ought to lie less with finding new spatial forms and aesthetic appearances than with "the advancement of a more socially just, politically emancipating, and ecologically sane mix of spatiotemporal production processes," challenging the general acquiescence to the forces of "uncontrolled capital accumulation, backed by class privilege and gross inequalities of political-economic power." His point is that the processes of urbanization (in terms of capital accumulation, deregulation, globalization, environmental protection, codes and regulations, market trends, and so on) are much more significant for the shaping of urban relationships than are spatial forms per se. Consequently, he argues that the search for new organizing structures and cities ought to derive from a Utopia of process rather than a Utopia of form. Here, the emphasis shifts from what things look like to how they work and what they do.

Now this is not to say that form and physical properties are unimportant; such an assertion would wrongly render the physical arts inert. An argument for process ought to recognize the profound effects form, space, and materials exercise upon the world. And yet an argument for process must also demand that physical form and material be valued not only for their aesthetic and qualitative aspects but also for their instrumental and productive effects. Thus, whereas practices of design and planning concerned with time and process are fundamentally material practices, landscape urbanism emphatically puts these materials to "work." This marks a clear pragmatic impulse, but less a generic, expedient pragmatism and more a tactical, insightful form of practice, both entrepreneurial and creative. This focus upon material agency demands equal concern for technique.

One good example in this regard is the very impressive and wholly integrated planning for the London Olympic Park in Stratford, London. [FIG. 2] This process began in 2003, with the Games opening nearly ten years later, in 2012, and the site still undergoing transformation and urban redevelopment through at least 2020. There are many interesting aspects to this project, both in terms of process and physical design, but the central interest here is the fundamental manner in which the entire site is treated as a large-scale landscape, as a kind of tissue and bonding agent that ties all the disparate parts together. Corridors, patches, mosaics, bridges, pathways, landforms, and matrices create a fabric within which the city can grow new roots.

### Techniques

Techniques of operation are crucial for the success of landscape urbanism in practice. Given the many social, economic, and logistical difficulties surrounding

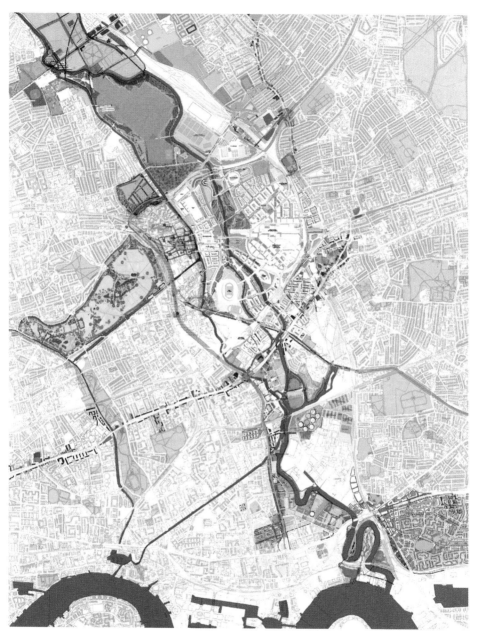

FIG. 2 — Integrated regeneration and development plan for the London Olympic Park and surroundings, by Design for London and the Olympic Park Legacy Company, 2011

large-scale projects today, practitioners must be quick and light on their feet. The art of rhetoric and persuasion is key, as is the capacity to work with multidisciplinary teams and experts, but so too is a wily sense of dance, or play. A designer can no longer walk into meetings as heroic author or master planner; one must be prepared to engage, converse, share, reflect, and revise. Increasingly, projects today demand collaboration and interdisciplinarity, with architects, landscape architects, traffic engineers, ecologists, economists, artists, and politicians all sitting around the table. While there is inevitably a tendency for such deliberations to stall through inertia, and to settle for the most familiar of common denominators (sameness), there is still the possibility of orchestrating a collective of experts and ideas toward a new synthesis. The art lies with the imagination and the capacity to lead—skills that are greatly enhanced through imaging and projection. Here, the pragmatic impulse might be cited again, for images are deployed not simply to "sell" or "get the job done" but more to query, explore, reorganize perceptions, and synthesize different insights. Thus, the project may unfold in a truly inventive and unique way, "getting the job done" but with new effects and consequences each time. Techniques drawn from landscape—such as mapping, cataloging, triangulating, surface modeling, implanting, managing, cultivating, phasing, layering, and so on—may be combined with urbanist techniques—such as planning, diagramming, organizing, assembling, allotting, zoning, marketing, and so on—to help create a larger bag of tools than the traditional planner has had in the past. Add to this Robert Rauschenberg's "flatbed" procedures, John Cage's "scorings," Buckminster Fuller's "projections," or Michel de Certeau's "microtechniques" and you might just have the beginnings of a landscape urbanist's toolbox. Together, these sets of techniques service a new art of instrumentality, an art that may prove to be ever more relevant in the face of a world where cities will continue to see exponential population growth, increased environmental stresses, complex demands upon space, and radically weakened control and planning authorities.

In striving to comprehend these complex urban issues while also looking to achieve Harvey's "advancement of a more socially just, politically emancipating, and ecologically sane mix of spatiotemporal production processes" in a world gone awry, landscape urbanism offers some of the most compelling future directions. It can offer direction because of its extensive scale and scope, its inclusive pragmatism and creative techniques, its prioritization of infrastructure and process, its embrace of indeterminacy and open-endedness, and its vision of a more wholesome and heterogeneous world. Underlying all of these claims, of course, is the soft world of ecology.

## Ecology

Ecology teaches us that all life is bound into dynamic and interrelated processes of codependency. Changes in the effects produced by an individual or ecosystem in one part of the planet can have significant effects elsewhere. Moreover, the complexity of these interactions escapes linear, mechanistic models or projections as layers of interrelationship create hidden cascades of effects to continually evolve forms in time. Such a dynamic, ongoing process of codependency and interaction is highlighted in ecology, accounting for a particular spatial form as merely a provisional state of matter on its way to becoming something else. In this sense, cities and infrastructures are just as "ecological" as forests and rivers. This may be a hard point for traditional environmentalists to swallow, but the fact remains that everything is connected to everything else, and if the "environment" is something always "outside," then we fail to realize the full codependency and interactivity of things. Hence, we might speak of ecology as describing not a remote "nature" but more integrative "soft systems"—fluid, pliant, adaptive fields that are responsive and evolving. A soft system—whether wetland, city or economy—has the capacity to absorb, transform, and exchange information with its surroundings. Its stability and robustness derive from its dynamics in its capacity to handle and process movement, difference and change. This is an attractive idea for landscape urbanism because it bears upon the continual need for cities and landscapes to be flexible, to be capable of responding quickly to changing needs and demands, while themselves projecting new sets of effect and potential. It also points to a revised activity in design practice: That is the active stirring of ecologies—eidetic and cultural as well as biological—in order to produce new combinatory mixes, new sets of effects, new transdisciplinary alliances, and new kinds of public space.

NOTES
1    David Harvey, *Spaces of Capital: Towards a Critical Geography* (London: Routledge, 2001).

297

FIG. 1 — Abandoned Vacant Lots, Brush Park Neighborhood,
by Alex S. MacLean, Detroit, 1989

© Alex S. MacLean / Landslides Aerial Photography

FIG. 2 — Abandoned Victorian house surrounded by cleared lots now overgrown with
grasses, Brush Park Neighborhood, by Alex S. MacLean, Detroit, 1989

© Alex S. MacLean / Landslides Aerial Photography

# LANDSCRAPING

The "Stalking Detroit" Project, and Charles Waldheim and Marili Santos-Munné's proposal "Decamping Detroit" in particular, prompt one to reflect on the reversal of traditional architectural approaches toward colonization and building to those of unbuilding, removal, and erasure.[1] These are important concerns not only because of the depopulation of certain urban areas, as in Detroit, but also the opposite extreme: the expansion of urban areas and the need to preserve or retain sectors of empty and open space. [FIGS. 1 + 2] If the former case implies decolonization, then the latter suggests an active process of anticolonization. Both are strategic operations that are crucial to the development of open reserves of space, reserves that are fast disappearing as low-density development sprawls unconfined across the surfaces of the earth. What character or program could be assigned to such reserves? Should they in fact be assigned any identity at all? And what mechanisms might be deployed to ensure the integrity and longevity of such spaces?

In considering the above questions with specific regard to Detroit, Waldheim and Santos-Munné look to two references. First is the city ombudsman's suggestion that blighted areas of metropolitan Detroit be closed down, voided, and left to nature. The second is the filmmaker Andrei Tarkovsky's enigmatic "Zone" in his film *Stalker*. Both references paint a picture of a cleared, decommissioned terrain that is essentially empty of references, representations, or programs. More importantly, these references also suggest that empty spaces are not simply the leftover results of desertion but rather of *construction*: They are intentionally "set up" and staged as open grounds for wholly indeterminate futures. The fact that such activity resides in the logistics of creating and

*Originally published in: Georgia Daskalakis, Charles Waldheim and Jason Young, eds.*
Stalking Detroit *(Barcelona: ACTAR, 2001): 122–26. Reproduced with permission.*

maintaining such spaces rather than in their appearance presents a real challenge to architects who have been long concerned with formal expression and
completion.

This notion of setting up reserves of indeterminacy points to a number of
significant issues with regard to the development of genuine open space. The
first issue raised is *management*. Decommissioning and reallocating resources
is an inevitable aspect of urban economy, as in "good housekeeping." Therefore,
a variety of precise organizational measures must be devised and implemented.
While many aspects of landscape and city, especially open space, may appear
to be quite simple, these structures are typically undergirded by an entire arsenal of instruments and mechanisms that derive from quite complex regimes of
organization. These infrastructural regimes are best described as "diagrams,"
or schematic frameworks that describe the codes and mechanisms necessary for
something to be enacted (including erasure). As such, they point toward a form
of architectural practice that is logistical and performative, as distinct from one
that is primarily object/form focused. These mechanisms of management raise
a second set of issues related to strategy and power. Power implies that there
will always be winners (typically the power authority, as in the State) and losers
(typically the lowest income groups) when territory is reorganized. However,
the diagrammatic emancipation of large tracts of land, the *deterritorialization* of
property, suggests a condition where there is in fact no single power or authority but rather a mass collection of individual choices and actions. In other words,
while there may well be a central agency that conceives and directs the deterritorialization of space, the ensuing result can be completely open and unregulated, thereby conflating questions of hierarchy, control, and power. The work
of deterritorialization moves away from both Modernist and New Urbanist
models of ordering the city (both of which believe that formal models alone will
remedy many of the problems of the city, stylistic differences notwithstanding)
to more open-ended, strategic models of radical emancipation through diagrammatic means. Thus, instead of "scaping" the land into a formal composition of
meaning and presence, I am suggesting the possibilities for "scraping" the land
of its various residues: symbolic, political, and material. The scraped ground
then becomes an empty field of absence that accommodates multiple interpretations and possibilities.

Waldheim and Santos-Munné's work demonstrates one such instance of
landscraping, but there are other examples as well, for instance: Rem Koolhaas's
and Office of Metropolitan Architecture's (OMA) proposal for the staged erasure
of La Défense in Paris and its subsequent overlay by an autonomous grid survey
framework. "The process of erasure could be scraped over time in a surreptitious

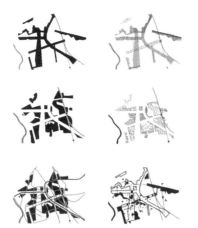

FIG. 3 — *Ville Nouvelle Melun-Sénart*, by Rem Koolhaas/ Office for Metropolitan Architecture, France, 1987

way—an invisible reality. We could gradually scrape whole areas of texture off the map, and in twenty-five years the whole area would be available...What to do with this new territory?"[2] In a different way, Koolhaas and OMA's proposal for the construction of five "linear voids" in the planning framework for the new town of Melun-Senart provides another useful comparison: "A system of bands, linear voids, is inscribed on the site like an enormous Chinese figure. We propose to invest most of the energies needed for the development of Melun-Senart in the protection of these bands, in maintaining their emptiness."[3] [FIG. 3] Here, a reversal is exposed, as the voids are the important vessels that are highly regulated, while the spaces left in between the bands become open for development with minimal regulation. A third project of erasure by Koolhaas is the Point City/South City plan, which speculatively reallocates density and distribution of settlement across the Netherlands in order to concentrate urban areas while preserving open space: "We systematically, deliberately, intentionally fabricate a Western metropolis, and at the same time create emptiness—a reservoir of void—in the rest of the country."[4] Adriaan Geuze and West 8 have proposed a similar strategy of empty scenarios, this time for the Randstad and Green Heart: "Empty scenarios are more sensible the more they are based on introducing guidelines and restrictions for developing each individual area than designating empty expanse: These can be related to excluding certain functions, limiting the height of buildings, density, noise, production, or incorporating ecological textures, and so on."[5] There are other instances of landscaping, for example: Peter Latz's concept of "residual" and "blank" space, Tony Smith's "unrecognizable space," Robert Smithson's "non-site," or Marc Augé's "non-space," and there is good reason to believe that practices of landscaping are constructing alternative grounds to that of either the traditional city or landscape.

These various practices of scraping and deterritorialization introduce voids. Regardless of how much the process tries, the decommissioning and erasure of sites still leaves a vacancy. It is impossible to completely remove space. As mentioned above, this void-space presents the city managers with multiple logistical and operational problems while providing the estranged residents with a vast range of unsanctioned and perhaps even hitherto unforeseen opportunities. However, it is important to note that these qualities are dependent upon the wholly undefined aspects of the void. The void cannot be earmarked as "nature reserve," "succession habitat," "recreational field," or any other such designate, because to name it is to claim it in some way. And what is potentially more socially liberating about the void is precisely the absence of recognition and the subsequent indifference toward it. One simply does not "see" it, even though it surrounds and enables performance, and is itself sustained by invisible mechanisms and regulatory infrastructures.

These issues challenge conventional architectural practice and the assumptions that underlie its methods and techniques. They also challenge society's acculturated assumptions about what is "good" and "bad" in a city, and what role landscape plays in the projection of urban morality. Ultimately, they suggest that the city is a complex and always emerging entity that can no longer be shaped through "architecture" or "landscape." In recognizing the dynamic, uncontrollable, and wild effects of contemporary urbanism, new techniques of intervention need to be devised that allow for the living entity of the city to be more creatively engaged. The move away from "master plans" to more tactical, improvisational, and provisional projects marks a shift in attitude from that of architect as super-authority to architect as adaptive entrepreneur: a social manager of sets and stages that enable the city to perform in newly dynamic ways. These sets and stages, these infrastructures, no longer aim to improve or correct the city (a position of power) but are rather aimed at establishing the conditions for the full liberating promise of contemporary urbanism to play out.

Two landscapes that come to mind with regard to the management, vacancy, and morality of the Detroit clearances are the English Commons and the Indian Maidan.[6] These vague, simple, and empty spaces, centrally located in towns and cities, escape easy definition or explanation: they simply *are*. Free of the excesses of design, composition, or representation, these blank and open fields invite the participation of all the city's residents. They function as blank slates, level terrains upon which differences may be negotiated in time. At once campground and nomadic field, these sites allow for the double experience of individual freedom and collective engagement. Anonymous and plain, the Maidan and the Commons belong to everybody and to nobody. They are readily accessible, openly shared, yet nondescript, banal, and ordinary. It is precisely these characteristics of blank space, the very lack of identity and (re)cognizance, that enable it to perform so adaptably and inclusively over time. It is in this generic form of space that we move away from architecture and landscape to something that is undesigned, unbuilt, and open.

This is not at all meant to suggest that space should simply be left alone, as in the politics of nondevelopment or ad hoc emergence. On the contrary, both the Maidan and the Commons have particular structures that undergird their existence: deterritorialized cuts and breaks, reterritorialized fields and frames, infrastructural points and lines of force, some visible, most invisible, hidden in the diagrams and regulatory apparatus of the various city managers, and, of course, the performative social patterns and group affiances that eventually colonize these surfaces in provisional yet deeply significant ways. Moreover, their very existence is dependent upon the density, intensity, and development of their surroundings. However, whereas these surroundings may continue to evolve according to typical processes of urbanization, including architecture and planning, the deterritorialized spaces are dependent upon a very different framework of mechanisms. Thus, to the degree that we might still speak about landscape and architectural design, it is more the design of managerial procedures, setups, and strategies of disappearance than it is the design of compositions.

NOTES

1   Charles Waldheim and Marili Santos-Munné's proposal for "Decamping Detroit" consisted of a four-stage decommissioning of land: (1) "Dislocation" of people and services in bounded "zones"; (2) "Erasure" through demolition and seeding aggressive plant species that would "hasten the natural deterioration of the city's building fabric as an effect of weathering"; (3) "Absorption," or "ecological reconstitution" through selective flooding as "an effective long-term solution to the contamination of the ground"; (4) "Infiltration" or a speculation on the recolonization of these zones, based on "open-ended responses to individual or collective demands placed on the landscape" (see Waldheim and Santos-Munné, "Decamping Detroit," in Georgia Daskalakis, Charles Waldheim and Jason Young, eds., *Stalking Detroit* (Barcelona: Actar, 2002), 104–20.

2   See Rem Koolhaas and Bruce Mau, *S,M,L,XL* (New York: Monacelli Press), 1090–135.

3   Ibid., 981.

4   Ibid., 891.

5   See Adrian Geuze, "Wildernis," in *De Alexanderpolder: New Urban Frontiers*, ed. Anne-Mie Devolder (Bussum, Netherlands: Thoth, 1993), 96–105.

6   See Anuradha Mathur, "Neither Wilderness Nor Home: The Indian Maidan," in *Recovering Landscape: Essays in Contemporary Landscape Architecture*, ed. James Corner (New York: Princeton Architectural Press, 1999), 204–19.

FIG. 1 — View of hard and organic surfaces blending together on the High Line, by James Corner Field Operations with Diller Scofidio + Renfro, New York, 2004

# TERRA FLUXUS

In the opening years of the twenty-first century, that seemingly old-fashioned term landscape is definitely back in vogue. [FIG. 1] The reappearance of landscape in the larger cultural imagination is due, in part, to the remarkable rise of environmentalism and a global ecological awareness, to the growth of tourism and the associated needs of regions to retain a sense of unique identity, and to the impacts upon rural areas by massive urban growth. But landscape also affords a range of imaginative and metaphorical associations, especially for many contemporary architects and urbanists. Certainly, architecture schools have embraced landscape in recent years, even though not long ago architects could not (or would not) even draw a tree, let alone demonstrate interest in site and landscape. Today, however, it is not merely an interest in vegetation, earthworks, and site planning that we see espoused in various schools of design and planning, but also a deep concern with landscape's conceptual scope—with its capacity to encompass sites, territories, ecosystems, networks, and infrastructures, and to organize large urban fields. In particular, themes of organization, dynamic interaction, ecology, and technique inspire a looser, emergent urbanism, more akin to the real complexity of cities—thus offering an alternative to the rigid mechanisms of centralist planning.

Leading schools of landscape architecture have traditionally understood the scope of landscape as a model for urbanism, embracing large-scale organizational techniques alongside those of design, cultural expression, and ecological formation. Recently, a few landscape architects have shed their professionally defined limits to expand their skills across complex urbanistic, programmatic,

*Originally published in: Charles Waldheim, ed.* The Landscape Urbanism Reader *(New York: Princeton Architectural Press, 2006): 54–80. Reproduced with permission.*

and infrastructural areas. So it seems that certain elements within each of the design professions—architecture, landscape architecture, urban design, and planning—are moving toward a shared form of practice, for which the term *landscape* holds central significance, as described through the formulation *landscape urbanism*. What is the precise nature of this hybrid practice and how are each of the terms *landscape* and *urbanism* altered?

This new disciplinary collusion was anticipated in the Landscape Urbanism symposium and exhibition in 1997, originally conceived and organized by Charles Waldheim, and has been further articulated through a range of publications.[1] It is a proposition of disciplinary conflation and unity, albeit a unity that contains, or holds together, difference—difference in terms of the ideological, programmatic, and cultural content of each of those loaded and contested words, "landscape," "urbanism." [FIG. 2]

Clearly, much of the intellectual intent of these manifesto-like propositions is the total dissolution of the two terms into one word, one phenomenon, one practice. And yet at the same time each term remains distinct, suggesting their necessary, perhaps inevitable, separateness. Such a dialectical synthesis is significant, for it differs from earlier attempts to speak of urban sites as landscapes, or from attempts to situate landscape in the city. The more traditional ways in which we speak about landscape and cities have been conditioned through the nineteenth-century lens of difference and opposition. In this view, cities are seen to be busy with the technology of high-density building, transportation infrastructure, and revenue-producing development, the undesirable effects of which include congestion, pollution, and various forms of social stress; whereas landscape, in the form of parks, greenways, street trees, esplanades, and gardens, is generally seen to provide both salve and respite from the deleterious effects of urbanization. A most canonical instance of this, of course, is Olmsted's Central Park, intended as relief from the relentless urban fabric of Manhattan— even though the catalytic effect that Central Park exerted on surrounding real estate development links it more closely with a landscape urbanist model. In this instance, landscape drives the process of city formation.

Jens Jensen articulated this sentiment when he said, "Cities built for a wholesome life…not for profit or speculation, with the living green as an important part of their complex will be the first interest of the future town-planner."[2] "Complex" is an important term here, and I shall return to it; suffice it to say that for Jensen, as for Olmsted and even for Le Corbusier in his Plan Voisin—this "green complex" comes in the form of parks and green open spaces, accompanied by the belief that such environments will bring civility, health, social equity, and economic development to the city.

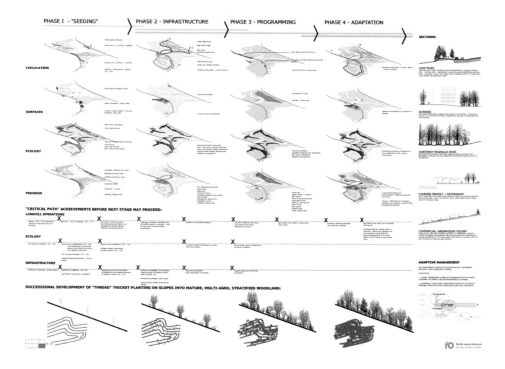

FIG. 2 — Fresh Kills Lifescape phasing sequence, by James Corner Field Operations, New York, 2004

More than aesthetic and representational spaces, however, the more significant of these traditional urban landscapes possess the capacity to function as important ecological vessels and pathways: the hydrological and stormwater system underlying the necklace-like structure of Boston's Back Bay Fens, for example, or the greenway corridors that infiltrate Stuttgart and bring mountain air through the city as both coolant and cleanser. These kinds of infrastructural landscapes will surely continue to be important to the overall health and well-being of urban populations. These precedents also embody some of the more significant potentials of landscape urbanism: the ability to shift scales, to situate cities in their regional and biotic contexts, and to design relationships between dynamic environmental processes and urban form.

The challenge in looking to these precedents for insight into our contemporary conditions is their invocation of a cultural image of "Nature," an image to which landscape is so firmly attached. Nature, in the above-mentioned examples, is mostly represented as a softly undulating pastoral scene, generally considered virtuous, benevolent, and soothing, a moral as well as practical antidote to the corrosive environmental and social qualities of the modern city. This landscape is the city's "other," its essential complement drawn from a nature outside of and excluding building, technology, and infrastructure.

A more complex and contradictory example is the Los Angeles River, which runs from the Santa Susana Mountains through downtown Los Angeles. The "river" is actually a concrete channel built by the U.S. Corps of Engineers in response to the serious flood threat posed by the springtime snowmelts combined with surface runoff from surrounding developments. The channel is designed to optimize the efficiency and speed at which the water is discharged. Its advocates view "nature" here as a violent and threatening force—and rightly so. On the other hand, landscape architects, environmentalists, and various community groups want to convert the channel into a green corridor, replete with riparian habitat, woodlands, birdsong, and fishermen. For these groups, "nature" has been defaced by the engineer's zeal for control. It is, I believe, a well-intentioned but misguided mission, and it underscores the persistent opposition in people's minds.

This contest goes both ways. The debate is not only concerned with bringing landscape into cities but also with the expansion of cities into surrounding landscape—the source of the pastoral ideal. In 1955, the megamall urbanist Victor Gruen coined the term "cityscape," which he posited in contradistinction to "landscape." Gruen's cityscape refers to the built environment of buildings, paved surfaces, and infrastructures. These are further subdivided into "technoscapes," "transportationscapes," "suburbscapes," and even "subcityscapes"—the peripheral strips and debris that Gruen calls the "scourge of the metropolis." On the other hand, "landscape," for Gruen, refers to the "environment in which nature is predominant." He does say that landscape is not the "natural environment" per se, as in untouched wilderness, but to those regions where human occupation has shaped the land and its natural processes in an intimate and reciprocal way. He cites agrarian and rural situations as examples, invoking an image of topographic and ecological harmony, bathed in green vegetation and dear blue sky. For Gruen, cityscape and landscape were once clearly separated, but today the city has broken its walls to subsume and homogenize its surrounding landscape in an economic and "technological blitzkrieg"—the various "scapes" now in conflict and with boundless definition.[3]

This image of one thing overtaking another (with competing values attached to each, as in either landscape permeating the city or the city sprawling across its hinterland) is reminiscent of debates surrounding the design of Parc de la Villette, in which many landscape architects initially decried the lack of "landscape" in the park's design, seeing only the buildings or "follies." More recently, landscape architects have revised this sentiment, suggesting that upon further inspection, the still maturing landscape has come to prevail over the buildings. This sentiment is very telling for—as with Jensen, Olmsted, Le Corbusier, Gruen, and their contemporaries, or indeed for the various groups contesting the Los Angeles River today—it keeps the categories of building/city versus green landscape as separate entities: The follies at la Villette are somehow not recognized as being part of the landscape, just as the concrete river channel is not recognized as a landscape element, even though its landscape *function* is solely hydrological.

Moreover, we know full well that each of these categories—landscape and urbanism—belongs to a certain profession, or institutionalized discipline. Architects construct buildings and, with engineers and planners, they design cities; landscape architects build landscapes, in the form of earthwork, planting, and open space design. Implicit in the sentiments of many landscape architects is indignation that the Parc de la Villette was designed not by a landscape architect but by an architect. Similarly, when a landscape architect wins a competition today that architects think belongs in their domain, there can be heard some rather cynical grumbling in that court, too. So this antinomic, categorical separation between landscape and urbanism persists today not only because of a perceived difference in material, technical, and imaginative/moralistic dimensions or these two media, but also because of a hyper-professionalized classification, a construction further complicated through competing power relations.

For example, it has been argued by others that landscape tends to be repressed by many architects and planners, or appropriated only to the extent that it frames and enhances the primacy of urban form. Landscape is employed here as a bourgeois aesthetic, or naturalized veil, typically in the form of greenery. Moreover, it is increasingly the case that vast developer-engineering corporations are constructing today's world with such pace, efficiency, and profit that all of the traditional design disciplines (and not only landscape) are marginalized as mere decorative practices, literally disenfranchised from the work of programmatic and spatial formation.

Conversely, of course, many ecologically aligned landscape architects see cities as grossly negligent with regard to nature. While the accomplishments of environmental restoration and regulation are both urgent and impressive, the exclusion of urban form and process from any ecological analysis remains extremely problematic. Moreover, so-called "sustainable" proposals, wherein urbanism becomes dependent upon certain bioregional metabolisms, while assuming the place-form of some semi-rural environment, are surely naive and counterproductive. Do the advocates of such plans really believe that natural systems alone can cope more effectively with the quite formidable problems of waste and pollution than do modern technological plants? And do they really believe that putting people in touch with this fictional image called "nature" will predispose everybody to a more reverent relationship with the earth and with one another (as if relocating millions from cities to the countryside will actually somehow improve biodiversity and water and air quality)?

At the beginning of the twentieth century, only sixteen cities in the world had populations larger than a million people, yet at the close of the century more than five hundred cities had more than a million inhabitants, many boasting more than ten million residents and still expanding. Metropolitan Los Angeles has a current population of approximately thirteen million and is projected to double in the next twenty-five years. Given the complexity of the rapidly urbanizing metropolis, to continue to oppose nature against culture, landscape against city—and not only as negational absolutes but also in the guise of benign, complementary overlaps—is to risk complete failure of the architectural and planning arts to make any real or significant contribution to future urban formations.

With this preface, we can begin to imagine how the concept of landscape urbanism suggests a more promising, more radical, and more creative form of practice than that defined by rigid disciplinary categorizations. Perhaps the very complexity of the forces that drive the contemporary metropolis demands a conflation of professional and institutionalized distinctions into a new synthetic art, a spatio-material practice able to bridge scale and scope with critical insight and imaginative depth.

By way of providing a schematic outline for such a practice, I can sketch four provisional themes: processes over time, the staging of surfaces, the operational or working method, and the imaginary. The first of these themes addresses processes over time. The principle is that the processes of urbanization—capital accumulation, deregulation, globalization, environmental protection, and so on—are much more significant for the shaping of urban relationships than are the spatial forms of urbanism in and of themselves. The modernist notion that new physical structures would yield new patterns of socialization has exhausted its run, failing by virtue of trying to contain the dynamic multiplicity of urban processes within a fixed, rigid, spatial frame that neither derived from nor redirected any of the processes moving through it. This emphasis on urban processes is not meant to exclude spatial form but rather seeks to construct a dialectical understanding of how it relates to the processes that flow through, manifest, and sustain it.

This suggests shifting attention away from the object qualities of space (whether formal or scenic) to the systems that condition the distribution and density of urban form. Field diagrams or maps describing the play of those forces are particularly useful instruments in furthering an understanding of urban events and processes. For example, the geographer Walter Christaller's diagrams of population distribution and city planner Ludwig Hilberseimer's diagrams of regional settlement patterns each articulate flows and forces in relation to urban form.[4]

In comparing the formal determinism of modernist urban planning and the more recent rise of neo-traditional "New Urbanism," David Harvey has written that both projects fail because of their presumption that spatial order can control history and process. Harvey argues that "the struggle" for designers and planners lies not with spatial form and aesthetic appearance alone but with the advancement of "more socially just, politically emancipatory, and ecologically sane mix(es) of spatiotemporal production processes," rather than the capitulation to those processes "imposed by uncontrolled capital accumulation, backed by class privilege and gross inequalities of political-economic power."[5] His point is that the projection of new possibilities or future urbanisms must derive less from an understanding of form and more from an understanding of process — how things work in space and time.

In conceptualizing a more organic, fluid urbanism, ecology itself becomes an extremely useful lens through which to analyze and project alternative urban futures. The lessons of ecology have aimed to show how all life on the planet is deeply bound into dynamic relationships. Moreover, the complexity of interaction between elements within ecological systems is such that linear, mechanistic models prove to be markedly inadequate to describe them. Rather, the discipline of ecology suggests that individual agents acting across a broad field of operation produce incremental and cumulative effects that continually evolve the shape of an environment over time. Thus, dynamic relationships and agents of process become highlighted in ecological thinking, accounting for a particular spatial form as merely a provisional state of matter, on its way to becoming something else. Consequently, apparently incoherent or complex conditions that one might initially mistake as random or chaotic can, in fact, be shown to be highly structured entities that comprise a particular set of geometrical and spatial orders. In this sense, cities and infrastructures are just as "ecological" as forests and rivers.

Since the publication in 1969 of Ian McHarg's *Design With Nature*, landscape architects have been particularly busy developing a range of ecological techniques for the planning and design of sites. But, for a variety of reasons, some outlined earlier, ecology has been used only in the context of something called the "environment," which is generally thought to be of "nature" and exclusive of the city. Even those who have included the city in the ecological

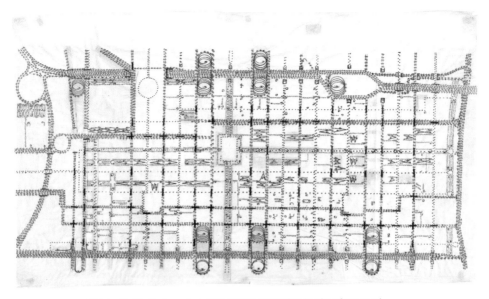

FIG. 3 — *Traffic Study, project, Philadelphia, Pennsylvania. Plan of proposed traffic-movement pattern,* by Louis I. Kahn, 1952, Ink, graphite, and cut-and-pasted papers on paper, 24½ × 42¾ inches (62,2 × 108.6 cm)

Courtesy The Museum of Modern Art, New York, NY, U.S.A. © The Louis I. Kahn Collection, The University of Pennsylvania and the Pennsylvania Historical and Museum Commission

equation have done so only from the perspective of natural systems (hydrology, air-flow, vegetational communities, and so on). We have yet to understand cultural, social, political, and economic environments as embedded in and symmetrical with the "natural" world. The promise of landscape urbanism is the development of a space-time ecology that treats all forces and agents working in the urban field and considers them as continuous networks of interrelationship. One model for such a conflation that comes to mind in this context is architect Louis Kahn's 1952 diagram for vehicular circulation in Philadelphia. [FIG. 3] With regards to this project, Kahn wrote:

> Expressways are like rivers. These rivers frame the area to be served. Rivers have Harbors. Harbors are the municipal parking towers; from the Harbors branch a system of Canals that serve the interior…from the Canals branch cul-de-sac Docks; the Docks serve as entrance halls to the buildings.[6]

Later, in Kahn's proposal for Market Street East came a whole repertoire of "gateways," "viaducts," and "reservoirs," each finding new expression in the urban field as iconographic figures illuminated in colored light at nighttime—allowing for both navigation and the regulation of speed.

Kahn's diagrams suggest the need for contemporary techniques of representing the fluid, process-driven characteristics of the city, wherein the full range of agents, actors, and forces that work across a given territory might be brought into consideration, mobilized, and redirected. This work must necessarily view the entire metropolis as a living arena of processes and exchanges over time, allowing new forces and relationships to prepare the ground for new activities and patterns of occupancy. The designation *terra firma* (firm, not changing; fixed and definite) gives way in favor of shifting processes coursing through and across the urban field: *terra fluxus*.

The second theme of the landscape urbanism project concerns itself with the phenomenon of the horizontal surface, the ground plane, the "field" of action. These surfaces constitute the urban field when considered across a wide range of scales, from the sidewalk to the street to the entire infrastructural matrix of urban surfaces. This suggests contemporary interest in surface continuities, where roofs and grounds become one and the same; and this is certainly of great value with regard to conflating separations between landscape and building—one thinks of the collaborations between Peter Eisenman and Laurie Olin in this regard. However, I would emphasize a second understanding of surface: surface understood as urban infrastructure. Unlike architecture, which consumes the potential of the site in order to project, urban infrastructure sows the seeds of future possibility, staging the ground for new promise. This preparation of surfaces for future appropriation differs from merely formal interests in single surface construction. It is much more strategic, emphasizing means over ends and performative logic over compositional design.

For example, the grid has historically proven to be a particularly effective field operation, extending a framework across a vast surface for flexible and changing development over time, such as the real estate and street grid of Manhattan, or the land survey grid of the Midwestern United States. This organization lends legibility and order to the surface while allowing for the autonomy and individuality of each part, and remaining open to alternative permutations over time.

Such urban surfaces register the trajectories of shifting populations, demographics, and interest groups over time, and enables people to provisionally stage a site for various and shifting programmatic events. This dynamic surface is not so much an object that has been "designed" compositionally, but rather a well-conceived organization or infrastructure that acts as both instigator and accelerator of process and action. Such a strategic approach, at once simple and conventional, endows residents the ability to configure sites according to changing seasons, needs, and desires. The thrust of this work is therefore less toward formal resolution and more toward public processes of engagement and future use. Concerned with a working surface over time, landscape urbanism anticipates change, open-endedness, and provides a platform for negotiation.

This leads in turn to the third theme of landscape urbanism, which is the working method. How does one conceptualize and work with an urban geography that functions across a range of scales and implicates a diverse host of people? Moreover, beyond issues of representation, how does one actually operate or put into effect this work, especially given the complex exigencies of contemporary development? There is no shortage of critical utopias, but so few of them have made it past the drawing board. It is both tragic and ironic that as designers we are all ultimately interested in the constructed reality of building, but that most who actually accomplish this have to do so through the confined strictures of conventional professional procedures. On the other hand, it would seem that the visionaries, while provocative and interesting, continue to evade real action: their utopias ignore the problem of an effective operative strategy.

In this regard, I believe that landscape urbanism suggests a radical reconsideration of traditional conceptual, representational, and operative techniques. The possibilities of vast scale shifts across both time and space; working with synoptic maps alongside the intimate recordings of local circumstance; comparing cinematic and choreographic techniques to spatial notation; entering the algebraic, digital space of the computer while messing around with paint, clay, and ink; and engaging real estate developers and engineers alongside the highly specialized imagineers and poets of contemporary culture—all these activities and more seem integral to any real and significant practice of synthetic urban projection. But the techniques to address the sheer scope of issues here are desperately lacking—and this area alone, it would seem to me, is deserving of our utmost attention and research.

This arrives at the fourth theme of landscape urbanism, which is the imaginary. There is simply no point whatsoever in addressing any of the above themes for their own sake. The collective imagination, informed and stimulated by the experiences of the material world, must continue to be the primary motivation of any creative endeavor. In many ways, the failing of twentieth-century planning can be attributed to the absolute impoverishment and incapacity of the imagination with regard to the optimized rationalization of urban development practices and capital accumulation. Public space in the city must surely be more than mere token compensation or vessels for this generic activity called "recreation." Public spaces are firstly the containers of collective memory and desire, and secondly they are the places for geographic and social imagination to inspire new relationships and possibilities. Materiality, representation, and imagination are not separate worlds; political change through practices of place construction owes as much to the representational and symbolic realms as to material activities. And so it seems that landscape urbanism is first and last an imaginative project, a speculative thickening of the world of possibilities.

In conclusion, I would return to the paradoxical separateness of landscape from urbanism. Neither term is fully conflated into the other. I do believe that this paradox is not only inescapable but also necessary to maintain. The failure of earlier urban design and regionally scaled enterprises was the oversimplification and reduction of the phenomenal richness of physical life. A good landscape architect must be able to weave the diagram and the strategy in relationship to the tactile and the poetic. In other words, the union of landscape with urbanism promises new relational and systemic workings across territories of vast scale and scope, situating the parts in relation to the whole, but at the same time the separateness of landscape from urbanism acknowledges a level of material physicality, of intimacy and difference, which is always nested deep within the larger matrix or field.

NOTES

1    Landscape Urbanism Symposium and Exhibition, April 1997, Graham Foundation,
     Chicago. See also, for example, my essays in *Stalking Detroit*, Georgia Daskalakis,
     Charles Waldheim and Jason Young, eds (Barcelona: Actar, 2001); *Landscape
     Urbanism: A Manual for the Machinic Landscape*, Mohsen Mostafavi and Ciro Najle,
     eds. (London: Architectural Association, 2003); and David Grahame Shane,
     *Recombinant Urbanism* (London: John Wiley, 2005).

2    Jens Jensen, *Siftings* (Baltimore: Johns Hopkins University Press, 1990). On Jensen's
     work and life, see Robert E. Grese, *Jens Jensen: Maker of Natural Parks and Gardens*
     (Baltimore: Johns Hopkins University Press, 1992).

3    Victor Gruen, *The Heart of Our Cities: The Urban Crisis, Diagnosis and Cure* (New
     York: Simon and Schuster, 1964). See also Gruen, *Centers for the Urban Environment:
     Survival of the Cities* (New York: Van Nostrand Reinhold, 1973).

4    See Walter Christaller's *Central Place Theory* (Englewood Cliffs, NJ: Prentice-Hall,
     1965); and Ludwig Hilberseimer's *New Regional Pattern* (Chicago: P. Theobald, 1949).

5    David Harvey, *The Condition of Post-Modernity* (Cambridge, England: Blackwell,
     1990).

6    Louis Kahn "Philadelphia City Planning: Traffic Studies," Philadelphia, PA, 1951–1953.
     These drawings and project papers are in the Louis I. Kahn Collection, Architectural
     Archives of the University of Pennsylvania.

Part Four

—

# PRACTICE

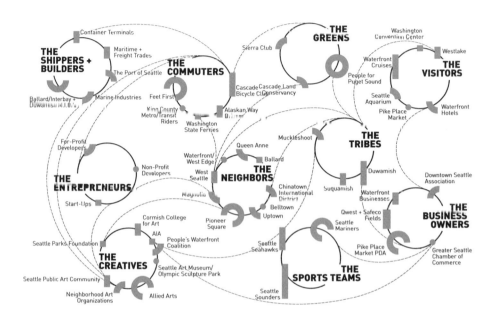

**THE SHIPPERS + BUILDERS**
- Container Terminals
- Maritime + Freight Trades
- The Port of Seattle
- Ballard/Interbay + Duwamish M.I.C.'s
- Marine Industries

**THE COMMUTERS**
- Feet First
- King County Metro/Transit Riders
- Washington State Ferries
- Alaskan Way Viaduct

**THE GREENS**
- Sierra Club
- Cascade Cascade Land Bicycle Club Conservancy
- People for Puget Sound

**THE VISITORS**
- Washington Convention Center
- Westlake
- Waterfront Cruises
- Seattle Aquarium
- Pike Place Market
- Waterfront Hotels

**THE ENTREPRENEURS**
- For-Profit Developers
- Non-Profit Developers
- Start-Ups

**THE NEIGHBORS**
- Queen Anne
- Ballard
- Waterfront/West Edge
- West Seattle
- Magnolia
- Chinatown/International District
- Belltown
- Uptown
- Pioneer Square

**THE TRIBES**
- Muckleshoot
- Duwamish
- Suquamish

**THE BUSINESS OWNERS**
- Downtown Seattle Association
- Waterfront Businesses
- Greater Seattle Chamber of Commerce

**THE CREATIVES**
- Cornish College for Art
- AIA
- People's Waterfront Coalition
- Seattle Parks Foundation
- Seattle Art Museum/Olympic Sculpture Park
- Seattle Public Art Community
- Neighborhood Art Organizations
- Allied Arts

**THE SPORTS TEAMS**
- Seattle Seahawks
- Qwest + Safeco Fields
- Seattle Mariners
- Pike Place Market PDA
- Seattle Sounders

FIG. 1 —"Seattle Agents" diagram of stakeholders and agencies invested in the waterfront, by James Corner Field Operations, Seattle, 2012

# PRACTICE:

## OPERATION AND EFFECT

### Why is it all so complicated?

My friends and colleagues outside of the architectural professions believe that designing buildings and landscapes is a mostly fun career, relatively clear-cut and enriching. To a large degree, they are correct. They may acknowledge that there are skills of design and building they do not possess—in ideation, visualization, and construction techniques, for instance, but they assume that good design education provides these in a straightforward way.

Yet there are many other, less obvious dimensions to landscape and architectural practice that can completely preoccupy good practitioners and make designing much more complicated. Relationships between site and program, form and function, appearance and performance, criticality and projection, and concept and implementation, for example, pose difficult and diverse challenges based on a project's unique characteristics (site, environment, program, client, budget, and so on). "Design innovation" poses a further difficulty. Everyone today seems to want this, but what exactly is it, and why is it sought (and then, paradoxically, often hindered in the process)? Practice realities continue to remain poorly understood and valued—from day-to-day organizational issues of budget, schedule, teamwork, regulations, client demands, and quality assurance (no small matters!), to the creative challenges of developing good design concepts and seeing them through to their (inevitably compromised?) realization. [FIG. 1]

No one can really understand the depth, difficulty, and challenge of practice until they have been intellectually and managerially in the trenches. There are three aspects of practice today that warrant more thought and care as we look ahead.

*Originally published in:* Harvard Design Magazine *33 (Fall/Winter 2010–2011): 100–2. Reproduced with permission.*

### Experimentation and delivery

Experimentation in design is often tied to avant-garde thinking that is abstracted and distanced from reality. Design experimentation frequently steps outside design disciplines to adapt other techniques (textual analysis, musical scoring, or algorithmic scripting, for example). While I do not want to restrict the freedoms and potentials of such open research, and would in large-measure encourage such work, I continue to believe that the most productive forms of design research happen in the field itself. In other words, the complexities that surround projects themselves ought to become the subject matter of experimentation and critique. Theoretical reflection and critique may be useful as means of propelling the imagination, but productive design thinking is focused on specific conditions.

This pragmatic formulation helps bypass the typical divide between high academic theory and avant-garde movements, on the one side, and the more prosaic conventions and habits of commercial practice on the other. Critical experimentation in action—informed by and informing the work at hand—allows for project- and practice specific modes of invention. Current issues in practice such as environmental sustainability, regionalism and globalization, and cross-disciplinary, team-based creativity—all demand new ways of working. The challenge is to evolve experimentation in practice that is always freshly responsive. Design is no longer formal stylization, iconicity, and expression, but more a highly customized, irreproducible *work*, based on creatively activating the potentials of a given situation.

### Public engagement and legibility

Landscape and architecture are public art forms. Projects are made to be shaped, interpreted, used, consumed, and revised over long periods of time. Great works of landscape and architecture continue to appeal to a diverse range of publics, sometimes centuries after their conception. This has led to the consensus today that citizen participation in design decision making ought to be integral to all public projects. While this democratic inclusiveness is to be welcomed for all of the good inclusive reasons (including the importance of building constituencies and future stewards), one of the challenges of this situation is how to make a design that is legible, memorable, and innovative when so many divergent voices tend to lead to conformity and the tried and true (which is inevitably safe and bland).

The difficulty of engaging publics in an effort to produce fresh work is enormous. The art of conversation and reasoned debate is critical, but many in the bureaucratic sphere are fearful of this, since it can quickly lead to situations

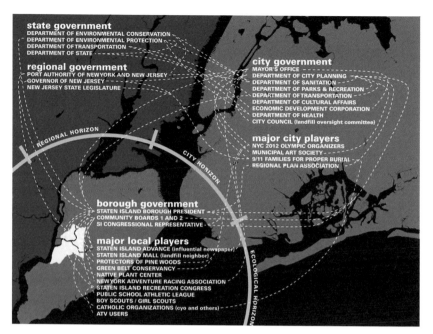

FIG. 2 — Map of the multiple agencies and stakeholders surrounding the Fresh Kills Park Project, Staten Island, New York, by James Corner Field Operations, 2002

that they cannot control. Designers of public projects are often coached prior to any public presentation about what they can or cannot say, and how messages are to be nuanced. To some degree, this is necessary, but the scripting of engagement can stifle authentic dialogue and exchange. Designers need much more sophisticated conversational, social and rhetorical skills if they are to authentically and productively engage the public in a process that supports imagination and innovation.

### Collaboration and disciplinarity

A third challenge to contemporary practice stems from the nature of collaboration and inter-disciplinarity. The world now demands team-based work. Many projects are so complicated that it would be naive to assume that any one professional can address all issues. Even in small projects, design is typically the result of a back-and-forth between office colleagues and the client. [FIG. 2] You wouldn't think that this was the case, given the rise of the "starchitects," but any of them will tell you (at least quietly over dinner) of their complete reliance on their teams, not to mention the responsiveness required to attend to client concerns. The starchitect is more than just a front-person, a brand, or a figurehead.

Most design professionals recognize the importance of collaboration and team-work but are puzzled about why the academy still pushes the idea of the individual star (in both studio teaching and academic literature).

Bigger projects require bigger teams from many disciplines and with diverse expertise. Landscape architects sometimes find themselves taking on the role of orchestrator, trying to ensure that all specialists feed into a final synthesis. This is a role not just of coordination and management but also of design, ensuring that the integrity of fundamental concepts, geometries, materials, and typologies remains intact. Effective collaboration requires superb listening and rhetorical skills, synthesizing multiple interests. [FIG. 3] As such, landscape architects and the landscape as a synthetic medium have exceptional opportunities to create freshly "integrated environments"—not freestanding objects but the fabric and matrix within which life nests and grows. Kenneth Frampton captures this idea:

> I am convinced that landscape proffers itself as a creative-cum-remedial modus both literally and metaphorically. The longstanding ideological division of labor between urban planning, urban design, and architecture can only be overcome, in my view, through what I can only call the self-conscious encouragement of a topographical/phenomenological disposition on the part of architects and planners, one that, while being against conventional expectations, is both technologically adept and economically realistic.[1]

If the academy and the profession want to have a significant effect on current practice, then their focus will need to be on the technical and operational aspects of working effectively in a multimodal world, seeking new effects from highly specific situations. In looking for new ways to creatively operate, to work in new ways with materials and technology, to effectively collaborate and communicate, and to approach and solve problems in freshly resonant ways, we may better chart new forms of practice and, by extension, new forms that shape our world.

NOTES

1    Kenneth Frampton, "Stocktaking 2004: Questions about the Present and Future of Design," in *The New Architectural Pragmatism: A Harvard Design Magazine Reader* (Minneapolis: University of Minnesota Press, 2007), 110.

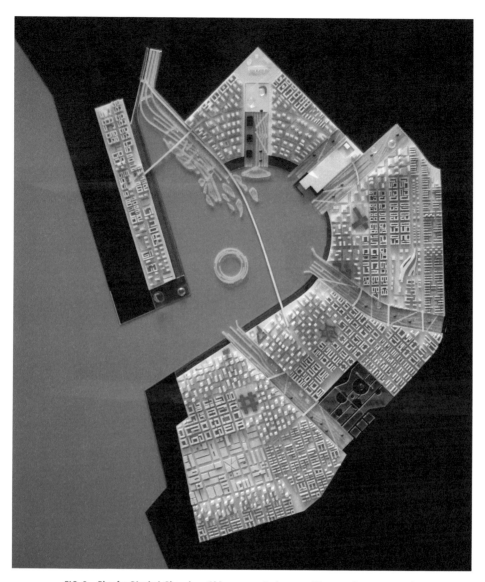

FIG. 3 — Plan for Qianhai, Shenzhen, China, a new city for two million people, as an example
of landscape serving as the primary shaper of new urban forms and as the nucleus organizing multiple
professional disciplines and stakeholders, by James Corner Field Operations, 2010

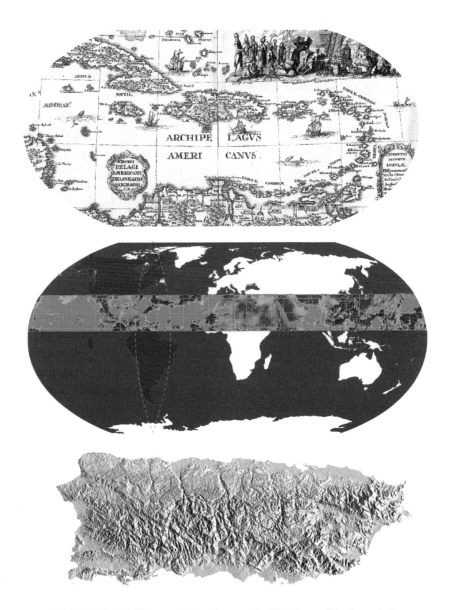

FIG. 1 — Tropical, Caribbean, colonial, and geographical histories condition the context
that is Puerto Rico today, lending it many characteristics both local and rooted, and global and hybrid.
University of Puerto Rico Botanical Garden, by Field Operations, San Juan, Puerto Rico, 2004

# BOTANICAL URBANISM

### Botanical urbanism

For those who are neither botanists nor avid admirers of horticulture, plants, and flowers, the topic of the botanical garden in the context of our media-saturated twenty-first century might at first seem a little antiquated—more a specialist subject for eccentric gardeners and historians perhaps. While many contemporary botanical gardens around the world are striving to find renewed vitality through conservation, education, and scientific research programs, attendance and revenue continue to decline in most cases. Is the botanical garden as a significant cultural place obsolete today, or at least outmoded in the face of modern science, technology, media, and globalization? Or is there scope for reinvention of the botanical garden as a cultural type somehow newly popular and relevant for the twenty-first-century imagination? [FIG. 1]

In what follows, I will sketch an outline for how the botanical concept, hybridized with current-day constructs of ecology and urbanism, might point to new directions in design and planning—not only for botanical gardens, but also for landscape architecture and urban design more broadly. For, like the city, the botanical garden is an exemplary hybrid form; it is a multiplicity, a collection of diverse and often disparate parts. Both the garden and the city are firmly rooted in the specificity of locality, and yet also freely rhizomatous (or spreading and infiltrating) in scope, invoking the foreign, the far-away, the exotic, and the other.

*Originally published in:* Studies in the History of Gardens and Designed Landscapes *25/2 (June 2005): 123–43. © 2005 Taylor & Francis, Ltd. (http://www.tandfonline.com). Reproduced with permission.*

A second characteristic of the botanical garden is its constructedness. It is not at all natural. It is instead a profoundly layered, ordered, and organized space. This organization is not simply a formal or geometrical patterning, but is more fundamentally derived from quite elaborate schemes of classification and taxonomy. Categories, trees, and tables govern how natural material is dissected, grouped, and arranged in the botanical garden—not according to nature, but according to rational tables of nomenclature. The botanical garden is all invention, fabrication, artificial orderings of nature, each highly organized and specific, and each producing very particular image ideas of culture's relationship to the vegetal world.

The constructed properties of botanical gardens can in many ways be related to the organization of larger urban patterns: the roman orchard grid preceding the squared city, for example; or measured plots and beds preceding larger scale patterns of land division; the axial Baroque Garden preceding civic planner Georges-Eugène Haussmann and the boulevard; even the tree-like hierarchy of Enlightenment botanical classification paralleling the rational organization in city planning. More recent ecological developments—botanical organization according to community and environmental relationships, or to collective ecosystems rather than to individual parts—has particular application to the city today, where processes of growth, interaction, and multiple temporalities are foregrounded.

All of the above suggests how the botanical concept might actually shed new insights upon more popular and contested terms of the urban and the ecological. As organizational models, the exotic artificiality of the botanical, the life-sustaining imperative of the ecological, and the programmatic spectacle of the urban exceed their own limitations when considered together as a kind of synthetic, hybrid model. Such a hybrid points to ways of not simply representing the natural and cultural worlds, but more to ways of *constructing* them in novel and freshly pertinent ways.

It is with regard to this introductory discussion that I will now describe a planning and design project that my office undertook for the Botanical Garden at the University of Puerto Rico between 2002 and 2005. The following remark made by historic preservationist Frank Matero could not apply better than to this garden:

> Recent advances in plant science and changes in public recreation have required these institutions to reconsider their contemporary role as valuable and relevant cultural landscapes. Increased recreational use, coupled with new methods of scientific research, have brought new problems including

accelerated deterioration, accessibility, interpretation, and scientific redundancy. Underlying these problems is the more fundamental question of the continued relevancy and practicality of these places as scientific institutions dedicated to specimen collection and display.

Originally founded in the late 1800s as an experimental research station, with a focus upon sugarcane and rum production, the botanical garden of the University of Puerto Rico today comprises a confusing amalgam of uses and identities, and certainly suffers from many of the same issues described by Matero, particularly the lack of an identity that is appealing and relevant for the city.

The garden is located close to the center of San Juan. It is bisected into two roughly equivalent parcels by a major road corridor, the PR-1. The north parcel is 141.1 acres in area, and is mostly flat land. This parcel is subject to frequent flooding by the Río Piedras, and is now a fairly underutilized area of overgrown meadow, tree collections, nurseries, and dilapidated rum research buildings. The south parcel is 144.3 acres in area and is quite varied topographically as the land rises to larger hills. This parcel is occupied by the University Central Administration and the original botanical garden display area.

Significantly, the whole site forms part of a much larger greenway swath, now legally preserved as the "ecological corridor." [FIG. 2] Proponents of the ecological corridor declare it an extensive, contiguous area of hilly forest and watershed, protected from any form of development or encroachment. On the other hand, the lack of any program or identity for this preserve makes it difficult for many in the metropolitan area to understand its value. The botanical garden, therefore, has the potential to present a model demonstration—or representation—of the larger ecological corridor in the context of the city.

Before any such potential is realized, however, the garden needs a significant amount of redesign and new construction. The existing site is disorganized, the result of many ad hoc additions and subtractions over the years. Entrances and circulation systems are confusing, and buildings seem random and disorganized. The garden display areas are run-down and in dire need of maintenance, signage, and provision of amenities. The use program for the site is also complicated and confusing, again the result of ad hoc accumulation over time. [FIG. 3]

The factors that have now led the University to reconsider and develop a master plan design for the future of the site are fourfold. First, the recent completion of a new light rail transit line linking the suburbs with Old San Juan, with a new station at Cupey on the corner of the north parcel of the site, represents a major opportunity for the University to tie into this lifeline and capitalize on the connectivity it affords. The garden could literally become a new destination on the line. Second, because of the new transit line and station, the University is anticipating major new development investment around it, including the building of an important biotechnology facility and, potentially, University housing and related mixed-use. The Governor of Puerto Rico has recently promoted the idea of a "knowledge economy," and has cited the garden project and surrounding development as a new "knowledge-leisure nexus." Here is envisaged an amalgam of new scientific research facilities with public education, leisure, recreation, ecological restoration, and urban amenity — a "botanical city." Third, the environmental lobby in Puerto Rico has recently signed into law the preservation of a huge segment of forest and related watersheds — known originally as the "Bosque Urbano," and now as the "Ecological Corridor" mentioned earlier — of which the botanical garden site is a central part. And fourth, the United States Corp of Engineers plans to channelize the Rio Piedras as it moves through the garden site for flood-control reasons, a project that the University wants to avoid and find alternative treatments for. In conjunction with the recent inauguration of a visionary University president, who has an eye for art and design as well as for developing the physical plant of the University as a whole, and a young, energetic governor with an ambitious new urban development agenda, and the reasons for designing and integrating the gardens anew with the city become evident. Moreover, given the ecological, touristic, and cultural richness of the Caribbean tropics, the cosmopolitanism of San Juan and the broad educational reach of the University of Puerto Rico, the president believes that there exists an opportunity to develop a world-class botanical garden of significant educational import as well as international distinction and prestige.

### A quick survey

In beginning our own thinking about the design of the garden, we first presented to the president and his advisory committee a historical survey of botanical garden themes. This survey begins with the sixteenth-century garden as global microcosm, reflecting the adventurous navigation and discovery of new lands together with the development of Enlightenment science. Collecting together the world's plants in a single place for study and exposition gathered the whole world into a single chamber. The circular garden enclosure, with four quadrants, one for each continent, served as a miniature representation of God's global creations and marked a triumph of human reason over the vagaries of nature. Later, of course, botanical gardens were laid out more in terms of topographical location to represent not only individual plant forms, but also the entire environment from which they derived (tropics, tundra, temperate forest, desert, etc.), pointing to the beginning of an ecological framework.

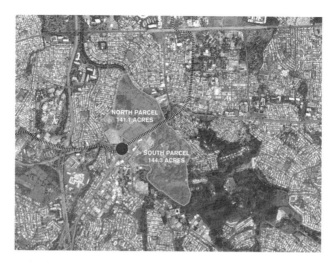

FIG. 2 — Site plan of the existing garden site in the context of the larger ecological corridor,
University of Puerto Rico Botanical Garden, by Field Operations, 2004

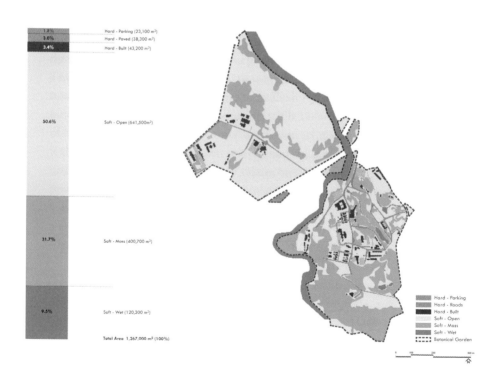

FIG. 3 — Site plan of the existing garden site, showing distribution of
ecosystems, pathways, and buildings, University of Puerto Rico Botanical Garden,
by Field Operations, 2004

The global theatre theme played itself out not only in the botanical garden, but also in various journals, books, and plays, wherein various plants—and later animals, birds, fossils, and crystals—would be represented in comparative discussion, effectively disputing individual species claims of superiority, beauty, sexuality, or utility. Here the colonial effect is particularly resonant in a place like Puerto Rico.

In the tradition of sixteenth- and seventeenth-century science, together with the colonial drive to map, name, classify, and tame, plants were moved around the planet and arranged according to taxonomic schemes, grouped by type and species, and exhaustively inventoried and recorded. Of course, as with any scheme of classification, individuals are subject to alternative forms of combination. The hypothetical 2001 proposal for Buga Park by the Dutch practice MVRDV, for example, proposes to use the alphabet as a means of collecting and grouping plants, thereby producing unusual and novel combinations while pointing tongue-in-cheek to the inevitable fiction of classification.

In contrast to taxonomic schemes of order, recent environmental collections arrange plants in terms of communities and associative habitats. The emphasis is upon individuals in relationship to others and to the dynamics of the ecosystem rather than to horticultural classification. As a consequence of greater emphasis on local environments, many botanical gardens have moved away from a global model to one of regionalist representation, using only native species and regional ecotones. Linked to this is greater emphasis on conservation and education, especially working with endangered or threatened species, for both research and conservation.

Botanical gardens are also great propagators, creating new hybrid plant forms and manufacturing large enough numbers for sale and distribution. Activities of cultivation, seeding, grafting, transplanting, pruning, and other horticultural techniques lead to the production of new species and forms and their subsequent sale for commercial use. Such uses include pharmacology, food production, ecological restoration, and home gardening. Since their inception, botanical gardens have been focused upon research and experimentation. Ranging from studies in taxonomy, speciation and hybridization, to medicinal and pharmacological uses, to ecological and interactive science, to food and fiber production, research continues to elevate the vegetable world to new levels of significance and potential. Botanical gardens have also long been associated with health, initially with the medicinal and herbal gardens, and more recently with pathways and facilities that allow for individual escape from the city with opportunities for exercise and meditation.

Many botanical gardens are of course designed to maximize the visitor's experience of plant material as an aesthetic medium. Sometimes, this desire may allow plant material to be used in increasingly artistic and synthetic ways, sometimes in novel combinations and at other times in completely abstract arrangements. In some cases, there may be a curious blurring of art and science, where new materials and technologies are used to produce new modes of production and reception. New movements in bioart, for example, point to new forms of manufactured nature, completely synthetic forms of propagating life and reproducing vegetal (and animal) forms, raising a host of related ethical and cultural questions. Clearly, this is no longer the representational world of Enlightenment science, the world of collection, signs, and meaning, but now the pure spectacle of production, invention, and virtual reality.

In conjunction with this brief historical survey, we also showed brief case studies of other botanical gardens around the world: the unsurpassed organizational and traditional depth in Kew; the contemporary design and environmental thrust in Barcelona; the tropical design and commercial success in Singapore and Sydney; the educational and urban focus in New York; the community outreach efforts in Missouri; and the novel ecological interpretation in Eden, Cornwall. This quick survey proved useful for the design team in Puerto Rico because it rendered visible the full range of cultural and programmatic possibilities the botanical garden type invokes. The garden can comprise multiple agendas and themes, a diverse environment of plants, settings, arrangements, open spaces, and amenities, providing for an extraordinarily wide range of uses, publics, programs, and meanings. This richness can be both further enhanced and focused by paying particular attention to the specificity of Puerto Rico, or to the context of a Caribbean botanical garden. Here again, we tried to situate future thinking about the garden in a broader cultural context.

In a colonial context, a botanical garden may carry negative connotations of plantation slavery: a landscape of labor and colonialization, on the one hand, and the dominance of European culture and settlement, on the other. Caribbean culture is caught in a sense between turning completely inward to the rooted localities of place and simply remaining displaced as a kind of transplant. And yet, in a postcolonial context, the Caribbean garden has the capacity to present a more unique, extroverted identity — a radically transformed version of the botanical garden, an ongoing, provisional, and experimental site that is both rooted and transplanted, mobile and static, placeful and displaced, recalling locality while fully taking part in global affairs.

The collection at the University of Puerto Rico's botanical garden boasts species from over sixty countries. Many species of nonnative origin have since hybridized and naturalized to become indistinguishable from original natives, and indeed many once exotic species have come to be considered and classified as native. The web of global cultures is mirrored by a network of botanical gardens that is increasingly exchanging information and material. Traditional distinctions of local, native, original, and stable, on the one hand, and global, exotic, transplanted, and mobile, on the other, are blurred and transformed, leading to new hybrid forms.

### Three provocations

The above-mentioned surveys, as well as additional presentations on Puerto Rico's climate and patterns of development, allowed the design team to provoke discussion with the University president and board about the future possibilities for their garden. In order to be more provocative, and encourage informed decision making along certain lines and priorities, we developed three future scenarios, each a purposeful provocation in its own right.

### Botanical Forest

Botanical Forest shifts the botanical emphasis on taxonomy and display to *ecosystem*—plants as complex system communities and living interrelationships. This shift is accomplished by placing emphasis on forest development and research, rather than on building and program, while keeping new structures and roads at a minimum on-site. [FIG. 4]

By capitalizing on its central role, Botanical Forest actualizes the larger ecological corridor in the context of San Juan. Linkages and interconnectivity with stream corridors, open spaces, and ecological systems help ensure a healthy self-sustaining ecosystem that also maintains significant educational and recreational impact.

Botanical Forest strengthens the connection to San Juan's green axis by emphasizing the growth of new forest. The ecological corridors of the forest and river would be accessible via trails and exhibits within. At the same time, the themes of urban ecology and forestry will be emphasized, rather than a return to an idyllic, preurban state. The reforestation effort, for example, would deploy contemporary silvicultural practices of systematic grid plantations, mixed-species, mixed ages, stratification, selective thinning, and adaptive management. Nature in education will be a focus of Botanical Forest, drawing on the resources of the Bosque Urbano and the University.

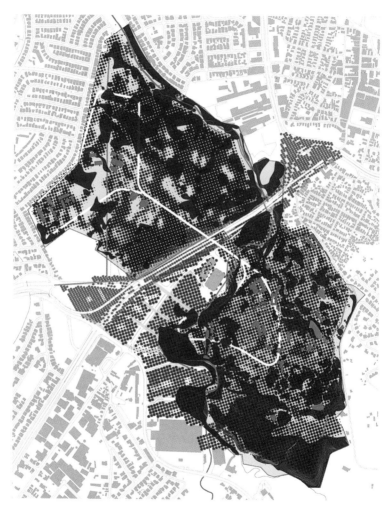

FIG. 4 — "Botanical Forest" was one scenario of development where themes
of reforestation, conservation, nature education, and ecology were foregrounded,
by Field Operations, 2004

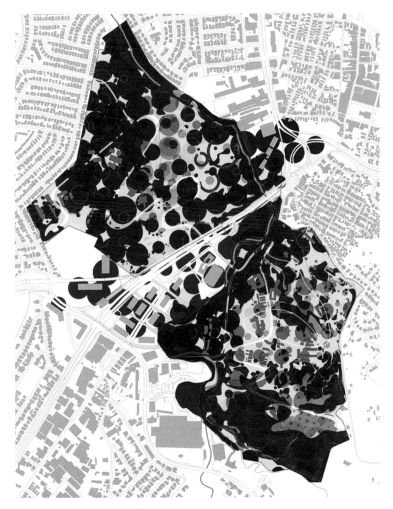

FIG. 5 — "Botanical Park" was a second scenario of development where themes of public space, leisure, spectacle, and exotic display were foregrounded, by Field Operations, 2004

FIG. 6 — "Botanical City" was a third scenario of development where themes
of commerce, research, science, agriculture, and technology were foregrounded,
by Field Operations, 2004

### Botanical Park

Botanical Park shifts the emphasis to maximize aesthetic and formal properties of plants as space-shaping groups and as settings for events. In order to achieve this shift, strategic display areas are enlarged and building use is redistributed across the site, with research buildings relocated to the north and public buildings throughout. [FIG. 5] Botanical Park is an integral part of San Juan's network of public institutional and green spaces, capitalizing on access along the Tren Urbano light rail line. Along with the Parque Muñoz Rivera and Parque Muñoz Marin, it would become a key public open space in the rapidly urbanizing city, providing much needed spaces for public amenity and expanding the programs of the garden.

Botanical Park emphasizes active use of both the north and south parcels, increasing spaces for large-scale events, display, gardens, and public amenities. Plantings and display areas are to be engaged, rather than viewed purely as aesthetic affect. Rooms, stages, platforms, and surfaces provide exotic settings for public event programming (concerts, exhibits, plays, etc.), set within a verdant landscape of layered tropical plantings and flowers.

### Botanical City

Botanical City shifts the emphasis to botanical production, research, and utility, with intensified urban edges. These shifts are accomplished by using the north parcel more actively for horticultural and nursery production and research, developing mixed-use structures in the center, and embedding both vehicular and pedestrian circulation throughout the site. [FIG. 6] Botanical City is the new center in San Juan's activity network, with an emphasis on urban development, education and research, and active, productive landscapes. The site is a link between the old city and the rapidly expanding suburbs to the south, east, and west. It is also strategically centered at the crossing of the city's major transportation arteries, Tren Urbano, PR-1, and Avenida Ponce de León. The river corridor is made as efficient as possible, urban density is encouraged around Cupey station, and density is increased on-site with research greenhouses, nursery plots, and commercial fields. A public promenade runs along PR-1 in the northern parcel, with amenities, parking, furnishings, and access to the gardens.

### Synthesis

These three purposefully provocative scenarios were extremely useful in eliciting an enthusiastic response from the president and board. Each provoked a debate on values, priorities, and desires. Each also allowed not only for philosophical reflection, but also for consideration of pragmatic decisions such as entrance locations, vehicular circulation, new buildings and investments, and degrees of public accessibility and relationship to the city. Each scenario possessed a range of characteristics and attributes that were equally desirable. By editing and rearranging several key features from each, we created a kind of hybrid graft, a combinatory synthesis that amalgamates the three into one.

In order to help unify the many disparate areas of the site, three organizational systems govern the formal and material fabric of the whole. The first of these is a mat-like surface of grasses, mown into concentric rings and waves of differing height and mix. Taller meadow mixes weave in and around shorter lawn mixes. The grain of the pattern is tighter and denser in areas of higher use and interest, and looser and coarser in more passive areas of the site. The same grain also governs how gravel and paved areas are treated. The second layer composes circulation loops. These new roads, paths, and trails allow for extensive movement around various parts of the site, while at the same time completing circuits so the visitor is constantly oriented, ending up at the place they started. These paths also string recreational users (walkers, runners, cyclists) in relation to garden exhibit visitors and other types of users, thereby intermixing the use and spectacle of the hybrid program. [FIG. 7] A third layer of forest overlays the landscape—a gauzelike plantation of differing spaces and layers to provide differential shade and volume. The planting is also conceived to be grown in time, with younger, smaller saplings intermixed with older species. And whereas the bulk of the planting is native to complement the continuity of the larger ecological corridor, strikingly exotic and unusual species are also concentrated in certain areas (or "clouds") for both display and contrast.

These three organizational layers work across the entire site and provide the matrix for the development of different programs. First, a new public park and event strip lines the road corridor and is tied into the newly expanded commercial nurseries and flower fields. Here the spectacle of plant marketing is highlighted as public space, with market and shade roofs, signage, special lighting, picnic areas, and furnished activity spaces. Second, the river corridor is reshaped for on-site flood control and water management. The corridor also supports terraces, new riverbank gardens, recreational spaces, and pathways. Third, the forest that extends along the river is restored and enhanced by new trails, nature education programs, and 140 experimental stations. Fourth, the original display gardens are renovated and enhanced. A focus upon tropical and exotic collections is foregrounded as existing and new gardens are woven across new interpretative pathways and loops. Spaces for theatre, concerts, education, and gatherings (such as weddings and parties) are integrated with the gardens. Research and experimental plots are also integrated into the garden displays,

FIG. 7 — View of the garden, University of Puerto Rico Botanical Garden,
by Field Operations, 2004

showcasing research in action. Fifth, the area around Cupey station is developed for scientific research, including new biomolecular laboratories, herbaria, and glasshouses. Plans for housing and other mixed-use development, including the revitalization of an adjacent neighborhood, are also aimed at integrating a diverse urban community into the garden itself. Taken together, the program for the site provides Puerto Rico with a new kind of social space—one of large-scale exposure to nature, education, recreation, and amenity, all set within exotic and unusual vegetal environments.

The planning and design for the botanical garden at the University of Puerto Rico is a work-in-progress—stalled in 2005 with a change in government and altered priorities within the University. The plans will likely change and be modified as the logistics of funding, leadership, and implementation are worked out over time. Nonetheless, this project articulates an ambition for a new form of botanical garden—a garden that continues to collect, research, and educate, but one that is also responsive to interpretative and interactive experience in the context of the cosmopolitan city, hybridizing the scientific and the artistic, the utilitarian and the exotic, the commercial and the civic, the local and the global. Importantly, the project might also point to new relationships among the botanical, the ecological, and the urban as producing a kind of hybrid model—not placing these territories in opposition (the botanical versus the ecological versus the city), but rather seeing their alternative constructs and schemes of organization as suggesting a new synthesis, relevant to our time. Moreover, these "new natures" are organized as both space and spectacle. In other words, the garden is not viewed simply as a composition of new forms on display, but more as a newly constructed social space, an exotic vegetal matrix within which the urbanism of difference plays out over time.

FIG. 1 — Gansevoort Overlook, the High Line, photograph by Barrett Doherty, New York, 2010

# HUNT'S HAUNTS:
## HISTORY, RECEPTION, AND CRITICISM ON
## THE DESIGN OF THE HIGH LINE

By "Hunt's Haunts," I am referring to the writings of John Dixon Hunt and the many discussions I have had with him over the years that have lingered with me in ways deeply enriching and, at the same time, oddly disquieting. After all, good criticism and difficult conceptual frameworks inevitably pose a challenge—one that can often agitate and haunt one's sense of direction if left unresolved.

This same point regarding the *reception* of fecund and challenging ideas could also be said of some of Hunt's favorite physical haunts—some of the great gardens and places from which he has derived inspiration and about which his work is focused. Such places include Stowe, Stourhead, Bomarzo, the melancholic and hidden gardens of Venice, and the many others that have gifted him the feeling of a "greater perfection."[1] As he has written, such places are "haunted by undeniable spirits, [wherein] the environment can become landscape."[2] By spirits, of course, he refers not to some mystical essence but rather to the human mind—to the imagination, to the fictions and designs that create a place of lasting presence, a presence that inevitably haunts precisely because of effects that tend to linger and escape any form of easy definition.

Good gardens haunt precisely because they inevitably exceed being thought. This phenomena of haunting excess—both as place and idea, and as developed through Hunt's writing on the subject—is both inspiring and elusive. It is a fascinating and fundamental topic of all art. Outlined here are three recurrent haunts in Hunt's work that I find particularly relevant for my own. In this context, I will use some images of the High Line project to suggest a certain striving in real-world practice to try and approximate certain ideas.

---

*Unpublished lecture given at "John Dixon Hunt—A Symposium," October 31, 2009*

First, is Hunt's work on site, the haunts themselves. Hunt has constructed an almost unassailable argument that the specificity of sites lies at the very core of any significant works of landscape architecture. In this vein, he has elaborated on key concepts such as the "genius of the place," "reading and writing the site," "placemaking as an art of milieu," "site mediation," and the nesting of "three natures" wherein the garden (third nature) is a focused concentration of its larger surroundings.[3] A close reading of a particular site's attributes—its history, its various representations, its context, and its potentials—conspires to inform a new project that is in some way an intensification and enrichment of place. Every site is an accumulation of local forces over time, and so, Hunt argues, any significant design response must in some way interpret, extend, and amplify this potential within its specific context. Averse to universal and stylistic approaches to design, Hunt demands inventive originality with regard to specific circumstance.

In the case of the High Line, a very close reading was made of the site's history and urban context. [FIG. 1] Two readings were particularly formative—one was the singular, autonomous quality of the transportation engineering infrastructure (its linearity and repetition, indifferent to surrounding context, and its brash steel and concrete palette), and the other was the surprising and charming effect of self-sown vegetation taking over the postindustrial structure once the trains had stopped running—a kind of melancholia captured beautifully in earlier photographs made by the artist Joel Sternfeld. [FIGS. 2-4] These photographs were later used to great effect by those who sought the preservation of the structure in the face of impending demolition.

The new design of the site, from its material systems (the lineal paving, the reinstallation of the rail tracks, the plantings, the lighting, the furnishing, the railings, etc.) to the choreography of movement; the meandering of paths, the siting of overlooks and vistas, and the coordination of seating and social spaces, is intended to reinterpret, amplify, dramatize, and concentrate these readings of the site. [FIG. 5]

The design is highly site-specific; it is irreproducible anywhere else without significant loss of origin and locality, partly owing to the history of the High Line itself, and partly to the unique characteristics of its urban context and adjacencies. The design aims to concentrate these found conditions, to dramatize and reveal past, present, and future contexts, and to create a memorable place for all who visit.

This brings me to a second theme of Hunt's Haunts, the concern for reception. Over the past few years, Hunt has brought into sharper focus the importance for how a visitor receives a given work—how they experience, understand,

**FIG. 2 — Historic view of the High Line,**
**Photographer unknown**

Courtesy Friends of the High Line, http://www.
thehighline.org/galleries/images

**FIG. 3 — Emergent vegetation on**
**the High Line, Photographer unknown**

Courtesy Friends of the High Line, http://www.
thehighline.org/galleries/images

**FIG. 4 — *Looking South on an Afternoon in June, 2000*, by Joel Sternfeld,**
**Negative: 2000, Print: 2009, Digital C-print, 39½" × 50" (100.33 × 127 cm)**

Courtesy of the artist and Luhring Augustine, New York

FIG. 5 — Washington Grasslands, the High Line, Photograph by Iwan Baan, 2011

value, and extend various interpretations of the work. He says that "landscape comes into being as the creative coupling of perceiving subject and an object perceived."[4]

As a landscape architect, it is very difficult to believe that a designed work can determine a particular behavioral response; a good designer can at best influence, steer, or guide a particular set of responses, but can never overdetermine or script reception. Hunt recognizes such a distinction in statements, such as, after W. H. Auden, that "a poet, especially a dead one, cannot control how we read and understand his poetry, but that—especially if it is good—we will constantly reread it in new ways; so even when later generations repeat the very same words that W. B. Yeats originally published, they will probably give them new meanings and new resonance." He continues the analogy: "When we are dealing with materials in a garden that have neither denotative basis (as words do in the first instance) nor precise declarations of idea or emotion, there is considerably more scope for reinvesting them with meanings, for seeing them in different ways than were originally intended or anticipated."[5] Thus, he suggests that a good design must harbor sufficient room for a wide range of receptions and interpretations, if not actually instigate, prompt, and support open and indeterminate readings. As he quite rightly points out, here is the palpable, haptic place, smelling, sounding, catching the eye; then there is the sense of an invented or special place, this invention resulting from the creation of richer and fuller experiences than would be possible, at least in such completeness or intensity, if they were not designed. Like cyberspace, a designed landscape is always at bottom a fiction, a contrivance—yet its hold on our imagination will derive, paradoxically, from the actual materiality of its invented sceneries."[6]

From such ideas, Hunt develops the concept of the *longue durée*, the long duration, the slow accrual of experience and meaning over time. Possibly one of the most fundamental, important, and difficult criteria for landscape architecture is the fact that the medium is bound into time. There can be no immediacy of appreciation, no fast way to consume landscape in any meaningful or lasting way. Landscapes can never be properly captured in a single moment; they are always in a process of becoming, as in a temporal quarry of accrual and memory—collecting experiences, representations, uses, the effects of weather, changes in management, cultivation and care, and other traces of layered presence.

In the case of the High Line, the experience of strolling is intentionally slowed down in the otherwise bustling context of Manhattan. [FIG. 6] Paths meandering in between tall perennial and grass plantings create an experience that can not really be properly captured in a photograph, or even video. Like so many other gardens, the place must be walked, with scenes unfolding in sequence and in juxtaposition. The dynamic plantings are different from week to week, with varied blooms, colors, textures, effects, and moods, combined with the changing light at different times of day, varied weathers and seasons, and with the different microclimatic effects of the surrounding cityscape. The visitor is almost always experiencing the High Line in newly nuanced ways.

Importantly, the design does not employ signs or symbols of narrative intent, it does not try to tell a story or to embed meaning—rather, its very materiality, its detailing, its artifactuality elicits or prompts different associations and readings. [FIG. 7] Hunt has spoken in numerous essays of triggers and prompts in design, describing a number of theatrical devices such as entry thresholds and liminality, the passage from outside to inside, dramatic frames and scenes, displacement and collage, inscription and marking.[7] [FIGS. 8-10] These precisely designed triggers and prompts are all concentrations of effect that draw the visitor into another world, heightening the allure and distinctiveness of a special place. The visitor becomes as much a performer as viewer, more deeply engaged in participating in the theatricality of urban life—the promenade as elevated catwalk, urban stage, and social condenser. [FIG. 11]

FIG. 6 —Chelsea Grasslands, the High Line, Photograph by Marie Warsh, 2011

FIG. 7 — Northern Spur Preserve,
the High Line, Photograph by Peerapod
Chiowanich, 2011
FIG. 11 — Diller-von Furstenberg
Sundeck, the High Line, Photograph by
Rik Panganiban, 2011

FIG. 8 — Gansevoort stair, the High Line,
Photograph by Iwan Baan, 2011

FIG. 9 — Tenth Avenue Square, the High Line, Photograph by Iwan Baan, 2011

FIG. 10 — 26th Street Viewing Spur, the High Line, Photograph by Iwan Baan, 2011

And here words bring us to the third haunt of Hunt, the critical. When he declares that "to theorize about gardens is justifiable for its own sake; moreover it increases the pleasures of understanding," he is establishing the basis not simply for passive contemplation but for actively energizing fresh developments in the ideas and practices of landscape architecture.[8] His insistence on historical perspective is well taken, but his commitment to concepts, to critical discourse, to informed argumentation, and—most important—to cultural enrichment through imaginative and inventive placemaking continues to challenge us all.
[FIG. 12]

Hunt's haunts are quite simply those remarkable places and ideas where content concentrates, lingers, and accrues. The combination of physical, material places with cultural ideas points to the unity of theory with practice, of design with reception, and of experience with intellect, all dialogues that we strive for in the best of our work. That such experiences might also haunt our imaginations is perhaps the highest calling of art, and in gardens, as Hunt has so eloquently taught us, we might find the greatest perfections.

NOTES

1    See John Dixon Hunt, *Greater Perfections: The Practice of Garden Theory* (Philadelphia: University of Pennsylvania Press, 2000). The title comes from Francis Bacon's "Of Gardens" (1625): "When Ages grow to Civility and Elegancie, Men come to *Build Stately*, sooner than to *Garden Finely*: As if *Gardening* were the Greater Perfection."

2    Ibid., 223.

3    Most of these ideas come up in *Greater Perfections* with a whole essay devoted to "The Idea of a Garden and the Three Natures" (32-75). See also Hunt's "Introduction: Reading and Writing the Site" in John Dixon Hunt, *Gardens and the Picturesque: Studies in the History of Landscape Architecture* (Cambridge, MA: MIT Press, 1992), 3-16.

4    Hunt, *Greater Perfections*, 9.

5    John Dixon Hunt, *The Afterlife of Gardens* (Philadelphia: University of Pennsylvania Press, 2004), 12.

6    Ibid., 37.

7    See Hunt's chapter "Triggers and Prompts in Landscape Architecture Visitation," in *Afterlife*, 77-112.

8    Ibid., 107.

FIG. 12 — Woodland Flyover, the High Line, Photograph by Iwan Baan, 2011

FIG. 1—Model of design for Qianhai Water City, by James Corner Field Operations, Shenzhen, China. 2011

# Afterword

## WORDSCAPE: THE WRITINGS OF JAMES CORNER IN THEORY AND PRACTICE

———

Richard Weller

During the mid-1980s, with Ian McHarg's call to global ecological stewardship still ringing in everyone's ears, landscape architectural discourse found itself worrying over the meaning of a grid of bagels set out in a Boston garden. Some called it Art, others called it rubbish. Both were wrong. The pendulum had simply swung to its counterpoint, from McHarg and ecology to Martha Schwartz and others seeking bold, artistic expression. The problem was not these poles per se, but the void in between.

For those of us who were serious about either saving the earth or making art, it meant looking far beyond the discipline in order to fill the void. At the time it meant reading theory—the likes of Lyotard, Foucault, Barthes, Baudrillard, Deleuze and Guattari, Jameson, Eagleton, and Virilio among others. These people were brilliant but, truth be told, they were hard to relate back to landscape architecture. It also meant understanding why "land art" had, in the space of a few short years while Robert Smithson was alive, produced more profundity about the topic of landscape than the discipline itself had done for decades. Additionally, because of architecture's cultural hegemony and the sensation of Deconstruction, one had to track what figures such as Eisenman, Libeskind, Koolhaas, Tschumi, and others were saying and doing, but again, these ideas and forms were hard to relate back to landscape architecture. Because of the burgeoning ecological crisis, landscape architects also felt a need to study the natural sciences as a wave of thinkers such as Lovelock, Capra, Berry, Dawkins, Jantsch, Prigogine, and Kauffman described a new world of self-organization and indeterminacy. As if all this was not enough, because we had neglected the city and urbanity loomed as the dominant cultural landscape of the *fin de siecle*, we felt it necessary to read urban design history and theory. This meant, for example, reading Mumford, Corbusier, Jacobs, Lynch, Rossi, Venturi, Rowe, and Harvey.

And as we groped about for a center, Norberg-Schulz's phenomenology, Frampton's critical regionalism, and the new geography of Cosgrove, Soja, and Harvey, provided useful and important signposts. Finally, figures such as Anne Whiston Spirn, Laurie Olin and, in particular, John Dixon Hunt, pointed out that in all this searching we were neglecting the history of our own discipline.

In this vast and disorienting atmosphere of postmodern thought, James Corner's writings served as a lightning rod. Corner, I think uniquely, seemed to be able to discuss the landscape architectural project through, and not in spite of, this broader, far richer, and more critical cultural milieu. It was Corner's writings that quite literally helped some of us navigate our way back to the discipline, and since then his writings have continued to demarcate the coordinates of landscape architecture as a contemporary cultural project.

### In Theory

Corner's intellectual impact began in the early 1990s with two essays in *Landscape Journal*. "Sounding the Depths — Origins, Theory, and Representation" provided a useful cursory history of the philosophy of science as a way of contextualizing landscape architecture's own narratives.[1] "Three Tyrannies of Contemporary Theory and the Alternative of Hermeneutics" went on to outline a contemporary philosophy of landscape architecture based on and borrowing from hermeneutics, the study of textual interpretation. These papers brought together wide-ranging interests in how history, art, design method, and poetics could relate to and inform landscape architecture toward the close of the twentieth century. They crystallized some of the deepest (and largely repressed) artistic and intellectual ambitions of landscape architecture at the time.

Hermeneutics, unlike scientific claims to objectivity, is concerned with the subjective and situated construction of meaning.[2] A quantum and poetic view of reality, hermeneutics begins with the truism that the subject is implicated in the formation of the object and that knowledge is only ever partial. Corner's appropriation of hermeneutics opened up landscape architecture as a textual field, that is to say, it writes us and we write it. The project was at once radical (in landscape architecture) because it insisted on representational self-consciousness, and simultaneously conservative because he positioned his postmodern hermeneutics against deconstruction and more broadly what he referred to as a world that was losing its "mystery and enigma." The philosophical promise of Corner's early writing and the magnitude of the landscape architectural project he foresaw is made clear when he declares that "to forge a landscape as a hermeneutic locus of both divination and restoration, prophecy and memory, is to help figure and orient the collective consciousness of a modern culture still caught in transition."[3] In an empty universe, against the tide of globalization Corner asks whether landscape theory and, by extension, praxis, could "rebuild an existential ground, a topography of critical continuity, of memory and invention, orientation and direction?"[4]

Finding McHarg's disdain for urbanism untenable and his methods excessively positivist, Corner could only maintain landscape architecture's grand narrative of reconciling modernity to place by transferring attention to poetics and art practices. Consequently, in the mid-1990s there was no way his belief in landscape as the topos of existential orientation could develop any further without engaging the full scope of the ecological crisis and, so, in order to "see" this first-hand he takes flight with Alex MacLean. In the resultant *Taking Measures Across the American Landscape* (1996), Corner attempts to turn the synoptic view of instrumental reason upon itself and take its measure. Whereas McHarg's overviews came with arrows and notations of what should go where, Corner finds a beguiling beauty in the sprawling, denatured world below. But aerial images are problematic representations, for they explain nothing of the real sociopolitical and ecological relations of the world they purport to lay bare.

In response, Corner starts making his own "maps" from aerial images and associated fragments of data. In a related essay, "The Agency of Mapping: Speculation, Critique, and Invention" (1999), he explains that instead of the accepted landscape architectural formula that defers design until after the data is collected, the entire process of collecting, assembling, and interrelating data is creative.[5] His definitive break with McHarg and the direction University of Pennsylvania would take under his chairmanship from 2001 to 2012 is established when he writes that mapping is not "the indiscriminate listing and inventorying of conditions as in a tracing, table, or chart but rather a strategic and imaginative drawing-out of relational structures."[6]

Two years earlier, in a daring and wide-ranging essay entitled "Ecology and Landscape as Agents of Creativity," he asks "How might landscape architectural creativity (informed through its representational traditions) enrich and inform the ecological idea in the imagination and material practices of a people?"[7] Following Henri Bergson, he recognizes that ecology is as much mind as it is matter. Collapsing the nature/culture divide by intellectualizing nature and naturalizing intellect, Corner claims that human creativity and ecosystems share the same tendency toward the increased "differentiation, freedom, and richness of a diversely interacting whole."[8] This philosophical conflation of culture and nature described a world that had become just that. By removing the oppositional referents that had for so long anchored landscape architecture's worldview and justified its actions, Corner opened the field to a new and more creative sensibility. His thinking on ecology is redolent with the creative potential of emerging scientific metaphors. Diversification, indeterminacy, self-organization, and emergence become liberating "ideas" for design processes that he not only writes about but also starts testing in his design studio teaching at Penn. He argues that "similarities between ecology and creative transmutation are indicative of an alternative kind of landscape architecture, one in which calcified conventions of how people live and relate to land, nature, and place are challenged and the multivariate wonders of life are once again released through invention."[9] Toward that end he urges landscape architects to develop a creative relationship with ecology in order to exploit a "potential that might inform more meaningful and imaginative cultural practices than the merely ameliorative, compensatory, aesthetic, or commodity-oriented."[10] His richly imbricated association of ecology with creativity was long overdue and his enigmatic comments and montages started appearing in landscape lecture halls around the world.

More or less a decade after his original paean to hermeneutics, he then publishes "Eidetic Operations and New Landscapes" in his edited volume *Recovering Landscape* (1999). Here his frustration with landscape's prelapsarian inclinations and its infrastructural impotence is palpable. In the text he moves across an axis from *landskip* (constructed scene) to *landschaft* (working place) because "little that is socially emancipating and enabling results from authorial, representational landscapes."[11] He quite rightly accuses mainstream landscape architecture of the "sentimental aestheticization" of places and declares a personal move toward "instrumental landscape issues" arguing that this requires a focus on organizational and strategic skills rather than indulgences in formal composition.[12]

But what is the contemporary working landscape? How can this landscape or anything designed by a landscape architect possibly be used to resist the dominant political ideology and aesthetic of landskip? In trying to move beyond this impasse and start to get his hands dirty, Corner turns to matters of "program, event space, utility, economy, and logistics." Along with what the Dutch were saying at the time, he argues optimistically that these aspects of a project can be foregrounded in the design process and turned through design toward "newly productive and significant ends."[13] What exactly these productive ends are he does not say, but echoing Koolhaas, he insists that the designer's attention should be focused on staging the "conditions necessary to precipitate a maximum range of opportunities in time," and that design be turned from aesthetics to "engendering strategies" and "strategic instrumentality."[14] Catalysts, not master plans; the fourth-dimension, not the third; instrumentality, not art.

Although his polemic lends itself to a potential polarization of art and instrumentality, it would be unfair to read his development in this direction as simply a case of either/or. Rather, in hindsight we can see that Corner is moving to all the edges of the field, gathering what he needs for what will ultimately become a holistic (and mature) landscape architectural design philosophy and methodology. As opposed to the connoisseurship of scenery (art) or the crude streamlining of development for profit (instrumentality), Corner's landscape architect is one who would both intervene in the symbolic order of things *and* simultaneously effect real socio-ecological change in any given place. For Corner this is not prescriptive, ideological, or utopian, this is just what good design should do.

To achieve this he has always stressed critical and creative attention to representation. He says "landscape as a culturally significant practice is dependent on the capacity of its inventors to image the world in new ways and body forth those images in richly phenomenal and efficacious terms."[15] Looking for models, he was not alone in reading much into Koolhaas and OMA's 1982 Parc de la Villette competition drawings. OMA's cartoon of indeterminacy for a Parisian park changed everything: Not only was this the end point of what had hitherto been the dominance of faux naturalism or Euclidean composition in park design, but more importantly, OMA's striations and confetti became a logo for a new conception of urbanism in general. Koolhaas referred to this new urban condition simply as "Scape." In this new condition, as we have seen with Corner's thinking on ecology, there is neither nature nor culture but only ever both, irreducibly interwoven.

In this new condition the spatial and professional boundaries between architecture, landscape, and infrastructure are no longer distinct. For better or worse, the subtraction of "land" liberated landscape architecture (momentarily) from its pastoral enslavement. So, too, architecture's traditional hegemony over the city through the agency of objects was loosened and ultimately set adrift. As Koolhaas so eloquently put it, "Architecture was a sandcastle and now we swim in the tide that washed it away." That tide is the tsunami of global urbanization and with it comes a deepening of the ecological crisis.

In 1997 Charles Waldheim conjured a similar semantic trick, although this time through addition, not subtraction. When the word "urbanism" was added to the word "landscape," a new disciplinary alignment in which landscape was now privileged in the urban design process was headlined. That brash move was fifteen years ago, with its early beginnings forged by Corner at Penn, where Waldheim studied architecture. What matters now is not whether landscape urbanism has become a clearly defined and agreed upon school of thought but that by bringing together such contradictory and yet relevant terms, landscape urbanism has become a provocative and stimulating idea, useful for advancing the field.

The conflation of landscape with urbanism ends (theoretically) the history of the city as a polarity of culture set against the endless and benign backdrop of nature. The new conception of the city that landscape urbanism implies is one befitting an age of ecological limitation, one where we are necessarily more concerned with the city's total metabolic performance than its formal composition. Despite some of its fuzzy and at times pretentious language, what landscape urbanism generates is a more concerted effort to retrofit old cities and design new ones so that open space systems and built form are spatially and systematically integrated in ways that offer a higher level of social and ecological performance. And if this remains vague it is only because the evolution of the city from a wasteful machine to a sophisticated ecology that landscape urbanists, and many others foresee, is no simple morphological thing.

By virtue of both eloquent and provocative writing, his inventive design teaching, and the publicity that his incipient practice was attracting at the time, Corner became synonymous with landscape urbanism. In his contribution to *Landscape Urbanism Reader* (2006) titled "Terra Fluxus," he set out a relatively clear encapsulation of its key characteristics. Firstly, he argued that landscape urbanism favors process over form, that is, following the failure of utopian modernism and David Harvey's critique of New Urbanism we recognize that cities are dynamic socio-ecological systems. Echoing Manual De Landa, Corner notes that "any particular form is merely a provisional state of nature." Reading the city as a "space-time ecology," the landscape urbanist does not seek to superimpose an ideal overarching form on the system, but rather applies design intelligence to the system itself. Secondly, Corner describes the "staging surfaces" of landscape, by which he means that the designer approaches a place as a field of potential rather than a fait accompli. In this regard, design is intentionally open-ended and resists closure while simultaneously seeking quite precise catalytic moves that set forth the conditions from which social, economic, and ecological growth can occur. Thirdly, as throughout all his writing, he reiterates the need for design tools and methods that keep up with contemporary understandings of social, economic, and ecological systems, methods that can engage the full complexity of these systems and productively redirect them. Finally, taking us back to his original musings in the early nineties, Corner insists that design is first and foremost an "imaginative project—a speculative thickening of the world of possibilities." Indeed.

This then summarizes Corner's "wordscape"—a palimpsest inscribed over an intense fifteen-year period. And while his conclusion that landscape architecture is an instrumental, ecological art is not in itself monumental or revolutionary. The way in which he arrived there helped to both demarcate and clarify the intellectual and creative cartography of the field as it entered the twenty-first century.

### In Practice

And so what happens when words try to become things?

Corner's fledgling practice Field Operations was first taken seriously on the occasion of the Downsview Park competition in 1999 (in association with Stan Allen), the same year his *Recovering Landscape* hit the shelves. Suddenly Corner was in the same frame as gurus Koolhaas and Tschumi and up against the likes of Peter Walker and Partners, the pinnacle of the formalist landscape establishment at that time. Moreover, the brief was not just asking for a nice park, it was asking for a philosophical landmark vis-à-vis culture and nature post–La Villette. Competitors were asked to treat "nature and humanity....as dynamic phenomena, constantly changing and interacting, no longer able to be described as a balanced state."

A collective testament to the impossibility of a return to sweet nature, all the schemes were about the rudiments of how to (painstakingly) grow a basic social ecology from an otherwise inert military field in the suburbs of Toronto. While the designs were simple in form and agricultural in technique, they were noticeably complex in their choice of language. As if straight out of Corner's "Ecology and Landscape as Agents of Creativity," the explanatory texts were breathless with references to Diversity, Unfolding, Emergence, Adaption, Mutation, Self-organization, Networks, and Flows.

Taking to a new level the practice of doing minimal to win a job, Koolhaas and Bruce Mau chose polka dots and a thousand pathways. Tschumi tried harder to meet the spirit of the brief by interweaving the digital and the vegetal, and Corner, with the barest economy of means, proposed a two-tiered system of "Circuits" (culture) and "Through Flows" (ecology). In essence, paths for humans and swales for the rest. He explained that the provision of this basic infrastructure would allow "the flows of both natural and cultural life to move through and colonize the site in multiple and flexible ways."

A vast array of social programming justified formal restraint in the finalists' designs and time developmental sections—particularly in the case of Corner and Allen—optimistically forecasted a process of biological and social succession that would ensue from meager initial investments. Reviewing the competition, Kristina Hill pointed out that in their enthusiasm for generating life on-site, the finalists had largely overlooked the more important ecological linkages off-site.[16] As to the social life of the park, no one would deny the importance of programming, but the lack of designed theatricality (the lack of landskip) whether bucolic or otherwise, suggested that the fourth-dimension had now swallowed the third.

Building on the successional approach used at Downsview, Field Operations won the Fresh Kills design competition in 2002 with a highly pragmatic method for converting the world's largest rubbish dump on Staten Island into a healthy ecosystem over a thirty-year period. Conventional techniques of landscape restoration—such as soil reconditioning through strip cropping and habitat reconstruction through endemic plantings—are integrated with earthworks that enhance the site's sublime qualities and circulation systems and programming that support the social life of the park. In the symbolic order of things, Fresh Kills quickly became the discipline's Central Park of the twenty-first century.

While Central Park and Fresh Kills both share a systematic pragmatism in terms of their base creation, they differ in their symbolic orientation. Where Central Park speaks of paradise lost, Fresh Kills can only look to a postindustrial future. Central Park is but a pretty folly in regard to the real world we have now created for ourselves. Fresh Kills, on the other hand, is the very embodiment of that world—a 2,200-acre experiment in "recovering" a toxic landscape. Indeed, to even breathe any life into this cornucopian corpse will be an achievement. As technology scholar Donna Harraway says, and Corner's Spartan images show, "the cyborg was not born in a garden."[17] Had its thirty-year process of artificial insemination begun as planned, Fresh Kills would have become the magnum opus of Corner's career, for here he answered his own question of "How might landscape architectural creativity (informed through its representational traditions) enrich and inform the ecological idea in the imagination and material practices of a people?"[18]

Much has already been said and written about Corner's hugely acclaimed High Line, but in this context it needs to be briefly discussed.

A place to be seen and a place from which to see, this Manhattan catwalk is New York's answer to the Promenade Plantée in Paris. It is a tourist attraction, a local shortcut, a meeting place, a linear park, a great way of saving industrial heritage, and yes, for better or worse a powerful catalyst for gentrification. It is also a beautifully crafted and restrained piece of landscape design, a subtle choreography of intra- and extraverted spaces held together by a richly nuanced planting palette. In this project Corner charts a path between the risks of too much spectacle on the one hand and romancing dereliction on the other. The line he finds in his writings between art and instrumentality is writ large through Manhattan's grid and the public has overwhelmingly voted with their feet in its favor.

At odds with public opinion (though always purporting to champion their interests against "high" design), Andrés Duany and Emily Talen in their new book, *Landscape Urbanism and its Discontents*, argue that the High Line is yet again a case of a celebrity designer's indulgence and the budget could have been better spent on making normal streets, for normal people. As even their own confidants tried to tell them before they went to print, this acerbic judgment is warped by their ulterior motive to find a scapegoat for *everything* they think landscape urbanism means—and nearly all of it bad. Skulking around the streets below, Duany and Talen protest that the High Line is a camouflaged modernist street in the air and that high art designers such as Corner don't care about people. In fact, for the huge numbers of people enjoying its pleasures above, the High Line is a unique, irreproducible, charming, and beautifully designed folly. No more, no less.

Our malcontents are, however, right to draw attention to the proliferation of hypocritical greenwash in other examples of contemporary urbanism. So, too, they are right to worry about whether the vogue for parametric ecoscapes and melting grids are fact or fiction. But they are mistaken in claiming ad nauseam that landscape urbanist theory is causal to such developments in design culture at large. In fact, if they could just restrain their Ivy League, avant-garde, modernist, antiurban, antisocial, eco-conspiracy theories for one moment, they would find that landscape urbanism emerges precisely from a critique of environmental superficiality and environmental exclusivity and has never sanctioned one particular urban morphology over another.

Because of their monomaniacal commitment to the nineteenth century, and in spite of their recent efforts to extend their relevance beyond Urbanism 101 by absorbing sustainability, the Congress for New Urbanism seems unable to see that "landscape" can ever be anything but an enclosed Victorian park. Similarly, that thing called Nature is for them best imprisoned in a National Park, lest it escape and attack the city. Landscape urbanism, however, sees "landscape" as the whole city and the entire ecosystem upon which it depends as an inextricably interconnected system—a system requiring design intelligence if it is to evolve beyond its current mechanistic incarnation.

Irrespective of whether the name endures, landscape urbanism as a rubric is an important development in reconceptualizing the city for the twenty-first century. But then we should also be able to begin to find evidence of its positive influence over major urban design projects where landscape architects/urbanists are now the lead consultants. And this, as its critics like to point out, is proving challenging for the incipient movement, so Corner's foray into large-scale urban design in contemporary China is doubly worth considering.

With their concept of a "Water City" Field Operations won the international design competition for the new city of Qianhai in Shenzen in 2010. [FIG. 1] Within a site area of 1,800 square hectares the city is expected to accommodate four million people. This means a density of just over 2,200 people per hectare. To be clear on what that means, low-density suburbia is around 22 people per hectare and high density Paris is around 450; Le Corbusier's Villa Contemporaine was 1,750. This density (which is not uncommon in the developing "world city") puts extreme pressure on public open space to offer both ecosystem and social services. The relationship between public open space and built form and the distribution and typology of that open space is therefore critical to the environmental and social success of this and any city. Additionally, from a landscape urbanist perspective the internal relationship of public open space and built form needs to also be organized in such a way that it links into and minimizes negative impacts upon the ecological systems beyond the site boundary.

The Qianhai Water City achieves the required density by maximizing the use value of a minimal amount of public open space. Carefully aligned with the region's drainage corridors, the public open space forms an interconnected network more or less within walkable catchments of future residents bound together by a coastal esplanade. This configuration organizes the city around the ecology of water filtration and recreational amenity.

For now, the master plan is just a structural diagram for a city: so much of what makes a good city is beyond its grain. What is important at this stage is that the big moves lock in a clear socio-ecological function for the main relationship between built form and open space. What matters is that these moves have the form and function to endure the uncertainties of the development process. As this new Manhattan matures and reaches a finer grain, one expects that its rigid geometry will adjust to site-specific conditions, that its streetscapes will filter water, mitigate heat, control traffic, and encourage life, and that its built form and invisible infrastructures will be designed so as to maximize livability and inversely minimize the ecological footprint necessary to sustain four million people. This is a big project that even in China will take a long time and, for all of the talk of process and indeterminacy in landscape urbanism circles, one wonders whether these qualities will be so welcome in the case of such large-scale urban design.

While some may pick at the inevitable discrepancy between some of Corner's words and his built works, I think both continue to highlight a creative conjoining of rational objectivity with inventive subjectivity. His wordscape has not only served to ground truth in the work his office produces, it has inspired a generation of landscape architects worldwide to be more erudite, more creative, and more ambitious. As a result, landscape architecture is on the ascendance as a leading-edge design profession everywhere. Of course, we should always continue to learn from and be critical of what is said and what is built, and Corner would have it no other way. But let us now, with this book, properly acknowledge and accord historical significance to the extraordinary intellectual achievement of these writings.

NOTES

1   James Corner "A Discourse on Theory I: 'Sounding the Depths'—Origins, Theory, and Representation," *Landscape Journal* 9/2 (Fall 1990), 60–78.

2   James Corner, "Discourse on Theory II: Three Tyrannies of Contemporary Theory and the Alternative of Hermeneutics." *Landscape Journal* 10/2 (Fall 1991), 115–33.

3   Ibid., 131.

4   Ibid., 116.

5   James Corner, "The Agency of Mapping," in *Mappings*, ed. Denis Cosgrove (London: Reaktion Books, 1999), 217.

6   Ibid., 230.

7   James Corner, "Ecology and Landscape as Agents of Creativity," in *Ecological Design and Planning*, ed. George Thompson and Frederick Steiner (New York: John Wiley & Sons, 1997), 88.

8   Ibid., 88.

9   Ibid., 100.

10  Ibid., 82.

11  James Corner, "Eidetic Operations and New Landscapes," in *Recovering Landscape: Essays in Contemporary Landscape Architecture* (New York: Princeton Architectural Press, 1999), 158.

12  Ibid., 158.

13  Ibid., 159.

14  James Corner, "Introduction: Recovering Landscape as a Critical Cultural Practice," in *Recovering Landscape: Essays in Contemporary Landscape Architecture* (New York: Princeton Architectural Press, 1999), 4; James Corner, "Eidetic Operations and New Landscapes," 160.

15  James Corner, "Eidetic Operations and New Landscapes," 167.

16  Kristina Hill, "Urban Ecologies: Biodiversity and Urban Design," in *CASE: Downsview Park Toronto*, ed. Julia Czerniak (Munich: Prestel, 2001), 90–101.

17  Donna Haraway, "A Cyborg Manifesto: Science, Technology, and Socialist-Feminism in the Late Twentieth Century," in *Simians, Cyborgs and Women: The Reinvention of Nature* (New York: Routledge, 1991), 149–81.

18  James Corner, "Ecology and Landscape as Agents of Creativity," 88.

# Acknowledgments

I first want to thank Alison Hirsch for her passionate and very close attention to collating and then finely editing this collection. We decided together to not radically rewrite or rephrase much of the original content, and to let each essay speak in its original voice, representative of the time when it was written. We only deleted parts that seemed repetitive or over-extended in an effort to make it easier for the reader. Alison's own introduction to this collection is in itself a remarkable contribution that both enhances and challenges my own sense of direction. I am grateful for her thoughtful dedication.

Second, it is important to cite those colleagues who have consistently enriched my own growth and maturation intellectually over time, mostly at the University of Pennsylvania School of Design. The larger-than-life Ian McHarg remains iconic and fundamental for me. He may not quite have fully appreciated this book, perhaps thinking it too effete and insufficiently actionable in his more positivist world; but, on the other hand, McHarg had such a huge imagination and love for the field more broadly that he might have at least accorded it a degree of respect for its larger intent. Much of this work is inspired by McHarg and simply seeks to advance his main mission, albeit on different terms; he believed that information, logic, and rational planning would ensure both nature's and humanity's sustained health; while I would simply like to add the ingredient of the imagination into that same project. A small but mighty factor.

Also, during my tenure at Penn, David Leatherbarrow, John Dixon Hunt, Laurie Olin, and Denis Cosgrove have been absolutely central for over twenty years now in shaping my own thought and writing. More recently, since 1999 or so, Stan Allen has been immeasurably significant in terms of broaching theory with practice, and linking landscape with urbanism.

Third are a diverse cohort of colleagues who have directly or indirectly had significant influence on me over the past two decades: Iñaki Abalos, Alan Balfour, Anita Berrizbeitia, Richard Burdett, Paolo Burgi, Julia Czerniak, George Descombes, Robin Evans, Kenneth Frampton, Christophe Girot, Adriaan Geuze, Kathryn Gustafson, Gary Hack, George Hargreaves, Richard Kennedy, Jeff Kipnis, Sanford Kwinter, Nina-Marie Lister, Alex MacLean, Sebastian Marot, Elizabeth Meyer, Mohsen Mostafavi, Peter Reed, Robert Slutzky, Anne Spirn, Fritz Steiner, Marilyn Jordan Taylor, Bernard Tschumi, Michael Van Valkenburgh, and Alex Wall.

In addition, a number of former students, now colleagues, continue to inspire, cajole, and enrich my work, and who have had significant influence on some of the essays contained herein. Most notably would be Charles Waldheim, who has worked strenuously to help advance landscape architecture, landscape urbanism, and critical practice. Anuradha Mathur has also been an important coconspirator for two decades now. Another close colleague, Lisa Switkin, continues to astound with her energy and dedication. I am also grateful for the continued creative contributions of Alan Berger, Tsutomu Bessho, Megan Born, Isabel Castilla, Tatiana Choulika, Philippe Coignet, Aroussiak Gabrielian, Lily Jencks, Wookju Jeong, Jayyun Jung, Ellen Neises, Chris Reed, Karen Tamir, Sarah Weidner Astheimer, and Hong Zhou, as well as all former and current colleagues in my practice.

I offer a special debt of gratitude to Richard Weller whose Afterword is so beautifully succinct and points toward necessary future chapters.

I am also thankful to Jennifer Lippert and her editorial and book design team at Princeton Architectural Press for undertaking this publication with such good care and attention to detail.

Anne-Marie has lent years of patience, support, and love—all of which I am eternally grateful for. Our daughters Chloe and Olivia continue to surprise, inspire, and delight.

I hope that any names I may have inadvertently missed will forgive me; any omissions, errors, or misreadings are my own. This is an imperfect book, but my hope is that it will instigate more thought, debate, and ideas that can only help to further enrich and advance the larger landscape imagination.

—*James Corner*

## Complete Bibliography of James Corner

### Books

Corner, James, Ric Scofidio, Joshua David, Robert Hammond, eds. *Designing the High Line*, New York: Friends of the High Line, 2008.

Margulis, Lynn, James Corner, Brian Hawthorne, eds. *Ian McHarg: Conversations with Students.* New York: Princeton Architectural Press, 2007.

Corner, James, ed. *Recovering Landscape: Essays in Contemporary Landscape Architecture.* New York: Princeton Architectural Press, 1999.

Corner, James and Alex MacLean. *Taking Measures Across the American Landscape.* New Haven, CT: Yale University Press, 1996.

### Chapters or Essays in Books

"Park as Catalyst." In *The Making of the Queen Elizabeth Olympic Park*, edited by John Hopkins and Peter Neale, 260–63. London: Wiley, 2013.

"Loft Space." In *City as Loft: Adaptive Reuse as a Resource for Sustainable Urban Development*, edited by Martina Baum and Kees Christiaanse, 88-94. Zurich: GTA Publishers, 2013.

"Lighting Landscape." In *Architectural Lighting: Designing with Light and Space*, edited by Hervé Descottes with Cecilia Ramos, 125–29. New York: Princeton Architectural Press, 2012.

"Agriculture, Texture and the Unfinished." In *Intermediate Natures: The Landscapes of Michel Desvignes*, edited by Gilles Tiberghien, Michel Desvignes, and James Corner, 7–10. Basel: Birkhauser, 2009.

"Creativity Permeates the Evolution of Matter and Life: The McHarg Event—An Unfinished Project." In *Ian McHarg: Conversations with Students*, edited by Lynn Margulis, James Corner, and Brian Hawthorne, 96–99. New York: Princeton Architectural Press, 2007.

"Foreword." In *Large Parks*, edited by Julia Czerniak and George Hargreaves, 8–22. New York: Princeton Architectural Press, 2007.

"Terra-Fluxus." In *The Landscape Urbanism Reader*, edited by Charles Waldheim, 54–80. New York: Princeton Architectural Press, 2006.

With Stan Allen. "Urban Natures." In *Theories and Manifestos of Contemporary Architecture*, edited by Charles Jencks, 261–63. London: Wiley, 2005.

"The Aerial American Landscape." In *Designs on the Land: Exploring America from the Air*, edited by Alex MacLean et al, 8–19. London: Thames & Hudson, 2003.

"Landscape Urbanism." In *Landscape Urbanism: A Manual for the Machinic Landscape*, edited by Mohsen Mostafavi, 58–63. London: Architectural Association, 2003.

"Field Operations." In *ArchiLAB: économie de la terre*, edited by Marie-Ange Brayer and Béatrice Simonet. Orléans: Claude Lefort, 2002.

"Landscraping." In *Stalking Detroit*, edited by Georgia Daskalakis, Charles Waldheim, and Jason Young, 122–126. Barcelona: Actar, 2001.

"Origins of Theory." In *Theory in Landscape Architecture: A Reader*, edited by Simon Swaffield, 19–20. Philadelphia: University of Pennsylvania Press, 2002.

"Theory in Crisis." In *Theory in Landscape Architecture: A Reader*, edited by Simon Swaffield, 20–21. Philadelphia: University of Pennsylvania Press, 2002.

"The Hermeneutic Landscape." In *Theory in Landscape Architecture: A Reader*, edited by Simon Swaffield, 130. Philadelphia: University of Pennsylvania Press, 2002.

"Representation and Landscape." In *Theory in Landscape Architecture: A Reader*, edited by Simon Swaffield, 144–64. Philadelphia: University of Pennsylvania Press, 2002.

"Downsview Park." In *CASE: Downsview Park Toronto*, edited by Julia Czerniak, 58–65. Munich: Prestel-Verlag, 2001.

"The Agency of Mapping." In *Mappings*, edited by Denis Cosgrove, 188–225. London: Reaktion Books, 1999.

"Introduction: Recovering Landscape as a Critical Cultural Practice." In *Recovering Landscape: Essays in Contemporary Landscape Architecture*, edited by James Corner, 1–26. New York: Princeton Architectural Press, 1999.

"Eidetic Operations and New Landscapes." In *Recovering Landscape: Essays in Contemporary Landscape Architecture*, edited by James Corner, 153–169. New York: Princeton Architectural Press, 1999.

"Ecology and Landscape as Agents of Creativity." In *Ecological Design and Planning*, edited by George Thompson and Frederick Steiner, 80–108. New York: John Wiley & Sons, 1997.

"The Landscape Project." In *The Designed Landscape Forum*, edited by Gina Crandell and Heidi Landecker, 32–35. Washington, D.C.: Spacemaker Press, 1997.

"Aqueous Agents: the (re)presentation of water in the landscape architecture of George Hargreaves." In *Hargreaves: Landscape Works—Process Architecture* no. 128, edited by Steve Hanson, 34–42. Tokyo: Process Architecture Co., 1996.

"The Obscene American Landscape." In *Transforming Landscape*, edited by Michael Spens, 10–15. London: Academy Editions, 1996.

"Time, Material, Event: The Built Work of Michael Van Valkenburgh." In *Design with the Land: Landscape Architecture of Michael Van Valkenburgh*, by Michael Van Valkenburgh, 5–8. New York: Princeton Architectural Press, 1994.

### Refereed Journal Articles

"Botanical Urbanism." *Studies in the History of Gardens and Designed Landscapes* 25/2 (June 2005): 123–43.

"Teaching Landscape Architectural Design." *Council of Educators of Landscape Architecture (CELA) 1992 Proceedings* (Spring 1993): 45–54.

"Landscape as Question." *Landscape Journal* 11/2 (Fall 1992): 163–4.

"Representation and Landscape: Drawing and Making in the Landscape Medium." *Word & Image* 8/3 (July–Sept. 1992): 243–75.

"Critical Thinking and Landscape Architecture," *Landscape Journal* 10/2 (Fall 1991): 159–61.

"Discourse on Theory II: Three Tyrannies of Contemporary Theory and the Alternative of Hermeneutics." *Landscape Journal* 10/2 (Fall 1991): 115–33.

"Discourse on Theory I: 'Sounding the Depths'—Origins, Theory and Representation." *Landscape Journal* 9/2 (Fall 1990): 60–78.

"The Hermeneutic Landscape." *Council of Educators of Landscape Architecture (CELA) Proceedings* (1990): 11–16.

### Other Articles or Publications

"Surface In Depth: Between Landscape and Architecture." Interview with James Corner in *VIA: Dirt*, edited by Megan Born and Helene Furján, 262–71. Cambridge, MA: MIT Press, 2012.

"James Corner Field Operations, Landscape Architecture and Urban Design, New York." *Harvard Design Magazine* 33 (Fall/Winter 2010-2011): 100–102.

"Green Stimuli." *A+U: Architecture and Urbanism* 5/476 (May 2010): 62–67.

"Landscape Urbanism in the Field: The Knowledge Corridor, San Juan, Puerto Rico." *Topos* 71 (2010): 25–29.

"Colonization." *VIA: Occupation*, edited by Morgan Martinson, Tonya Markiewicz, and Helene Furján. Philadelphia: PDSP/School of Design, University of Pennsylvania, 2008: 34–50.

"Botanical Urbanism: A New Project for the Botanical Garden at the University of Puerto Rico." *A+T* 28 (Autumn 2006): 134–57.

"Field Operations." In *Design Life Now*, edited by Barbara Bloemink, Brooke Hodge, Ellen Lupton, and Matilda McQuaid. New York: Cooper-Hewitt Design Museum, Fall 2006.

"A New U.S.—Mexico Border." *New York Times Magazine* (September 2006).

"Field Operations, New York, USA." *A+T* 25 (Spring 2005): 98–117.

"Fresh Kills Lifescape." In *Groundswell: Constructing the Contemporary Landscape*, edited by Peter Reed, 156–61. New York: Museum of Modern Art, 2005.

"Lifescape: Fresh Kills Parkland." *Topos* 51 (2005): 14–21.

"Not Unlike Life Itself: Landscape Strategy Now." *Harvard Design Magazine* 21 (Fall 2004/Winter 2005): 32–34.

"Re-envisioning Ground Zero." *New York Times Magazine* (April 2004).

"Field Operations." In *INDEX Architecture*, edited by Bernard Tschumi and Matthew Berman. New York: Columbia University, 2003.

"Field Urbanism." In *The State of Architecture at the Beginning of the 21st Century*, edited by Bernard Tschumi. New York: Monacelli Press, 2003.

"Urban Density." *Lotus* 119 (Summer 2003): 120–130.

"The Contemporary Landscape." *Environment and Landscape Architecture* (Korea: Fall 2002).

"Earthwork." In *A New World Trade Center*, edited by Max Protetch, 38–39. New York: HarperCollins, 2002.

"Lifescape: Field Operations." *Praxis 4: Landscapes* (Fall 2002): 20–27.

"Lifescape: Fresh Kills Reserve." *Lotus* (May 2002): 34–42.

"Field Operations." In *Dimensions: Michigan School of Architecture Review*, edited by Caroline Constant. Ann Arbor: University of Michigan, 2002.

"Downsview Park." *Lotus* (Spring 2001): 52–59.

"The Älvsjö Project." *Landskab* (March 2000): 34–41.

"Field Operations." *Architectural Design Profile 140: Architecture of the Borderlands* (Fall 1999): 52–55.

"Suburban Landscapes." *Casabella* 673–674 (December 1999): 82–89.

"Formgiving as Ecological Craft." *Magasin for Modern Arkitektur* 19 (Spring 1998): 42–47.

"Operational Eidetics: Forging New Landscapes." *Harvard Design Magazine* (Fall 1998): 22–26.

"Landscape Matters." *GSD NEWS: Harvard University Graduate School of Design* (Fall 1996): 33–36.

"Map." *Maps* (London: International Institute for the Visual Arts, 1996): 45–46.

"Paradoxical Measures: The American Landscape." *Architectural Design Profile 124: Architecture and Anthropology* (Fall 1996): 53–60.

"The Finding and Founding of Urban Ground: The Built Urban Work of Robert Hanna and Laurie Olin, 1981–1991." *VIA 13: Simultaneous Cities* (unpublished, 2000).

"On the work of Michael Van Valkenburgh." *GSD News: Harvard University Graduate School of Design* (Winter/Spring 1994): 33–36.

"Taking Measures Across the American Landscape." *AA Files* 27 (Spring 1994): 47–54.

"Drawing: Projection and Disclosure." *Landscape Architecture* 83/5 (May 1993): 64–67.

"Layering and Stratigraphy." *Landscape Architecture* 80/12 (December 1990): 38–39.

**Book Reviews**

Review of *Invisible Gardens: The Search for Modernism in the American Landscape*, by Peter Walker and Melanie Simo. *Journal of Garden History* 16/3 (1996): 227–29.

Review of *Minimalist Gardens: Peter Walker*. *Land Books* (Winter 1996): 10–11.

Corner, James and Ruth Cserr. Review of *Nature Pictorialized: The History of the "View" in Landscape Architecture*, by Gina Crandell. *Design Book Review* (Winter 1994): 6–8.

**Unpublished Manuscripts**

"Hunt's Haunts." Paper presented at John Dixon Hunt—A Symposium, Philadelphia, Pennsylvania, October 2009.

"Time and Temporality in Landscape Construction." Unpublished paper, 1993.

"Sediments and Erasures: Landscape as Quarry." Unpublished manuscript, 1992.

"Absence and Landscape." Unpublished manuscript, 1991.

"Twelve Questions—A response to Gary Dwyer." Unpublished response to questions by Gary Dwyer, 1991.

"Free Association—A Mechanism in Landscape Architectural Studio Teaching." Paper presented at the American Collegiate Schools of Architecture Conference, Princeton, New Jersey, October 1990.

"A Future of Resistance." Unpublished paper delivered at the GSFA Centenary Symposium, 1990.

PUBLISHED BY
Princeton Architectural Press
A McEvoy Group company
202 Warren Street
Hudson, New York 12534

Visit our website at www.papress.com

© 2014 Princeton Architectural Press
All rights reserved
Printed and bound in China
20 19 18 5 4 3

EDITOR: Meredith Baber
BOOK DESIGN: Paul Wagner

SPECIAL THANKS TO: Mariam Aldhahi, Sara Bader, Nicola Bednarek Brower,
Janet Behning, Megan Carey, Carina Cha, Andrea Chlad, Barbara Darko,
Benjamin English, Russell Fernandez, Will Foster, Jan Hartman, Jan Haux,
Diane Levinson, Jennifer Lippert, Amrita Marino, Katharine Myers, Jamie Nelson,
Lauren Palmer, Jay Sacher, Rob Shaeffer, Andrew Stepanian, Sara Stemen,
Marielle Suba, and Joseph Weston of Princeton Architectural Press
—Kevin C. Lippert, publisher

LIBRARY OF CONGRESS CATALOGING-IN-PUBLICATION DATA
Corner, James, 1961– author, editor.
The landscape imagination : collected essays of James Corner, 1990–2010 /
James Corner and Alison Bick Hirsch, editors. — First edition.
367 pages : illustrations (some color), color maps ; 24 cm
Includes bibliographical references.
ISBN 978-1-61689-145-9 (alk. paper)
1. Landscape architecture. I. Hirsch, Alison Bick, editor. II. Title.
SB472.4.C67 2014
712—DC23
                                        2013028719